Johnny Weissmuller

"Twice the Hero"

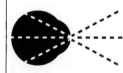

This Large Print Book carries the
Seal of Approval of N.A.V.H.

JOHNNY WEISSMULLER

"TWICE THE HERO"

DAVID A. FURY

Thorndike Press • Waterville, Maine

AUG 1 0 2001

Copyright © 2000 by David A. Fury

All rights reserved.

Published in 2001 by arrangement with Artist's Press.

Thorndike Press Large Print Biography Series.

The tree indicium is a trademark of Thorndike Press.

The text of this Large Print edition is unabridged.
Other aspects of the book may vary from the original edition.

Set in 16 pt. Plantin.

Printed in the United States on permanent paper.

Library of Congress Cataloging-in-Publication Data

Fury, David.
    Johnny Weissmuller : "twice the hero" / David Fury.
      p. (lg. print) cm.
    Originally published: Minneapolis, Minn. : Artist's Press,
2000.
    ISBN: 0-7862-3384-2 (lg. print : hc : alk. paper)
    1. Weissmuller, Johnny, 1904– 2. Motion picture actors
and actresses — United States — Biography 3. Swimmers —
United States — Biography. 4. Large type books. I. Title.
PN2287.W4556 F87 2001
791.43′028′092—dc21
    [B]   2001027651

Dedicated to . . .
my wonderful friends and family

Thank you one and all for your
encouragement and
support during this challenging and
exhilarating climb

Contents

"Not Good for Man to Look at Sun"

First things first . . . Before telling you about Johnny Weissmuller, my Tarzan father, and my "Jungle Family," I want you to know a little about my real family. I was BLESSED with an extraordinary and wonderful childhood with caring, loving, teaching parents who were probably the most popular mother/ father combo among all the children in the neighborhood. Quite aside from being GREAT parents, my father, Reginald, was a successful English stage and screen actor, director, and producer whose work you may have seen and my mother, Louise Van Loon, was a "Vassar Girl" with a liberal arts education who LOVED books and lectured.

Mother was my data bank and father taught me his profession. He had me "On the Boards" early and on Broadway in the starring role of "Pud" in *On Borrowed Time*

9

at 6½ years. I had a beautiful and charming older sister, Mary Alice, and still have my younger brother, William. They gave me some great nieces and nephews and we all are connected through the Internet. Patty, my cherished wife, and I have three treasured children, Patrick, Stewart, and Regina. No grandchildren, yet. So as a child growing up, I enjoyed the best of TWO family lives; one real and one fantasy. BOTH were, and still are, very near and dear to me.

NOW A REQUEST . . . I have wondered whether "Twice the Hero," the title of this new book, is HERO enough when it comes to the GREATNESS of Johnny Weissmuller. TWICE may be a little conservative. Perhaps it should be THRICE or MORE. It's MORE for me; I truly believe it's a LOT MORE! You be the judge. After reading this biography, as carefully written by David Fury, please let me know how many heroes Johnny Weissmuller is for you.

DAVID FURY — movie fan, collector, author, biographer, and publisher . . . Over the years I came to recognize David Fury as a fan/collector. He made his written requests on his personal letterhead which featured a rather distinctive profile of the bearded author wearing what I would describe as a Van Gogh hat. This pleasing profile caught my eye, so one day I gave David my Internet address. Through e-mail I came to know more about Dave and recognized him as a serious movie fan, historian, author, and publisher. Our friendship grew until 05:55:01 on January 8,1999, when I received the following request via "Electronic Drums."

"Would you consider writing a Foreword for *Twice the Hero*? I'd be greatly honored if you would; I think it would be appreciated by everyone who reads the book. I think you could say some things to honor Johnny that no one else on this planet could . . ."

I knew David was working on this biography and have encouraged him along the way. I wanted to read it. So, when David dropped it on me to write the Foreword for *Twice the Hero* I was flattered! This request came as a surprise. I thought for a moment and wondered what Big John would want me to do. The answer came fast: "Umgawa, Boy, Umgawa!"

I quickly answered: "I would be honored to write the Foreword." I always read the entire foreword in any book I start, but if you, the reader, feel I am "Padding the Part" too much, the option is wide open to skip on ahead and read this later.

I am not a biographer nor a literary critic. Many biographers fail to research thoroughly their subject and fail to separate fact from fiction. They perpetuate stories and events that are untrue or just never happened. There are some "Tall Tales" included in this volume which are entertaining and to be expected in material dealing with "Show Business." Enjoy them; we won't blame you if you are suspicious. I know first hand only the small portion of Big John's life covering the times we were together making Tarzan films. This is a faithful and accurate work with respect to our shared experience.

The book speaks for itself. I am hopeful you will appreciate the thoroughness and skill that went into its making. The enlightening quotes and graphics that warm these pages remind me of the time I was an INSIDER, when I was actually involved in the Life Story of Johnny Weissmuller. Personally, I have learned from this biography much about Big John's life I didn't know before. I think you will too.

I was seven-years-old when I first met Johnny Weissmuller and in the next nine years we made eight Tarzan pictures together. We were CLOSE. I knew he was an Olympic champion and ALL that, but I didn't know a great deal about his life history as revealed in this wonderful book. It has taken 50+ years to fully understand how spending my formative years (seven years to 16 years) under the wing of a world champion has affected my life. I would like to share some of that with you here.

FOR OPENERS . . . It's always the same when I am interviewed about Tarzan. Since I was seven-years-old to the present, my answers have changed, but the questions remain the same. It didn't matter where I was in the world or where I am today the FIRST question is: "Are you REALLY the Johnny Sheffield who played 'Boy' on TARZAN with Johnny Weissmuller and Maureen O'Sullivan?" And the SECOND question is ALWAYS: "What was it like working with Johnny Weissmuller?"

My answer is YES to the first question. In this Foreword, after having had 61 years to think about it, I want to share with you my current response to Question #2.

WHAT WAS IT LIKE working with Johnny Weissmuller? I knew one day I would become the last living member of my "Jungle Family" and I could then say anything I wished about those times without fear of contradiction. Yes, Big John had a BAD SIDE! You never saw it, but it was there.

Johnny Weissmuller was a Superstar whether he was performing on the "Silver Screen," in the water "Swimming for Gold," or just walking around. Wherever he went Big John gave off a special light and it shown for all of us to see. Fortunately, some of that light got into me.

I first met Big John 62 years ago at M.G.M.

He has been with me ever since, creating a lasting influence on my life. I didn't know it then, but as time passed I could see very clearly how Big John was different from most and how being around him started a clock ticking in my head a lot like the one in his. Here, right in my life, was a champion, an UNDEFEATED Olympic world champion. There are a lot of us who feel he is UN-BEATABLE as the character of Tarzan as well.

The most important thing for me about Johnny Weissmuller is he always had time for Boy/me. This man might well have been aloof with no time for me other than what was called for in the script. This was not the case. Johnny Weissmuller loved me and I knew it and I loved him. When I was near, he always had a kind word for me when I might easily have passed by unnoticed.

FUN & GAMES WITH TARZAN . . . Big John loved to PLAY. He liked good-looking women, flashy clothes and toys. He owned a Lincoln with the "Continental Pack" on the back; he loved that Lincoln. He drove it on the studio lot and to and from location. In the trunk he kept his golf clubs and practice balls as well as some swimming gear (i.e., trunks, face plate, and swim fins).

Behind the scenes Big John would play with me. On location, when I wasn't in school, he would call me and we would go over to that Continental trunk for some golf gear and would "hit a few balls" together. Tarzan loved golf. We played "Hollywood frisbee." We used the lid from a 35mm film can as that was before there were commercial frisbees on the market.

Big John loved to WIN and he gave me HIS WINNING ATTITUDE. He said to think of it this way: "When they step up look down the line and SEE that there are two kinds there (swimmers, golfers, card players, etc.) — the ones who are going to LOSE and ME!" Hey, it worked for Big John.

On the set, Big John taught me how to play gin rummy. He always wanted to WIN and usually did. He got a special TWINKLE in his eye when he got a FAST GO DOWN hand and stuck me with a lot of cards. He loved to lean forward a bit and get in my face and say: "GIN! Count 'em up, Boy!" Sometimes I caught him with a fist full of cards and I KNEW what to DO, FEEL, and SAY! Big John gave me his love for winning.

I am often asked, "What was it like swimming with Tarzan?" Well, Big John was NEVER DEFEATED in his swimming career. I know I never beat him! He was like a motorboat in the water. Carl Curtis at his Beverly Hills Swimming School taught me how to keep from DROWNING and TARZAN taught me how to SWIM.

15

The thing I remember most about swimming with Johnny Weissmuller was that he was always playing around in and with the water. He would come up close to you, put his face down in the water, and start turning his head from side to side blowing bubbles and making very loud incomprehensible sounds. Suddenly, he would sweep his head up in your face with an EXPLOSIVE shout ASKING: "How old are you!?" This startled me and we would laugh. In the water together we always made "Oink Oink, Ahhnnk Ahhnnk" and other seal-like noises antiphonally to each other. That was a GIVEN among "water men."

Big John would cup his two hands together underwater and pull water into his palms. Then he would lift them above water and, through an orifice made where his little fingers lapped, he would SQUIRT a steady stream of water right in your eyes. He would repeat that a couple of times and then as if by mistake, he would let the water come out backwards through his thumbs and squirt HIMSELF right in the face! Then we really laughed! It makes me feel good all over just thinking about it. This little SQUIRT business was always good for a belly laugh between us and from the spectators and crew.

When we swam together Big John would instruct me in ways to improve my stroke. He had other swimming tips for me. He showed me how to swim in the Chicago river. That was really funny and informative. Because of the debris and fecal matter, he instructed me to do a sort of breast/splash stroke using my cupped palms to splash water away from my head when reaching out for the power stroke.

As yet I have not swum in the Chicago river, but armed with this Weissmuller technique I have swum safely in other waters. So have many of our fighting men who were taught, by Big John, the same technique to swim safely in Flaming Waters during the 2nd World War. He showed me where to hold the water on my forehead for racing and how to hold my head out of the water while swimming for the camera. That was difficult, but Big John showed me a little trickwhen he instructed me to "slip on these Owen Churchill swim fins for the camera." You couldn't see them and it made me feel as powerful as a crocodile! Some of the swimming we did for the camera was difficult and scary; Big John coached me through it all and I improved over the years. Imagine what it was like as a BOY to have Johnny Weissmuller as my personal Swimming Pal! Swimming was PLAY with Tarzan and Boy.

When Big John gave me instruction, he swam or stood close to me. He held my hand or shoulder and engaged my eyes with his, smiled and spoke to me softly. He encouraged me always. He instructed me and said,

"You can do it, Johnny; go ahead and try." It was good for me being with and doing things with this champion.

Whether on location or at the studio cafeteria, Big John had a place for me at his table. We didn't always eat together, but there was a place for me. My real father saw the importance of this relationship and would allow me to go places alone with Big John. Big John took me to swimming and diving competitions, to the beach for a rough water swim; they would be having a diving contest off a pier somewhere and we would go. When we went off together, Big John was accompanied by his friends. They were all champions. Imagine being at a diving or swimming event and being introduced right along with Johnny Weissmuller, Stubby Kruger and Sammy Lee. You hang around champions like that and it rubs off — especially if you are young. You start to think you are a Champion, too! Sometimes we went out to lunch together. Sammy liked "Stink Fish" and Big John would take us all to lunch at an old oriental cafe in downtown Los Angeles to try the Stink Fish; Stubby and I liked the Duck!

The point is Johnny Weissmuller was happy, buoyant, generous, playful, unassuming, loved people and sports, and most of all he had a positive winning attitude ticking away in his inner self that made him a champion. That clock never lost a beat no matter what was going on around him. By working, playing and being with Johnny Weissmuller I was able to see and understand that and start a little clock of my own ticking away in me. You can start one too.

Fun and Games with Big John for me was an opportunity of a lifetime. He was Tarzan, I was Boy, he was my coach, and most important, Big John was my friend. To this day, wherever I go, he goes with me!

JANE . . . I think in a Johnny Weissmuller Foreword it is fitting that I add a word about Big John's first Jane, Maureen O'Sullivan. She was my first Jungle mother and Tarzan and I loved her a lot. Maureen was the Jane of the much quoted "Me Tarzan, you Jane" scene and without her in *Tarzan Finds a Son*, Tarzan might have named me "Elephant"! Jane prevailed and I was named Boy and the movie days of my Tarzan, Jane, Boy, and Cheetah family began. There was Tarzan with "Jungle Wisdom" and the physique of a world champion and Jane with a calming voice and a "figure" that could stop an elephant! Imagine growing up with such parents! You may have noticed we all had a pretty good (GREAT) time together in our Edgar Rice Burroughs' escarpment hangout. Maureen and Big John shared a common desire to do other films and not be forever typed as Tarzan and Jane. At that time, Maureen O'Sullivan wanted to be remembered for her acting abilities which she felt were limited by the role as Jane, so she left my Tarzan family for bigger and better roles.

The last time I saw Maureen personally was February 15, 1993, while attending the annual American Cinema Awards charity banquette in Hollywood. I was talking to Uncle Milty (Milton Berle), who was seated across from me, when I felt a hand on my shoulder and heard a voice say, "Hello, Boy, how are you?" That voice, Maureen's voice, took me back 51 years. Before I turned around to look, I could see all of my jungle family in my mind. Tarzan, Jane, Cheetah, Bulie, Leo, and myself all together in our escarpment paradise. What a moment. In the course of that evening, Maureen confided in me that in spite of all the roles she had played in her life, she now felt fortunate to have played Jane with Johnny Weissmuller in the Tarzan series and fortunate the Weissmuller Tarzan series became a Classic and that she was reconciled to that fact. Maureen was a working actress all her life and played many other roles, but she will be remembered for "All Time" for her role of Jane in the Weissmuller Tarzan adventures. I love and remember her as my Jungle mother and all that that means to me.

SEX & THE JUNGLE . . . My sexual education was not lacking as Boy. As a lad, when my father, Reginald, was teaching me about the "Birds and the Bees," Tarzan was teaching me about the "Crocodiles and the Flamingos." So, by the time I reached adolescence I was pretty well informed on the subject. I remember one day while rehearsing a scene Big John caught me STARING at Jane's curves. I came out of it when he nudged me on the shoulder. I looked up at Big John and he was smiling. He said quietly to me: "Pretty nice, Boy, huh?" I had to agree, but boy was I embarrassed. Tarzan then said for ALL to hear: "Boy growing up, now!" I guess it was pretty obvious to the whole crew the discovery I had made. After that my education grew.

That one was on me and this one is on Big John. There was a time when we had a CALL other than the Tarzan yell on the set. "Brenda Swims Tonight" echoed around the sound stage. Perhaps it is time that you be let in on it. Big John was training a young woman swimmer, Brenda, for a series of races. (Please understand this "Brenda" was not Brenda Joyce, my second Jane.) She was under his care and in STRICT TRAINING. The idea was to reserve all her strength for the competition and that meant NO SEX just before a race. This approach was not working as Brenda was not winning. Big John told me he was going to try something new. So when Tarzan told me, "Brenda Swims Tonight," I knew what that meant. She WON! Soon the crew caught on and were delighted when Big John came on the set and announced: "Brenda Swims Tonight."

My jungle schooling has stood me well. Patty, my beautiful wife, and I just celebrated 41 years of marriage. On the escarpment or anywhere else, Big John taught me a healthy attitude about SEX. He had a little trouble with the marriage thing at first; I have not, so far, thank God!

BEST SIDE FORWARD . . . Remember I said Big John had a "Bad Side"? Well, it's true; at least he thought so. He told me that in his youth he was struck in the throat by a blow dart which left a very visible scar on the side of his neck. Big John thought it was UGLY and would not permit himself to be filmed close-up from that angle as he preferred to put his "Best Side" toward the camera. Well, I can tell you he looked GREAT from any angle. You always got the best side from Big John. Do you remember the side from which Big John was never shot close up?

BIG JOHN was a Superstar with a capital "S" . . . he was a world champion Olympic swimmer, a champion Tarzan among some great Tarzans, and he NEVER endorsed cigarettes or whiskey. These endorsements were there for him and would have brought him $$$$ BIG BUCKS $$$$ when he needed money, but he refused to take them. Now that's a genuine HERO for you. When Big John died I called a news conference which was picked up by most of the news services. You may have read about it. I wanted the world to know how I loved him and that he was a great father for "Boy" and me.

The last time I saw Big John alive I was hitting six-irons on the practice fairway at the Riviera, my home golf club in Los Angeles. The word came down that my Jungle father, TARZAN, was getting ready to tee off on #1 above me. When I saw Big John's foursome crossing the Barranca coming down the fairway toward me to make their second shots on #2, I cut loose with Boy's Tarzan yell and Big John answered with his famous Tarzan yell. The golf course stopped. He left his group and came over to me and we talked. Big John watched me hit a couple and encouraged me and hit a couple himself. It was like old times by that Continental trunk. I looked at him and he looked at me. We both looked down to the practice green where our shots were resting. Then we looked at each other again and had a Great Laugh. We both hit 'em pretty darn good. He ruffled my hair. On the way back to rejoin his foursome he turned and smiled. It never mattered what Big John was doing — he always had time for me. That was the last time I saw my jungle father alive.

FAME . . . Tony Curtis said it best. You find something you like to do and learn how to do it well enough to gain recognition. If you are LUCKY you attain FAME. Then you have to learn another profession; how to DO fame. Maybe you can have a private life, but you must learn to do FAME first. Big John LEARNED to do FAME like the champion he was.

AND NOW . . . Umgawa, my dear Reader, Umgawa . . . ende

Johnny Weissmuller: Twice the Hero

[signature: Johnny Weissmuller]

The name, *Johnny Weissmuller*, has a magic ring to it. Many people around the world think of the tall young man who couldn't be defeated in a swimming contest, including winning five gold medals in the Olympics of 1924 and 1928. Millions of movie fans are reminded of the jungle king Tarzan, whom Johnny portrayed on the big screen for seventeen years (1932-1948). We all remember the handsome man with the high-pitched voice and infectious laugh, who loved people and made friends wherever he went on his journey through life.

Johnny Weissmuller was an undefeated swimming champion and American hero as a five-time Olympic gold medal winner, and then continued his own brand of heroism on the silver screen — first as Tarzan and then later as Jungle Jim. He was even a true-life hero in 1927, and was credited with saving the lives of eleven people after the tragic capsize of the Lake Michigan excursion boat, *Favorite.*

Johnny was also an exemplary role model to his adoring fans, who spent more than three decades worshiping his every move in the pool and on the screen. Johnny's squeaky clean image resulted in his being chosen as a central figure in the first Wheaties ad campaigns in 1933, along with Babe Ruth and Jack Dempsey. His adoring public — men and women alike — would always forgive any minor sins he might commit in his lifetime because of his genuine purity of heart and kindness of soul.

Chicago in the 1920s had two of the most talked about and written about "celebrities" in America. Johnny Weissmuller was a hero for his swimming exploits, while gangster Al Capone was infamous for his mob rule of Chicago. Johnny was Chicago's hero of the 1920s — all of America, really. Meanwhile, Al Capone was America's shame. And these two diametrically opposed people, one good and one evil, both called Chicago "home."

The city of Chicago after the turn of the century was a slice of Americana — this was where the American dream was coming true for many immigrants. Many millions of people had lost all hope of happiness in their homelands, and braved the arduous journey by boat to the United States for the opportunity to be part of the greatest country in the world. Johnny Weissmuller was one of these myriad immigrants, coming to the United States as an infant and becoming one of America's most beloved and enduring celebrities and heroes.

The "Roaring '20s" represented an era of giants in American sports, and home run slugger Babe Ruth of the New York Yankees was perhaps the biggest "giant" of them all. Some of the other sports heroes of the decade included Jack Dempsey, heavyweight boxing champion from 1919 to 1926; former Olympic decathlon winner Jim Thorpe, a pioneer in the early days of football; Bobby Jones, the world's greatest amateur golfer; and Bill Tilden, seven-time winner of the U.S. Open in tennis. In the swimming world, the name of Gertrude Ederle would be etched in sports history in 1926 when she became the first woman to swim the English Channel, and in a time that was *two hours faster* than the men's record.

And then there was the six-foot three-inch Adonis of swimming, Johnny Weissmuller. An American legend before his 20th birthday, Johnny was the darling of the printed media in the 1920s, earning nicknames like

"Human Hydroplane," "Prince of the Waves," "Flying Fish," "Aquatic Wonder," "King of Swimmers," "America's Greatest Waterman," and "the Illinois Flash."

Chicago has always been one of the greatest sports towns, and this was the beginning of an era of sports history in the "City by the Lake." Comiskey Park, home of the White Sox, came into existence in 1910, and Wrigley Field, home of the Cubs, opened in 1916. The Chicago Staleys, coached by George Halas, became the Bears in 1922 and also played their home games at Wrigley Field. In 1927 heavyweight boxers Gene Tunney and Jack Dempsey fought for the championship at Soldier Field before a crowd of 105,000 people, as Dempsey failed to recapture his crown from Tunney.

The "Black Sox" scandal of 1919 made an indelible black mark on the city of Chicago and the sport of baseball itself, when eight White Sox ballplayers, including "Shoeless Joe" Jackson, were bribed by gamblers to lose the 1919 World Series. A year later, Jackson departed the courthouse in Chicago after admitting his guilt in the bloody affair, his eyes downcast and unable to return the disbelieving gaze of his fans. Legend recalls that a small boy with tears in his eyes, tugged at his sleeve and pleaded of his hero, "Say it ain't so, Joe."

In the aftermath of the Black Sox scandal,

Johnny Weissmuller was a breath of fresh air to a shell-shocked Chicago. But it was more than a breath. It was more like a hurricane of vitality, competitive energy, and an unequaled level of skill in swimming pools across the country in which he competed against America's best swimmers. This young teenaged phenom had all of America opening their collective eyes, and marveling at the phenomenal skills that would make him a legend.

Through it all, the good and the bad of sports history in Chicago during the 1920s, one thing and one person could be counted on: Johnny would give his best in each and every race he entered and would win them all. Few athletes in the history of sports can lay claim that they retired undefeated, as was the case with Johnny, who never lost a freestyle race in his amateur swimming career. From his official debut in competitive swimming in August of 1921, when he won his first A.A.U. championship in the 50-yard freestyle, Weissmuller was the winner in every freestyle race he ever entered through 1929, when he retired from competitive swimming.

As difficult as it is to achieve fame and reach the pinnacle of success in a particular field, Johnny Weissmuller did it twice: He was the greatest swimmer of all-time, and then became eternally famous and internationally loved and remembered as "Tarzan" on the silver screen. As an undefeated swimming and Olympic champion, he was a hero to millions of Americans. His fan adulation eventually spread around the world, and knew no boundaries by country or creed. As Edgar Rice Burroughs' jungle god in twelve Tarzan adventures, he was the ultimate screen hero. Tarzan didn't use guns to fight his enemies; instead, he used his cunning, guile, and superior physical prowess to send his enemies to their ultimate demise. Weissmuller continued to wear the mantle of heroism with his role of "Jungle Jim," another pulp fiction character brought to the big screen for sixteen thrilling adventures (and one TV season) during an eight-year run from 1948 through 1956.

Johnny was in the right place at the right time for the screen role of Tarzan — it was simply a matter of fate. Those closely entwined cousins of fate, serendipity and fortuity, certainly helped guide Johnny through his magical life. You could also say that Johnny got lucky when Maureen O'Sullivan was cast as "Jane" in the first MGM Tarzan picture in 1932, *Tarzan, the Ape Man*. This turned out to be a brilliant stroke of casting, as the duo enjoyed unequaled popularity during the decade that they shared top billing in the treetops in six Tarzan films.

As the guest of honor at the 1971 Edgar

Rice Burroughs convention, Johnny recalled that an MGM executive wanted to change his name when he was being considered for the role of Tarzan. "Weissmuller," advised the producer, "is too long for the marquee. You've got to have a shorter name." When the gentleman was informed and enlightened to the fact that Johnny's name was known around the world for his swimming heroics and Olympic gold medals, the producer relented. "Okay, we'll lengthen the marquee . . ." If the movie people had foolishly changed his name to the contemplated "Jon Weis," it just never would have been the same.

Johnny lived and enjoyed life to the maximum, during all of his nearly eighty years here on Planet Earth. He loved swimming and athletic competition, which was his first love. Swimming made him a star to an adoring public, which was captivated by the feats of the young man who couldn't be defeated in his watery domain. He reveled in the role of Tarzan, which kept him in the limelight for more than two decades as a silver screen hero and matinee idol. He appreciated the beauty of women, and was married five times to five different women who each brought something special to his life. (The pressures of Hollywood broke up each of his first four marriages, but his loving union to Maria Weissmuller lasted for more than twenty years until his death.) Johnny loved a good joke, and he possessed a wonderful sense of humor and a marvelous laugh that rang out and filled others with their own laughter.

Johnny Weissmuller was and still is remembered as one of America's legendary heroes, one of sports' greatest undefeated champions, and one of the movies' most memorable screen legends, Tarzan. But knowing these facts, what pertinent information must we know about Johnny that we don't already know? Better still, what inaccuracies, falsehoods, and distortions of the truth can we correct at the beginning of this biography? When we have accomplished this mission with the initial pages of this volume, we can then continue on with the thrilling story of one of America's most beloved heroes.

This is the *Johnny Weissmuller story: Twice the Hero*.

David Jury

CHAPTER ONE

The Truth of the Matter

Johnny was born on June 2, 1904, in the town of Freidorf in Eastern Europe. (Until the end of World War I, Freidorf was within the boundaries of the Austro-Hungarian Empire — it is now part of the Banat region of Romania.) Reproduced at the end of this chapter is an entry for Johnny's birth from the original parish register for Freidorf, indicating he was born Janos (Johann or John) Weissmuller to his parents, Peter and Elizabeth.

For virtually his whole life Johnny related the story that he was born in Windber, PennsylvaniaWindber, Pennsylvania (which indeed was the birthplace of his brother Peter, 15 months after Johnny's birth). For the reason behind this fictional account of his birthplace, a somewhat convoluted distortion of the truth, we must fast-forward ahead to a few months prior to the 1924 Olympics, to be held in Paris, France.

At some point in his young life, perhaps not long before these same Olympic games, Johnny's mother informed her son that he had been born in Freidorf, and thus he was an immigrant like his parents. The Weissmuller's journey from their original homeland to the United States was only a few months after Johnny was born, when he was an infant.

This meant that Johnny was technically not an American citizen, and the Weissmuller clan — Johnny, Peter, and their mother — greatly feared that he would not be allowed to compete in the Olympics under the flag of the United States. So this is the moment when a little white lie, a distortion of the truth, was concocted to allow Johnny to compete in the Olympics without fear of his secret being discovered. Needing a passport to travel to Paris for the Olympics, Johnny was given his younger brother Peter's birth certificate indicating his birthplace to be in Windber, Pennsylvania. In the baptismal records of St. John's Cantius Catholic Church is a handwritten entry for "Petrus (Peter) Weissmuller" on the date of September 3, 1905. Between the first and last names is written "John" in a noticeably different ink and penmanship. Church officials were never able to determine when the church records were altered — or by whom — to provide Johnny with a documented American birthplace.

(The sad thing about this whole situation is that it could have been completely avoided, if Johnny had learned of his birthplace at an earlier date. He would only have needed to take the citizenship test and recite the oath to become an American citizen. A similar situation existed with swimmer Martha Norelius, who was born in Stockholm and yet competed for the United States in the 1924 Paris Olympics, and was a teammate of Johnny's. Miss Norelius was only 15-years-old at the time of 1924 Games, and yet had her U.S. citizenship. Johnny also could have easily gained his legal citizenship, and it never would have been a problem for him.)

Johnny, his mother, and brother Peter were certainly in on this little drama of subterfuge. One would assume that William Bachrach, Johnny's swimming coach and mentor, would have straightened out the whole mess had he been informed of Johnny's true birthplace. And if so, it would have saved Johnny from carrying around this particular "demon" his whole life — this deep-rooted fear of having his gold medals taken from him by the powerful Olympic committee.

Johnny very well knew the story of the great American Indian athlete, Jim Thorpe, who had won both the decathlon and pentathlon in the 1912 Olympics in Stockholm, only to be later stripped of his gold medals when it was discovered he had accepted a few dollars for playing baseball one summer. This was an injustice of epic proportion, and Johnny feared the same type of repercussion from the Olympic committee if it was discovered that he had misrepresented his United States' citizenship. (Note: Jim Thorpe's medals and records were restored posthumously in 1982.)

Johnny never revealed his true birthplace during his lifetime, even after he had become a legal citizen sometime after his swimming career ended. The reason that Johnny did not get into trouble over this situation was that everyone loved Johnny Weissmuller, who was as American as "apple pie." He had never harmed anyone with this untruth, and it didn't affect his amateur status. He was respected by his competitors and adored by fans around the world. And thus years later upon discovery it was treated as an oversight by the Olympic Committee, and not a violation of Olympic rules.

One other untruth that should be corrected at this point concerns Johnny's father, Peter Weissmuller. Johnny always told the story that his father had contracted "black lung" disease after working in the coal mines during the time they lived in Windber, and later died of the affliction when Johnny was in the 8th grade.

In reality, Peter Weissmuller left his wife and two sons, John and Peter, and took up a separate residence in Chicago sometime around 1916 (when Johnny was indeed in the

8th grade). In those days it was extremely difficult to divorce when one was a member of the Catholic religion, and Mr. Weissmuller's departure from the family was explained by his "death." And thus Johnny, brother Peter, and their mother Elizabeth grew even closer when the family became just the three of them. For their own personal reasons, they always stayed with the story that Mr. Weissmuller had died around the time of their separation just prior to World War I.

The man who was supposed to be the "bread winner" in the Weissmuller family apparently never supported his two sons after the separation. Thus, Peter Weissmuller was ostracized and considered "dead" by his legal wife, Elizabeth, and sons Johnny and Peter. And so when Johnny later recalled becoming the man of the family when his father "died," it is clear now that he was speaking figuratively of his father's desertion. (A 1984 *Sports Illustrated* article by Arlene Mueller concerning the 1984 Olympics, states that the elder Weissmuller was alive in 1937 when he became a U.S. citizen. This article strongly supports the evidence that Peter Weissmuller, Sr. was alive many years after his purported death.)

In Johnny's own 1930 autobiography, *Swimming the American Crawl*, he virtually ignores the existence of his father. His only reference to his father in the book is as follows: "I resemble my father, Peter Weissmuller, who has always been fairly tall and slender, but was not so tall or so heavy [muscularly developed] as I have grown. Both my father and my mother liked the water, but they never did much swimming."

The fact that Johnny told the story of his life and his swimming career, with little or no mention of his father, revealed that the rift between father and son was very deep. These wounds were obviously never repaired, and Johnny took with him to his grave his true feelings about his father. Johnny was a tough kid and he could have taken abuse from his father and survived, emotionally speaking. Johnny loved his mother immensely, and any physical or mental abuse that his father heaped upon her, could never have been forgiven.

Decades later, when Johnny was interviewed by Narda Oynx for the 1964 biography, *Water, World, and Weissmuller*, he was still embittered with memories of his father, and stuck with the story of his death when he was a teenager. "I had to quit school after my father died," he recalled. "You know, your guts get so mad when you try to fight poverty . . . I told myself, 'I'm going to get out of this neighborhood, if only because he's got a quarter and I haven't.' I fought my way out . . . Maybe it is this drive to better oneself and one's surroundings that makes a champion out of the less-fortunate boy, instead of the one born with a silver spoon in his mouth, as the saying goes. With but few exceptions . . . it is always the underdog who wins through sheer willpower."

The consequences of these two untruths concerning Johnny's birthplace and his father's "death" are virtually nonexistent. In reality, they concerned only the nuclear Weissmuller family. But at the time that these events occurred, they were no small matters to Johnny, Peter, and Elizabeth Weissmuller. The first untruth protected Johnny and his quest to be an Olympic champion; the second protected the family from what Mrs. Weissmuller felt would be shame and embarrassment for herself and her sons, Johnny and Peter.

Now that the record is set straight on these matters, let's go back in time to the place and day of Johnny's birth: the town of Freidorf on June 2, 1904. The baptismal register indicates that a baby boy, Janos (Johann) Weissmuller, was born on this date to parents Peter Weissmuller and his wife, the former Elizabeth Kersch. The Catholic priest who conducted the infant John's baptism on June 5th was Wendel Ochsenfelder, and the godparents were Janos Borstner and Katharina Zerbesz.

Peter Weissmuller had been a soldier, reportedly a captain and engineer, and served with Franz Josef's army in Vienna prior to his marriage to Elizabeth Kersch. Weissmuller was employed as a brick worker at the time of the birth of his first son, Johann, in 1904. (Documents from Freidorf also indicate that Peter Weissmuller, from the town of Varjas, had married Elizabeth Kersch, of Freidorf, on June 7, 1903. These documents are written in Hungarian because Freidorf was ruled at this time by the Hungarian monarchy.)

The turn of the 20th Century was a period of unrest and political upheaval in Eastern Europe, and immigrants were flocking by the tens of thousands to the "Promised Land" of the United States. The Weissmuller couple and their infant baby traveled to Holland at the beginning of 1905, where they arranged passage in steerage on the Dutch ship S.S. *Rotterdam*, bound for the United States. The ship sailed from Rotterdam on January 14, 1905, and arrived in New York at Ellis Island on January 26, 1905, after an ocean voyage of twelve days.

The immigration manifest indicates that Peter Weissmuller and his wife Elizabeth were both 24-years-old, and that the only money they had was ten dollars. Their sponsor in the United States was a brother-in-law, Johann Off, who lived in Windber, Pennsylvania. They traveled by train from New York City to Windber, and each individual was given a bag lunch for the trip to their new home in the United States. After gaining their legal status as immigrants, the Weissmullers and their infant son began their new lives in America in January of 1905, when Johann was seven months old. As an infant they called their baby "Hansi," and eventually he was called the English version of Johann, "John."

A local history entitled "The Windber Story" states that the Weissmullers boarded with the Fritz Fronyak family during their years in the town of Windber, and that Mr. Weissmuller worked in the Windber mines as a coal miner. Records at St. John's Cantius Catholic Church in Windber indicate that Elizabeth Weissmuller gave birth to a son, Peter, Jr., on September 3, 1905.

The plan all along was to move to Chicago, where a Freidorf colony of immigrants, including the parents of Elizabeth Kersch Weissmuller, had established themselves. There would be friends and relatives from the "old country" in Chicago, thus reducing the fear of the unknown in the new frontier. With the ultimate goal being the move to Chicago, the Weissmuller family lived in Windber until 1908.

(In 1967, Johnny was inducted into the Cambria County War Memorial Sports Hall of Fame, and the Windber Hall of Fame in 1979. In September of 1999, an historical marker honoring "JOHNNY WEISS-MULLER" was dedicated in Windber.)

Previous biographical accounts of the life of Johnny Weissmuller refer to his address in Chicago during his childhood as 1921 Cleveland Avenue North. However, the Chicago address directories for the years 1910-1915 list the home of Peter Weissmuller as 1521 Cleveland Avenue North. Obviously in these past accounts, a simple typographical mistake or error in transcription (1921 — 1521) moved the Weissmuller home (on paper) four blocks from its actual location just off of North Avenue.

(According to information on microfilm at the Cook County Recorder's office in Chicago, there was only a vacant lot at 1921 Cleveland Avenue during this period of time. Also, the home where the Weissmullers lived at 1521 Cleveland was owned by a Mr. Holleson from 1902-1921, and then after that the owner was a Mr. Jurdik. Obviously, the Weissmuller family rented during their years in Chicago, and probably only a single floor of this multi-floor home.)

The house where Johnny Weissmuller lived his childhood on Cleveland Avenue was unfortunately just a vacant lot by the year 1999. The lots are very narrow on this street — barely 25-feet wide — which is why the homes were originally built straight up some two and three stories high. A few of the original houses in the neighborhood were still standing as the Millennium approached, but most had fallen prey to the wrecking ball to make way for new homes and townhouses.

Peter Weissmuller's occupation in the Chicago directories is listed as "laborer." Also, the 1916 Chicago directory lists a new address for Peter Weissmuller at 1627 Sedgwick, a few blocks from where his wife and children lived on Cleveland Avenue. This same year a saloon purchased by Peter Weissmuller is listed at 1501 Cleveland (corner of Cleveland and Weed). One could easily assume that the acquisition of the saloon and Mr. Weissmuller finding separate living quarters for himself are related events. Certainly, the boys hanging out at their father's saloon just down the street from their home, rather than at St. Michael's church, would factor in the split of Mr. and Mrs. Weissmuller.

Finally, there's one minor mystery that is more difficult to completely resolve. Johnny only mentioned five wives in his lifetime, although some biographical sketches of Weissmuller include a sixth matrimonial partner, Camille Lanier (also spelled Louier in some references). There are no public records of a marriage between Johnny Weissmuller and Camille (who was also known by her nickname of "Toni").

Camille was born in 1907, and was one of Florenz Ziegfeld's showgirls for several seasons. A dark-haired beauty, she was billed as "the girl with the million dollar legs" with the Ziegfeld Follies in the late 1920s. She also appeared as a Follies' showgirl in the motion pictures *The Great Ziegfeld* (1936), and *Ziegfeld Follies* (1946). After marrying Eddie Mannix, a powerful vice-president and financial controller at MGM, Camille went by "Toni" for the rest of her life.

If Johnny was indeed involved with Camille, it probably happened in 1929 when he was single, lonely, and staying in New York while appearing in his first motion picture, *Glorifying the American Girl*, a Ziegfeld production. Since Camille was a Follies' showgirl, she undoubtedly appeared in the various Follies' production numbers in the picture. Johnny turned 25-years-old in June of 1929, and Camille was three years younger. It is certainly probable an affair of some degree happened at this time, although it is highly unlikely that the relationship was a legal marriage.

Johnny Weissmuller, Jr. recalled that he ran into Toni Mannix (dressed in a fur coat) at MGM in 1958. After surprising the younger Weissmuller with a bearhug, she confirmed that there had been a relationship between herself and Johnny, Sr., many years in the past. (Johnny, Jr., an accomplished sailor who has earned his living as a long-shoreman and part-time actor for many years in the Bay area, lives in San Francisco with his wife Diane. Weissmuller said his sister, Wendy Weissmuller, also lives in California.)

This will have to remain one of Hollywood's lesser unsolved mysteries as all the principal players are dead and gone. In this case we will give Johnny the benefit of the doubt on this matter and include in this biography only his five confirmed legal marriages.

It is interesting to note that Toni Mannix was also involved in one of the most intriguing of Hollywood's unsolved mysteries: the tragic death of George Reeves in 1959. Although Toni was married to Eddie Mannix, she was romantically involved with Reeves for ten years beginning around 1949. Reeves is indelibly remembered as portraying "Superman" on television in the 1950s.

A few months after the breakup of the affair between Reeves and Toni Mannix, George Reeves died of a gunshot wound in his home. Officially called a suicide by police, there is some evidence that Reeves may have been the victim of foul play: murdered with evidence planted to make it look like death by his own hand.

(Holding with the murder theory, Eddie Mannix was a strong suspect in the alleged murder of Reeves. Another theory had Toni

Mannix hiring the killer of her ex-lover Reeves, in retribution for being dumped and replaced by a sultry New York debutante, Leonore Lemmon. Also considered a suspect by police was Ms. Lemmon, who was at the home of Reeves' on the night of his death.)

Johnny Weissmuller, like most everyone else, was only a distant spectator to the sad and unfortunate death of the popular Reeves, whose Superman character made him a pop icon to the present day. Johnny was friends with Reeves, who portrayed a fortune hunter in the first *Jungle Jim* feature in 1948. Johnny was also very familiar with Eddie Mannix, who controlled the financial strings at MGM for several decades until his death in 1963.

CHAPTER TWO

Chicago: Johnny's Home Town

In 1908, the Weissmuller family journeyed west to Illinois and were finally reunited with the parents of Elizabeth Kersch Weissmuller. This was a heartfelt reunion for Elizabeth and her parents, who lived on a farm on the outskirts of Chicago. The times spent visiting at the Kersch farm in these early years in Chicago were happy ones for the family. It also allowed an opportunity for the boys, Johnny and Peter, Jr., to become closely acquainted with their maternal grandparents. (In later years, when Johnny fondly spoke of his grandmother, he used the German word "grossmutter," which translates to "grandmother" in the English language.)

The house where Johnny and his family lived in Chicago was located in the heart of an area known today as Old Town. The two and three-story frame and brick houses of the neighborhood were built after the Chicago Fire of 1871, which burned the wooden houses of Chicago like kindling. First settled around 1850 by German immigrants, the neighborhood was originally called North TownNorth Town (also German Town). North AvenueNorth Avenue, just one-half block north of the Weissmuller home, was known for many years as "German Broadway" and the neighborhood was primarily of German heritage.

The area north of the German Broadway had been potato and cabbage fields tended by immigrants who became farmers. Around the time that the Weissmuller family moved to Chicago, an influx of Hungarian and Russian immigrants began to change the face of the neighborhood. According to author Vivien Palmer, between 1910 and 1920 the old German Broadway had gradually transformed to "decidedly a Hungarian shopping street, its stores owned by Russian Jews . . . but replete with advertisements to attract the Hungarian trade."

Many decades later, in 1976, the Chicago City Council designated the Old Town Triangle area (bounded by North Avenue, Clark Street, and the Ogden Avenue Mall), as a landmark district. In support of the designation, the pastor of St. Michael's parish noted that, "The real strength of Chicago lies not in the Sears Towers, or the Hancock Centers, but in the neighborhoods such as this one. Chicago, to be humanly alive, must sustain little homes inhabited by the common man."

Johnny and his brother Peter (who was called "Petey") went to school at St. Michael's parochial school, which provided a complete education system from grammar school through high school. The tradition of St. Michael's parish is historically one of the richest in Chicago, and their first house of worship was built by German Catholics in 1852 at the corner of North and Hudson. Land for a new parish was donated by wealthy German brewer Michael Diversey at the corner of what is now Cleveland and Eugenie.

The second St. Michael's was begun in 1866 and completed in 1869 in splendid red brick. Gutted by the Chicago Fire in 1871, the church was rebuilt and rededicated in 1873 when a magnificent 200-foot clock tower was added to the original structure. St. Michael's was designed in the grand fashion of Bavarian Baroque architecture, and the altar is an extraordinary monument of carved wood capped by a figure of the patron saint with sword and jeweled crown. St. Michael's towers above the smaller structures of the neighborhood, and is one of the most stunningly impressive churches in any city around the world. Chicago folklore states that you are within the boundaries of Old Town if you can hear the pealing of St. Michael's five bells.

Chicago, like many big cities after the turn of the century, was a human mosaic of ethnic and cultural diversity. North Town was predominately German, while other ethnic neighborhoods included Polish, Ukrainian, Russian, Lithuanian, Swedish, Irish, Hungarian, Italian, French-Canadian, and African-American. The population of Chicago burgeoned from 1.7 million at the turn of the century to 2.7 million in 1920; a great majority of these one million new residents were immigrants.

JAddams, Janeane Addams, winner of the 1931 Nobel Prize for her 46 years of service to poor immigrants at Hull House in Chicago, had this to say about the ethnic diversity around the turn of the century: "Between Halsted Street [six blocks east of Cleveland] and the river live about 10,000 Italians. In the south on 12th street are many Germans, and side streets are given over to Polish and Russian Jews. Still farther south, thin Jewish colonies merge into a huge Bohemian colony, so vast that Chicago ranks as the third Bohemian city in the world." (The original Hull House, founded in 1889 by Jane Addams, is preserved and located on Halsted near the University of Illinois at Chicago, about two and a half miles south of the former Weissmuller home on Cleveland Avenue.)

The numerous youth gangs of Chicago were based on ethnic heritage; if you lived in an Italian neighborhood, your friends and gang buddies were also Italian. Johnny was never more than on the fringe of the gang activity in his German neighborhood of North Town. By the time he was old enough to have his life influenced by gangs (easily a possibility without a real father-figure), Johnny was devoting his teenage energy to swimming and other sports. Johnny was a smart kid who learned his lessons early in life, and knew the difference between right and wrong.

In retrospect, Johnny recalled the thought processes that pushed him to work hard at his every endeavor, rather than choose crime (as many did) when gangsters and Prohibition moved into Chicago when he was an impressionable teenager:

"It's the way you start," said Johnny. "All through the years one always knows that nothing good will follow something evil. One might call it conscience, but I think it's more than that — it's an inbuilt heaven or hell."

According to Johnny, there was an Irish cop in his neighborhood named O'Malley that befriended the young man. In Chicago in those days there was probably an Irish cop named O'Malley walking the beat in most every neighborhood! But maybe, just maybe, this particular O'Malley was enough of a positive influence on Johnny to help him overcome the lack of a strong father-figure in his life. "When I was a kid," said Johnny, "if I

51

thought about what I would be when I grew up I probably would have said cop — or maybe a hood. Hoods were real big in those days, back in Chicago." (I guess you could say that Johnny chose the right path — his future career as Tarzan was the ultimate good guy.)

In his early youth Johnny was kept on the straight and narrow path by his mother Elizabeth, with her unequivocal love and devotion to both of her sons. Johnny occasionally had discipline impressed upon him during his school years at St. Michael's, where he also served as an altar boy. He learned some hard lessons from the Catholic brothers and the priest, whenever he stepped out of line by their rigid standards. (When Johnny later joined the Illinois Athletic Club, his coach, Bill Bachrach, became the father-figure he had lacked up to that point in his life on a continuing basis.)

At age twelve, Johnny left St. Michael's School and enrolled in Manierre Public School on Hudson Avenue, located a block from his house. This was a new experience for Johnny, after attending the all-boys parochial school at St. Michael's — his new classmates included members of the opposite sex. However, at this stage of his life he only cared about swimming (with little time for girls).

"I wish I could have stayed a middle-of-the-roader between my early apprehensions towards girls, and my later infatuations," said Johnny. "It might have saved a few fireworks." (While Johnny said "fireworks" in this later reminiscence, he undoubtedly meant "heartbreaks.")

In the early years in Chicago, Peter Weissmuller, Sr., worked for Keeley's Brewing Company, which was located on the South Side at 28th near Cottage Grove. Around 1916 he purchased a saloon in North Town, on Cleveland Avenue, just down the block from the Weissmuller home. Not a great deal is known about this latter venture, other than the fact that the elder Weissmuller ran it on a course that ended in financial ruin. The saloon eventually went out of business sometime before ProhibitionProhibition began in 1920.

Mr. Weissmuller was a drinking man, whose love of the bottle was greater than any love he would ever have for his family. His frustrations in life, compounded by the inevitable manifestations of alcoholism, were often taken out on Johnny and Peter in the form of violent beatings for disobeying even the simplest of his demands. It is little wonder that Johnny had no problem considering his father "dead" when his parents separated when he was a teenager. Terrible arguments between Peter Weissmuller and his wife Elizabeth were most often one-sided, with alcohol giving the man of the house all the courage he would need to win every fight.

One of the few times Johnny ever broke through the shell and spoke of his father, it was a bitter memory: "I ran away once and slept under an elevated railroad — but then came back to the beating I knew he would give me."

Perhaps the only good that ever came out of his father's saloon for Johnny was a pair of boxing gloves that he won as a prize, for collecting an extraordinary number of beer-bottle caps off the floor of the saloon. With the new gloves as an inspiration, Johnny became an accomplished pugilist at an early age, a skill that served him well in neighborhood fights with other young "toughs." The boxing gloves meant a lot to Johnny, as did his growing love for swimming. Johnny later recalled a childhood memory: "At Manierre School, I thought only about swimming, and went to bed with my pair of boxing gloves."

Interestingly, saloon keepers in those days were often aldermen as well. The last and most famous of this unusual breed of politician was Mathias "Paddy" Bauler, who ran the 43rd Ward's Democratic affairs for almost a half-century from his saloon at North Avenue and Sedgwick Street (approximately three blocks from the Weissmuller saloon). He began in the days of mayor Bill Thompson and gangster Al Capone in the Roaring '20s, and his most famous quote was, "Chicago ain't ready for reform." He also liked to tell reporters, with a sly grin, "I'll talk about anything, as long as the statute of limitations has run out."

While Mr. Weissmuller seemingly could do no right in money matters, Elizabeth carried the family financial burden and paid the bills with her job as the head cook for the Turn-Verein Society, a famous social organization located in northwest Chicago. The society held regular business meetings and gymnasium classes to promote a healthy mind and body. There was also a Ladies Section that helped to raise money for various charitable causes. The drum and fife corps gained great popularity, as did the fencing team. Perhaps the most noble achievement of the organization was the important role it played in introducing public playgrounds in the city of Chicago (as well as gymnastics into the public school system).

Mother Weissmuller was a wonderful cook and the dinner table always offered an abundance of healthy, delicious foods. Johnny and Peter, Jr. were well-fed and well-loved by their mother. Elizabeth Weissmuller was famous in the neighborhood for her apple strudel, a delicious recipe she had brought with her from the "old country." When it was "strudel day" at the Weissmuller house, the local children would all come by to join Johnny and Peter in enjoying a portion of this delicious treat.

Mrs. Weissmuller also instilled a love of music in her sons, and whenever possible took them with her when she was able to attend local opera productions. Being present at a live production of one of German composer Richard Wagner's classic operas, or a symphony by Viennese composer Franz Joseph Haydn, was one of the great joys of her life, especially if her sons were able to accompany her. Chicago was very much a center for the arts in the early years of the century, as it is now.

Chicago's own opera company was organized in 1910, with Cleofonte Campanini as musical director and first conductor. Artists for the new company were recruited from Hammerstein's disbanded Manhattan Opera, plus a number of premiere guest stars from the Metropolitan, including celebrated Italian tenor Enrico Caruso, who dropped in to sing in one performance of *The Girl of the Golden West*.

Architects Adler and Sullivan built The Auditorium in 1889, which had a 175-foot dining room and a magnificent 4,000-seat opera house, as well as the 400-room Auditorium Hotel. Opera singer Mary Garden later thrilled and enraptured Chicago audiences at The Auditorium, with her performance in

Pelleas et Melisande and many other productions. French actress Sarah Bernhardt also appeared at The Auditorium, and later proclaimed the city of Chicago to be "the pulse of America."

There would be plenty of music at the neighborhood picnics that would take place each summer in the North Town neighborhood (along with the traditional pig roast and gunnysack races). A yodeling contest was a much-anticipated event at the festivities, and these exhibitions later became the basis for part of the Weissmuller legend. Johnny listened and learned from the local masters of this "sport," which was a custom of Swiss and Tyrolese mountaineers. (Webster's dictionary defines yodel as "to call or sing with repeated transitions to the falsetto.")

The famous Weissmuller Tarzan yell, which according to this account from Johnny, was inspired by his participation in these mostly-for-fun yodeling contests. Eventually Johnny became quite proficient at the art of yodeling, as he recalled:

"My family came from Vienna, and in Chicago we would go to the German picnics on Sundays. And they had yodeling contests and I learned to yodel pretty well myself. It took me a few months to learn to yodel, but I eventually perfected it. I had a very high voice when I started out in athletics — but I wasn't the only one. Jack Dempsey and Gene

Tunney both had high voices and I did too, until I received some voice training when I went into the movies.

"But when I was chosen to do Tarzan, they were looking for a yell for the ape-man to do in the pictures, as the character created by Edgar Rice Burroughs did in the books. So I said, 'I know a yell, a yodel, from my childhood.' So I did the yodel and they modified it and turned it over to the MGM sound boys to create what you hear in the Tarzan pictures. But I practiced the yell for a couple of months and by the second Tarzan picture I was able to do it by myself."

Johnny was also an avid reader as a youth, and years later he recalled reading the first few Tarzan books written by Edgar Rice Burroughs. Johnny was probably around 12-years-old by the time a secondhand copy of Burroughs' first novel, *Tarzan of the Apes* (which had been published in book form in 1914) came into his hands. The first Tarzan motion picture was released in 1918, and starred Elmo Lincoln, whom Johnny would meet years later. Johnny was only 14-years-old when Tarzan first reached the silver screen, and a silent screen at that.

It is interesting to note that the Weissmuller home in North Town was less than one mile from the Biograph Theatre, where the death scene of John Dillinger was played out in deadly fashion in 1934. Johnny plunked down his quarter at the Biograph many times during his youth to enjoy the silent films of his heroes, Douglas Fairbanks, Sr., Lon Chaney, and William S. Hart. He often would sit through as many as five shows in a row, changing seats at the end of each feature to avoid the ushers.

(On the night of July 22, 1934, Dillinger was gunned down by Chicago police and FBI agents, when he left the Biograph after watching Clark Gable get the electric chair in *Manhattan Melodrama*. His female companion that evening was Anna Sage, the fabled "Lady in Red," who had betrayed her lover to the FBI in hopes of avoiding deportation to her native Romania. Elsewhere in America on that fatal night during the midst of the Depression, theater patrons would be watching Johnny Weissmuller and Maureen O'Sullivan in their classic adventure, *Tarzan and His Mate*.)

Johnny, like many youngsters of poor families, went to work at an early age to help with the family finances. One of his earliest jobs was delivering packages for a church supply company. One could just picture this young, tall and skinny lad with a mop of dark hair, riding the Chicago trolley-cars with his bundles of packages, resolute in accomplishing his mission and happy in the knowledge he would bring home a few pennies to help out his mother. This could be dangerous work for a young lad like Johnny, as English author William Archer noted in his book, *The Green Goddess*: ". . . you take your life in your hands when you attempt the crossing of State Street, with its endless stream of rattling wagons and clanging trolley-cars."

Johnny also earned baskets of fresh vegetables and fruit, working for a produce peddler with a horse-drawn cart. Riding around the neighborhood with the old man on mornings before school, Johnny would call out in his high-pitched voice, "Fresh fruit and vegetables! Tomatoes . . . cucumbers . . . beans and cabbage!" Perhaps this was Johnny's first taste of show business, hawking produce with a voice that would someday be famous.

There were many of these horse-drawn businesses-on-wheels roaming the streets of Chicago in those days, as author George Ade noted in his *Chicago Stories*. Besides the vegetable carts and young Weissmuller's high-pitched hawking, there were also "the red wagons of waffle men, wheeled street pianos, mobile cobblers, carts selling straw for bedding, buffet carts specializing in ham-and-egg sandwiches and other tasty treats such as fresh lemonade, sweets, pies, and even chewing-gum wagons in the city of Wrigley."

Johnny would give most of his earnings to his mother, but each week he would save a few pennies until he finally had enough to buy a secondhand sled that became his most cherished possession. Johnny and his brother Peter took the sled to the local park to glide down a snowy slope, and they took turns hauling each other along the icy neighborhood streets. Seeking additional speed, Johnny hooked his sled rope to a delivery truck and then held on for the most exciting ride of his life.

The sled careened along the city streets at breakneck speed, and Johnny held on for dear life! Suddenly the speed was too much, and hitting a bump in the road he was thrown off the sled to the snow-covered pavement. He skidded to a halt and to his utter horror and chagrin, the precious sled remained tied to the back of the truck and disappeared from his sight forevermore.

"I remember sitting in the snow, crying my heart out," lamented Johnny years later. "It was so cold that tears froze on my cheeks."

CHAPTER THREE

Swimming: A Legend Begins

Chicago around the turn of the century was a pretty decent place for a kid to grow towards adulthood, and provided plenty of areas to run, jump, play and swim (the beaches along Lake Michigan). By the year 1893, the city fathers had spent $24 million dollars on eight large and twenty-nine small parks and squares, connected by thirty-five miles of boulevard.

The largest of the parks in Chicago was Lincoln Park on the North Shore of Lake Michigan, a marvelous park that was no more than four short blocks from Johnny's house on Cleveland Avenue. (Lincoln Park was originally called Lake Park, and was renamed in 1865 after Lincoln's assassination by John Wilkes Booth.) The Lincoln Park Zoo, founded in 1874 with a solitary bear cub (valued at ten dollars), was also within the boundaries of Lincoln Park. This provided a wonderful opportunity for youngsters like

Johnny and his friends to visit one of the world's finest zoos — a splendid collection of species that was practically in their own backyards.

As an adult Johnny recalled his fascination with the ferocious big cats of the zoo: the lions, tigers, and panthers. Little did he realize these big cats would become an integral part of his future as Tarzan in the Hollywood jungle. Johnny also loved horses and learned to ride bareback at the old Armory, where he volunteered to exercise the noble creatures. (This experience also proved useful to Johnny, when he mounted a stallion and rode bareback in the 1943 feature, *Tarzan's Desert Mystery*.)

There were many activities and celebrations held in Lincoln Park, such as the annual Fourth of July picnic, that were primarily aimed at familiarizing European immigrants with American customs and traditions. In a glowing tribute to Lincoln Park, author Ade, GeorgeGeorge Ade said, "No Chicago millionaire has such a magnificent front yard." Fortunately for Johnny, there was also the mighty Lake Michigan to complement Lincoln Park. Graceful swan boats moved slowly about the lake, carrying young lovers out for a cruise. The park's iron bridge was a sight to behold, and was often lined with pedestrians enjoying the sights and sounds of the park and lake.

Johnny's lifelong affair with water started at the age of eight-years-old, when his mother brought him and little brother Petey to the "Baby Beach" (also known as Fullerton Beach) in Lincoln Park for their first swimming lessons. The water at Fullerton Beach is shallow and calm, on the west side of a protected bay that juts in from Lake Michigan. Mrs. Weissmuller bought a pair of water wings for the boys to share, and they took turns in the water splashing around with the other children. Johnny eventually came to love the water so much that he practically lived at Fullerton Beach during the summer months.

Johnny made friends with other boys who gathered at Fullerton Beach, and as they collectively grew older and bolder, they moved northward up the beach to a rugged breakwater of massive craggy boulders, appropriately called "the Rocks." Strong waves pushed by the winds gusting across Lake Michigan would crash against the Rocks, and this watery playground was a proving ground for the boys who were now confident in their swimming abilities. Johnny recalled years later the excitement and danger of the Rocks: "Swimming had come naturally to me," said Johnny, "and like all kids I had yearned for adventure. Swimming over the Rocks was dangerous, but it was exciting."

The frothy waters at the Rocks were cold

and rough, and Johnny and his friends learned to dive and perform stunts off of the mighty projecting boulders into the deep waters. Johnny recalled these days as being unforgettable and mostly carefree. "We used to swim when no one was looking," recalled Johnny with a laugh, "because we didn't have any swim suits."

Johnny, a fierce competitor even at this early stage of life, entered all of the boys' races sponsored in the summer months by Lincoln Park. One of the officials in charge of those races was George T. Donoghue, who would later become chairman of the athletic committee of the Illinois Athletic Club.

Stanton Park was part of Johnny's neighborhood, and he and his buddies "Hank" Miller and "Hooks" Miller joined the team at the Stanton Park Pool one summer when they discovered the exhilaration of swimming competition. According to Johnny, he and his two friends dominated those junior team championships.

As the years passed, Johnny became obsessed with swimming; he simply had to be in the water every single day. The beaches along Lake Michigan became his playground, and the waters of the lake became his domain. The North Avenue Beach was the closest to his house, but Johnny would sprint the extra half-mile or so down the shoreline to the Oak Street Beach. This particular beach was a sweeping stretch of sand at the south end of Lincoln Park, which became his favorite hangout and swimming hole.

Johnny's childhood companions included his own brother Peter, the Miller brothers, and Fred Lauer, who went by the nickname of "Pal." (Lauer, a tall handsome lad with a mop of black hair, would later be a teammate of Johnny's on the United States water polo team that competed in the 1924 Olympics and claimed a bronze medal.)

Often accompanying him on his daily excursions to the beach was his childhood pet, a Dachshund named "Hans." Considering Johnny's love of the water, it is humorous that his dog was afraid of the lake and couldn't swim a stroke. The proof of his lack of swimming ability came when he accidentally fell in the lake one day and Johnny was fortunately close by to save his life. The phrase "loyal as a dog" was never more true after Johnny's canine rescue, and Hans' adulation for his master increased tenfold. Johnny would always have a love for animals, and this affinity would become dramatically important when he would later work with the chimps, big cats, and elephants, in his Tarzan movies.

Once the outdoor swimming season was over and the chill of fall was in the air, it was necessary for Johnny and friends to find an indoor pool to further their watery ambitions.

The North Side YMCA on Larrabee Street was the logical choice, but for Johnny there was one small problem: the age to join the "Y" was twelve, but Johnny was younger.

Years later, Johnny admitted the chicanery that allowed him to join the "Y" team at a premature age: "I started out in the 'Y' and eventually became YMCA champion," said Johnny. "You had to be twelve to join, but I was tall for my age and got in at eleven. We didn't have any indoor pools in Chicago, so I couldn't wait any longer to be old enough to join the 'Y'. That lake was darn cold!" Johnny swam at the "Y" until age 14, and not only won all of his swimming races but also was the champion at running and high jumping. Johnny also recalled: "The only thing about the 'Y' was that we could go in only twice a week, and that wasn't enough for such fish as we were turning out to be!"

The summer before Johnny joined the YMCA, he reached his eleventh birthday on June 2, 1915. About seven weeks later, on July 24th, one of worst tragedies in United States history happened in Chicago, on Lake Michigan. History recalls that on this date the excursion steamer *Eastland* was loaded with over 2,000 passengers, mostly employees and family members of the Western Electric Company. They were bound for a cruise around Lake Michigan and then an after-

67

noon picnic along the Indiana Dunes.

The crowds of spectators watching from shore were thrilled to see this marvelous ship filled with hundreds of happy people about to embark on a fun-filled adventure. Unfortunately, the vessel was perilously overloaded and top-heavy, as the crew had emptied ballast tanks to allow additional passengers to board beyond capacity. As the *Eastland* began to ease away from its Chicago River dock between the Clark and La Salle Street bridges, the ship began to list dangerously to the port side, where a majority of the passengers had crowded to watch the passing river traffic. As this terrible tragedy unfolded before the eyes of the shocked spectators, gravity sent hundreds more frantic passengers to the port side of the vessel, which overturned violently in the shallow waters. The *Chicago Daily News* reported the horrific scene the following day:

"The river seemed covered with struggling forms. Life preservers were thrown from other boats, lines from shore, boxes and barrels from the commission houses on South Water Street and everything movable that would float by frantic spectators on shore, but dozens of those in the water disappeared under the waves or were dragged down by others."

Meanwhile on shore, policemen and volunteers leaped to quick action to form human chains and pull survivors from the water and drag them to safety. The *Eastland* death toll, the single worst disaster in Chicago history, was 835 victims, including 22 entire families. Many of the passengers were trapped below the main deck and drowned, while others were trampled in a panicked stampede to escape death via a staircase.

Johnny would never forget the lesson that he learned this sad day, after this cataclysmic event happened very near the beaches where he and his friends spent virtually every summer day. His entire life, he advised and advocated that swimming be taught to all youngsters at a very early age, to avoid what happened to many of the unlucky passengers who simply could not swim to save their own lives. Perhaps the impact of this tragic day was a major motivating force that helped to turn him into a champion swimmer and Olympic hero. (Twelve years later, almost to the day, Johnny would save the lives of eleven people, after the similarly tragic capsizing of the excursion boat, *Favorite*, on Lake Michigan.)

As these early years passed and Johnny's swimming skills grew stronger, his audience began to grow in size and admiration of the talented young man. An assistant coach named Peters from the Hamilton Club spotted Johnny one afternoon cutting through the waves off the Oak Street Beach, and invited him to try out for their swimming team. Johnny trained at this club for a period of months, and his raw talent eventually allowed him to achieve respectable times around 58 seconds for the 100-yard sprint. The coach at the Hamilton Club admitted to Johnny that he would have to join a big-time program like the Illinois Athletic Club, where both the coaching and competition would be at the highest level.

As Johnny approached his sixteenth birthday, he was an awkward six-feet tall, broad in the shoulders, and his gangly frame carried around 160 pounds. Both Johnny and his brother Peter had wiry builds, and later in life he disclaimed the story that he was "sickly" or suffered in ill health as a youth:

"That was something we put out to inspire the kids," Johnny admitted. "I was skinny, all right, but there was nothing sickly about me. I would have filled out even without swimming."

Johnny also quit school during this period of time, after his parents' separation. The only things of importance at this juncture of his life were swimming and a new job he had landed as a bellboy and elevator operator at the Plaza Hotel (located in North Town at 1553 N. Clark Street, a few blocks from his house).

But being a bellhop/elevator operator for a

small salary and tips wasn't his life's ambition; it was a necessity to help out his mother and younger brother, as well as putting a few coins in his own empty pockets. This young man had visions of being a champion, and getting out of the old neighborhood and rising to heights a boy could only imagine in his wildest dreams.

Although this was the end of his formal schooling, Johnny was now getting his education at the "school of hard knocks." A dropout by necessity at an early age, Johnny was never truly in danger of becoming a "bad" kid. He simply had too much drive to become a champion, determination to make a better life, and talent — above all, Johnny had an immense amount of talent in his chosen field.

At this point in time, what Johnny needed most was a big-time coach, who could squeeze the most out of the gifted young man. Johnny longed to join the Illinois Athletic Club where his buddy Hooks Miller had made the team and was training under William Bachrach. When Miller helped to arrange an audition for Johnny with coach Bachrach to try out for the I.A.C. team, young Weissmuller's stars were beginning to align in the heavens. Fate was taking its course, and the bonding of pupil and teacher would soon have extraordinary consequences.

Before continuing with the saga of Johnny Weissmuller, we should briefly tell the story of the politics of the city of Chicago during this era of Prohibition and the Roaring '20s. William "Big Bill" Thompson served three terms as mayor of Chicago between 1915 and 1931, and sadly was one of the most notoriously crooked politicians in the history of the United States. William Hale Thompson is necessary to mention here because his administration affected the lives of all Chicagoans, including the Weissmuller family. He even lightly touched Weissmuller's career as an amateur swimmer, when Johnny won the "William Hale Thompson" trophy in 1927 for winning the three-mile Chicago River Marathon.

Thompson was elected mayor in 1915, and then served two terms through 1923. A contemporary critic boldly stated: "Thompson has given the city an international reputation for moronic buffoonery, barbaric crime, triumphant hoodlumism, unchecked graft and a dejected citizenship. He nearly ruined the property and completely destroyed the pride of the city. He made Chicago a byword of the collapse of American civilization." (Judge William E. Dever, an honest politician, served as mayor for the next four years as the criminal element fought desperately to remain in control.)

Thompson eventually became friends with Al Capone and formed an unholy alliance with the up-and-coming mob kingpin. (Although the Illinois Athletic Club removed Thompson's photograph from its hallowed halls, the same portrait of the Chicago mayor did hang in the hotel suite of Al Capone, where he lived at the Lexington Hotel during the 1920s.) In 1927, with the backing of Capone and his crime syndicate, Thompson was reelected for a final four-year term of crooked politics.

The beginning of the end for "Scarface Al" and the crooked regime of William Thompson was the arrival on the Chicago scene in 1929 of Eliot Ness and his small band of loyal bravehearts, branded "the Untouchables" by the Chicago press. In his own words from his 1957 book, *The Untouchables*, Mr. Ness said:

"That was Chicago in 1929, a city ruled by the knife, pistol, shotgun, tommygun, and 'pineapple' of the underworld, a jungle of steel and concrete clutched fast in the fat, diamond-studded hand of a scar-faced killer named Al Capone."

Eliot Ness may have been using dramatic license here to emphasize his point, but it was all true. However, this biography is not the place to tell the unholy tale of William Thompson and his crooked administration, or the equally sordid story of Al Capone. Suffice to say that while all the negative headlines were created in Chicago by these men of evil doings, a young man of seventeen years, Johnny Weissmuller, began creating headlines in 1921 that enthralled all of America with his brilliant athletic achievements.

CHAPTER FOUR

Johnny & Big Bill: Mutual Admiration Society

Before Johnny Weissmuller began training with Bill Bachrach, he was — metaphorically speaking — a lump of clay. To be sure, a lump of clay with vast potential. But he needed the loving hand of a skilled sculptor to realize and mold his potential as a swimmer. Bachrach was undoubtedly the most influential force, and made the largest contribution of any single person, to Johnny's unequaled success as a swimmer. The "Great Bach" was arguably the best swimming coach in America, and the pool at the Illinois A.C. was one of the finest in the country — a dual enticement that had Johnny salivating at the prospect of becoming a member of the team.

Bachrach was a father-figure to all of this swimmers, male and female, and the numerous champions he developed would win 120 national A.A.U. championships during his years with the Illinois Athletic Club (often shortened to I.A.C.). When Johnny first was introduced to Bill Bachrach, whose official title was Swimming Director, it was October of 1920. Bachrach, born in 1879, was approaching his prime of life at age 41, and lived at the Morrison Hotel in downtown Chicago.

William Bachrach was of the Jewish faith, a big man at six-feet tall and a solid, muscular physique of three-hundred pounds. Bachrach had red hair complemented by a bushy moustache, and was usually dressed in a weathered bath robe. He got his nickname, Big Bill, from his size and he invariably had a cigar sticking out of his mouth, even in the swimming pool area. "Bach" was an imposing figure of a man, but he also had an aura about him that manifested his wonderful capabilities as a coach. He had the critical ability to communicate with his students — to get inside their heads and know what they were thinking. Although at first glance Bachrach appeared to be gruff, his heart was made of pure gold and inside he was smiling — on occasion the smile even showed upon his face, rimmed by his crimson moustache and customary stogie.

You could call this first meeting of master and pupil an audition, but Bachrach had heard enough about young Weissmuller that he wasn't about to let him get away.

Bachrach knew talent, and he had a "sixth sense" about Johnny — he had a gut feeling this was that once-in-a-lifetime opportunity for greatness. And this tall, skinny kid was standing in front of him, hoping to impress the "Coach" enough to make the I.A.C. team.

Little did Johnny know, he had nothing to worry about on this particular autumn afternoon. "I'll never forget him that day," recalled Johnny. "Bachrach was dressed in a tattered bath robe, chewing a cigar, and his hands were perched on his spacious hips. He took a cool, unfriendly glance at me."

"So you're the great swimmer I've been hearing about," muttered Bachrach through his cigar. "You think you're good, eh? Well, let's see what you've got. Get into the pool and swim 100-yards."

Johnny later recalled this fateful moment in time. "I plunged in while Bachrach watched me, and I ploughed through the water with the terrible stroke I had in those days. I could make good time because I was so long and skinny, shooting through the water like a stick. But I was willing to try to swim five times my accustomed distance at top speed.

"As I look back now, my stroke was terrible. I plunged into the water and started to swim my head off. At the end of the 25-yards — and 75-yards from my goal — I was completely exhausted. I was ashamed of myself. It was then that I received the most important lesson — in swimming or in life. Bachrach told me to swim for form and not for speed. Throughout my career I swam for form. Speed came as a result of it."

Johnny had admitted that the best thing he had going for him was his immense desire, and a willingness to learn! Despite this young stringbean's lack of form, "Bach" was impressed with the raw talent of his new protégé. "He had the gawkiness of an adolescent puppy, and he was awkward," recalled Bachrach. "Also the stroke he used was the oddest thing I ever saw — no form, no nothing. But the stopwatch told it all; nearly record time, and the kid wasn't even trying. By the time he got out and dried off, he was an official member of the Illinois Athletic Club."

At that moment Bachrach handed him a membership card for the Illinois Athletic Club swimming team. Johnny was a little stunned and somewhat in awe of this small square of heavyweight paper that answered his most immediate dream — he was in!

Johnny could only nod his head, as all words seemed to have frozen in his mouth as Bachrach began his mesmerizing speech: "Well, you'll have to do everything I say, without question for a long time. You are terrible now. But because of your long, slender body, you have possibilities. I'll try if you will. And if you work hard enough, you'll be champion."

Coach Bachrach pulled Johnny off to one side, away from the other swimmers, and said: "Now you come down tomorrow and I will start you on a real course of training. You are going to get something that I have never given anybody before — these other boys will not be in your class at all. Now I'm going to change your stroke all over, and I want you to do everything I say to the letter, without question." Johnny agreed without hesitation.

"At that time my stroke was all wrong," he recalled. "I crossed over my arms in front: that is, I reached across what would be an extended line in front from my shoulder, reached across my head with each hand in turn. I held my arms straight and swept them wide; I didn't make a full stroke with the arms. My legs were used in a 'mongrel' way, and I had no system about breathing, body position, or anything else."

Bachrach began his new pupil's training by working with the arms only, and completely ignoring his mongrel leg kick, as Johnny had called it. For these initial months, all he learned was the arm stroke, and what would turn out to be the most critical part of his education — relaxation. These two facets (arm stroke and relaxation) were so important that Bachrach told Johnny to kick or not to kick — it didn't really matter. So Johnny would just let his legs trail behind in the water — his feet encased in a rubber tube to make them float — during these daily arm stroke sessions.

The key to relaxation, as taught by Bachrach, was to get rest within the stroke. In theory, this meant to be able to relax while still maintaining the stroke and swimming at optimum speed. In practice, Bachrach's method of relaxation could only be learned after many long hours in the pool, and following to the letter the technical points of his instruction.

The mental aspect of swimming was continually pounded into Johnny by his mentor. He would stop him from time to time and ask: "What are you thinking about, John?"

"I'm thinking about not crossing over with my hands out in front," replied Johnny. "I'm thinking about keeping my elbow bent; about not reaching too far out in front."

Johnny would go back to practicing his arm stroke, while maintaining relaxation, and Bachrach would stop him again with the same question: "What are you thinking about now, John?"

Johnny would answer that he was thinking about how and when to bend his elbows; about not holding his arms straight; about keeping his shoulders flat, and not dipping down with either shoulder on the arm he was stroking with; about keeping the shoulder and elbow higher than the hand when making the catch of the hand; about keeping the head up.

While Johnny worked hard in the pool, the Coach puffed on his cigar and appeared to be dozing from time to time. Suddenly he would blare out at Johnny:

"What are you doing with your right arm?"

"Digging with it," was the pupil's reply.

"Why?" shouted Bachrach as Johnny swam on.

"Because it gives me more power. I must put my hand in first to keep my shoulder up above water, so that the water will pass under my arm and not retard me."

When the question of relaxation was posed, Johnny was ready with his answer. Yes, he was thinking every minute of his time in the pool about relaxation. Bachrach would constantly extol the virtues of relaxation in regard to swimming technique, and the utter importance of keeping it in the forefront of your mind. As the months passed, Johnny learned Bachrach's critically important relaxation lessons well, as he later recalled:

"It's the greatest secret of my success," noted Johnny. "Relaxing at the same time you are swimming at maximum speed."

Bachrach also imparted to Johnny the secret of the arm stroke — it is simple yet difficult to master.

"The arm stroke is a pull and a push; not a thrash or a sweep or a chop or anything else," said Johnny. "Bachrach showed me just how to get this 'pull and push.' The pull part comes first. After making the catch of the hand in front, not reaching too far out in front, but reducing the reach by bending the elbow, and keeping the elbow and shoulder higher at all times than the hand, you pull almost straight down in the water on a line with the shoulder. When the hand comes under the shoulder and to the breast, the pull ceases and it becomes a push.

"At this point the hand is about eight or ten inches separated from the breast, and the elbow is pointed out. From here you carry on the stroke, pushing backward and outward. The push ends at the hip and then you relax your arm. You bend the elbow still more, and in recovery your upper arm is carried parallel to the water, the lower arm and hand flopping loosely at an angle of forty-five degrees. Here the lower arm, wrist, and hand are getting their relaxation. As the arm arrives to the forward position, it straightens somewhat, and here you get your relaxation in the upper arm and shoulder.

"Always I am thinking about getting this relaxation, keeping easy and loose all over. I developed a great arm stroke during these months when I never used my legs and feet, but forgot about them as much as possible."

When Johnny started his training, the world's champion sprinter was Duke Kahanamoku of Honolulu. The Duke, the current Olympic champion in the 100-meters, swam with his back arched and his head up so he could see where he was going. He was a champion at short distances because of his powerful leg kick, a kick that Bachrach taught to his pupils.

Eventually, Bachrach started Johnny on the leg stroke. Johnny spent one hour of each day in the pool holding a board and practicing the perfect kick of the Duke. Bachrach taught him to flutter the legs up and down at the rate of six beats of the legs with each revolution of the arms. That meant three leg beats on each arm as it was making its pull. Johnny would count "one-two-three, four-five-six," for many hours in the pool, every day, for many months in this initial training period.

In his own words, Johnny described the importance of adding the leg kick to the arm stroke, as at this point he became a whole swimmer once again: "Now getting the legs into play changed the position of my body. The legs drove me higher in the water, lifted my whole body up so that my chest was hydroplaning on the surface; my head was up high, and that part of my back between the shoulders, and almost to the waist, was clearly out of the water.

"Lots of swimmers can get their heads up, but this throws their feet down so that they are swimming more at an angle than I do. My whole torso rides on the surface of the water, and only my hips and legs are submerged. This position is achieved by arching the back up and getting tremendous power with the leg drive.

"Once you get up to this position, you ride with great ease, except for the fact that you've got to keep going fast to hold the position. If I swam slower, I'd use just as much effort in getting the reduced speed, because I'd be lower in the water, encountering more resistance."

A fellow swimmer at the I.A.C. was Norman Ross, a Bachrach disciple who was also an Olympic champion in the 400-meters (1920 Antwerp Games). Ross was noted for his perfect starts; Johnny was able to learn his secrets firsthand by watching his teammate. Ross would coil his body like a giant spring, and launch himself into the pool with one leg low. His leg would hit first and break the plunge, and the body would then glide over the surface of the water. By the end of the glide the arm-and-body stroke and leg kick would be in motion. Johnny watched and learned, copying the starting technique of an Olympic champion.

Johnny also learned the techniques of another champion, Harry Hebner, who was the world's tank champion. Hebner's strengths included the ability to make a perfect turn at the end of each lap in the pool. Swimming at top speed as he neared the edge of the pool, Hebner would use his arm as a rudder to turn his feet for a quick kick-out underwater. Johnny quickly learned the perfect turn developed by Hebner, as Bachrach sat back and smiled at the abilities of his pupil.

And so it went these first months of training for Johnny under Bill Bachrach. He was not allowed to race another swimmer, nor to even race against the stopwatch. The Coach had his master plan for his prize student, and he did not want his ego bruised with defeats in the pool before he had completed his initial training. Bachrach didn't need a stopwatch to see that Johnny was the fastest swimmer he had ever seen, and that his form was now nearly perfect.

During his training period, he had successfully learned the strongest techniques of the best swimmers in the world. In most cases he had improved upon these techniques, as his own natural ability took over. Johnny could dive into the pool with the power and grace of Norman Ross, and make the turns at the end of the pool as well or better than Harry Hebner. He had adopted — and improved upon — the powerful leg kick of the Duke, and the relaxation techniques taught by Bachrach allowed Johnny to swim with a relaxed, rolling body motion. He swam with his head up, like the Duke; however, the arch in back was not high enough to impede his speed in water or exhaust him.

Johnny had learned his lessons well, and it would soon be time for his first formal competition. He would have to compete against some of the best swimmers in the country, but Bachrach mentally acknowledged that he would soon be ready. Bachrach also visited Johnny one day at the Plaza Hotel where he was employed as a bell boy and elevator operator. He noticed Johnny lugging heavy suitcases around the hotel for the guests, and realized that he might hurt himself.

Bachrach asked Johnny if he would give up the job and concentrate on his swimming training, at his request. The wise mentor drove home a point to Johnny that he could do a lot better for his family by becoming a swimming champion, perhaps even an Olympic champion, than the few bucks he earned each week at the hotel. Johnny listened and agreed with some reluctance, knowing that the money had helped out at home. But Johnny was willing to tighten his belt, so to speak, and thus that was the end of his job at the Plaza. It was good advice, and Johnny always listened to the Coach.

CHAPTER FIVE

Print the Legend!

A true part of the Weissmuller legend was his undefeated swimming career from his official debut in A.A.U. competition in August of 1921, through his final race in January of 1929. But before that, before becoming something beyond a mortal being, Johnny was as capable of defeat as anyone else on this planet. When he joined the I.A.C. swim team, several of his senior teammates were faster than "the new kid on the block" in the various freestyle races. Bachrach suspected that Johnny would become a champion in the future, but he was keeping him under wraps until he was ready to handle all comers.

On January 6, 1921, coach Bachrach allowed Johnny to swim in a meet held at the I.A.C. pool, as some Central A.A.U. championships were being contested on that Thursday evening. In the January, 1921, issue of the I.A.C. club magazine, Johnny's name appeared in print for the first time, noting him as "the coming champion."

The account of the meet in the club magazine contained one paragraph which mentioned Johnny, albeit a nervous Johnny, competing in his first meet: "Herbert Topp, of the C.A.A., defeated J. Weissmuller in the men's junior hundred-yard championship in 57.4 seconds. Weissmuller is a schoolboy of sixteen, and he is new to open competition work. He made three false starts, jumping in the water each time, which, with his somewhat erratic swimming, showed his over-anxiety."

One published report of the meet noted that Johnny finished second in this non-sanctioned race not because of a lack of speed — but because of his shaggy hair! Weissmuller tried out a swimming cap for the only time in his career, to try to control his unruly mop of hair. During the race the cap suddenly slipped down over his eyes, and half-blinded he finished a close second. Coach Bachrach gave Johnny the obvious edict: "Lose the cap and get a haircut!"

Johnny was also allowed to participate in a meet for a second time at the Great Lakes Naval Training Station on March 17, 1921. His name appeared in the April issue of the club magazine, this time listing him as the winner of the open hundred-yard freestyle race, defeating teammate Jamison "Jam" Handy in a time of one minute, 1.4 seconds.

A one-column photograph of Johnny was captioned "one of the most promising of our young swimmers." Johnny was also mentioned as finishing second to Norman Ross, of the I.A.C., in the national championship at 500-yards freestyle. There was no shame in losing to Ross, a triple gold medal winner at the 1920 Olympics with his victories coming in the 400 and 1500-meter freestyle events, as well as the 4x200-meter freestyle relay.

According to Bill Bachrach, these two races were "preliminary tryouts," and should not count as losses against Johnny's record. Basically, coach Bachrach just threw Johnny into "shark-infested waters" to see how he would do — and he did just fine after his initial case of nervousness subsided. After testing Weissmuller in these two tryouts in the winter of 1921, Bachrach kept his protégé out of all competitions during the next five months of intensive training. As Johnny's technique improved over the coming summer months, so did his speed in the pool. Johnny followed the training of Bachrach to the letter, as he had demanded many months before, and now the results were beginning to pay dividends.

History records August 6, 1921, as Johnny's official debut in competitive swimming at the Duluth Boat Club in Minnesota. Many of the best swimmers in the world were at Duluth for this meet, including top U.S. swimmers Teddy Cann and Norman Ross.

(Cann held the world record in the 50-yard freestyle, while Ross held the world indoor record in the 100-yard freestyle.) Both Johnny and coach Bachrach were confident that he was ready to take on the best swimmers in the world, who were present this afternoon. He had his arm around Johnny, as he imparted a few last moment words of wisdom:

"Don't lose your head," whispered Bachrach. "Don't try to outswim them. You can swim faster than any of them. Let them pace you until you reach the three-quarters mark. Then you sprint. When you start out in front, the little man with the lead hammer will hit them on the head, and then watch them fall back."

As Johnny strode to the edge of the pool to assume his starting position, he snapped a salute to Bachrach, who smiled back proudly at the young man. Once the starter's whistle blew, Johnny blew by the competition! He won his first A.A.U. championship in the 50-yard freestyle, and he did it in smashing style! His time of 23.2 seconds was within one-fifth of a second of the world's record! He also won the Central title in the 100-yard freestyle, with a time of 55.2 seconds — his best time to date in this particular length race and several seconds faster than when he started training under Bachrach just ten months prior. Capping off his incredible performance in his first officially sanctioned meet, he also easily won the 120-yard and 150-yard freestyle races.

The other top swimmers were stunned by Johnny's performance, as he won every race he entered with ease. Cann couldn't believe it, and thought perhaps it had been a fluke. Teddy Cann was a great champion himself, and also a real-life hero. Cann was awarded the Congressional Medal of Honor during World War I for risking his own life while repairing a hole in a sinking ship that had been sabotaged. But Johnny did all the sabotaging on this date, and his wins were no fluke — he wouldn't lose an individual freestyle race for the balance of his lengthy career.

On August 27th and 28th, a schedule of A.A.U. outdoor championship races were contested at the Edgewater Beach Hotel in Chicago. (Located on the lake's edge at 5349 N. Sheridan Road, this luxury hotel was built in 1916 and was a favorite dining and dancing spot for Chicagoans as well as visitors to the Windy City.)

Coach Bachrach kept Johnny out of the individual competitions, but he was part of the I.A.C. relay team competing in the 400-yard relay. On the first day they won the title (with Johnny swimming second) in a time of three minutes, fifty-one seconds — a new world's record! On the second day of the meet, Johnny anchored the relay team that won the

400-yard Central title, in a time just one second slower than their record-breaking performance of the previous day.

The handsome young phenom from Chicago was an instant celebrity in his own city after his triumphs at Duluth, and at these national championships. The next A.A.U. meet for Johnny and the I.A.C. team would be in Brighton Beach, New York, in the last week of September. Newspaper stories originating in Chicago calling Weissmuller "the next world's champion" were met with an amount of incredulity in the "Big Apple," as Johnny recalled:

"With these two meets I had made my debut in regular competition successfully, in Central and National championship events, and won some recognition in the Middle West. I had come near a world record, but had not yet broken one. Comments from the East [N.Y. newspapers] indicated some skepticism of the stories they had heard about me. Experts in one section of the country are always a bit doubtful about the timing of performances announced in other sections, and in other countries.

"It was only natural, therefore, that I went East in the latter part of September, anxious to make a good showing and convince the world that my first performances were not a false alarm. This anxiety, felt also by my teammates, keyed me up to the point that I not only won every race I entered, but established my first world's record."

Johnny's first two world's records were set at Brighton Beach on September 27, 1921. In the prestigious 100-meter freestyle, Johnny was once again up against Ross and Cann, both of whom were bent on redemption after their previous loss to the young upstart from the I.A.C. Halfway through the race the three young champions were neck-and-neck in the water, until suddenly Johnny shot into high gear, arms and legs furiously orchestrating that beautiful Weissmuller crawl. This was a world record-setting performance in a spectacular time of one-minute and four-tenths of a second!

Not content with one world's record, Johnny raced to another in the distance of 150-yards. His time of one-minute, 27.4 seconds, knocked 2.2 seconds off of the previous record held by Teddy Cann of New York. Johnny also set a record in the 120-yard freestyle, and won the 300-yard freestyle race by a comfortable margin over the frustrated competition. (Eventually, over the course of his career, Johnny would set so many records and earn enough trophies that his trophy room would be literally filled to the brim!)

As the 1921 outdoors season progressed,

Johnny also won the 220-yard national championship at Indianapolis, Indiana. Johnny defeated Ludy Langer of Hui Nalu, Hawaii, and his own teammate, Norman Ross, in a time of two minutes and 28 seconds (a very fast time, but not a record). He also won the fifty-yard National, and the Central hundred-yard freestyle, as well as being the dominant cog on the National and Central championship 400-yard relay teams.

The records and championships for Johnny began to pile up, and his next freestyle world's record was set in late November, in the sixty-foot pool at the I.A.C. An article in the *'Tri-Color'* magazine for December of 1921, described Johnny's sterling day:

"On November 21, Johnny took it upon himself to make a mark in swimming history. The I.A.C. staged an open swimming meet for the benefit of a visiting delegation of A.A.U. officials from all over the country. These officials were here to pass on new records for the year, and also to award various athletic events to clubs bidding for them.

"Bachrach had a premonition that something was going to happen. He felt that certain records were threatened, so every precaution was taken to see that any records made would be authentic. The A.A.U. officials measured the tank to the fraction of an inch. The stopwatches used for timing — and there were plenty — were all previously tested for accuracy. All the possibilities for a fluke were eliminated.

"Johnny was nervous and made a false start, but when he actually started, good-night! He made the fastest time ever negotiated through water by a human being, covering one hundred yards in fifty-two and three-fifths seconds. Think of it — fifty-two and three-fifths seconds for one hundred yards!

"After the race, spectators were more out of breath than Johnny was. Timers, judges, and watches all agreed that then and there a record was made that will remain a record for some time to come. It is safe to say that those who were so fortunate as to witness that marvelous exhibition of swimming will never forget the thrills it afforded them."

After his stunning, record-setting performance in front of the numerous A.A.U. officials in attendance, the name of "Johnny Weissmuller" quickly became known not only in the United States, but around the world. A 17-year-old teenager from Chicago was suddenly the fastest swimmer in the world, and before long he would erase every important record in the book. Johnny would dominate the sport like no one ever had — or ever would in the future.

Sprint swimming is a short duration sport — similar to track or even horse racing. It requires pure unadulterated speed, power, and stamina, which Johnny gained through superior athletic ability and his famed methods of relaxation. Johnny Weissmuller had everything it took — including determination and mental toughness — to excel in his sport.

During the next few years of the decade, Johnny would be "Mr. Everything" for Bill Bachrach and the I.A.C. Multifaceted and durable are adjectives that would accurately describe Johnny, who would swim in every distance including 50-yards, 100, 220, 300, 500 (yards), and later would add the backstroke and the pentathlon (five swimming and diving events) to his mighty arsenal! Johnny also swam the anchor position on all the relay teams for the I.A.C., and played on the water polo team! Weissmuller was simply a great athlete, and his range of versatility was amazing.

1921 was obviously a breakthrough year for Johnny, and after the November 21st meet at the I.A.C., he had much to be thankful for at the Thanksgiving and Christmas holidays. He enjoyed the small break during the holidays with his mother and brother, Peter, with a realization that his life would probably never be the same.

Fame and celebrity status often carry a hefty price to pay, but Johnny would usually handle it well because of his down-to-earth personality. With coach Bachrach always close by to keep his head "out of the clouds" and continue his training, 1922 would be the next domino in a series of record-breaking years for Johnny.

CHAPTER SIX

A Very Good Year

In 1922, Johnny's string of victories begun the previous August continued unabated into the New Year . . . and continued . . . and continued. 1922 also began a seven-year barnstorming tour of the United States (and eventually the world), orchestrated by coach William Bachrach, the master strategist. Cities along the road who were treated to the firsthand presence of this young champion included Honolulu, Philadelphia, Columbus, Milwaukee, Sacramento, Atlanta, New York, Buffalo, Indianapolis, Kansas City, and Chicago.

Johnny continued to run roughshod over all competitors in the pool, and some of the highlights of the year 1922 included the following A.A.U. national championships and records:

National Championship 50-yards, outdoor
    pool (time 23.0)
National Championship 100-yards, outdoor
    pool (time 52.8)

National Championship 220-yards, outdoor
pool (time 2:22.4
National Championship 440-yards, outdoor
pool (time 5:16.4)
National Championship 220-yards, indoor
pool (time 2:17.4)
National Championship 500-yards, indoor
pool (time 5:46.8)
National Championship 200-yard relay,
indoor pool (time 1:39.2)
National Championship 400-yard relay,
indoor pool (time 3:43.6)
National Championship Pentathlon (five
swimming events)

Johnny set the following world records
during the calendar year 1922:

World records — 20-yard pool: 150-yards,
April 6, Chicago, IL (time 1:25.4); 220-
yards, May 26, Honolulu, HI (time 2:15.6);
400-meters, April 6, Chicago, IL (time
5:05.2); 440-yards, April 6, Chicago, IL
(time 5:05.2); 500-yards, April 6, Chicago,
IL (time 5:46.8)
World records — 25-yard pool: 50-yards,
Aug. 1, Columbus, OH (time 22.8); 100-
yards, May 27, Honolulu, HI (time 52.6);
100-meters, May 2, Culver Military Academy, Indiana (time 59.4); 200-meters, May
26, Honolulu, HI (time 2:15.6); 300-yards,
March 25, Philadelphia, PA (time 3:35.2);

500-meters, Sept. 30, Milwaukee, WI (time 6:24.2); 100-yds backstroke, Nov. 4, Milwaukee, WI (time 1:05.4); 100-meters backstroke, Nov. 4, Milwaukee, WI (time 1:12.6); 150-yards backstroke, April 20, Milwaukee, WI (time 1:45.4)

World records — 100-yard or 100-meter pool: 100-yards, June 23, Honolulu, HI (time 52.8); 100-meters, July 9, Alameda, CA (time 58.6)

World records — Open Water: 100-yards, June 23, Honolulu, HI (time 52.8); 150-yards, Sept. 9, Atlanta, GA (time 1:27.8); 200-meters, June 24, Honolulu, HI (time 2:17.2); 220-yards, June 24, Honolulu, HI (time 2:18.4); 300-meters, June 22, Honolulu, HI (time 3:45.0); 400-meters, June 22, Honolulu, HI (time 5:06.6); 440-yards, June 22, Honolulu, HI (time 5:07.8); 500-yards, June 22, Honolulu, HI (time 5:47.6)

The world indeed seemed to be his playground — or rather his swimming pool. Johnny also set an incredible 39 American records to add a pronounced exclamation point to his dominance in the sport of swimming. Johnny hadn't, as of yet, had the opportunity to go up against international competition, but the world records he was setting at the tender age of seventeen (reaching his eighteenth birthday on June 2nd), were strong indicators that he was already the best swimmer in the world.

But in order to be crowned the best in the world, you have to beat the best in the world. Johnny had already defeated I.A.C. teammate Norman Ross, an Olympic champion who had won the 400-meter freestyle in the 1920 Antwerp Olympics, as well as the 1500-meter freestyle. But the acknowledged "best swimmer in the world" was Duke Kahanamoku of Hawaii, who had won the 100-meter freestyle in the 1912 Stockholm Olympics, as well as the same event in the 1920 Olympic Games held in Antwerp. (The 1916 Olympics were canceled because of World War I.)

Everyone knew that only a match between Johnny and Duke would determine the greatest swimmer in the world. There was great anticipation when it was announced that such a contest would take place in June in the Duke's homeland of Hawaii, to coincide with the Shriners Convention in Honolulu. Coach Bachrach was trepidatious that it was too soon for such a match to take place, but Weissmuller was ready for the challenge. "Let's go," said a fearless Johnny. "The Duke will probably lick me, but I'll never know for sure if we duck him."

The Chicago Shriners volunteered to pay for the expenses of Johnny and coach Bachrach, expecting to see the local lad stand tall against Kahanamoku. The I.A.C. team also went along to Hawaii to participate in the

A.A.U. national championships for 1922, which were scheduled for the final week of June.

Johnny and coach Bachrach were welcomed upon their arrival in Hawaii, but the people of the Islands loved their "Duke," who was a national hero. The locals were confident he couldn't be beaten by the talented teenager from Chicago, who was known on the Islands as the "Illinois Flash." Given the unique name of Duke Paoa Kahinu Makoe Hulikohoa Kahanamoku, he was born in Honolulu on August 24, 1890, in the palace of Princess Ruth.

The head-to-head race between Johnny and the Duke was to take place between two huge shipping barges in the Honolulu harbor, anchored approximately 100-meters apart. The day before the race Johnny and the Duke met face-to-face on the beach, the two swimming stars eye-to-eye at well over six-feet tall. The Duke, fourteen years older and powerfully built in the shoulders and chest, smiled at his wiry, broad-shouldered adversary and said:

"Hello, sonny," quipped the Duke good-naturedly. "I'll give you a good trimming tomorrow and send you back to Chicago."

Johnny smiled back at the Duke, a living legend in the swimming world. He still wasn't intimidated, and neither was coach Bachrach, who had a great deal of respect for the Duke and didn't want to embarrass him in his homeland. He pulled the Duke off to one side for a private conversation, away from the ears of Johnny.

"Duke, my friend, I'll be honest with you," confided Bachrach. "The kid can beat you tomorrow. I've never let Johnny extend himself yet. If you knew how fast he's been racing in practice, you'd think twice about this race."

The confident Duke could hardly control his mirth, at the thought of losing to a teenager whom he felt wasn't even wet behind the ears. Duke was ready to walk away when Bachrach produced his own timepiece and said: "Okay, Duke. Here's a stopwatch. Time him yourself."

Bachrach sent Johnny into the 25-yard Punahou pool, and he swam at his top speed as the Duke timed him for 100-yards. Kahanamoku was stunned as he watched Johnny swim faster than the Duke had ever done, confirmed by the stopwatch held by his own trembling hand. There was fear in the Duke's heart, because he knew if he raced on the morrow he would be beaten by this relative newcomer to the swimming wars.

The next day, all the newspapers announced that the Duke had taken ill, and had left Honolulu to recuperate. There would be no race against the youngster from Chicago on this day, and Johnny and Bill Bachrach were the only ones who knew the real reason: Duke was afraid of racing against Johnny, whom he knew was the coming champion. But a showdown was inevitable, no later than the 1924 Olympics, that would determine who was the best swimmer once and for all.

Though the Duke was absent, there were other big-name swimmers in Honolulu that weekend in June, and Johnny was ready to take on all challengers. When the smoke had cleared after an incredible three-day meet, Johnny had set seven international records in distances from 100 to 500-yards, as well as nine American records! It was the greatest swim meet of his career, and Johnny was brimming with confidence when he looked Bachrach in the eye and said, "I'll see Duke later." Johnny was willing to bide his time for an Olympic showdown with the Duke, in a match that would surely crown the champion swimmer of the world.

On July 9, 1922 in Alameda, California, Johnny made swimming history when he became the first swimmer in history to break the one-minute mark in the 100-meter freestyle with a time of 58.6 seconds. This incredible record would be equivalent to the first runner breaking the four-minute barrier in the mile run!

Life was wonderful for Johnny during these record-breaking 1920s, and he had most everything he could ask for — except a girlfriend. Coach Bachrach later recalled that the distractions of the fairer sex began around this time in Johnny's career. "He never failed to be there when the starter raised his gun," said Bachrach, "but in between times it was sometimes hard to locate him. He had discovered girls — among other things."

By this time Johnny was easily the most eligible teenaged bachelor in Chicago, perhaps all of America. He was literally adored by girls he met everywhere he traveled, but as of yet no young lady had managed to tie him down. He had female friends among the swimmers at the I.A.C., but no one who made his heart pound like a jackhammer. But this would change when he met a slender blonde-haired beauty named Lorelei on a Chicago beach one summer day.

They soon became a couple, and dancing was the language of their romance. Johnny and Lorelei frequented clubs like the College Inn, and danced the "Swing" and "Hip-Hop" to Isham Jones and his 15-piece band. The city of Chicago swayed to the marvelous saxophone and piano music of "Ish," and the popular songs he wrote included "It Had to Be You" and "I'll See You in My Dreams." It is easy to see why Johnny and Lorelei, and thousands of other young dancers, were so drawn to dancing in the 1920s. The music in the Windy City was new, it was wild, it was JAZZ!

Another hot spot for Johnny and Lorelei was Marshall and Fox's posh Drake Hotel, located near the Oak Street Beach at the juncture of Michigan Avenue and Lake Shore Drive. The new Drake had been built for $8.5 million dollars, and the vast Silver Forest ballroom ran the whole length of the hotel's north side. The lively music of Fred Waring, Hal Kemp, Jack Hilton, and Alec Templeton, as well as Phil Spitalny and his All-Girl Orchestra, were among the nation's best orchestras. It was the "Roaring '20s" and "that Toddling Town" had swing to spare!

Louis Armstrong moved from New Orleans to Chicago in the summer of 1921, to join King Oliver's Creole Jazz Band and play his brilliant coronet for the amazing sum of thirty dollars a week. Armstrong entertained at the Lincoln Gardens, the Royal Gardens, and the Plantation Cafe, and thrilled Chicagoans and visitors alike with the black jazz he brought with him from the South. According to author Henry Osgood, the Jazz Age was born in Chicago. In his book, *So This Is Jazz*, he states that Chicago introduced the white world to the new music: ". . . the craze for jazz in the North and East appears to have come out of New Orleans via Chicago."

World famous band leader Paul Whiteman and his 80-piece orchestra entertained at the

$1,500,000 Trianon Club, which opened in 1922. The great Rudolph Valentino danced the tango at the Trianon on February 18, 1923, as 6,000 adoring fans crowded the floor to dance along with Valentino. Johnny and Lorelei often honed their skills on the marble dance floor of the Trianon, which was America's most luxurious public ballroom. They eventually entered popular dance contests and won five trophies, proving Johnny had the same championship moves on a dance floor as he did in the swimming pool!

Johnny was smitten by the love bug and assumed that Lorelei would be his wife someday and that they would spend the rest of their lives together. Meanwhile, coach Bachrach knew that this first love probably wouldn't last. He advised Johnny as much, a lad he loved like a son, but Johnny was unconvinced. This would be the first of many times Johnny would take his lumps in the romance department. For now he had a girl, and he was in love.

Johnny continued to live with his mother and brother at their 1521 Cleveland Avenue home when he was in Chicago, which was perhaps only half the time. Johnny was 18-years-old and still a growing lad, and spent many weeks out of the year on the road with Bill Bachrach and other members of the team (including his younger brother Peter, who had also become a member of the I.A.C. swimming team). Johnny was getting a marvelous education just visiting the many cities in America that became part of Bill Bachrach's traveling aquatic exhibition.

Johnny later recalled the adventure and excitement of life on the road. "I got to meet people and see places I never even dreamed about as a kid in Chicago. I wasn't getting rich, of course; amateur athletes don't get paid — and even professional swimmers couldn't make much of a buck in those days."

It could easily be stated that Bill Bachrach was the greatest pitchman since P. T. Barnum! During these days, an amateur athlete received seven dollars a day, plus expenses, while on the road. Back home in Chicago, there was no pay — period — except for free training meals at the I.A.C. Many wealthy businessman and store owners would dine at the Illinois Athletic Club, and Bachrach would swoop in on them like a vulture. Coach Bachrach, with Johnny in his stable of swimmers, would gather contributions from these strong supporters of Chicago amateur athletics, in the form of "freebies" for the top athletes. If Johnny needed a new suit, Bachrach would make a call to a local haberdasher who was only too glad to outfit young Weissmuller in the latest men's fashions.

Bachrach would propose that Johnny would break a record for these wealthy benefactors, in exchange for meals, clothes, and new shoes. The master coach and strategist would of course prepare his protégé to win each and every race, and set a record if possible — but only by the slimmest of margins. That way Johnny would continually be setting new records, which kept his name in the newspapers and the contributions flowing into the I.A.C., care of Bill Bachrach! And every time that his star swimmer broke another record, a steak dinner with "Bach" would be the reward — with Johnny breaking records every week, the "Illinois Flash" ate hearty and was always well-dressed.

As an amateur athlete, Johnny wasn't allowed cash prizes for winning races. But trophies, medals, and gold watches were given to the winners of major competitions, including national championships. Before long, Johnny had won so many of these prizes that he was able to give a gold watch to each of his teammates, as well as his brother Peter. Weissmuller, estimated to have swum over 1000 winning races in his career, probably was awarded more wrist and pocket watches than any other athlete in history!

Johnny began to garner a great deal of national publicity by this time, including the following from the *Literary Digest* for May 27, 1922:

"Every now and then, at long intervals, the

sports fraternity is startled by the sudden rise to fame of some unknown athlete whose extraordinary skill enables him to leap almost overnight from obscurity to international leadership. So observes L. DeB. Handley, in the *New York World*, introducing John Weissmuller, a Chicago boy who has broken nearly every record in sight, and hasn't had to exert himself very much, apparently, to do it. He belongs to the Illinois Athletic Club of Chicago, and the *World* sports writer calls him 'the greatest all-around swimmer of all-time.' "

The *Digest* article continued with more comments from Mr. Handley, a sports writer and top swimming coach, who was stunned by the talents of Weissmuller when he made his "Big Apple" debut at Brighton Beach in September of 1921:

"Competing in open water he thrashed 100-yards straightaway in the amazing time of 52 seconds, or one full second under the world's record. The feat was received with quite general skepticism and, unfortunately, conditions prevented official recognition of the new standard. But developments since make it decidedly probable that Johnny actually attained the pace credited to him, for indoors under less favorable conditions he has covered the century officially in 52.6 seconds in a 60-foot pool. The famous Duke Kahanamoku of Honolulu never beat 54 seconds for the distance in a short bath, although he holds the straightaway world's standard at 53 seconds.

"Weissmuller hung up his first international marks at the Brighton Beach Bath in September when he turned 100-yards in 53.2 seconds, 120 yards in one minute, 8.4 seconds, and 150-yards in one minute, 27.4 seconds, all new figures for a regulation 75-foot pool, and he has kept on smashing records ever since. His greatest feats, achieved in 75-foot pools also, include 100-yards in 53 seconds, 210-yards in two minutes, 17.8 seconds, or exactly two seconds under Teddy Cann's former standard; 300-yards in three minutes, 35.2 seconds, a great slash of ten seconds from Norman Ross's listed record; and 500-yards in five minutes, 56.6 seconds, or 2.2 seconds faster than the latter's registered mark.

"The 500-yard record, set in the national championship pentathlon at the Brooklyn Young Men's Christian Association recently, is earnest of what might be expected of the Chicago youth hereafter. That very evening he had taken part in four races before the 500-yard event was called, and so did not have to extend himself to win it. In fact, he plodded along leisurely, stopping at every turn to survey the field, and there is no doubt whatsoever that he could have gone 15 to 20 seconds faster had circumstances required.

None who witnessed the contest questions Johnny's ability to put great dents in all other world's records, from 500-yards to one mile. His speed and stamina are almost unbelievable.

"Norman Ross, the recognized all-around international swimming champion, said to the writer some time ago: 'Johnny has everything I ever had plus youth. He is enjoying also the advantage of more efficient methods than known when I started swimming. It is my firm belief that he will do 100-yards freestyle in 50 seconds, and with backstroke in 60 seconds before long. I am convinced, too, that if he trains for all distances every world's record for both styles of swimming will be at his mercy. He is absolutely a marvel.' "

"Weissmuller is tall and rangy, it seems, ideally built for swimming," continued Handley. "He stands six-feet one-inch, weighs 170 pounds, and he tapers gracefully from broad, powerful shoulders, to narrow hips and slight, agile legs. He uses the stroke known technically as the six-beat double trudgeon crawl, and his form is well-nigh perfect. His action is so smooth and easy that it appears effortless.

"Johnny is a happy-go-lucky lad, totally unspoiled by the worldwide fame suddenly fallen to his lot. He loves swimming, and lives in the pool most of his spare hours, but he takes lightly the honors he is winning. After his final achievements here, Bachrach, who was in charge of Illinois swimmers, ventures to congratulate him. 'That's all right,' said Johnny with a grin. 'But are the rigors of training discipline lifted now? Can I have a real feed of frankfurters and ice cream at last?' Still a big boy despite the international prominence earned."

In the July 1922 issue of *Outing* magazine, Johnny was featured in a photographic display that also included 17-year-old swimmer and diver Helen Wainwright, and 20-year-old golfer Bobby Jones. The caption under Johnny's photo, poised to dive into competition, boasted of his virtues in the pool:

"Johnny Weissmuller is seventeen and he is reported to have broken twenty-three swimming records since January 1. Recently he set a new indoor record of 53 seconds, equaling the Duke's mark outdoors. Two other world's records he holds are the hundred meters and the hundred and fifty yards indoors. These are only samples."

Another photographic display page in the *Current Opinion* for September 1922 featured Walter Hoover, a peerless oarsman and winner of the English amateur sculling trophy, the Diamond Sculls, as well as teenaged swimmer Ethelda Bleibtrey, captioned, "A Modern Mermaid with No Rival." Meanwhile, Johnny's poolside photo was captioned: "THE FASTEST SWIMMER IN

THE WORLD! Johnny Weissmuller, at 17, holds a score of national and international records. Never defeated."

And from the December 1922 issue of *Country Life*, high words of praise for young Weissmuller, who had finally reached his eighteenth birthday by this time:

"The outdoor swimming season of 1922 left no doubt as to whom we may crown 'King of the Seas' for the season of 1922. Johnny Weissmuller, of the Illinois Athletic Club, has proven himself no mere flash, but a consistent record breaker, so far superior to all others that there is no one worthy of the name of rival to him. Weissmuller started as a schoolboy marvel and few believed that he could last at the fast pace he set . . .

"But when Weissmuller had finished his tour of the Hawaiian Islands and then east to New York there was no doubt that America had produced the greatest swimmer of all time, no less than thirty-six records already having been credited to him."

Once again, another great action photo of Johnny poised to dive for another swimming record, was captioned in glowing terms: "Johnny Weissmuller, one of the brightest stars that ever flashed across the swimming firmament, who has no less than thirty-six records to his credit."

1923 started out the same as the previous

year for Johnny — victory after victory after victory. He looked invincible and indestructible — after all, wasn't he? Once again he collected national championships and world and national records like some people collected stamps or baseball cards.

New cities that were part of the 1923 tour included Minneapolis, Newark, Decatur, Great Lakes (IL), New Haven, and South Bend. Johnny also recorded the following A.A.U. national championships during the year: 100-yards, outdoor pool (time 54.6); 440-yards, outdoor pool (time 5:37.4); 50-yards, indoor pool (time 23.6); 100-yards, indoor pool (time 54.8); 220-yards, indoor pool (time 2:22.0); 500-yards, indoor pool (time 5:43.6); 150-yard backstroke, indoor pool (time 1:42.0); 400-yard relay, indoor pool (time 3:42.0); 880-yard relay, outdoor pool (time 10:05.4). (Johnny also tied with Stubby Kruger, a teammate on the I.A.C., for the pentathlon national championship which consisted of five swimming and diving events.)

By this time Johnny already held most of the world's swimming records in distances from 50 to 500-yards. In 1923 he added nine new world records, as well as 15 new American records. Through the first half of the year, Johnny was invincible and certainly looked like he was a "Superman" from another planet. (In the words of Nietzsche, Superman was "an idealized man with greatly superior physical and mental qualities." Wow . . . he must have been referring to Johnny Weissmuller!)

All the gears of the machinery were well-oiled and running smoothly, at least until the beginning of the summer, 1923. In mid-June, Johnny spent a week at Lake Geneva doing preparatory work for the new outdoor season, and then competed at Great Lakes on June 27th, setting a new world record of five minutes, 50.4 seconds at the distance of 500-yards. On June 30th the team was in Newark, New Jersey, where he narrowly missed breaking his own world's record at 300-meters, falling just six-tenths of a second short of his previous mark.

Johnny competed in the races in Decatur on July 4th, winning all five of his races without a problem. It was an average performance for Johnny, who only broke one record during the meet (setting a new American record for 500-meters in open water in a time of six minutes, 55 seconds). There was no clue at this point that by the next day, Johnny would be in the hospital with what was feared to be a heart ailment!

While Johnny spent a few days in the hospital with this "mysterious" ailment, the I.A.C. club magazine reported the following:

"Either there is nothing wrong with Johnny Weissmuller and a false alarm has been sounded, or something strange, remarkable, and exceptional in the realm of athletics has happened. The issue remains for specialists to decide. In the mean time, Johnny is resting in the hospital.

"Following the races at Decatur, Illinois, on the Fourth of July, Johnny experienced a weakness, slight fever and fatigue, something he had never known before as result of swimming. What is it and what caused it? That is the problem. His performance that day was not of unusual severity."

Johnny showed no signs of a problem at the scene of the races in Decatur, and he rode back to the hotel with coach Bachrach by automobile. "Are you all right, kid? You look a little pale to me," said Bachrach. Johnny nodded that he was okay, but Bachrach was unconvinced. At dinner that evening Johnny, a notoriously big eater, had no appetite whatsoever, a sure sign that something was wrong with the young man.

Bachrach knew that his star swimmer was ill, and advised him to go right to bed. Johnny, however, wanted to wait until the race prizes were passed out. He did collect his prizes for the Decatur races, and then obviously weary went directly to bed. The team was scheduled to leave by train at midnight, and after the trip to the station, Johnny spent the balance of a restless night in a sleeping-car berth.

They arrived back in Chicago early the next morning, and upon arrival at the club a physician was called. After examining Johnny, it was advised that he be taken to a hospital. After two days in the hospital of tests and exams, the medical staff thought that something was wrong with the action of his heart — possibly a dilation of the heart. At this point specialists were called in to examine Johnny, to hopefully determine the problem.

By this time Johnny was so tired of lying around in a hospital room, that he begged Bachrach to take him home. To prove his point that he felt fine, Johnny ran around the hospital room like a madman, leaping over his bed, and scaring the doctors and nurses alike! After this maniacal display, Bachrach relented and took Johnny out of the hospital. He did take him over to the University of Chicago to see the football team doctor, who gave Johnny a clean bill of health (prescribing only rest). Johnny spent the next few weeks resting and recuperating at home, with lots of love and care from his mother, Elizabeth.

The final diagnosis was what they called in those days, a case of the "grippe" (flu-like symptoms). Johnny was feverish and unable to get any rest, so the original doctor who examined him administered a drug to put him to sleep. Unfortunately, this doctor gave Johnny an overdose of the drug, which in turn was the cause of his "heart problem." What started out as a mild case of the grippe, could have turned into a tragic scenario because of a faulty diagnosis and treatment by the doctor. Johnny did indeed make a rapid recovery and was ready to return to action only a few weeks after his illness.

Near the end of August of 1923, a new outdoor swimming pool was being opened at DeKalb, Illinois, and Johnny and the I.A.C. team were invited to participate in the swim meet and dedication. The highlight of the meet was a new American record set by Robert Skelton, in the 220-yard breaststroke. But more importantly, Johnny made his successful return to competition, winning his only race in the 100-yard freestyle by a wide margin.

Once again, the I.A.C. magazine recalled the details of the momentous occasion of Johnny's return: "Second only in importance to the shattering of the world's record [by Skelton], was the appearance of Johnny Weissmuller, world's champion swimmer and holder of forty-two records.

"It was Weissmuller's first public appearance since he was ordered by physicians to quit swimming because of an ailing heart, some six weeks ago. That his recovery had been complete was demonstrated by his performance in the 100-yard freestyle event, the only event in which he competed. He won in

55.8 seconds, which is only three seconds over his own world's record."

The highpoint for the 1923 swimming season was the A.A.U. national indoor championships that were held in Chicago the first week of April. Johnny was in fine form in winning the freestyle races at 50, 100, 220, and 500-yards, and was the dominant member of the relay team in the 880-yard freestyle race. What more could he possibly do?

A still-hungry Johnny asked one of the race officials, "What's left on the show?"

"You're done for the day, Weissmuller," said the official. "The last race is the 150-yard backstroke, and that's not one of your events."

"It is tonight," said Johnny with a smile. Incredibly, although he wasn't known as a backstroker, he stunned the crowd and the competition and set a new world record in the race in a time of one minute and 42 seconds flat!

Coach Bachrach, puffing on a victory cigar, acknowledged to one of the writers covering the race, "Johnny doesn't care what the event is, just as long as they have a tank, timers, and a finish line!" (Oh, and water. Let's not forget the water, coach!)

The low point for the year had been Johnny's illness that had knocked him out of competition for six weeks. Bachrach somewhat limited Johnny's participation in the pool for the balance of the year when he returned to action, but in November he did set an American record in the 100-meters with a time of 59.2 seconds.

Both Johnny and Bill Bachrach knew that the real test was coming up in only a few months in Paris, in the 1924 Olympics. Long before the end of 1923 Johnny was back to his usual superb health, and once again his goal and dream was to win a gold medal in the coming Olympics.

CHAPTER SEVEN

Olympic History Beckons

Since 1924 was an Olympic year, everything for Johnny was geared towards Paris, the site of the summer Games. The outdoor season was sharply truncated for Olympic athletes, but Johnny did win seven national championships during the calendar year, including: 50-yards, indoor (time 24.0); 100-yards, indoor (time 53.8); 220-yards, indoor (time 2:14.8); 500-yards, indoor (time 5:50.4); 200-yard relay, indoor (time 1:38.8); 400-yard relay, indoor (time 3:41.4); 880-yard relay, outdoor (no time available).

It was also becoming more difficult for Johnny to break his own world and national records, and thus he "only" set two world records and four national records during the year. But Johnny did make history on February 17 at the A.A.U. swim meet held in Miami Beach, Florida. He set a new record in the 100-yard freestyle, with a time of 52.4 seconds. But it was his performance in the

100-meter freestyle that was monumental, as he set a new world record in a time of 57.4 seconds, breaking his old record by 1.2 seconds.

The proof of Johnny's dominance of the sport of swimming, and the significance of this record, was that this particular record in the 100-meters would last for ten years before being broken! Imagine, no other swimmer in the world could touch this record for a full decade. This was like Babe Ruth hitting 60 home runs in 1927, a stupendous record that would last for many years. Johnny's record was of a similar stature, and it further established him as the favorite in the sprint events in the coming Olympics.

Coach Bachrach was given the honor of coaching the American men's swim team for the 1924 Olympics, and the "Final Olympic Tryouts" were held in Indianapolis at the Broad Ripple Pool over a four-day period, June 5-8. With his many records and championships over the previous three years, the expectations were up in the treetops for Johnny (as well as for his teammates, many of whom were record holders and past Olympic medal winners). All the top United States swimmers were in Chicago for the tryouts, including Duke Kahanamoku, his brother Sam, and Jack Robertson of the Olympic Club of San Francisco.

On June 6, 1924, the *Honolulu Advertiser*

reported the following concerning the Olympic time trials: "WEISSMULLER NOSES OUT DUKE IN RECORD TOPPING SWIM IN THE 100 METER EVENT . . . Sam places third in event when the 'Illinois Flash' makes time of 59.4; one second lower than Duke's Antwerp time." Johnny had gone head-to-head with the Duke and won the race in convincing fashion! The Duke was still the Duke, but in the swimming world there was a new King! The Olympic re-match would be far more important than these time trials, but Johnny was now confident that the results would be the same in Paris.

(Chicago had been the site of the Olympic tryouts for the 1920 Antwerp Games, which were held in Johnny's very own Lincoln Park Lagoon in Lake Michigan. He had just turned sixteen, was not yet a member of the I.A.C., but he had big dreams of some day becoming an Olympic champion. Johnny watched the tryouts from a distance, far enough away to avoid the 50-cent admission price, and at one point swam out to open water beyond the roped-off area that was restricted to competitors. From this vantage point he was able to get a closer look at the best swimmers in the world like Olympic champion Duke Kahanamoku, and Chicago's own Norman Ross. All he had then were the dreams of a kid with a big heart and the determination to be a champion. Now, four years later, the dreams had come true and he was on his way to the Olympics in Paris to compete for his beloved America!)

Johnny's girlfriend, Lorelei, along with his mother, were among the small party that bade farewell to the small Chicago contingent headed for Paris. In his suitcase, Johnny had a sports coat and a scarf his mother had given him for his 20th birthday, only a few days prior to his departure.

During the 1920s, cross-country travel was accomplished by train, and Johnny, coach Bachrach, and other members of the I.A.C. who qualified for the Olympic team, arrived in New York on Sunday, June 15th. After spending the night in the Park Avenue Hotel, there was a great farewell demonstration at the pier at Hoboken the following morning. At noon, the U.S. Olympic squad set sail for France aboard a huge ocean liner, the S.S. *America*. Sailing out of New York harbor, past the Statue of Liberty, the crowd of well-wishers waved good-bye to the members of the Olympic expedition.

Among the 263 athletes, mostly male, were 66 swimmers and divers, 110 track and field men, 25 boxers, 16 wrestlers, 15 oarsmen, 11 gymnasts, and 20 fencers. Women athletes competed in swimming and diving, as well as fencing and tennis. (On the U.S. fencing team was Adeline Gehrig, sister of baseball player Lou Gehrig, who would become a legend with the New York Yankees and would eventually become known as the "Iron Horse.")

Others in the Olympic party included 12 coaches, 10 team managers, 10 trainers, and 6 masseurs (or "rubbers" as they were called). Officials associated with the Olympic team included manager John T. Taylor, and the president of the American Olympic Committee, Robert M. Thompson. Also on board were wives and husbands of athletes and coaches, other relatives including parents, siblings and children, along with friends of the athletes and officials totaling another 250 individuals.

This wasn't the entire U.S. Olympic team, as many athletes had arrived earlier to compete in team and individual events scheduled in May and June. The Navy athletes were making the journey across the Atlantic via battleship, and the Yale crew competing in the eight-oared rowing event traveled over the following Saturday on the S.S. *Homeric*. (It is interesting to note that one member of this Yale rowing team, destined to win the gold medal, was Benjamin Spock, who would later gain fame as Benjamin Spock, world-renowned author and "baby expert.")

There were great expectations for the American Olympic team, which had dominated the 1920 Olympics in Antwerp, winning a total of 41 gold medals to the next highest total of 17 for the Swedish team. The swimming team had done especially well, winning 11 gold medals out of the 15 swimming and diving events for men and women.

The head swimming coach for the men's swimming team was William "Big Bill" Bachrach, who had molded Olympic champion Norman Ross, and his current star, Johnny Weissmuller. Members of the I.A.C. on the Olympic team included Robert Skelton, Fred "Pal" Lauer, John Faricy, Oliver Horn, Jam Handy, and Stubby Kruger. Female swimmers included Sybil Bauer and Ethyl Lackie, both of whom were strong medal contenders for the U.S. squad.

The American swim team also boasted Hawaiian stars Duke Kahanamoku and his 19-year-old brother Sam, along with brothers Warren and Pua Kealoha (both of whom had earned medals in previous Olympics). U.S. swimmers of reputation included Paul Wyatt and William Kirschbaum, both top contenders in the backstroke and breaststroke, respectively. Wallace O'Connor of the Venice A.C., Harry Glancy of Pittsburgh, and Ralph Breyer of Northwestern U., were all members of the 4x200-meter freestyle relay team (along with Weissmuller). Others included Jack Robertson and Lester Smith of the Olympic Club; Richard Howell of Northwestern U.; and Adam

Smith of the Erie YMCA.

One of the new friends that Johnny made during his Olympic adventure was Ulise Joseph "Pete" Desjardins, a member of the diving team who at five-feet three-inches was surely one of the shortest male competitors in France! Desjardins and Johnny would become close friends and in later years performed diving exhibitions, including the famous "Mutt and Jeff" comedy routine.

When the 16-year-old Desjardins competed in Chicago for the 1924 national indoor diving championship, the press dubbed the little man from Miami "The Little Bronze Statue from the Land of Real Estate, Grapefruit and Alligators," a nickname that would stick his entire career. (Desjardins would win the silver medal in springboard diving in this Olympics, and would later win double-gold at the 1928 Games at Antwerp.) Other world class divers for the United States were Albert White, Clarence Pinkston, and David Fall. The diving coach was Ernst Brandsten, who was the U.S. Olympic diving coach four times and was considered the "Father of Modern Diving" for his coaching dedication and innovations such as the tapered springboard and movable fulcrum.

The top swimmers for the women's team included Gertrude Ederle, Mariechen Wehselau of Honolulu, Martha Norelius,

Helen Wainwright, Florence Chambers, Agnes Geraghty, Euphrasia Donnelly, and Aileen Riggin (who competed in both swimming and diving). Female divers hopeful of medals included Helen Meany, Elizabeth Becker, Caroline Fletcher, and Caroline Smith.

The women's swimming coach was L. deB. Handley, who had spoken so glowingly of Johnny Weissmuller after his magnificent display of skill at Brighton Beach, New York, a few weeks after his debut in the summer of 1921. Handley was a swimming journalist who was simultaneously bylined by the *Times, Tribune, World,* and *American,* as well as being the author of five books on swimming. Louis deBreda Handley was also a coaching genius, and many of the girls he coached at the New York Women's Swimming Association later became members of the Swimming Hall of Fame, including Gertrude Ederle and Eleanor Holm.

This group of comrades from all over America comprised the U.S. swimming and diving team, many of whom became friends with Johnny during the long sea voyage from New York to Paris. During the many weeks of competition they would be rooting for each other, and finally, they would share the journey home. But home was a great distance away, as at this moment their trials and tribulations — and the glorious triumphs — were just at a beginning.

The swimming team trained in a small canvas tank that was rigged on deck, large enough only for two swimmers at a time. With limited space in the tank, coach Bachrach pulled out his bag of tricks and used an overhead rope and a rubber inner tube in the pool to anchor each swimmer during a series of training exercises. Built upon the promenade deck was a 220-yard cork running track for the runners, as well as boxing rings and wrestling mats. Daily calisthenics and regular walks around the deck of the S.S. *America* helped to burn excess energy, along with shipboard games like shuffleboard and badminton. Suffice to say that this was the best-conditioned contingent of American Olympic athletes in history, and the ship itself was a veritable athletic training center.

A nine-day journey by sea between two continents must have seemed like an eternity when the adventure of a lifetime awaits at the other end. Memories made on this trip and during the course of the Olympic games at Cherbourg would surely last forever for most of the participants. There were friendships made between the athletes, and romances that bloomed between the opposite sexes.

Emotionally speaking, spirits were high and the young athletes had the time of their lives. Any jostling between the young men was all in fun, but just in case of any minor trouble there was a policeman on board. Pat McDonald, a genial giant who was a New York City policeman was taken along as a guest of Colonel Robert Thompson. He was appointed "Chief of Police" for the journey and also dubbed "The Prince of Whales" (in good fun, referring to his massive size). McDonald had been to previous Olympic Games as an athlete, but his specialty — the 56-pound weight throw — had been eliminated. (Wow . . . try throwing a 56-pound weight to see if you are in shape!)

A dance held on Saturday night was an opportunity for everyone to mingle and have a great time. The normal ten o'clock bedtime was relaxed on this one night only, as the dancers reveled in the joy of the moment. (Not too late though, as the Reverend Ralph Spearow, a pole vaulter from the University of Oregon, would be conducting church services the following morning.)

The closely knit members of the Illinois Athletic Club, including Johnny and his boyhood companion, Fred "Pal" Lauer, shared one of the cabins which were set up to sleep eight individuals in four double-decker bunkbeds. They shared the cabin and they shared their dreams of winning medals and returning home to Chicago triumphant. Johnny talked fondly of his girlfriend Lorelei, whom he missed dearly and would be without for many weeks.

Possibly the only true excitement on the trip was the discovery of a stowaway, a Nebraska hurdler who had failed to make the team. Realizing his own dream was slipping away, the young man had smuggled himself on board, determined to make the trip by hook or crook! Some of the athletes learned of the resolute young man's illegal presence, including Johnny and his friends, and helped to smuggle food to keep him from starving. After he was discovered by the crew there was no way to send him home, so he was allowed to complete the trip to Paris. The would-be athlete was only a spectator at Cherbourg, but perhaps his dreams were fulfilled enough to make his desperate chicanery worthwhile.

And finally the trans-Atlantic odyssey was completed. The S.S. *America* arrived in the harbor in Cherbourg on June 24th, and was greeted at the pier by a throng of jubilant Americans as well as several journalists and photographers angling for the early stories. The band from the U.S.S. *Pittsburgh* was at the dock to welcome the Americans with a rousing musical salute. Upon disembarking with their luggage, the athletes were spirited off to two waiting trains, specially chartered for the Olympians.

Their arrival in Paris was once again to a large cheering crowd of Americans and Parisians alike. Johnny was one of the brightest stars on the American Olympic team, and he swelled with pride at this tremendously warm welcome.

Johnny by nature was usually easygoing, but occasionally his temper would flare up and get him into trouble. One such incident happened shortly after their arrival, as the U.S. team was traveling by train within Paris. A deranged heckler riding his bicycle alongside the train tracks was shouting anti-American insults, replete with obscene gestures. The attention of the I.A.C. swimmers was caught by the lunatic, and finally enough was enough! Johnny was nominated by his teammates to defend America's honor, and he jumped from the train with the thought of only giving the rogue a scare. However, when he jumped from the train he bumped the man on the bike and soon the troublemaker lay by the tracks in a tangle of arms and legs and bicycle wheels.

Later, Johnny apologized to Olympic officials who considered disqualifying him from the American team. This notion was quickly dismissed, after learning the circumstances of the verbal assault by the heckler. An impassioned plea by coach Bachrach to the Olympic Committee on behalf of Johnny was enough to satisfy officials that the incident would not be repeated during the Olympics. Bachrach claimed that he would have done the same to the brute if Johnny had not done it first, to defend the honor of America from the insult-shouting bicyclist.

Fortunately, that was the end of any repercussions for Johnny. If the Olympic Committee had indeed gone through with their threat to suspend Johnny from the games, the equally headstrong Bachrach would surely have pulled the entire American swim team in protest. That in itself would have caused an international incident of epic proportion, much larger than the trainside mishap. The eyes of the world were on Johnny and other American star athletes, and those eyes were anxiously awaiting the thrill and excitement of the contests between the best athletes from 44 nations.

After the arrival in Paris at the Gare St. Lazare, fresh off the incident with the heckling bicycle rider, the athletes and coaches dismounted the train to find 70 motorcars waiting to take them to their headquarters at Rocquencourt, an estate that had once been the residence of Prince Joachim Murat, a French marshal and later the king of Naples. (Murat was a brilliant military officer and major cog in Napoleon's coup d'etat of Brumaire in 1799. Joachim Murat was executed after Napoleon's downfall at Waterloo in 1815.)

The United States Olympic Committee had constructed 11 concrete barracks to house the American athletes during their stay at Rocquencourt, while the officials lived like aristocrats in the beautiful chateau. Everyone was ready for a quiet evening their first night in France, but were interrupted from a peaceful sleep by the clanging of a fire alarm. It was a major fire in the neighboring village, burning brightly and belching smoke to the sky. The Americans jumped into their clothes and went to the aid of the firemen.

When the fire was finally extinguished, one French firefighter had died and a dozen houses had burned to the ground. The local residents were extremely grateful to the Americans, who had risked themselves in helping to control the blaze before it burned the entire neighborhood. The next day, learning of the man's death, the Olympians dug deep into their pockets and raised $200 for the widow and children of the blaze's victim. Not surprisingly, the Americans were treated with gratitude and kindness during their stay by their neighbors at Rocquencourt.

It turned out that Rocquencourt was too crowded for all the athletes, so coach Bachrach volunteered to move the American swim team to Colombes, the actual site of the Games. Here were adequate living quarters for his swimmers, as well as a practice pool. Unfortunately, the pool leaked and the swimming practices had to be moved to Tourelles in Paris, some 12 miles by bus from Colombes.

The Olympic swimming events would begin in earnest after the opening ceremony, leaving almost two weeks after their arrival for practice sessions and perhaps a little bit of Paris sight-seeing. Practice sessions for each competing team were allocated on an equal basis, normally one session per day for each nation.

The newly-constructed swimming arena at Tourelles featured seating for 10,000 spectators and an Olympic-sized pool — 50-meters in length, 100-feet wide, and a depth gradually deepening from four to fifteen feet. The deep end was where the tower and diving board were located and the diving events would take place. Competitor lanes were separated by ropes supported by cork floats, an innovation for these Games.

Finally they were settled in their new home, a so-called "Olympic Village," and they were ready to begin practicing for the events that each athlete hoped would culminate in a gold medal. Johnny was used to spending many nights away from home, as he had done in his travels around the country from meet to meet the past three years. He and his cohorts spent their evenings talking of home, playing cards, and reading American newspapers and magazines that were supplied each day. Whenever possible, Johnny would send postcards to Lorelei and his mother.

According to Johnny, one fellow snuck in a bottle of liquor and opened up a "speakeasy" from underneath his mattress. (This was during Prohibition, and United States citizens could not legally drink — especially in the Olympic Village!) Years later, Johnny recalled some of his memories from his first Olympic experience:

"They kept us locked up, under constant guard, and all the guys called Olympic Village a high class Boy Scout camp. We younger men did not mind it too much, but some of the older fellows complained. Still, no one tried to sneak out. We knew that our officials had some spies running loose in the bars, and if one happened to spot you taking a champagne cocktail, or something — pow! You were thrown off the team without mercy. We were carted around like tourists, never allowed to separate, always in groups of twenty-five or so. Most of us wanted to see the Moulin Rouge but we all wound up on top of the Eiffel Tower. That was that! Anyway, most of the time we were too nervous to care much for anything except the Games. We had come to the Olympiad to do a job and training for it was foremost on our minds . . . I guess I was one of the few swimmers who had to compete in so many events that I never got a breather until I left Paris."

Johnny was right about being far too busy for any "monkey business." Between practicing for the three events in which he was scheduled to compete, he was also a member of the water polo team! Besides, after the incident on the train with the bicyclist, Johnny had promised coach Bachrach that he would keep his nose clean for the balance of their time in France. His thoughts, for the most part, were concentrated on winning Olympic gold.

CHAPTER EIGHT

Let the Games Begin!

The official opening ceremony at Colombes Stadium for the 1924 Olympics was scheduled for July 5th, with the Games continuing through July 27th. A Fourth of July party was presided over by General John Pershing, the U.S. Chief of Staff, with entertainment provided by motion picture comedienne Marie Dressler and vaudeville singer Nora Bayes. On the morning of July 5th, religious services were held in historic Notre Dame Cathedral, as Cardinal DuBois praised the attending athletes by pronouncing, "You are upholders of modern chivalry."

Matt McGrath, point winner at the Games of 1908, 1912, and 1920, carried the American flag during the opening ceremony, while Pat McDonald (the ship's policeman) carried the sign with the name of the country "Etats-Unis" (United States). The Olympic Committee had supplied all the athletes with navy-blue blazers bearing an embroidered Olympic crest, as well as several pair of white khaki trousers, which was the uniform of the day for the opening ceremonies. In the parade were 1,430 athletes representing 44 nations from the four corners of the world.

As the athletes marched into Colombes Stadium through the Marathon Gate, a battery of 75's thundered forth a salute and Boy Scouts released dozens of pigeons to honor the participants. It was undoubtedly the proudest moment of Johnny's life, as he humbly represented his country as well as the Illinois Athletic Club.

More than 40,000 cheering spectators watched the opening parade that afternoon, including French president M. Gaston Doumergue. Among the dozens of royalty and honored guests were Edward, Prince of Wales (who later became king and abdicated); Prince William of Sweden; the Crown Prince and Princess of Romania; and the Regent of Abyssinia. Four French bands and two choirs rendered musical selections, including a stirring rendition of "La Marseillaise." Representing all his fellow athletes, the Olympic oath was spoken by George Andre, a French runner who had won points at every Olympic Games since 1908.

At the conclusion of the pomp and pageantry of the opening ceremony, President Doumergue declared the Games open, as the Olympic runner entered Colombes Stadium carrying high the blazing Olympic torch. It was time for the Games to begin! Enthusiastic crowds of 60,000 or more came out daily to watch the events, often cheering loudly for the favored American athletes. Although television was still just a vision of the future, this would be the first Olympics where events could be followed through live radio broadcasts. A French schoolmaster coined the new Olympic motto: *citius, altius, fortius* ("faster, higher, stronger"), an appropriate maxim for an Olympics where numerous world and Olympic records were established.

As an indication of how times have changed since 1924, there were 2,956 men participants from the 44 nations represented, but only 136 women! One nation absent from competition was Germany, still exiled from the Games as they had been in 1920. Despite the efforts of former I.O.C. president Pierre de Coubertin to forgive the sins of the "Fatherland" during World War I, they would not be reinstated until 1928. (Coubertin was quoted as saying in 1896, the year of the First Olympiad: "The important thing in the Olympic Games is not to win but to take part; the important thing in life is not the triumph, but the struggle.")

Track and field were the first events to be contested, and Paavo Nurmi of Finland was the champion of these thrilling events. Nurmi not only won five gold medals (three individual, two team), but he won the 1,500-meter and 5,000-meter races on the same day, both in Olympic record times! The events were scheduled back-to-back with less than an hour break between the two long-distance races, but Nurmi was unfazed by the scheduling snafu.

The Americans fared well in track and field, winning gold medals in 12 of the 27 events, including the rare double of the decathlon and high jump by Harold Osborn. Clarence "Bud" Houser also grabbed two golds for the Americans in the discus and shot put, the last man ever to achieve this difficult double victory. History was also made by William De Hart Hubbard, who became the first black athlete to win a gold medal, in the long jump event.

Meanwhile, a Scottish clergyman named Eric Liddell declined to compete in his specialty — the 100-meters — because the event was held on a Sunday. However, he did set a world record in the 400-meters, upsetting the favorite, Horatio Fitch of the United States. Liddell's teammate, Harold Abrahams, also pulled an upset when he defeated the man known as "the world's fastest human being," Charley Paddock, in the 100-meter sprint.

The dramatic story of these two races was immortalized in the 1981 motion picture, *Chariots of Fire*. Paddock also pulled a boner in the 200-meters, with his friends Douglas

Fairbanks, Mary Pickford, and Maurice Chevalier hoping to root him on to victory. With a slim lead, Paddock turned to check the other racers near the finish line, only to have his teammate, Jackson Scholz, lunge by him for the victory.

For Johnny Weissmuller and his teammates in swimming and diving, the anxiously awaited contests began on Sunday, July 13th, coinciding with the conclusion of the track and field events. Johnny had been training for these specific races for many months, under the watchful guidance of coach Bachrach. The mental aspect of the training had intensified during the days of practice leading up to the actual races, and the day had finally arrived for the preliminary, or "heat" races.

Johnny knew what he would have to do to make his coach, his mother back home, his girlfriend Lorelei, and all of America proud — win every race in which he was entered. His mind was set, he clearly recalled every ounce of technique and wisdom that Bill Bachrach had imparted to him, and he had his lucky piece — a wooden finger ring that he touched for luck before every race in his career. Johnny was confident, but a little "knock on wood" never hurt!

The first race for Johnny would be the 400-meter freestyle, in which his main competition was expected to come from Borg, ArneArne Borg, the world record-holder in the event. (Four years earlier at Antwerp, Norman Ross of the I.A.C. had won this race, but wasn't competing in the Olympics this time around.) The only strong contender in the third heat was Charlton, "Boy" Charlton of Australia, along with Kohler of Holland, Peter of Great Britain, and Pellegry of France.

Johnny won this heat easily, with Charlton also qualifying for the next round of eliminations. In the first semifinal, Weissmuller had little problem winning over Charlton, Vernot of Canada, and Antos of Czechoslovakia. (The fifth qualifier, Ralph Breyer of the United States, was unable to start for reasons unknown.)

The finals were set for July 18th, and the world was waiting for the showdown between Weissmuller and Arne Borg, the European crowd-pleaser known as the "Swedish Sturgeon." Was the kid from Chicago really unbeatable, or would Borg or Charlton prove him a mortal being after all? The finalists in the 400-meter sprint were Weissmuller, Charlton, Hatfield of Great Britain, Arne Borg, and his twin brother, Ake Borg.

But now the moment had come and speculation would soon become reality. The combatants began to coil in their lanes like springs about to explode, as the starter announced in French, "On your mark!" Time stood momentarily still for Johnny as he heard the next command in his head, "Get set!" Suddenly the starter's gun barked out, and the racers shot into the water like five torpedoes launched into a clear blue ocean.

This event turned out to be one of the closest races of Johnny's career, and indeed it proved to be a two-horse race between America's best champion and Arne Borg of Sweden. At 100 meters, Borg led by six inches over Weissmuller as Charlton stayed close to the leaders. At the halfway mark, Johnny had inched ahead of Borg by less than a foot. At 300 meters, it was Borg by the length of a finger over Weissmuller and Charlton still hanging close. As they sped through the water for the final quarter of the race, they were neck and neck and it was still anyone's race! With only 20 meters to the finish, Johnny put on a superhuman burst of speed and edged Borg by only four feet! Johnny had set a new Olympic record of five minutes, 4.2 seconds, and edged out Arne Borg by 1.4 seconds. Charlton had managed to stay close, and won the bronze medal only one second behind Borg.

It's hard to truly imagine what an athlete feels after winning Olympic gold, but Johnny surely felt elation and satisfaction after beating the best in the world. Later, when Johnny mounted the winner's block and accepted the gold medal for America, he had accomplished his first goal. But he still had two more swimming events in which to compete: the 100-meter freestyle, perhaps the most prestigious event in the world; and the team event of the 4x200-meter freestyle relay. As always, Johnny was ready, willing, and able to become a champion!

Johnny's huge popularity in these Paris Olympics was due in part to a comedy diving exhibition which he performed several times during breaks between races and water polo matches. Johnny did the routine with a partner, Harold "Stubby" Kruger, who was on the U.S. Olympic diving team in both 1920 and 1924. Kruger was a champion in his own right, and at one point held the American fancy diving and pentathlon championships, as well as setting a world's record in the backstroke event. Johnny was the straight man and Stubby was the comedian of the act, as the duo earned the adulation of the crowd and tickled their funny-bones with a hilarious display of showmanship!

Johnny and Stubby performed a series of trick dives and stunts, which warmed up the crowd. Then for a finale, Johnny performed four classic dives in his best form — while Stubby mimicked the same dives, wearing clown makeup, in a crowd-pleasing slapstick performance. Johnny's dives included the classic and graceful swan dive, the jackknife, a one-and-a-half somersault, and finally, a full gainer. The latter starts as a forward dive, with a complete backward somersault before entering the water head first. Meanwhile, Stubby broke up the crowd with his antics, doing a comedic version of each dive, sometimes with eyes closed, legs pumping in mid-air, and always crashing into the water in the most ungraceful and laughable positions!

This diving routine was a building block of Johnny's reputation and of his legend. Only Weissmuller could have talked his coach into allowing him to do these dives, many of them dangerous, while still waiting to compete in other swimming events. But coach Bachrach knew that this would help to fuel the kid's immense popularity, and besides, Johnny loved doing it and he was having the time of his life!

At one point after one of Johnny's comedic diving routines, the water polo matches were delayed by the clamor of the audience, who threw their derby hats into the pool in hopes of seeing more of their new American hero, Johnny Weissmuller. These exhibitions were so popular with the fans and had so many encores that they were banned at all future Olympic Games!

Johnny's busy schedule included being a member of the United States water polo team. His teammates included Fred "Pal" Lauer, a Chicago friend whom Johnny recalled in his own book, *Swimming the American Crawl*, as "the greatest goal tender in water polo the United States has produced." Oliver Horn was also an I.A.C. teammate, as was John Faricy. (Unfortunately, Faricy had sprained an ankle when he first stepped off the train in Paris, and was unable to compete in the water polo matches.) Jamison "Jam" Handy was also from the I.A.C., and had competed on the 1904 U.S. Olympic team as a swimmer. Now twenty years later, he was back in the Olympics as a member of the water polo team.

The water polo team from the I.A.C., including Johnny, had won the U.S. national championship in 1924 (they would also repeat as champions in 1927). The balance of the team included Clarence Mitchell, George Schroth, Herbert Vollmer, Arthur Austin, John Norton, and Wallace O'Connor.

The U.S. water polo team had finished fourth at the 1920 Antwerp Olympics, and now with the addition of Weissmuller and Lauer they expected to at least take home the silver or bronze medal. The Belgian team was favored for the gold medal, but the French team was the choice of the Parisian crowd. Surprisingly, France defeated Belgium 3-0 for the gold medal, much to the delight of the French partisans.

Meanwhile, the U.S. team led by Weissmuller and Lauer did indeed win the bronze medal for third place. They had a shot at the silver medal, but lost in final elimination to Belgium by the score of 2-1. The American team seemed to feel that Belgium had not played fairly, and lodged a protest, which was upheld. The match was replayed, and the Belgians won again by the same score, 2-1. (Johnny later recalled that some of the foreign opponents played some very "dirty" tricks in these matches — including scratching and grasping below the surface, and a one-legged player who used his "stump" to pin Johnny underwater!)

The next race for Weissmuller would be the 100-meter freestyle, a sprint race in which he owned the world record (57.4 seconds set in the previous February). All things considered, Johnny was the prohibitive favorite to win the gold medal. But some of the best competition in the world perhaps had other ideas, including Arne Borg, who had given Johnny all he could handle in the 400-meter freestyle event. A rising star was Sam Kahanamoku, younger brother of Duke. And last but not least of the top contenders was the Duke himself, who had won this event twelve years before in Stockholm, and in the 1920 Games at Antwerp. They all hoped to dethrone Weissmuller as the top swimmer in the world, but Johnny was the world record-holder and thus was the favorite in this race.

Placed in the fifth heat against Pinillo of Spain, Pycock of Great Britain, Vanzeveren of France, and Christie of Australia, Johnny won this elimination race with relative ease. In the semifinal heats the competition was tougher, including Arne Borg, as well as Pycock, Stedman of Australia, and Zorilla of Argentina. Once again Johnny won this heat well ahead of the other racers, hardly breaking a sweat.

The finals on July 20th looked to be a tougher challenge for Johnny, but still he felt confident. The other top swimmers who had made the finals were Arne Borg, Katsuo Takaishi of Japan, and Johnny's American teammates, Duke and Sam Kahanamoku. Borg, the "Swedish Sturgeon" who between 1921 and 1929 set 32 world records at distances between 300-yards and one mile, was the darling of the European fans. Borg's strongest race was the 1500-meters, and in a sprint race he was given little chance of beating Johnny Weissmuller.

Of the challengers, Johnny had the most respect for the Duke — after all, he had won this race twice in previous Olympics. The lane assignments had Weissmuller in between the two Hawaiian stalwarts, which could possibly spell trouble for the favorite. Johnny had conferred with his coach over the possibility that Duke and his brother Sam would swim a "team race" against him — in order that one of them would win the gold medal. Bachrach looked at Johnny, and then the brothers Kahanamoku, and reassured his star swimmer that nothing like that would happen on a team that he coached.

As if to quell that notion once and for all, Duke turned to Johnny as they moved to their starting positions, offered his hand and said, "Johnny, good luck. The most important thing in this race is to get the American flag up there three times. Let's do it." Johnny smiled back at the Duke and nodded his agreement, a firm commitment in his mind to win this race for America!

The 100-meter freestyle only takes approximately one minute to complete, but it is the most exciting swimming event because the racers are moving at the fastest speed possible in the water for any human being. The starter's gun banged and Johnny jumped to an immediate lead over Duke and Sam, who were battling for second place with Arne Borg.

The crowd cheered in awe as Johnny blazed through the water, swimming a magnificent race in a new Olympic record of 59 seconds flat! And sure enough, the Duke placed second and Sam third, only a split second behind his big brother. Johnny's heart was pumping as he gasped for enough air to make up for the intense exertion of proving

151

he was the fastest swimmer in the world. Meanwhile, Bachrach had forgot to breathe for almost one minute, but now he breathed a sigh of relief. Johnny's victory margin was 1.4 seconds, winning the race by three meters over the Duke.

The Americans had swept the three medal positions just as they had planned, putting a smile a mile wide on the face of coach Bachrach, who couldn't have been prouder of his valiant warriors. Johnny was presented with the gold medal, Duke the silver, and Sam the bronze. They made an unforgettable portrait on the presentation blocks, Johnny highest in the center, as three American flags were raised on the masts of honor. If it hadn't been official before, it was now — the world had a new hero and champion in Johnny Weissmuller.

This was just a beginning, as his worldwide fame and popularity would continue to grow to legendary proportion over the next 30 years! After Johnny's stunning victory in the 100-meters, the crowd of 7,000 stood and cheered and called for him to reappear for almost three minutes, calming only when it was announced that he would appear again later that same afternoon.

The final event for Johnny in this Olympics was scheduled to be the 800-meter freestyle relay: four teammates each swimming 200-

meters against the competition. In the 1920 Olympics, Norman Ross and the Duke had been members of this winning relay team. This time around the Duke was in the cheering section as Johnny anchored the team, along with Wallace O'Connor, Harry Glancy, and Ralph Breyer. The U.S. quartet had one distinct advantage over the other nations: Weissmuller was the fastest swimmer in the world!

In the first heat and the semifinals, the U.S. team disposed of the competition with little resistance, setting a new world's record in the process. Other teams in the finals included Australia, anchored by "Boy" Charlton; Sweden, including both of the Borg brothers; and also Japan, Great Britain, and France.

In the finals on the afternoon of July 20th, Breyer started for the United States and opened up a lead over Australia. Glancy swam the second leg against Charlton, with the Aussie pulling the teams back to even at the halfway mark of the race. O'Connor swam the third leg for the U.S. team as the race stayed close, with America gaining a small advantage. But with Weissmuller swimming the final 200-meters from the anchor position, it was clearly no contest: the American relay team defeated Australia for the gold medal by almost nine seconds! The official time was 9 minutes and 53.4 seconds, a new world record for the event. Meanwhile,

Charlton of Australia and Borg of Sweden led their teams to the silver and bronze medals, respectively.

After pulling himself from the water, Johnny looked at Charlton and Borg and realized he had defeated the best swimmers in the world in this Olympics. Moments later, Johnny accepted the gold medal for the United States, as he beamed with pride at coach Bachrach and his teammates. When he stepped down from the block, he accepted final congratulations from these two tough competitors, knowing they would both be back in four years at the next Olympic Games. Johnny, too, would be ready for the challenge!

CHAPTER NINE

An Olympic Hero

It was quite an Olympics for Johnny Weissmuller. In addition to his three gold Olympic medals and the adulation of fans around the world, he was given a special commendation and medal for his athletic excellence by French President Doumergue. If Mr. Weissmuller had indeed committed a diplomatic *faux pas* concerning the incident with the heckling bicyclist, he had turned it all around by the end of the Paris Games. Johnny's Olympic medals crowned him a champion to sports fans worldwide, and his comic diving routine with his partner made him a lovable hero as well.

The following quote is taken from the 1973 book, *Young Olympic Champions*:

"Clearly, everyone agreed, Johnny Weissmuller was the star of the 1924 Olympic Games. For the first time a swimmer had stolen the show from all other great athletes. Johnny had his place in history. Everyone knew that. At nineteen years of age, Johnny was a world-famous champion." (Johnny had actually turned 20-years-old just prior to the Olympics.)

And if there was a star nation in these Olympics, it was clearly the United States. They dominated many of the competitions, and won the team championship by a wide margin. American athletes won a total of 45 gold medals, compared to fourteen for second-place Finland and thirteen for France.

Nearing the conclusion of the Games the Paris daily newspaper *Liberte* offered this interpretation for the French losses, under the heading "Why We Were Beaten":

"The Americans are following exactly the same severe training regime here as at home (in America). You never see them at any of the amusement, drinking, smoking or dancing establishments. They will win because they are doing everything possible to win." Clean living will do it every time, and the Americans were squeaky clean at the Eighth Olympiad. The gold medals went to Johnny and his victorious teammates, and the victory cigar went to Big Bill Bachrach, trainer of champions.

The U.S. swim team performed especially well, led of course by Johnny Weissmuller. An account of the swimming events at the Olympics in Paris, appearing in the *Tri-Color* magazine for July, said that, "American swimmers, both men and women, showed great superiority over all their rivals." The article continued:

"Chicago swimmers were well up to the fore. Of the seventeen swimming events for both men and women, thirteen were won by the United States, two by Australia, one by England, and one by France. Chicagoans won five of the eleven individual victories. Johnny Weissmuller was the outstanding star, winning two individual races and swimming on the championship eight-hundred-meter relay.

"A new Olympic record was set in every swimming event, which is setting a record for breaking records that will be hard to beat. Andrew Charlton, of Australia, proved himself the greatest distance swimmer of all time by taking nearly two minutes from the world's best performance [in the 1500-meters]; while Weissmuller sustained his reputation as the world's greatest sprint swimmer.

"Of the eleven records set, America accounted for nine. An Australian and an English girl accounted for the other two. The men made a clean sweep of the first three places in three events, the 100-meter freestyle, the springboard diving, and the fancy high diving. The girls cleaned house in the 100 and 400-meter freestyle events and the springboard diving.

"The clean-up made by the girls was more

complete than that of the boys. Out of a possible one hundred and twenty-four points, the girls scored one hundred and six. A perfect score for the men would have been one hundred and seventy-two, but they rolled up only one hundred and fourteen. The women scored nearly as many points in seven events as the men did in ten.

"In the men's events, Warren Kealoha successfully defended his backstroke title, Duke Kahanamoku, twice Olympic winner in the hundred, was forced to take second to Weissmuller, and Clarence Pinkston, fancy high diving champion, placed third behind his schoolmates, White and Fall.

"Four Illinois Athletic Club swimmers won individual championships, two of them swam on the winning four-man relay team, and four played on the seven-man water polo squad.

"Winning the 400-meter swim, Weissmuller proved his right to be called a champion, for he was forced every inch of the way by Arne Borg, of Sweden, and had to take several seconds from the record to win. Johnny's Olympic record time in this event was five minutes, four and one fifth seconds. In the 100-meter freestyle, he recorded the time of 59 seconds. The 800-meter relay team, on which he swam anchor, made the new record of nine minutes, and 53.2 seconds.

"Several surprising performances were put up by the other Chicagoans. Chief among these was the victory in the 100-meters freestyle for women scored by Miss Ethel Lackie, of the I.A.C., the world's leading understudy of Weissmuller's style. She defeated Miss Mariechen Wehselau, of Hawaii, holder of the world's record, in the new Olympic time of one minute, 12.4 seconds."

Sybil Bauer of the I.A.C., who at 20-years-old was exactly the same age as Johnny, was also an undefeated champion, and was the world record-holder in all the women's backstroke events. She dominated the 100-meter backstroke event in Paris and won the gold by an impressive margin of 4.2 seconds.

Sybil and Johnny were good friends and teammates in Chicago and on the Olympic team, both champions and gold medal winners. She was such a tremendous backstroker that at a swim meet in Bermuda in 1922, she became the first woman to shatter an existing men's swim record. Sybil chopped six seconds off the record in the 440-yard backstroke that was held by Stubby Kruger, another teammate from the I.A.C. (It would be a serious blow to Johnny, and the swimming world, when Miss Bauer would die of intestinal cancer in January of 1927 at the age of twenty-two.)

Nineteen-year-old Helen Meany was at her second Olympics, as she placed fifth in the platform diving event for the United States. She met Johnny during the weeks in Paris and became friends, and later during the 1928 Olympics in Amsterdam, they would become very close friends. In the 1987 book, *Tales of Gold*, Miss Meany recalled some highlights from the 1924 Games:

"I was very excited to be on an Olympic team. In 1924, the British and the American men were winning most of the medals in track and field, except for the long distances, and Americans were also winning the swimming and diving events. At the swimming stadium, the American flag was going up, and 'The Star-Spangled Banner' was playing after practically every event. There were a lot of Frenchmen in the audience, and they all wore straw hats with colored bands on them. The Frenchmen didn't stand up and didn't take their hats off at any time. We became kind of indignant about it, so the swimmers got together, and the next day they brought some trackmen to the pool who were finished with their races. When the American anthem played and the flag went up for the first time, these men rushed the Frenchmen, grabbed all their hats, and sailed them into the pool. There were all those hats with the colored bands bobbing up and down in the water. It was beautiful! There could have been an international incident over that, and I don't know how it was avoided.

"After the swimming events, some people wanted to see more high diving. No one would dive, so my coach, Charlotte 'Eppie' Epstein, asked if I would do it, and I agreed. They rigged up a derrick next to the Seine, and they had to put two ladders together so that I could climb up. It was at least 40 feet high, higher than I had ever dived before. On ladders like that, I often froze, but I made it up and did three dives."

Another female competitor at these Games was a butcher's daughter from Brooklyn named Gertrude Ederle. Miss Ederle won a bronze medal in the 100-meter freestyle, and was a member of the gold medal winning team in the 4x100 relay. (However, Gertrude's greatest fame would come on August 6, 1926, when she became the first woman to swim the English Channel. In a marvelous feat of endurance, Gertrude Ederle's time of 14 hours and 31 minutes was almost *two hours faster than the men's record* for the Channel swim!)

After the Olympics, one of the secrets of Johnny's championship ability was revealed in an article by Grantland Rice, one of America's foremost sports authorities. The article, "Loose People" was printed in *Collier's Weekly*, and spoke of the importance of loose-jointedness in different kinds of athletic activity. Mr. Rice commented on the 400-meter freestyle race at the 1924 Olympic games, and some of the famed contestants:

"There were, among others, Arne Borg and Andrew Charlton, the great Swedish and Australian stars, keyed up and ready for the big test. They were all set and eager to get away. Suddenly another entry, who had been talking and laughing with a nearby group, threw aside his bathrobe and strolled into line. He still had a broad grin and his hands were also dangling at his sides as if hung there by strings. There was only a second or two before the starter's gun would bark. And yet this latest arrival was about as tense as a loose towel. Just before the gun cracked he turned, and said, 'Come on, fellows, let's go!' And he hit the water with the loosest-looking body and the loosest-looking pair of arms one could ever expect to see. His name was Johnny Weissmuller. On that occasion he won another Olympic championship and broke another world's record as he outsped Borg and Charlton through the last few yards.

"Weissmuller knew the competition that he faced. He knew that he had to break another world's record to win. And yet there wasn't a single sign of nerve strain or tautness or physical stiffness either in arms or body. He remained loose and willowy and elastic on his way through the air into the pool."

★ ★ ★

Johnny was very "loose" all right, and as many people observed over the years, he was "happy-go-lucky." Perhaps this inner child-like happiness was the real secret to his success as a swimmer. The following quote is from the 1996 book, *Olympic Dreams . . . 100 Years of Excellence*:

"The 1924 Games also marked the Olympic debut of one of the greatest, if not the greatest, freestyle swimmers of all time. Not only did American Johnny Weissmuller never lose an Olympic race, he never lost any race of any sort. In all he won a total of five Olympic gold medals. In Paris he finished first in the 100 and 400-meters and contributed to the team victory in the 4x200-meter freestyle relay, and also won a bronze medal in water polo. Four years later in Amsterdam he repeated his 100-meters and relay victories.

"In addition to his superior skill Weissmuller had perfected what was known as the American crawl. In the early days of competitive swimming most contestants utilized a sort of combination dog paddle/breaststroke technique to propel themselves through the water. This changed late in the nineteenth century when an Englishman named Frederick Cavill observed South Seas Islanders swimming overhand and kicking their legs scissors style. This technique became known as the Australian crawl.

"By the early twentieth century American coaches had modified this style by replacing the scissor kick with straight-legged flutter technique. It was this new style, known as the American crawl, of which Weissmuller became the acknowledged master."

In the August 9, 1924 issue of *The Literary Digest*, an article entitled "American Youth Vindicated at Colombes" made the following observations:

"It is not only the most interesting news of the day to millions of Americans, thinks the Pittsburgh *Sun*, that the United States Olympic team retains the world's athletic championship by winning the eighth modern revival of the ancient games at Colombes, France, but it is perhaps the most important news of the day, too, 'for it indicates that American youth, despite much head-shaking and lamentation, is able to hold its own with the youth and stamina of the rest of the world, and incidentally to break a collection of records set by past generations. It indicates that an age that is commonly said to be going soft is not entirely flabby.' "

An accompanying photograph of Johnny Weissmuller was captioned, "OUR CHAMPION SWIMMER." The article later noted the "bulldog tenacity of the Yale crew, the imperturbability of Helen Wills, and the *dazzling* speed of Johnny Weissmuller."

Among all the superlatives that could be

applied after this Olympics, *dazzling* certainly described Johnny. Perhaps one could also say that America's new hero was overwhelmed by all the attention he received from near and far. Men, young and old, admired his athletic skills and achievements. Women, the young as well as the not-so-young, adored him for his apparent innocence and his unadulterated male radiance and virility.

The world was waiting for young Mr. Weissmuller, and even though he wanted to go HOME, he and his coach accepted an invitation to tour Europe after the Olympics. For the time being, Lorelei and the shores of America would have to wait.

CHAPTER TEN

Just a Vagabond Swimmer

For Johnny Weissmuller and his teammates on the swimming squad, their Olympic experience concluded with the finals held on Sunday, July 20th. The official closing ceremony would be on July 27th, as events such as weightlifting, tennis, cycling, and equestrian would be the final events to be contested during the last week of competition. The S.S. *Leviathan* departed port with the track and field men on July 15th, with the S.S. *George Washington* and the S.S. *President Roosevelt* scheduled to head for the good old U.S.A. with the balance of the athletes on the 23rd and 28th of the month, respectively.

Meanwhile, the A.A.U. had accepted an invitation for the entire swim team to compete in Belgium on July 22nd, at the Royal Circle of Natation of Brussels. (Webster defines the word "natation" simply as "the act or art of swimming.") Johnny and his teammates performed before Albert I, King of

Belgium, and the royal family. Naturally, Johnny's comedy diving routine was the hit of the exhibition as his popularity continued to grow outside of the United States. Once again another medal was bestowed upon him, this time by the Belgian king, for his swimming achievements at Colombes.

Johnny was disappointed when the rest of the team headed for home, while he and his comedy diving partner, Stubby Kruger, along with coach Bachrach, began a barnstorming tour of Europe that was sanctioned by the A.A.U. Naturally, Bachrach had orchestrated this European exhibition to show off his young champion. He wanted the world to see his great swimmer, Weissmuller, first hand. But Johnny longed for the familiar streets of Chicago, his mother's home cooking, and his girlfriend, Lorelei. Despite the fact that he had written her several times from Paris, he had received no letters in return. He was worried, but obligated by the tour, so he concentrated on enjoying some of the sights of Europe.

In reality, this was a chance of a lifetime for a young man to see the world without having to join the Army! Johnny and his traveling road show visited many of the great cities of Europe, including German cities Hamburg, Magdeburg, Dresden, and Berlin. Johnny knew that his parents were immigrants of European heritage, so this was a homecoming of sorts for him.

In every port that they stopped, including Budapest and Prague, the crowds cheered Johnny as he performed his aquatic skills in the pool, demonstrating the American crawl, the backstroke, and his incredible speed swimming. The comedy diving routine of Johnny and Stubby was the highlight of every show, bringing each and every audience to their feet to laugh and applaud for these talented, and funny, Americans. Johnny shared the applause with Stubby, but he was the man they had come to see. They were never disappointed.

Exhibition races against local champions always resulted in the same victor — Weissmuller. The exhibition matches included several against Hungarian champion Istvan Barany, who claimed that in his long career the only man to ever defeat him in a freestyle race was Johnny Weissmuller. Barany was such a legendary swimmer in Europe that he was known as the "Hungarian Weissmuller," perhaps the ultimate compliment to Johnny.

Johnny's legend continued to grow and one particular incident added fuel to the fire of his fame. Prague, the capital city of Czechoslovakia, is located on the banks of the Moldau River. After the exhibition matches in this famous city, a Czech swimming coach approached Bachrach with a bet of one-hundred dollars that Johnny couldn't swim upstream in the Moldau, whose powerful currents had prevented all previous attempts to achieve such a feat. Bachrach accepted the bet, confident that the best swimmer in the world could do what others had failed to accomplish.

That evening Johnny and Bachrach went to the site of the proposed trial by water, where he was to swim along the length of a 50-yard bathhouse. His first attempt ended in exhaustion for Johnny, as the turbulent waters and strong current prevented any appreciable headway. Undaunted, Johnny tried again using the best techniques of relaxation that Bachrach had taught him. This was truly a Herculean task, but he made enough forward progress to reach his goal, a nearby cabana pole. Johnny had achieved through relaxation what brute force had failed to do. Weary from his efforts, he smiled at Bachrach and gave him the "thumbs up" sign, confident that he could do it again.

The next day Bachrach and the bettor met on the banks of the Moldau, and Johnny once again made the difficult swim upstream to the cabana pole. The Czech swim coach grudgingly paid off the bet to Bachrach, shocked that Johnny had accomplished what he had thought was impossible! But for Johnny, the impossible was achieved with regularity, while the difficult was merely mundane!

A tour of several weeks seemed like an eternity to Johnny, but eventually he and his companions were homeward bound. The triumphant trio headed for America on the S.S. *Rotterdam*, a Dutch passenger vessel. (Coincidentally, the S.S. *Rotterdam* was the same ship in which the Weissmuller family had emigrated to America in 1905. As an infant, Johnny and his parents had made the transAtlantic voyage in steerage — space reserved for the very poorest of travelers. Now twenty years later, he was a national hero and traveling in first class.)

Back home in America, Johnny was given a hero's welcome. He was immediately invited to the White House, where he was given a special citation by President Coolidge for his outstanding achievements at the Olympics in winning three gold medals and representing America with honor. The Olympic team — sans the touring Johnny — had been invited to the White House after the Olympics, for a formal ceremony. But now, a private audience and words of congratulations from the President of the United States — this was perhaps his proudest moment.

From the highest emotional peak of an audience with the President, to perhaps the lowest valley. Johnny's presumed romantic relationship with Lorelei turned out to be just smoke. His heart moved up to his throat and stuck there when he was told — second hand — that Lorelei had gotten married! Johnny would have taken it like a man if she had written him a "Dear John" letter, but this was almost too much. He had taken his first chance with love and gotten badly burned. It would be some time before he would take another chance, after this romantic disaster.

Several weeks later she phoned Johnny and asked him to meet her at Lincoln Park. By this time he was concentrating on swimming again, but he reluctantly agreed out of an aching curiosity to learn the truth. The disloyal Lorelei offered an explanation — but no apology. She told Johnny that she had met a man who offered her security, a man who also wanted a home and children as she did. She felt that Johnny couldn't give her these things — in less than kind words she had referred to him as a soldier of fortune who had dropped out of school and didn't even have a job.

Johnny couldn't believe it. He was a hero to his nation, but the girl he thought he loved considered him a vagabond who couldn't even earn a living! Johnny had heard enough. The stinging words were ringing in his ears as he turned and walked away. He never looked back, and he never saw Lorelei again. But he would see love again — in the distant future.

1924 had been the longest year of Johnny's

life, but it finally ended. He had gone to the Olympics and triumphed, and toured most of Europe after the Games. He had found love — he thought — and lost it. The most important thing Johnny gained from Paris were the friendships with his fellow Olympians that would last a lifetime.

An admirer of his who became a friend was Douglas Fairbanks, Sr., who along with his wife Mary Pickford had attended the Games in Paris. They had come to watch the track and field events and cheer for their friend, sprinter Charley Paddock, but they left mesmerized by the performances of Johnny Weissmuller.

After participating in swim meets on the west coast, Johnny was invited by Fairbanks to Hollywood to visit him on the set of his new movie, a swashbuckling adventure called *The Black Pirate*. Motion pictures were still "silent" at this time, but this innovative film deviated from "black and white" photography and used an early Technicolor process. It was a big thrill for Johnny to meet Fairbanks, who in this particular story portrayed a nobleman who becomes a pirate after being victimized by cutthroats.

After watching some of the scenes being filmed, Johnny was invited to have lunch with Fairbanks and another man, introduced as producer Sol Lesser. (Little did Johnny realize at this moment, that a few years later he would be a bigger star than the aging Fairbanks and that Sol Lesser — later still — would be producing his Tarzan pictures!)

Lesser brought up the idea of Fairbanks starring in a film about Tarzan, the fictional character that had been created by Edgar Rice Burroughs in 1912. Fairbanks by this time was over 40-years-old, and he scoffed at the idea of playing the ape-man. Many years later, Johnny recalled to the best of his memory the scenario on that particular day:

"I was on my way to Honolulu to swim in a championship meet," said Johnny. "Sol Lesser was then trying to get Fairbanks to do the Tarzans. But Fairbanks said, 'I don't think I should do it. Too many people know me and know that I've grown out of that type of role. You should put a new face on the scene. Someone people don't know.'

"And he turned over to me and said 'Get a fellow like that!' He pointed right at me, and everyone laughed! I said I didn't know anything about jungles!"

Johnny was also invited to the palatial home of Fairbanks and Pickford, which was nicknamed "Pickfair." Fairbanks was known as a congenial host who invited many of the biggest stars of Hollywood to his home for parties during the years of his marriage to Mary Pickford. Johnny was requested to perform his comedic diving routine with Stubby Kruger, and the dynamic duo were filmed by

Fairbanks with his home movie camera. Later, Fairbanks added some reverse footage of himself popping out of the pool completely dry and serving tea, a bit of "trick photography" that showed off his offbeat sense of humor. Fairbanks later sent a copy of the film to Johnny in Chicago as a remembrance of his visit to Pickfair.

This Hollywood experience certainly got Johnny interested in the motion pictures. After leaving Tinseltown his thoughts returned to swimming and the immediate tasks at hand — winning more championships. But a seed had been planted in his brain, and the idea that he could someday be a movie star now seemed a little more realistic. After all, hadn't the great actor Douglas Fairbanks himself pointed out swimming star Johnny Weissmuller as the man to star as the next Tarzan?

1925 was a usual year for Johnny in that he was still the best swimmer in the world, and he won his share of A.A.U. national freestyle championships, including: 50-yards, indoor (time, 23.2); 100-yards, indoor (time, 52.2); 100-yards, outdoor (time, 52.0); 440-yards, outdoor (time, 5:22.5); 400-yard relay, indoor (time, 3:45.0); and 880-yard relay, outdoor (time, 11:12.0).

The national championship in the 100-yard freestyle was a new world's record of 52 seconds flat, set in Seattle on August 1, 1925.

Perhaps Johnny's best meet of the year was in early December in Pennsylvania, where he set a world's record in the 150-yard freestyle and also broke the world's record in the 220-yard freestyle.

For the year his production was "down" a little bit: only three world records and nine American records were credited to Johnny for 1925. Of course, most swimmers would have traded a career for any one of Johnny's years, including the present one.

As great a champion as Johnny was, he was simply one of a kind. His brother Peter, on the other hand, was an underachiever. As the younger brother of Johnny Weissmuller, coach Bachrach had gladly added Peter to the I.A.C. team a couple of years after Johnny had joined in 1920. Bachrach was hoping to catch lightning in a bottle a second time, but with Peter it never happened.

Peter trained with the team for several years, competing in the junior championships. Bachrach saw some of Johnny in Peter, but he knew he would never follow in his big brother's footsteps. Something inside of Peter told him the same thing. After finishing in second place in his first national contest, he quit the team and never swam in another competition. Peter obviously felt that second place was not good enough for a Weissmuller, considering that his brother had never lost a race. The comparisons made between Johnny and Peter were unfair, and the expectations too high. Peter realized if he continued to pursue swimming, he would be considered a failure by the high standards already set by Johnny. And whereas Johnny reveled in the spotlight, Peter was more of the shy unassuming type.

Johnny's constitution was as strong as Lou Gehrig, the "Iron Horse." Peter Weissmuller, shorter and more slightly built than Johnny, told his big brother that he felt he didn't have the stamina for competition. He felt his body couldn't hold up to the stress and strain. Peter still loved the water and swimming, so he accepted a job as a lifeguard at the Oak Street Beach. Peter wanted to be close to home, and that was as close as one could possibly get.

Johnny accepted his brother's decision to quit the team. He knew in his heart that he had to follow his own star, and that Peter would have his own destiny. But they remained good friends and nobody was a bigger supporter of Johnny than his little brother. Peter was always very proud of the accomplishments of his now famous older brother.

Coach Bachrach had never let Johnny swim in any distance events longer than 500 meters. After his retirement from competition, Johnny recalled when that finally changed:

"Bachrach had always insisted that I was a sprint, not a long-distance swimmer," said Johnny. "At any rate, my speed at the shorter distances assured me of victory, while the longer distances offered room for doubt. Bachrach insisted that in my youth I should keep to the sprints, because they were less of a strain on the growing body, leaving the longer grinds to older men."

This philosophy of Bachrach's changed in July of 1926, due in part to pressure from Johnny. He wanted to break the record for the three-mile Chicago River Marathon, which was held by Richard Howell of the Chicago Athletic Association. Bachrach wanted the thousand-dollar prize for the I.A.C., and had entered George Schroth, who had twice won the Golden Gate Marathon in San Francisco Bay. Bachrach also wanted a guarantee of winning, and that meant entering Johnny who was always "money in the bank."

Although Johnny was the favorite to win the event, it would prove to be a difficult task. It was obvious from the start of the race that conditions would be against a new record that day. A strong breeze blowing in from Lake Michigan created a choppy sea, which would constantly slap the faces of the swimmers as they strove for progress. Thousands of spectators watched from every available perch, including motorboats, wharves and bridges along the length of the race which began on the shore of Lake Michigan on the north side of the Municipal Pier. The racers entered the Chicago River from the lake's ship channel, as Johnny jumped to an early lead of 50 yards over Solomon Adler of the Covenant Club.

Despite the rough water and difficult progress, Johnny gradually increased his lead over Adler. Meanwhile, his brother Peter was acting as his pilot in guiding him along the course in a row boat. (The other pilot in the Weissmuller boat was S. C. Jennings, who had won the first Chicago River Marathon.)

Again, the rough waters created problems for swimmers and pilot boats alike. Peter was rowing the boat, and the strong wind kept pushing the small vessel into Johnny's path in the river. Unable to correct the course of the row boat, Peter kept yelling at Johnny to bear off. (This undoubtedly cost him time in his attempt to break the record.)

By the time that Johnny reached the fifth and final bridge at Wells Street, his lead had grown to an insurmountable distance. The nearest competitors were Adler, who finished almost six minutes back, and Schroth, nearly 10 minutes behind the winner. Johnny won the prize money for the I.A.C., and coach Bachrach had his "sure thing." His time of 56 minutes, 48 seconds was only 28 seconds slower than the record set by Howell (who declined to enter the event this year).

Johnny's time was eight minutes faster than Howell's time the previous year, but he failed by less than 30 seconds in his efforts to break the record due to the strong winds and choppy water. Howell was on hand to shake the hand of the winner, after following the race in an official motorboat. But having proved that he was indeed a long-distance swimmer, Johnny knew that the record would be his the next summer.

In the meantime, something extraordinary happened in the world of swimming in 1926, and for once it was accomplished by someone other than Johnny. Gertrude Ederle, who had been a teammate of Johnny's at the 1924 Paris Olympics, became the first woman to swim the English Channel. The following from *Time-Life Books, 1920-1930*, shows how this incredible feat affected Johnny, at least for a short period of time:

"In 1926, when 19-year-old Gertrude Ederle swam the English Channel, it was front-page news across the nation. Not only was 'Our Trudy' the first woman to conquer the Channel, but her time — 14 hours and 31 minutes — was almost two hours faster than the men's record. She was lionized with a huge ticker-tape parade when she returned to New York.

"But by the following year she was slipping into obscurity and the headlines once more belonged to handsome swimming idol Johnny Weissmuller. Between 1921 and 1929 — when he 'retired' from competition at the age of 24 — Weissmuller set some 67 world records."

Gertrude Ederle paid a high price for her superhuman feat, in spending more than half a day battling the ocean to accomplish what had never been done by a woman. She later became temporarily deaf as a result of her Channel swim, and suffered a nervous breakdown. She also spent four and a half years in a body cast as the result of a serious back injury. But she eventually overcame these tragedies, and devoted much of her later life to teaching swimming to deaf children. When she was inducted into the Swimming Hall of Fame in 1965, it was noted that "Gertrude Ederle was the female counterpart of Johnny Weissmuller, in that they were discussed in every household as the two greatest swimming figures of the 1920's, idols of the Golden Age of Sport."

There was no change in the pecking order in 1926 of the world's finest sprint swimmers. Johnny was still on top, with George Kojac and Walter Laufer standing in the wings but unable to ever defeat the reigning "King of Swimmers," as he was dubbed by members of the press (along with many other nicknames, all complimentary). Other up-and-coming American sprinters included Austin Clapp, Raymond Ruddy, and a young fellow by the name of Clarence "Buster" Crabbe.

After adding the Chicago River Swim to his calendar of events for the year, Johnny also cut back on the rest of his schedule. He did win national championships in his two specialty events, the 100-meter freestyle in a time of 59.6 seconds; and the 440-yard freestyle in a time of five minutes, 21.8 seconds. Once again the I.A.C. relay team won the national championship, with Johnny as the anchor, in a time of nine minutes and 43 seconds. His best performances of the year included setting new American records in the 100-yards, 200-yards, and 220-yard freestyle events, as well as new standards in the 100-yard 0backstroke in both the 20-yard course and short course.

By the fall of 1926, Johnny had spent six years of his life training with coach Bachrach, and winning championships for the Illinois Athletic Club. Johnny was an institution and it looked like he could go on forever as the premiere sprint swimmer in the world. After all, he was still only 22-years-old. But change is inevitable, and the faces at the I.A.C. were gradually changing. Johnny's boyhood pal Hooks Miller had given up competitive swimming and taken a job in the business world. Peter Weissmuller had left the team, leaving the broad shoulders of his brother to carry the load for the Weissmuller name. Also added to the I.A.C. team was Arne Borg, the Swedish champion. Borg wanted the opportunity to train with Bachrach and swim on the same team as Johnny, his friendly rival from the 1924 Olympics.

It was also a difficult time for Johnny and his I.A.C. teammates when Sybil Bauer had to leave the team for severe health reasons in late 1926. Sybil, who was a senior at Northwestern University in Chicago, was engaged to Ed Sullivan, a sports writer from New York. Sullivan had interviewed her at a national event in 1925, and a mutual attraction sparked between the young swimming star and the reporter (who would years later go on to fame with his own television variety show). Two months after their engagement in 1926, Sybil fell from a touring car during a victory parade after winning her final championship at St. Augustine, Florida. She didn't appear to be seriously injured, but as the weeks went by her health deteriorated rapidly. By the fall of 1926, Sybil was diagnosed as having inoperable intestinal cancer.

At the time of her death on January 2, 1927, Sybil was the reigning Olympic champion in the 100-meter backstroke, as well as holding all the world records in her specialty.

She had won six successive national championships between 1921 and 1926 in the 100-yard backstroke, and had won nationals in the 100-meter, 150-yard, and 220-yard backstroke.

The members of the Illinois Athletic Club were like family, and this was a tragic death in the family. It was a difficult loss for everyone concerned, including her close friend Johnny Weissmuller. Her fiancé, Ed Sullivan, was at her bedside when she died. The pallbearers at her funeral included six swimmers who were some of her closest friends, including Johnny, Robert Skelton, Hugo Miller, Weston Kimball, Dick Howell, and Ralph Breyer.

Quoting her obituary in the *Tri-Color*, the club magazine of the Illinois Athletic Club: "Sybil's early passing is saddening beyond human expression; but had she lived a hundred years, she could hardly have added anything to her glorious athletic career, nor strengthened her hold upon the hearts of all who knew her. She was a champion of women swimmers, the greatest of all in her field, and as such she will always be remembered."

CHAPTER ELEVEN

Disaster of the "Favorite"

The year 1927 started out in a spectacular, triumphant manner for Johnny. On January 6th, an invitation swimming meet was held at the Illinois Athletic Club pool, in which high school, college, and club stars appeared. Johnny was already the world record holder in the 100-yard freestyle event, and this evening he would swim this distance faster than he, or anyone else, had ever done.

Johnny was primed and ready on this Thursday night, as he talked casually with coach Bachrach poolside before the event. When it was time for the race to begin, Johnny assumed his starting position and the gun fired by R. E. Davis signaled his charged plunge into the water. His form was perfect and his speed brilliant, as the five lengths of the pool went by like a blur to Johnny. The crowd, strongly pro-Weissmuller, cheered wildly the final two lengths to encourage their hero to even greater speed.

This was the fastest Johnny would ever swim this distance, and the crowd was in disbelief at his incredible time of 49.8 seconds — of course this was a new American record in this event. (This was an invitation meet and not an internationally sanctioned meet, and therefore this new American record was not considered a world record by the A.A.U.)

Charles A. Dean, a national authority on amateur athletics, was quoted in the *Tri-Color* as saying about Johnny's performance on this date: "Greater than swimming the English Channel!"

Dean, a former president of the Amateur Athletic Union of the United States, was the manager of the American team at the 1924 Olympic Games, and for a number of years was chairman of its track and field committee. He had also officiated at hundreds of events around the United States.

"Weissmuller's performance," declared Dean, "is the greatest I have ever witnessed in any line of athletics. It outclasses running one hundred yards in nine seconds, something that many experts declare will never be done. His feat of cutting one and two-fifths seconds from his own world's record for the event lacks the dramatic features of battling wind, wave, and tide to catch the public fancy, which attaches to Channel swimming, but to those who know their aquatics it is a much more significant performance.

"It represents a triumph of perfection in technical skill, of mental preparation and determination, of the scientific application of strength, energy, and power. Weissmuller's triumph is rightfully shared by his coach, William Bachrach, who thereby reached the peak of a long and brilliant career of producing record breakers.

"Many swimmers have negotiated the English Channel. Only Weissmuller has paddled one hundred yards in forty-nine and four-fifths seconds, or anything near it. I never expect to see anybody break this record, except Weissmuller himself."

Meanwhile, Johnny set the official world record of 51 seconds in this event at the University of Michigan Union pool at a swim meet at Ann Arbor, Michigan on June 5, 1927. Johnny wasn't finished thrilling the customers on this spring date, as he also set world records in the 200-meter and 220-yard events.

In the 1970 book, *The Super-Athletes*, author David P. Willoughby mentions this record-setting performance by Weissmuller in a most favorable light:

"As to who is, or was, the greatest sprint swimmer, it is the man whom most sports experts and sports followers alike have long regarded as such: Johnny Weissmuller. A glance at Figure 13 (not shown) bears out this assertion. Where the plotting of the records on this graph shows an erratic distribution up to about the year 1915 — due to the early records being far below the potential — from 1915 on there is a reasonably good correspondence of the curve with that of population increase.

"In relation to the curve, Weissmuller's record of 51 seconds flat, made in 1927, is the outstanding performance. It is 1.2 seconds faster than would be expected in the year 1927; and it stood for nine years (another record, for the event) before being equaled. Steve Clark's present world record of 46.8 seconds, made in 1961, is a fine performance, but it is doubtful whether it will stand as long as Weissmuller's mark stood."

The outdoor national championships were held in Honolulu in late June, 1927, at the War Memorial Auditorium at the eastern end of Waikiki Beach. America's greatest swimmers were present for these championships, including Hawaii's own Buster Crabbe, George Kojac, Walter Spence, Harry Glancy, and Walter Laufer. Also competing was Japan's champion, Katsuo Takaishi, and the man known in Hawaii as the "Illinois Flash," Johnny Weissmuller.

The first race was the mile event, and winning the first national championship of his career was Crabbe, who came within two seconds of Arne Borg's national record in the event. Johnny won his first race of the meet in the 110-yard freestyle, and the following day he would be squaring off in the 440-yard race against Crabbe, who more than anything wanted to beat the acknowledged master of the pool. Both swimmers would be competing in the 1928 Olympics, and these nationals were an early showdown to determine supremacy. Johnny was the undisputed king, but a hungry Crabbe was hoping to force Weissmuller to abdicate the throne!

From his autobiography, *A Self Portrait*, Buster recalled swimming against Johnny in this particular event, and the importance that he had placed on the possibility of beating the "King of Swimmers" at his own game:

"My first race that afternoon was the 440-yard event, swimming against Johnny Weissmuller. Johnny was an Olympic champion at the time, having won three gold medals in 1924 and quite the national hero for American water enthusiasts.

"I was kind of nervous about swimming against him, as much impressed by his reputation in the water as I was with my own first national title, which I wanted to live up to. Beating Weissmuller would skyrocket me to national attention far more than the mile championship would do.

"As the gun sounded in the 440-yard freestyle event Johnny was off like a flash. He paddled with a roar as we raced through the four laps of the 110-yard pool. By the end of the final lap he had beaten me and the rest of the field by a good 20 yards. He was terrifically strong and I knew I didn't have much chance of beating him by the time the race was half over. I had won one event and came in second in the 440, to give me a total of eight points.

"Johnny had won the 110-yard freestyle on the first day and with his victory in the 440 he had a total of ten points, to give him the lead for the high-point medal, which was awarded to the swimmer with the most total points in the overall meet.

"Both Johnny and I were entered in the half-mile race the next evening and a win for me would give me the high-point medal, plus the glory of having defeated the king of swimmers. The fact that he so thoroughly overpowered me in the 440 event earlier didn't dampen my enthusiasm any. I was having a great time during the nationals, undoubtedly spurred by my opening day victory in the mile and two second place finishes behind great swimmers. By the time the half-mile was ready to begin, I felt rather cocky. Weissmuller was serious — I don't recall him ever being jocular when he was racing, perhaps because he was too concerned about somebody beating him.

"When the gun sounded, he was off like a bullet, churning water like a paddlewheeler. This time he didn't beat me by 20 yards, but only by about 10. With the win, Johnny got five more points to finish the meet with 15. I came in second and was runner-up for the gold medal at 14 points.

"Hell, I was happy as a kitten. In my first outdoor national I'd won a swimming title and came only one point away from tying the great Johnny Weissmuller for the high-point medal. It was enough for a 19-year-old Hawaiian lad to live on for months."

Crabbe would get another shot at beating Johnny at the 1928 national championships to be held in San Francisco, as well as in the 1928 Olympic Games to be held in Amsterdam. But try as he might, and despite Crabbe's positive thinking, Buster could never beat Johnny in a swimming match. When it came to freestyle swimming, Weissmuller was the undisputed king — and the crown was still firmly on his head.

The title of this chapter forebodes a "disaster," and indeed the tragedy that struck the pleasure boat *Favorite* on July 28, 1927, was one of the worst in Chicago history. Johnny was involved in this dark hour in history, as a real-life hero who risked his own life to save the lives of others.

On this particular date, Johnny and his brother Peter were training for the up-and-coming Chicago River Marathon in late July. Each day they would meet at the Oak Street Beach, and take to Lake Michigan to train for the event: Peter rowing a boat alongside his brother as they would do in the coming three-mile race. They had laid out a course along the lakeshore, approximately one and half miles in length, and by the time they completed the round trip they had covered the three-mile distance of the marathon.

On many of these afternoons they would also see the passenger steamboat, *Favorite*, on its daily pleasure excursion around Lake Michigan. On this bright and sunny Thursday, the double-decker vessel carrying 71 passengers, mostly women and children, started at the Lincoln Park Pier with a destination of the Municipal Pier some five miles distant.

Johnny and Peter had just completed the first half of their training route, when the weather suddenly turned dark and ugly. This was to be no ordinary thunderstorm, and in fact the weather bureau later described the storm as a "squall with cyclonic force, accompanied by heavy rain." As the brothers were preparing to head for the safety of shore, they noticed that the *Favorite* was in desperate straits itself.

When the gale force winds struck the *Favorite*, it was approximately abreast of North Avenue. The strong winds and violent waves caused the boat to suddenly roll over into the lake, throwing most of the upper-deck passengers into the turbulent waters. Even more tragically, by the time the boat righted itself it had sunk to the bottom of the lake, leaving only the second deck barely above the angry surface of Lake Michigan.

By this time Johnny and Peter were rowing frantically to the scene of the disaster, reaching the *Favorite* in a matter of minutes. Johnny later recalled this grim scene as being almost surrealistic: the captain of the boat, obviously in shock, was seated on the top deck — still smoking a cigarette — while holding the hand of a small boy! Meanwhile, below the surface of the water, dozens of people were trapped on the main deck of the boat.

Realizing the magnitude of this catastrophe, Johnny and Peter both dove into the lake, intent on saving lives. Johnny brought up two children, and Peter was moments behind with another two. Seeing that the shell-shocked captain was going to be little help in the rescue, Johnny barked out an order to his brother Peter: "Start pumping them out — or they'll die!"

And so Johnny dove repeatedly into the turbulent waters and brought up the victims — children and adults — as Peter used his lifeguard training to try to revive as many as possible. Together they worked to the point of exhaustion — minutes passed that seemed like hours — until they had rescued approximately 20 children and adults. By the time a rescue team arrived to help them, it was too late to save the unfortunate others still submerged in ghastly repose in the desolate waters.

Wearily, Johnny pulled himself out of the lake a final time. His eyes were burning from oil in the water leaking from the wounded *Favorite*, and his lungs ached from the many minutes below the surface searching for and claiming a fortunate few. Of the nearly two dozen individuals they had brought to the surface, eleven lived. Of the 71 passengers on board the *Favorite* this day, 27 died as a result of drowning.

Exhausted both mentally and physically, Johnny and Peter rowed slowly back to shore as the rescue team (that had finally arrived) continued searching for more bodies in the frothy waters of Lake Michigan. This was a very traumatic experience for Johnny, and something he would never forget his entire life. The similar lake tragedy of the *Eastland*, some twelve years before, still burned in his memory banks. Every Chicagoan was a part of that disaster, if only as spectators and witnesses in the aftermath and shock waves that echoed through the city.

But this fresh tragedy was so close to him that he vowed to help everyone to learn to swim. His entire life Johnny advocated that youngsters should learn to swim at an early age, to avoid tragedies like the *Favorite*. The

Weissmuller brothers were called heroes for their bravery, and were credited with saving the lives of eleven who survived. But it was with heavy hearts that they accepted a scroll for their heroism from the mayor of Chicago, as well as gold watches in a ceremony held in their honor at the I.A.C.

Many of the survivors and families of the survivors, thanked Johnny and Peter for their efforts. A 1962 letter received by Johnny, epitomized the heartfelt gratitude for this real-life heroism. A young girl back in 1927, the woman penned the following:

"I have seven children and one day, my seven children will have their young ones. This circle of life will continue forever or as long as God grants this earth to remain fertile within the atmosphere. But only you, Mr. Weissmuller, are responsible for this vast miracle that has come to touch my life, because it is you who rescued me from certain death, and enabled me to marry and have my children. I shall always impress upon the minds of my young ones to say a prayer of thanks on your behalf and, God willing, these prayers will last through a part of eternity."

Johnny's life seemed to be guided by fate. It was surely fate that placed him and his brother closest to the scene of the tragedy of the *Favorite* on this particular day. Perhaps no one else was better equipped to save lives on this day, than the world's greatest waterman. He had proved his courage many times over in rising to the challenge of competition, but on this date he had the courage to save lives and was a real-life hero. Peter also proved his own courage under fire, "pumping out" the victims as his brother brought them to the surface, singly and sometimes in pairs.

Johnny put his life on the line diving into the depths of the lake time after time; with each dive he could have succumbed to the exhaustion permeating his bones and possibly drowned himself. Fate, however, was indeed watching out for Johnny, as he dove and dove until there was no one left who could be saved. Johnny earned the mantle of hero this time, more than any other time. But once this tragic event was over, he only wanted to forget and move on in life. And so he did.

The memory of the *Favorite* was fresh in his mind on Saturday morning, as Johnny prepared for the Chicago River Marathon just two days after the tragedy. In his heart he was dedicating this race to the victims, and he was determined to win the race in a record time for the I.A.C. His brother Peter would be piloting the escort boat for Johnny, along the same course they had traveled in winning the race the previous year. Of the nineteen years this event had been held, I.A.C. swimmers had finished first a total of 14 times, including Perry McGillivray four times, W. L.

Wallen three times, and Norman Ross was twice a winner.

There was a thousand dollar prize for the winning club, as well as the William Hale Thompson trophy. (Coach Bill Bachrach coveted the cash prize for the I.A.C., although he had little regard for the shady mayor of Chicago, namesake of the trophy prize.) Johnny was the solitary hope for the I.A.C., as teammate Robert Hallaran had injured his arm in the rescue mission of the *Favorite*, and was scratched from the race by Bachrach.

Witnessing the race that day was journalist Clarence A. Bush, who later collaborated with Johnny on his book, *Swimming the American Crawl*. Through the eyes and words of Mr. Bush, here's how the race looked that day:

"Thousands banked upon barges, bridges, and the two levels of Wacker Drive yelled themselves hoarse, sirens shrieked, bells clanged, and horns tooted Saturday, July 30, as the long arms of Johnny Weissmuller, of the Illinois Athletic Club, flashed through murky, green water to a record-breaking finish in Chicago's greatest aquatic spectacle, the nineteenth annual Chicago River Three-Mile Marathon. From the start at the north side shore line of the Municipal Pier to the finish at Wells Street Bridge, Weissmuller, leading the way, was acclaimed by some fifty thousand spectators, the greatest crowd in the history of this swimming event.

"It was a performance worthy of the crowd which lined the sides and the ends of the pier, massed upon the breakwaters, and upon the docks. Wacker Drive offered seats to many more thousands on its two decks, to get a good view of the finish of this sporting classic of Chicago waters. Hundreds followed the course of the race and the leadership of Weissmuller in excursion boats, undaunted by the shadow of the tragedy of the *Favorite*. For the benefit of these thousands, Weissmuller trimmed nearly two minutes from the record for the course.

"The champion employed a leisurely modification of his famous crawl sprint stroke. He slowed down the leg beats and indulged in a more restful roll from side to side. Piloted by his brother, Peter Weissmuller, who rowed the escort boat, Weissmuller assumed the lead at once. He battled his way through a mass of driftwood brought in by steamers docking at the Municipal Pier. Here the water was roughened by a fresh breeze from the northeast that sent waves crashing against the pier and caused considerable backwash that bothered the swimmers not a little.

"When he rounded the northeast corner of the pier, three quarters of a mile on his way, Weissmuller built up a hundred-yard lead on Solomon Adler. The latter advanced fifty

197

yards ahead of A. J. Thomsen, of the Milwaukee Athletic Club, and Cyril Nelson, of Griffith Natatorium, who were destined to swim the closest battle of the spectacle.

"After turning the northeast corner of the pier, Weissmuller swam south half a mile to the end of the Chicago River Breakwater which extends east into the lake almost as far as the Municipal Pier. When he turned west around the end of this breakwater, Weissmuller had increased his lead by fifty yards more.

"Under the south lea of this breakwater, Johnny found smoother water, and he made splendid time westward toward the mouth of the river. As he approached the river mouth, he sprinted for about two hundred yards. Hitting the current which flows into the river from the lake, Weissmuller stretched his lead over Adler to three hundred yards, and the latter had no chance to make it up.

"Though very few, even among the contestants themselves, appreciate it, the race to the beginning of this favorable current is the real test of the Marathon. The contestant who reaches it first automatically stretches out his lead without extra effort, for while he is being carried downstream, his slower rivals are still fighting the more stable and rough lake waters. When the slower swimmers finally reach the current, they get no advantage from it as far as the leader is concerned, for he enjoys the same current.

"From this point on, the Weissmuller *entourage* was picked up by a boatload of Hawaiian ukulele players and singers, who added much to the gaiety and color of the occasion by chanting: 'Clap hands — here comes Johnny!'

"These Hawaiians were out there primarily to root for their countryman, John Kaaihu, of the Healani Boat Club, Honolulu, but this invader finished well back in the field, so they sang about Johnny while waiting for their comrade to paddle into view.

"From every angle it was one of the greatest spectacles in the history of the event."

And indeed it was. Johnny set a new record of 54 minutes and 29 seconds, eclipsing the 1922 mark set by Richard Howell of the I.A.C. At the finish line to congratulate Johnny were his brother Peter and Robert Hallaran, his injured teammate who rode in the pilot boat with Peter. Also present were coach Bachrach, and Johnny's mother, Elizabeth.

Years later, Johnny humorously recalled that his mother refused to pose with him for photographers waiting at the finish line, because of the stench of the Chicago River sewage that now had permeated her son's handsome physique! Playfully pushing Johnny away from her, Mrs. Weissmuller told her son to shower for a week before coming home! Peter laughed, Johnny smiled, and Mrs. Weissmuller was as proud as a peacock of her champion swimmer son. It was quite a portrait for the photographers as they recorded history set once again by Johnny Weissmuller.

As the year 1927 drew to a close, Johnny looked back on the highs and lows of the year. The tragedy of the *Favorite* had dampened his record-breaking victory at the Chicago River Marathon. Johnny had harvested his fair share of national championships, including the outdoor freestyle events of 100-meters, 440-yards, and 880-yards, as well as the indoor events of 100-yards, 220-yards, and 500-yards. Also as usual, he was the anchor on the I.A.C. national relay championships in the 880-yards (outdoor), and the 300-yard (indoor) medley event.

Johnny's incredible 51 seconds flat in the 100-yards on June 5th was his most significant world record of the year, in fact of the decade. Johnny also set four additional world records in 1927, as well as a magnificent 19 American records for the year.

But the coming year, 1928, would be the most significant year of his career because it would be his final year in competitive swimming. The decision hadn't yet been made in his mind, but every great athlete must eventually decide when it is time to retire. Johnny wanted to go out on top, and his undefeated string had now stretched for over six years. Weissmuller had an undying competitive fire that had made him the greatest champion of them all in the swimming world. The challenge now for Johnny was to stay up on the "high-wire." Could he maintain his winning streak indefinitely without falling off?

Foremost in his mind at this point in time, however, was the coming Olympics to be held in Amsterdam. After the Games, he would make a decision on his future. At this juncture, it was simply time for reflection on the past twelve months and the anticipation of what would be his final Olympic competition during the coming year.

CHAPTER TWELVE

Dutch Treat: Two More Golds

Winning gold at Amsterdam at the Ninth Olympiad was Johnny's foremost goal for the current year of 1928. It was business as usual as he prepared for the coming Olympic Games, winning his share of national championships and adding to his staggering total of world and national swimming records. Weissmuller had been recognized as the world's foremost sprint swimmer since shortly after his debut in 1921, and his undefeated status was in no danger from any of the present day challengers. However, Buster Crabbe felt that if anyone was ready to knock Johnny off of the mountain, it would be Buster himself.

To that end, Crabbe would get his opportunity at the outdoor nationals held in mid-May, 1928 at the Fleishhacker pool west of downtown San Francisco, just off the beach. The pool itself was gigantic — over 1000 yards in length — with high towers and springboards for diving. A bulkhead had been placed to section off 110 yards from the shallow end, thus creating the course for the nationals meet.

All the best swimmers in the country were present to challenge for the outdoor national championships, especially with the Olympics only two months away. The meet began on a Thursday, and Johnny won the 110-yard event (100-meters) in a time that was only a fraction of a second slower than his world record time of 57.4 seconds. Johnny's rival, Buster Crabbe, won his specialty of the mile event and also broke the existing record. The following day Johnny and Buster would meet in the 440-yard freestyle, and once again Crabbe felt that this would be his best chance to dethrone the champion. In the words of Buster Crabbe:

"I couldn't help wonder how I'd fare against Weissmuller the next day when we met for the 440," reflected Crabbe. "Johnny was getting up in age — he was twenty-four, while I was twenty — and he had to know his time was running out as a strong competitor. I was still impressed with him and he wasn't to be taken lightly, but his peak of performance was at its fullest, if not behind him. He'd never be better than he was. I always felt Weissmuller was good up to about 300 yards and after that he just didn't have it, even though he held the records in the 440 and 880 for a time. As it turned out, they weren't hard records to beat.

"We nodded to each other from adjoining lanes as we mounted our starting blocks with the other four competitors. He was a tall son of a gun — a good three inches more than me — and he appeared relaxed, though quiet. With the starting gun we both hit the water. He pulled and kicked in his unorthodox style, something he liked to call 'hydroplaning.' I've come to the conclusion that if Johnny had discarded that discoordinated style of his, he'd have set more records than he did. Hydroplaning works fine if you're an experimental navy ship hovering on jets of air, or a motorboat being pushed by a powerful engine. Working with the water by utilizing your buoyancy has always been preferable to trying to hold yourself above the water ala Weissmuller, a feat that can only slow you down because of the waste of energy in accomplishing it. My criticism notwithstanding, his style worked for him and that was all that really counted.

"He jumped way out in front of me, as he'd done the year before, but about one lap from the finish he seemed to lose something from his stroke and I pulled steadily closer to him. I caught up just before the finish, but he out-touched me by the length of his hand to win the race. Had the course been two yards longer, I know I'd have taken him. We rested a moment in the water before climbing out onto the deck. 'You know, John,' I said, 'this race was a little short for me. But I'll see you on Sunday in the 880.'

"I meant it as a friendly challenge, but Johnny wasn't amused by it. I knew he had to show up for the 880 in order to win the high-point medal and on the strength of my 440 showing, I knew I was finally going to beat the master. It was obvious that I'd grown stronger as a swimmer since our first meeting in Hawaii and there wasn't *any way* Weissmuller could beat me on Sunday. 'Kid,' he said, without smiling, 'I'll never swim you again.' He hoisted himself out of the pool and left.

"The next day — Saturday — Weissmuller left the San Francisco outdoor nationals and flew back to Chicago. I was amazed that he'd do that — give up the high point medal and maybe another national title. But it reinforced the rumors that had been going around the swimming circles at the time: his reputation meant more to him than his desire to compete. I guess he'd won enough titles, anyway. With Weissmuller out of the meet, I won the high point medal in 1928, plus a couple of national titles."

What Buster didn't know at the time — in fact not even coach Bachrach was aware — that Johnny was nursing a pulled tendon in his leg that he feared might keep him out of the Olympics. It bothered him so much during this meet that Johnny had what he called the closest race in his life, to George Kojac of the New York A.C. in the 100-meter freestyle.

"I looked up with about two strokes to go and there was Kojac," reminisced Johnny. "I just about leaped out of the water to beat him. 'Bach' raised the devil about that. But my time of 57.2 on a long course (100-meter straightaway) was a world record." Kojac was a great swimmer who was expected to challenge Johnny in the coming Olympic time trials at the Detroit Boat Club pool — however, he finished a distant second to Johnny.

Crabbe may also have been unaware of the fact that Johnny had never competed in the 880-yard freestyle event in any national championship, so thus there was no reason for him to break precedent this particular year. Crabbe was only trying to goad Johnny into swimming in an event that Crabbe was superior, so he could simply claim that he had beaten Weissmuller.

But Johnny was too smart to be taken in by Crabbe, who was well known for attempting to "psyche out" his opponents with mind games. Unfortunately for Buster, he would never race against Johnny again. He knew he couldn't compete with Johnny in the shorter races like the 100-meters, and Johnny didn't train for the long-distance races. Crabbe had given it his best shot, and now his chance to beat his hero was forever gone. They would both be at the coming Olympics, but would not compete in the same events.

Johnny would not be competing in the Chicago River Marathon this summer, as it conflicted with the trip to Amsterdam. And thus the coming Olympics in Holland (now called The Netherlands) would be the final mountain of his career for Johnny to climb. He knew he would be facing the best swimmers in the world in this ultimate test of competitive fitness. The United States Olympic swim team, again coached by William Bachrach of the I.A.C., was selected at the final tryouts held at the Detroit Athletic Club in early July. The swim team spent several days in New York prior to sailing, and coach Bachrach had his swimmers giving exhibitions for the public. The small admission fees charged to watch the U.S. squad swim practice heats helped to defray the expenses that would be incurred in Amsterdam.

The American contingent left Pier 86, New York harbor, on the S.S. *President Roosevelt* on July 11, 1928. "American Olympic Team" was painted on both sides of the ship, as some two thousand well-wishers waved and cheered as the *Roosevelt* chugged off to sea. General Douglas MacArthur, as the President of the A.O.C, was accompanying the American athletes on the voyage to Amsterdam, with the Games set to open on the 28th of the month. After the team boarded the *Roosevelt* for the trip across the Atlantic, MacArthur announced his confidence in the U.S. athletes:

"The opening of the Games finds the American team at the peak of form. We have assembled the greatest team in our history." MacArthur came around to introduce himself to the various groups of athletes on board, and he had a special hello for Johnny, whom he had met during the 1924 Olympic expedition.

Many of the same friends Johnny had celebrated victory with in the Paris Olympics, including divers Pete Desjardins and Helen Meany, and shot put and discus champion Bud Houser, were on board to renew old friendships. Also entered in these Games was Clarence "Buster" Crabbe of the Outrigger Canoe Club of Honolulu, who dreamed of winning a gold medal and also beating his arch nemesis, Johnny Weissmuller. The Amsterdam Olympics would be a continuance of the long-running rivalry between the two men who would both be future "Tarzans."

Members of the men's swim team included George Kojac and Raymond Ruddy of New York; Walter Laufer of Chicago; Austin Clapp of Hollywood; Thomas Blankenburg of Oakland; Harry Glancy and Paul Wyatt of

Pennsylvania. Other members of the Illinois Athletic Club on the team, besides Johnny, included swimmer Paul Sampson as well as Ogden Driggs, Samuel Greller, and Wallace O'Connor on the water polo team. A longtime member of the I.A.C., Perry McGillivray, was chosen as coach of the men's water polo team.

The women's swim team, coached by Robert Kiphuth of Yale University, included Eleanor Garatti and Marion Gilman of California; Albina Osipowich of Massachusetts; Jane Fauntz of Chicago; Margaret Hoffman, Susan Laird, and Josephine McKim of Pennsylvania. A large contingency from the New York Women's Swimming Association included Martha Norelius, Ethyl McGary, Adelaide Lambert, Lisa Lindstrom, Agnes Geraghty, and Eleanor Holm. (Miss Holm would be Johnny's future partner in the Aquacades of 1937 and 1939.)

The men's diving team was coached by Ernst Brandsten, and included Peter Desjardins of Miami; Michael Galitzen and Harold Smith of Los Angeles; and Walter Colbath of Chicago. Lady divers included Helen Meany of New York, competing in her third Olympics; Betty Becker of Detroit; Georgia Coleman, Dorothy Poynton, and Clarita Hunsberger of California.

The American Olympic team consisted of 3014 athletes — including 290 women —

competing in 109 different events. It is interesting to note that women were allowed to compete in the track and field events for the first time since the modern Olympic Games began in 1896. The track and field events had been considered too "strenuous" for women athletes by the I.O.C., allowing them to compete only in "ladylike" events like swimming, diving, tennis, and fencing. However, in 1928 five new events were scheduled for the ladies, including the 100-meter sprint, 800-meter run, 4x100-meter relay, high jump, and the discus throw. German athletes were also allowed to compete in the Olympic Games for the first time since 1912, ending a bitter exile caused by lingering political animosities in the aftermath of World War I.

The spirits of Johnny and his teammates were high on the trip over, as they had every reason to believe that this great Olympic adventure would be a major success. They arrived in Amsterdam on the afternoon of July 21st, and were greeted by a band and a formal salute from the guns of the U.S.S. *Detroit*, which was headed out to sea.

During their stay in Amsterdam, the American team lived aboard the *Roosevelt*, which was anchored in the middle of Amsterdam Canal, and it was necessary to take a ferry to shore each day. MacArthur, a strict disciplinarian, had a rule that all athletes had to be in their staterooms by 9:30 each evening. After each day's events, the athletes would go to dinner in Amsterdam and relax, as well as celebrate the day's high points and victories. If you missed the last tender (small transport vessel) to the ship at about seven o'clock, you had to hire one of the Dutch lads to row you out to the ship in a row boat to make curfew. Meanwhile, everyone else would be standing at the ship's rail, and would join in a spirited rendition of "Row, row, row your boat . . ."

MacArthur, not seeing the humor in this from his spot on the top deck, would bark out through the horn: "Now hear this! Have whoever came in on that rowboat report to me immediately!" According to American track star Ray Barbutti, MacArthur's bark was worse than his bite, and that he was well-liked and admired by the team members. Also recalling Major General Douglas MacArthur was assistant swimming team manager Dr. Francois D'eliscu, who said of the American leader of the Olympic expedition: "He alone (MacArthur), can be set aside, as an inspiration for other athletes to follow. Just sit with him as a spectator! Quiet and reserved, firm and forceful, friendly and sympathetic, and a born leader!" Dr. D'eliscu also had strong words of praise for William Bachrach, coach of the men's swimming team, when he called him "one of the greatest coaches living today . . . a man with experience, practical business ability, and a keen knowledge of swimming."

Barbutti also noted in the 1987 book, *Tales of Gold*, that handsome swimmers Weissmuller and Crabbe "got all the women . . . the rest of us didn't do much of anything." Johnny was romantically linked to diver Helen Meany during this Olympics. Perhaps this liaison was Barbutti's reference to "all the women." Most of the young female swimmers and divers did tend to admire Johnny and Buster, who as we all know, were great athletes and had movie star looks as well. That unbeatable combination acted like a magnet for the opposite sex, although Johnny himself was mostly concerned with winning gold — not girls — in Amsterdam.

The trip was not all fun and games for Buster Crabbe, who developed a case of influenza on the fifth day out. Crabbe's flu was also aggravated by the rocking motion of the waves of the Atlantic, and he was confined to his cabin for the final five days of the voyage. Fed a steady diet of soup by his roommate, George Kojac, Crabbe dropped twelve pounds from his normal weight of 185. Unfortunately, Crabbe would not be at full strength during these Olympics, and for many years he was bitter that his illness had cost him his chance at a gold medal at these Games.

The team was raring to go after arriving in

Amsterdam, however, finding a pool to practice their swimming techniques was another matter! The water in the harbor was "foul and unpleasant," and thus the swimmers could not swim near their floating resort home. According to John T. Taylor, the manager of the U.S. swimming team, the two pools that were assigned to the Americans were completely unsuitable as practice facilities.

Taylor and his two assistants spent two entire days wearing out their wooden clogs on the cobblestone streets of Amsterdam, before they located a pool in Haarlem that met the minimum standards for practice. Even this pool created a problem, as it was sixteen miles from the harbor, thus wasting time in travel each day. Taylor later noted that the same type of problem existed in Paris in 1924, and once again they had to deal with this adversity.

The actual competitions were to take place at the new Swimming Stadium, which had stands on either side of the Olympic pool to accommodate approximately 6,000 spectators. The pool itself was the official Olympic size of 50 meters long and 18 meters wide. The deepest end of the pool, where the diving competitions would take place, was 15 meters in depth. Since this was an outdoor pool, there was a facility located at one end with dressing rooms for the swimmers and divers;

on top of this building were stands reserved for official visitors, contestants, and members of the press.

The Games officially opened on Saturday afternoon, July 28th, with Prince Hendrik of Holland presiding over the opening ceremonies at the newly built Olympic Stadium. An eager and excited crowd greeted I.O.C. president Henri de Baillet-Latour, of Belgium, who had succeeded Pierre de Coubertin in September of 1925.

A crowd in excess of 40,000 spectators were present during the opening festivities, while outside the stadium another 75,000 fans were disappointed that they could not obtain tickets at any price. More than 4,000 athletes and officials from the 46 competing nations marched in the parade, which took longer than one hour to pass the reviewing stand.

Johnny Weissmuller was chosen to represent America and carry the designation standard bearing "Vereenidge Staten" (United States), while Clarence "Bud" Houser followed Johnny and carried the American flag in the procession. Marching right along with them was General Douglas MacArthur, the diplomatic leader of the American team, in full military regalia. (Later in life Johnny would recall that this particular moment, marching with General MacArthur and Bud Houser in representing the United States, was the proudest moment of his life. A second special memory for Johnny was "standing on the champion's platform at the Olympics, listening to the 'Star Spangled Banner' being played.")

For the first time ever, a flame was ignited on the 150-foot Marathon Tower, thereby introducing the Olympic Flame to the Games. As Prince Hendrik pronounced the Games open, the Olympic flag was raised and a thousand pigeons were released, signifying peace and good will to all nations and all peoples on earth.

Anticipation began to mount as Harry Denis, captain of the Dutch soccer team, took the Olympic oath for the assembled athletes of the 46 nations. Johnny breathed a sigh of relief as he and his teammates left Olympic Stadium at the conclusion of the ceremony. The pomp and pageantry was now over, it was now time for the Games to begin!

The track and field events were the first to be contested, and by the time of this Ninth Olympiad the rest of the world had caught up to the United States in athletic ability. The Americans won only three gold medals out of thirteen track events, including the 400-meter sprint by Ray Barbutti, and two relay events (4x100-meters, 4x400-meters). They fared considerably better in the field events, winning gold in the high jump, long jump, pole vault, shot put, and the discus throw. Meanwhile, 16-year-old Elizabeth "Betty" Robinson became the first American woman to win a gold medal in track and field with her victory in the 100-meter sprint.

The Americans were favored to win in many of the swimming events, as both the men's and women's swimming teams were considered very strong components of the U.S. squad. Olympic champion Johnny Weissmuller was planning to compete in the same events in which he won gold in 1924: 100-meter freestyle, 400-meter freestyle, and the 4x200-meter relay.

However, coach Bachrach wanted Johnny to compete on the water polo team instead of the 400-meter freestyle, hoping that this squad would be strong enough to win a gold medal (after capturing the bronze medal in 1924). In addition, Bachrach wanted Arne Borg, who had been competing with the I.A.C. for the past two years, to have a shot at the gold medal in the 400-meter event. There can be only one winner, so Johnny was forced — reluctantly — to give up what looked like a strong gold medal event for him in favor of his close friend, Borg.

This turned out to be a bad break for Johnny, as a relatively weak U.S. water polo team did not medal at all. In fact, the Americans had the unfortunate luck of drawing European champion Hungary for their first match, and lost 5-0. It was a disappointing loss for the team, especially considering that Bachrach had handpicked Perry McGillivray from the I.A.C. as the coach of the team, and many of the same players from the bronze-medal winning squad of 1924 were back. (A disheartened John Taylor went so far as to say that perhaps the U.S. should give up the sport unless the quality of competition was elevated to a level as to be able to compete with the European teams.) In the finals, Germany and Hungary were tied 2-2 in regulation, with Germany winning the gold medal in overtime by a score of 5-2.

Not one to cry over spilt milk, Johnny still would be competing in the two swimming events in which he was confident of gold medals: the 100-meter freestyle sprint, and the 4x200-meter relay. Johnny was the world record holder in the 100-meter event, and with Johnny as the anchor, the American relay team was an overwhelming favorite in this team event. Meanwhile, Alberto Zorilla of Argentina would win the 400-meter freestyle, edging out Charlton, Borg, and Buster Crabbe in that order. Johnny had defeated Zorilla, Charlton, and Borg in the 1924 Olympics, and he certainly would have been favored to grab the gold in this event this time around.

The swimming preliminaries began on August 4th, one day before the conclusion of the track and field events. That moved the swimmers, and Johnny Weissmuller, to the center of the stage in the eyes of the world. Johnny had set the Olympic record in the 100-meter freestyle in 1924 in 59 seconds flat, and he also held the world record in the event at 57.4 seconds (a record that would stand for ten years, 1924-1934). The swimming events, always a spectator favorite, drew capacity crowds for the eight days for a total of 50,826 in paid attendance.

In Johnny's first heat he competed against — and readily defeated — Walter Spence of Canada, Brooks of Great Britain, and Heinrich of Germany, in that order. The competition was tougher in the semifinals, which included Istvan Barany, the Hungarian champion that Johnny had met on his European tour in 1924. But Johnny was up to the challenge, setting a new Olympic record in a time of 58.6 seconds, as he was trailed by Barany, Heitman of Germany, Olsen of Norway, and Polli of Italy.

The finals were held on August 11th, and the best swimmers in the world were intent on dethroning Johnny as the world's premiere sprint swimmer. American challengers George Kojac and Walter Laufer had qualified for the finals, along with Barany of Hungary, Spence of Great Britain, Katsuo Takaishi of Japan, and Alberto Zorilla of Argentina.

Conspicuous by his absence from this race was Arne Borg, who had opted to enter the 400-meters and the 1500-meters — events that Johnny would not be competing. Borg had lost out to Johnny in this event in 1924, and realized that this race belonged to Weissmuller. (But it also looked like a further trade-out on the part of Bachrach, that Arne Borg did not compete in an event in which he was a top contender.)

This particular race is perhaps Johnny's most famous race, and one that he would always gladly talk about in an interview. It was a race he nearly lost, because he swallowed a mouthful of water which came close to being his swan song! But a loss was not in the cards, as Johnny recalled in his own words:

"I had always dreaded swallowing a mouthful of water," said Johnny reflectively. "I knew the lights would go out and I wondered what I'd do if it ever happened to me. Sure enough, my time arrived as I did the turn, the only turn in the race. I dipped down and came up with a throatful of water! We [the racers] were all even. I felt like blacking out. I swallowed the stuff and lost two valuable yards. Lucky for me, we still had some forty meters left to go — with only ten or so I'd never have made it. But — well, I guess I had to win for America, to come in first."

A Herculean effort in those final forty meters by Johnny regained the lead he had temporarily lost, and he edged out Barany, who won the silver, by 1.2 seconds. His time of 58.6 tied the Olympic record he had set in the semifinals, although he surely would have set a new record if not for the now famous "gulp" of water! Claiming the bronze medal was Takaishi of Japan, followed by Kojac, Laufer, Spence, and in dead last place, Zorilla. (This was the same Alberto Zorilla who claimed the gold medal in the 400-meter free-style, a throne abdicated by Johnny after the unfortunate decision for him not to enter that particular race.)

The *Tri-Color*, magazine of the I.A.C., later recounted the exciting race that was perhaps the most memorable of his career:

"The redoubtable Johnny Weissmuller was certainly one man who did not let the Americans down, but he did not have an easy job of it. Takaishi, the bearded Jap, was only third, but a new menace pressed Johnny in the last lap, Barany, of Hungary. Weissmuller went out and just beat him to the cement by one and a fifth seconds.

"The race was swum in a glistening pool under a sun-scorched sky. In the deep shadows at the far end of the tank, Takaishi seemed to beat Weissmuller to the cement at the last turn, but after a submerged turn, Johnny's long brown arms appeared flashing in the sunshine, leading Takaishi by a body's length, with the Hungarian cutting

220

the water at their heels.

"The last twenty meters brought Barany away from the fishlike Takaishi, the Hungarian leaving a wake behind like a motorboat. Barany's spurt broke up at about the same instant Weissmuller tapped the finish."

The gold medal that Johnny claimed in this 100-meter freestyle was the fourth of his Olympic career, and now there was only a final competition left — the 4x200-meter relay. Although this is a team event, the anchor (final swimmer) is the most important position. The anchor can win or lose the race for his team, and Johnny always swam the anchor. And thus it is the anchor swimmer who most richly deserves the kudos for winning a gold medal in the Olympics. By the time of the final leg, it is merely a 200-meter sprint between the anchor swimmers — and Johnny was the top sprinter in the world.

Buster Crabbe had hoped to be a member of the six-member relay team that would be competing in the 4x200-meter event (four men would compete, two were alternates). When the trials for the event were held two days after arrival in Amsterdam, Crabbe was still weak from his shipboard bout with the flu, and he was unable to gain one of the six spots on the team. Crabbe wanted a gold medal more than anything in the world, and he realized that the relay team with Weissmuller at anchor, was a cinch to win the gold medal.

Crabbe later recalled his feelings and disappointment at being left off the relay team, and missing out on the opportunity to win a gold medal on the same relay team as the man he desperately hoped to equal in accomplishments, Johnny Weissmuller:

"I tried again to talk Bachrach into giving me a spot on the [relay] team, but he said the teams were all established, that he was sorry I had been sick, and that it wouldn't be fair to remove someone else and go against the results of the trial.

"Damn it! He was right about being fair, but I felt I was right, too, because there wasn't any reason for holding the trials so soon after landing in Holland. At 90 percent of my normal strength, I could beat several of the relay swimmers.

"As expected, the American team won the 800-meter relay and each swimmer received a gold medal. I was bitterly disappointed that I wasn't one of them."

In the preliminaries, the U.S. team was represented by Weissmuller and Paul Sampson of the I.A.C., David Young, and Austin Clapp. With Johnny swimming the anchor, the Americans were in command of the heat in defeating a strong Japanese team, followed by Sweden, and Argentina. Their time of 9 minutes, 38.8 seconds chopped almost 15 seconds off the Olympic record set in 1924 by the American team led by Weissmuller, and also set a new world's record in the process.

The relay finals were to be held on August 11th, the same day that Johnny won gold in the 100-meters. For these finals, America needed their very best swimmers in the race, so Young and Sampson were replaced by Walter Laufer and George Kojac. Rounding out the foursome was Austin Clapp, with Johnny swimming in the critical anchor position. The strongest competition was expected to come from the Japanese swimmers, along with the Hungarian team anchored by Barany, and the Swedes with their all-world swimmer, Arne Borg, at anchor.

In the final Olympic race of his career, Johnny again proved why he was the best waterman in the world. He turned a close battle into a five-second victory for the United States, as he and his teammates set a new Olympic record of 9 minutes, 36.2 seconds. Finishing second was the Japanese team, with Canada, anchored by Walter Spence, grabbing the bronze medal.

When Johnny accepted the gold medal for the United States and his teammates, his fifth gold in two Olympics, it was the culmination of one of the greatest Olympic careers in history. He had recently celebrated his 24th birthday, and he was literally on top of the world! Watching the ceremony, coach

Bachrach was like a proud father. The young man he had trained and nurtured to adulthood over the previous eight years, had done himself and his American teammates proud.

The assistant manager of the swim team, Dr. Francois D'eliscu, also had high words of praise for the American swimmers as a whole, as noted in the official Olympic report:

"Never in the history of athletics have a finer group of men and women ever been selected as this special team that presented the finest and best in the United States. It can only be said by the writer who had the extreme honor and privilege to be on the starting line and take care of the personal wants of each swimmer and watch their positions; that the comments of distinguished people, athletes and officials, were so pleasant and inspiring, that it made one proud not only to be an American but happy to be with such a team.

"Every swimmer was considered a gentleman or a perfect lady, respectively. They all won a place in the hearts of officials and spectators, and it is sincerely hoped that some day when they return to these United States, that we can demonstrate, prove and express, the same appreciation as they have manifested throughout our entire meetings."

The American team of swimmers and divers also performed extremely well in these Olympic competitions, helping the United

States to the overall championship with a total of 22 gold medals to 10 for runner-up Germany. Of the 22 gold medals, the swimmers and divers accounted for 10 of the first places achieved by the team! General MacArthur, in summing up his pride in the accomplishments of the American athletes, said in his official report: "Nothing is more synonymous of our national success than is our national success in athletics. The team proved itself a worthy successor of its brilliant predecessors."

In addition to Johnny's successes, the Americans enjoyed a clean sweep in the 100-meter backstroke event: George Kojac won the gold medal, Walter Laufer the silver, and Paul Wyatt accepted the bronze for the United States. Meanwhile, diminutive diver Peter Desjardins won both the springboard and platform diving events. Desjardins, at five-foot three-inches tall, was by this time a good friend of Johnny's, and they later teamed in the comedy diving act that Weissmuller had made famous at the 1924 Paris Games.

Longtime Weissmuller rivals Arne Borg and Andrew Charlton also did well in this Olympics: Borg won the gold in the 1500-meter event, while Charlton settled for silver medals in the 400 and 1500-meter events. Meanwhile, a bronze medal in the 1500-meter freestyle was the best that Buster

Crabbe could do in this Olympics. (However, his gold medal in the 400-meter event in the 1932 Los Angeles Olympics would lead to his long career as a Hollywood stalwart in B-pictures and serials like Flash Gordon and Buck Rogers.)

The American women enjoyed phenomenal success in the pool, winning gold medals in five of the seven swimming and diving events. In the 100-meter freestyle, Albina Osipowich won the gold and her teammate, Eleanor Garatti, placed second for the silver medal. The 400-meter freestyle was captured by Martha Norelius, while Josephine McKim finished third for the bronze medal. (Miss McKim was introduced to Johnny Weissmuller during these Olympics, and later worked as a stunt "double" for Maureen O'Sullivan in underwater swimming scenes in the 1934 film, *Tarzan and His Mate*.) The United States also won the gold medal in the 4x100-meter freestyle relay, with Adelaide Lambert joining Osipowich, Garatti, and Norelius on the team.

The lady divers were perhaps the most successful of all, winning five of the six medal positions in the two diving events. In highboard, Elizabeth Pinkston-Becker won the gold, with Georgia Coleman in second place for the silver medal. In the springboard competition, Helen Meany led an American sweep of the medal positions, followed by teammates Dorothy Poynton and Georgia Coleman.

It is interesting to note that Helen Meany, competing in her third Olympics, finally won her one and only gold medal in the springboard diving event. She had placed fifth in the platform event in Paris in 1924, and had also made friends with a certain young swimmer named Weissmuller. Johnny had spent much of his free time in Amsterdam watching Helen perform at her competitions, and she likewise was Johnny's number one fan for his races and competitions.

Johnny had not had a serious romance in his life since his breakup with Lorelei four years before, and he welcomed the friendship and company of Helen during their Olympic adventure. They seemed like an ideal couple, the handsome swimmer and the lithe and pretty diver. At this point in time they were a couple, and they would also be traveling together on a tour of Japan shortly after the Olympics.

CHAPTER THIRTEEN

Twilight of a Brilliant Career

At the conclusion of the Amsterdam Games on August 12th, Johnny was presented with his gold medals by Queen Wilhelmina of Holland, along with a special award for his athletic excellence. The queen presented the gold medals to all the winning athletes, while Prince Hendrik and I.O.C. president Henri de Baillet-Latour awarded the silver and bronze medals, respectively. After the Games were pronounced closed by Count Baillet-Latour, a salute of five guns was fired as the Olympic flag was lowered. Queen Wilhelmina left the stadium to polite applause as her loyal Dutch subjects sang, "Wilhelmus van Nassauen."

On August 13th, the entire American team bade their farewells to the host country and friends they had made from the competing nations. The athletes once again boarded the S.S. *President Roosevelt* and sailed for the United States, which they reached on August

22nd after a rough voyage. A New York City ticker tape parade down Fifth Avenue was next for the triumphant American Olympic team, as thousands of fans applauded and cheered their appreciation of the American athletes. A farewell luncheon was held for the team at the Hotel McAlpin, and Johnny received all the accolades that an American hero deserves, including his second Presidential citation. New York governor Smith added to Johnny's collection of medals with a special commendation for his great Olympic achievements, and the keys to the city were presented by the "Big Apple" mayor, Jimmy Walker.

Back home in Chicago, it was a hero's welcome for Johnny, as their favorite son had once again made all of America proud with his accomplishments in Amsterdam. It was nice for Johnny to see his mother and brother, after an absence of several weeks. But he wasn't home for long, as Johnny and the other Olympic gold and silver medalists had been invited to participate in an international swimming competition in Japan, in the month of October. Representing the Japanese swimmers as host was Katsuo Takaishi, who had finished third to Johnny and Istvan Barany in the 100-meter freestyle in the recent Games.

Johnny was looking forward to this particular tour, as diver Helen Meany was also traveling on the S.S. *Taiyo Maru* to participate in the swimming and diving exhibitions. Johnny and Helen were constant companions during the voyage, as a friendship that grew in Amsterdam bloomed towards a full-blown romance during the ship's journey to the Orient. Helen Meany later recalled the greatest thrill of her magnificent diving career to be "an invitation to participate in a three-day meet in Tokyo in honor of Prince Chichibus' wedding. 1928 Olympic winners were invited to participate including Johnny Weissmuller, Wally Laufer, and Arne Borg. I was the only woman invited."

Among those that accepted the invitation of the American-Japan Society was Arne Borg, who had won the gold medal for his native Sweden in the 1500-meter freestyle in Amsterdam. Borg was accompanied by his fiancee, whom he planned to marry in Japan in prelude to a honeymoon in the United States. Johnny and Borg had been teammates for two years on the I.A.C., and thus he gladly accepted his friend's invitation to be his best man at the wedding. The upcoming nuptials would also be an opportunity for Johnny to show off his own girlfriend, Helen, who was growing fonder in his heart with each passing day.

After Johnny and coach Bachrach arrived at their Tokyo hotel, Katsuo Takaishi discreetly asked for a confidential meeting with the two Americans. Takaishi confided that a powerful Japanese official had planned to derail the Weissmuller express, by holding the swimming events in frigid water that would cause cramps in all of the participants except the Japanese, who were used to training in similar conditions.

It was this warning from one Olympic competitor to another that allowed Johnny to prepare for the adverse conditions of very cold — almost freezing — pool water. Bachrach concocted his own unscrupulous plan to counteract the subterfuge, by fighting ice with ice! He ordered many buckets of ice to be sent to his room, which in turn were dumped into a bathtub of water. Now Johnny and his teammates took turns in the tub, acclimating themselves to the frigid water in which the competitions would take place. This unique training plan continued for several days until the hour of the meet, and by that time Johnny was fully acclimated!

Johnny won all of his races, held in the Tamagawa Pool, including his Olympic gold medal event of 100-meters. The Japanese people loved Johnny Weissmuller and loudly cheered his winning efforts, while journalist Shunjiro Kojima called him the greatest champion to ever compete in Japan. Culminating the accolades bestowed upon him, the Crown Prince of Japan presented Johnny with a prestigious medal that was the highest honor a foreigner could receive.

At the conclusion of the Japanese exhibitions on the main island of Honshu (as well stops on the islands of Osaka and Kobe), Johnny was surprised by an invitation from a Japanese official to become their head swimming coach. With politeness, Johnny turned down the offer (as did Bachrach, who later received a similar request). Johnny realized that coaching may be in his future at some point, but if and when it happened he would be coaching American athletes. More importantly, he already missed his homeland and he was plenty tired of the frigid water of Japan!

The trip home by ship was a final opportunity for Johnny and Helen to determine if they were two lovers that were meant to be, or just "ships passing in the night." Helen promised to write Johnny from her home in New York, but the inscription on her photo was less than encouraging: "To Johnny — in Memoriam, Helen."

Conspicuous by its absence from the photograph was the word "love." Back home in their respective concrete jungles of Chicago and New York City, time blurred their days together and the letters became the correspondence of friends, not lovers.

It would be difficult to express on these pages the emotions that Johnny felt for Helen, but he would always remember her fondly. In the 1987 book, *Tales of Gold*, where past Olympic stars spoke of their Olympic memories, Helen Meany submitted a photo of herself and Johnny, arm in arm, on board the *President Roosevelt* during the voyage home from Amsterdam. They say a picture is worth more than a thousand words, and almost 60 years after the Ninth Olympiad, this photo undoubtedly represented one of her fondest memories of her romance with Johnny.

Home in Chicago once again, Johnny pondered his future. He realized that he had to start earning a living some day, and as an amateur athlete, he virtually had no income of his own. His spending money, the clothes he wore, every meal that he ate in a restaurant, were paid for by William Bachrach and the I.A.C. Wealthy financial supporters of the I.A.C. donated money to the club; because of Johnny's immense popularity, there was enough money flowing into the club to take care of the athletes. Johnny was a premiere athlete — in fact the premiere athlete at the club for more than seven years. A great deal of money was donated each year so that he could be a champion and not have to worry about working jobs to make ends meet.

But Johnny knew that the time was near to consider his retirement from amateur athletics. He competed in a swim meet in Honolulu in November, and set an American record (long course) in the 150-yard freestyle in a time of one minute, 26 seconds flat. This was the final record of his career, and shortly after this meet Johnny came to the decision to retire. It was not an easy decision, but after conferring long and hard with coach Bachrach, it was decided that January 3, 1929, would be the final swim meet of his career.

Bachrach later recalled that Johnny's retirement in 1929 was necessitated by the need to earn a real living, not by any lessening of his competitive fires. "He was 25, healthy, and athletic training can go on just so long," said the Coach. "You can't do that (earn a living) and stay an amateur athlete, or, anyway, you couldn't in those days."

1928 had been a great year for Johnny Weissmuller. He had won two gold medals in the Olympic Games held in Amsterdam, and also won his usual share (the lion's share!) of national A.A.U. championships. For the year he won titles in the following: 100-meters, outdoor (time, 57.8); 440-yards, outdoor (time, 4:58.6); 100-yards, indoor (time, 50.8); 220-yards, indoor (time, 2:10.4); 500-yards, indoor (time, 5:35.0); 880-yard relay, outdoor (time, 9:32.6); 300-yard medley relay, indoor (time, 3:05.6); 400-yard relay, indoor (time, 3:32.6).

Johnny's retirement was announced in the newspapers on December 26, 1928, as well

234

as in an article in the *Tri-Color* by Clarence Bush. The official press release announcing his retirement read as follows:

"John Weissmuller, of the Illinois Athletic Club, the 'Prince of Waves,' is planning to abdicate his amateur crown. The 'human hydroplane,' who has dominated sprint swimming for eight years, will make his last appearance in amateur competition at the I.A.C., January 3, in connection with the twenty-second annual Cook County Interscholastic Swimming Championship meet.

"Johnny finds it necessary, approaching his twenty-fifth birthday, to devote more time to earning a living. To remain an amateur champion, keeping in constant training and making frequent extended trips to distant cities, would delay his business career.

"After dominating the amateur aquatic world for eight years or more, Weissmuller retires undefeated. With few exceptions, he holds all freestyle world's records in pools of all sizes at distances from fifty yards to eight hundred and eighty yards, indoors and outdoors. Coach Bachrach says he could probably go on indefinitely breaking records and winning titles."

Johnny also composed a letter to W. Gibbons Uffendell, chairman of the athletic committee, revealing his reasons for his impending retirement:

"I am planning to give up my career of

235

swimming competition. My last appearance as a competing amateur will be in the Illinois Athletic Club swimming meet January 3. I am getting to an age where I must look to the future and try to earn some money, something an athlete in constant training finds hard to do, and so it is with a great deal of regret that I must take this step.

"I wish to take this opportunity to thank the athletic committee and all the members of the I.A.C. and Coach Bachrach for the wonderful encouragement they have given me since I joined the club's swimming team in 1920.

"I joined the club as a poor boy, unknown, and through the support of the members of the I.A.C. and my coach, Mr. Bachrach, I have had a glorious time, a chance to see the world, and get a real education. No athlete could ask for any better treatment than that accorded me by the Illinois Athletic Club.

"The club has given me the opportunity to meet many representative business men of Chicago and I have made many friends in the club whose friendship I prize very highly.

"While I will not be competing for the I.A.C. in the future, I will still be a member and interested in anything the club does, especially in its athletic teams. I will be pulling for the I.A.C. teams with all my heart, and hope to continue my many friendships among the club members.

"Again I wish to say that I regret it is necessary for me to take this step, but I am sure that Coach Bachrach will find and develop another champion as he always has in the past."

Mr. Bush's article in the December *Tri-Color* also contained an account of the "farewell" dinner that was given to Johnny by the club, which was attended by more than fifty of Johnny's friends and biggest supporters throughout the years. C. F. Biggert, president of the club, made the keynote speech, and called Johnny "the greatest champion of champions the club has ever had." Biggert thanked both Johnny Weissmuller and coach Bachrach for "the honor and glory they earned for the club, spreading its fame around the world."

Coach Bachrach, with a sincere pride, said of his protégé: "Weissmuller brought to a new perfection of style the American crawl stroke. He became the stylist of champions, getting more speed than any rival with a comparable amount of effort. His stroke reduced water resistance to a minimum, facilitated breathing, put the body in a position to make unimpeded use of all its strength and leverage, and got the most propulsion for the effort expended."

Bachrach also recalled one of Johnny's outstanding performances, at the national A.A.U. championships in Honolulu in August of 1927, a race that typified his efforts throughout his career: "Our team," said Bachrach, "had to have a first in the 880-yard swim in order to win the meet. That is outside of Johnny's regular line and he had done no training for the distance. No teammate had a chance to win it, and though he had already been through his regular strenuous racing program, Johnny plunged in and won the half-mile title in world's record time."

Many important speakers climbed the podium to praise Johnny, each admitting he would be irreplaceable at the I.A.C. George T. Donoghue, the new chairman of the athletic committee, declared with a wry sense of humor that he felt he was inheriting a deficit, having a "whole team" such as Johnny walk out at once. Mr. Uffendell, retiring chairman of the athletic committee, admitted his desire to "trade places" with Johnny, and then presented to him on behalf of the club a handsome engraved watch. He noted that when Johnny came to the I.A.C. in 1920, he was "a gangling, unsophisticated youth . . . and now he displays physical development comparable to the gods of mythology, and a charm of personality that wins him a host of friends wherever he goes."

John Banghart, president of the "Otters" (fraternal order), presented Johnny with a substantial check to start him down the road to financial success, and noted that in the world of athletic competition, "he was unmatched for his competitive ability."

Andrew McNally stated that Johnny had "remained modest, despite the avalanche of flattery that has descended upon him. He has always conducted himself as a gentleman, always been a good fellow in the highest meaning of that term." McNally also admired Johnny for his discipline, strict obedience, and remaining "an unspoiled, lovable boy."

Johnny, indeed still boyish at age 24, was practically without words when it was his turn to address the gathering of friends that had come to honor the retiring champion. Later, Johnny recalled the moment: "In my response I found myself almost speechless, but managed to thank the club for all it had done for me, the friends it made me, and I asserted that as long as I live there is nothing I would not do for the club and its members. And that goes."

It was obvious that Johnny was still a humble soul, even after the incredible successes of his long career in swimming. He totaled more than 50 individual world records, and at least 75 American records in distances from 50-yards to 880-yards; this included three world records in the backstroke, which was certainly not his specialty. He also accumulated 52 national championships between 1921 and 1928, including eight in his final year of competition.

One of the public's fascinations with Weissmuller during his swimming career was his incredible unbeaten streak from 1921 until his retirement in 1929. Every time Johnny would race in swim meets across the country, people would grab the sports section to see if he had indeed done it again. And of course he always won, and remained unbeaten.

It was a wonderful saga that lasted for almost eight full years, and it mesmerized the sporting nation. Johnny endured for almost an entire decade — undefeated — as he built a huge worldwide fan following. Everybody loves a winner, especially a humble one. Johnny was the best of both worlds.

Johnny took on all challengers in cities across the country, defeating would-be champions in their home pools as easily as in his own home pool at the I.A.C. Even the best in the world bowed to the greatness of Johnny, including Arne Borg, Andrew Charlton, Duke Kahanamoku, Buster Crabbe, and many others who discovered to their admiration and chagrin, that Weissmuller was undefeatable. His five gold medals in the Olympics of 1924 and 1928 speak for themselves, and Johnny could have easily added to this total if he hadn't unselfishly played on the U.S. water polo team in both years.

It had been a great career — and that's an

obvious understatement. But after his final swim meet on January 3rd held before his home fans at the I.A.C., he was officially retired. Now it was time for Johnny to find himself a career, but he wasn't exactly sure which direction his life was going to take.

Johnny was certainly interested in the movie business, but the Hollywood agents weren't exactly beating down his door just yet. One of the offers that came his way after his retirement was for a scholarship to a flying school, and at the time he did have an interest in becoming a commercial pilot. In his heart Johnny also felt that swimming, after all that he had accomplished in the sport, would continue to be a big part of his life.

Johnny's final words on his swimming career, from his own book, *Swimming the American Crawl*:

"I've certainly had a great time swimming, and if I had my boyhood days to live over again, I can't imagine anything more interesting to do than just what I've done."

For the immediate moment Johnny was retired. He would sit down with coach Bachrach, and talk about the various possibilities of the future. Sports enthusiasts around the world always lament the retirement of a great champion, but they have great respect for one who retires before he becomes an embarrassment to himself and his sport. Johnny Weissmuller — undefeated champion — retired as the greatest freestyle swimmer ever, leaving behind a legacy that would never be matched. He was the acknowledged master of the "American crawl," a stroke that was imitated by many in order for young swimmers to pattern themselves after the greatest swimmer in the world.

Little did Weissmuller know that he would have a completely different career in the not-to-distant future, in which he would also be indelibly remembered. But for now, he was just another retired athlete with a somewhat uncertain future. Johnny hoped he could be successful in other fields of endeavor, but of course he had no concrete idea what fate had in store for him.

CHAPTER FOURTEEN

No Crash for Johnny

Nineteen-twenty-nine was a significant year in world history because of the Great Stock Market Crash. Men lost their paper fortunes, and jumped from windows from the highest available skyscraper. As a result, the Depression arrived and unemployment in America soared to an all-time high. However, the dire straits of the economy hardly affected Johnny at all. After his retirement in January, he didn't have a job to lose and he didn't own any stocks. But he was famous and the world loved him, and there were boundless opportunities for America's Olympic hero.

Johnny also had his friend and mentor, Bill Bachrach, working on his behalf. Bachrach arranged for Johnny to give swimming and diving exhibitions at the finest hotels in Florida's finest leisure cities, Miami Beach and Coral Gables, and also in Bermuda. It was a nice life, and Johnny was getting paid rather handsomely for the Sunday afternoon exhibitions he would give at hotels like the Roney Plaza in Miami Beach and the

Biltmore in Coral Gables.

Johnny was a "professional" now and getting paid for performing his swimming and diving tricks, and thus he had irrevocably given up his previous amateur standing. However, when friends Helen Meany, Pete Desjardins, and Martha Norelius joined Johnny for a nonsanctioned water show in Miami Beach, those three all lost their amateur standing with the A.A.U. It was an especially tough break for Desjardins, who had planned to defend his double gold medal crown in the 1932 Los Angeles Olympics.

Many years later Johnny recalled giving swimming lessons to a young boy at the Roney Plaza for several weeks during this period of time. The lad had been in ill health, but the daily swimming lessons from Johnny helped to make him stronger as well as improve his frail emotional state. Johnny thought it strange that the boy was always accompanied by a man in a trenchcoat, who always stayed in the background. Johnny rightfully assumed that the man was a bodyguard for the boy, who said his father traveled around the country a lot.

One day the boy showed up with tears in his eyes and said that he was leaving town with his father. He handed Johnny a small wrapped package that was from his father, in gratitude for the swimming lessons and friendship Johnny had shown toward the boy.

After the boy left, Johnny opened the package to find a bejeweled gold belt buckle that looked like the genuine article.

Some time later Johnny got two surprises. He pawned the buckle for $150, which was far more than he thought it was worth (obviously the gold and diamonds were real). He also saw a photograph in a Chicago paper of the boy he had befriended, along with the ever present bodyguard. The photo caption identified the boy as Al Capone's young son, Albert Francis Capone, "Sonny" Capone. (Sonny Capone was indeed a sickly lad, suffering a series of illnesses and maladies during his childhood.)

Capone had been living in Miami during this period of time, having been chased out of Chicago and other major cities that had refused to allow the crime boss to take up residence. Capone and his wife Mae had purchased a luxurious yet secluded villa near Biscayne Bay, where most of the chic homes in the neighborhood were owned by Miami's leading socialites. It is also true that Capone's trademark gift was the diamond-studded belt buckle which he gave to anyone to whom he felt indebted.

Did Johnny give swimming lessons to Sonny Capone, or was this the "stand-in" boy that Capone used as a decoy so that his own son would not be murdered by his most bitter enemies? An interesting story, to say the least. Whether the boy was Sonny or not, the belt buckle undoubtedly came from Capone. Johnny never met Capone, although the two men were the most famous residents of Chicago in the 1920s.

The best deal that William Bachrach ever negotiated for Johnny was with B.V.D. swimwear, who wanted the best swimmer in the world to wear their swim suits exclusively. B.V.D. gave Johnny a five-year contract at $500 per week to be their worldwide representative and spokesman. He would be required to devote a certain number of weeks of each year to promotional work for his new employer; the balance of the time was his own to further other goals and ambitions.

This sum of money — 26 thousand dollars a year — was staggering to Johnny. He hadn't had a legitimate job since the days of hustling for tips as a bellboy at the Plaza Hotel in Chicago, when he was 16-years-old. Suddenly, with the country battered by the Wall Street crash, Johnny was rolling in the dough! He'd been perilously close to broke his whole life, and now the money was in the bank! (It also meant a check each month for his mother, who was overjoyed that her son's great popularity as a swimmer now also meant financial success.)

Young Weissmuller, an American sports hero for ten years but still only 25-years-old, would appear in magazine ads dressed in the finest of B.V.D. apparel, and make promotional appearances around the country. Johnny's clean-cut All-American image was perfect for B.V.D., and he was one of the most recognizable athletes in the world. Johnny began a tour of the country with a stop at the B.V.D. headquarters in Piqua, Ohio, and then the barnstorming began in earnest.

In each city Johnny would make personal appearances in department stores, signing photographs of himself wearing his B.V.D. swim suits, and shaking hands with wide-eyed youngsters and admiring adults. Another part of his duties was with the B.V.D. Swim Club, which gave lessons to young swimmers. What greater way to promote swimming than to have the great Johnny Weissmuller personally instructing the youngsters. Johnny made friends wherever he went, and in general was a wonderful ambassador for B.V.D. He was earning his money.

One of the stops on the tour was in New York City, where Johnny had his first brush with the motion picture business. Florenz Ziegfeld was producing a picture in New York for Paramount called *Glorifying the American Girl*. The artistic director was John W. Harkrider, who was a costume designer for the Follies and other Ziegfeld stage productions. Harkrider introduced himself to Johnny at one of his personal appearances, and offered the Olympic champion a small role in this early talkie musical revue as "Adonis."

A number of celebrities of the era appeared in roles as themselves including Ziegfeld himself, along with Eddie Cantor, Helen Morgan, Rudy Vallee, Noah Beery, Ring Lardner, and New York Mayor Jimmy Walker. The film's actors and actresses portrayed various great figures of history, in what amounted to a brief collage of historical characters. As a member of one of the Follies' production numbers, Johnny portrayed a living statue of Adonis while Evelyn Groves played his Aphrodite.

The standard plot followed the rise of showgirl Gloria Hughes (Mary Eaton), who has to leave her boyfriend behind to make it big on the New York stage. The story culminates in a typical Ziegfeld Follies' extravaganza production number, with the young heroine reaching stardom as her former boyfriend has gotten married to her best friend. Highlights included a number of marvelous song and dance routines performed by Mary Eaton, as well as songs by Rudy Vallee and Helen Morgan. Eddie Cantor did a very funny bit as a cheap tailor, who does his best to sell a suit to a customer who really doesn't want to buy. Ziegfeld interspersed some two-color Technicolor sequences for the production numbers that were considered highly innovative for the period.

It was a small role for Johnny as the handsome Greek mythological character who was loved by Aphrodite, but he did get his "feet wet" in the picture business. There was one problem that arose for Johnny after appearing in this film. His employer, B.V.D., complained about the use of their star contractee without their permission. Johnny didn't realize that there was an exclusivity clause in his contract that allowed B.V.D. veto power over any activity that didn't meet with their approval. (Of course, anything to do with swimming, dressed in a B.V.D. swim suit, was fine with them.)

Shortly thereafter, still not calling himself an "actor," Johnny starred in *Crystal Champions*, one of several Grantland Rice sport shorts in which he was featured. Johnny's swimming sequence was produced using slow motion, an early special effect that showed off the talents of Weissmuller demonstrating his world famous American crawl, and several other strokes. (This time Johnny was dressed in his B.V.D.s!)

Grantland Rice also filmed Helen Meany, Pete Desjardins, Martha Norelius, Stubby Kruger, and Weissmuller at Silver Springs, Florida, in a segment of *Crystal Champions* that presented diving as the new glamour aquatic sport to the current generation.

In his 1954 book, *The Tumult and the Shouting*, Grantland Rice noted that his long series of *Sportlight* films usually played in around eight-thousand American theaters, along with at least an additional 1,000 theaters in the British Isles. Rice noted that the stars of these films were not actors, but the greatest sports heroes of the current age:

"We've built action around Ty Cobb, Red Grange, The Four Horsemen, Babe Didrikson, and such famed horses as Man O' War, Twenty Grand and Greyhound, the trotting marvel. Johnny Weissmuller gave our cameras excitement during the boomtime 1920's — in Miami and then at Silver Springs, Florida, where we made *Crystal Champions*, a great grosser.

"The four Olympians, Helen Meany, Martha Norelius, Pete Desjardins and Weissmuller, plus Stubby Kruger, the diving clown, helped put Silver Springs on the map with that picture."

Rice also reminisced that Johnny and his close pal Stubby went slightly overboard with their penchant for the practical joke, getting into a bit of trouble that resulted in a few hours of detention in a Miami jail for the two Olympic heroes. "During that trip Weissmuller and Kruger went on a spree in Miami and turned on a fleet of fire alarms," said Rice. "Steve Hannagan, rest his brilliant promotional soul, bailed them out of the hoosegow."

With Johnny's movie star looks, it was obvious that Hollywood would eventually come calling. It appeared his first major role would be in 1929, when he was offered a lead role in a new "talkie" starring Jeanne Eagels, then a rising star in Hollywood. Shortly after production began, tragedy struck down Miss Eagels, who died of an overdose of sleeping pills and alcohol on October 3, 1929. Jeanne Eagels at age 35 was in the prime of her life and had just completed her finest film, *The Letter*. (For her superb portrayal in *The Letter*, Jeanne Eagels received a posthumous Oscar nomination for Best Actress.)

This would not be the last such tragedy to affect the life of Johnny, but it was only a bump in the road of his movie career. For the time being he was too busy with his B.V.D. nationwide tour, to seek out a career in motion pictures. He would have to wait for fate to intervene.

Whenever Johnny was in Chicago he would do his swimming at the Medinah Athletic Club at 505 N. Michigan, which was constructed in 1929. The Medinah was a luxury men's club for members of the Shrine organization; Johnny had been a favorite of the Chicago Shriners since his beginning days at the I.A.C., and was always welcome as a guest at this new club. In fact, when Chicago's "favorite son" came back home during the years after his retirement from swimming, the town rolled out the red carpet for their celebrity hero. (The Depression took its toll on the Medinah, which closed its doors in 1934. The property made its debut in 1944 as a hotel, and has remained ever since under various names.)

Facilities in the original athletic club included a gymnasium, running track, bowling alleys, golf driving range, and the one feature that really interested Johnny, a junior Olympic-sized swimming pool. This pool was considered an engineering marvel in 1929 because it was above ground (on the 13th floor). The original pool in all its glory remains to this day as part of the Inter-Continental Hotel, a beautiful reminder of an earlier age; brilliant blue tiles surround the marble and terra cotta fountain of Neptune on the east wall of the pool area. It is easy to see why Johnny enjoyed swimming in this pool: the beauty of the architecture and the warmth of the sunlight flooding the pool area made for a peaceful place to exercise the human body and relax the mind.

In the early part of 1930, Johnny completed his own autobiography, *Swimming the American Crawl*, which was written in collaboration with Clarence A. Bush and published by Houghton Mifflin. This 190-page hardcover book (plus photos) was the quintessential handbook for aspiring swimmers. Johnny detailed his techniques, as taught to him by Bachrach, WilliamWilliam Bachrach, in every phase of the sport. Included were in-depth chapters on proper form for the leg kick and arm stroke, relaxation, breathing, as well as diet and exercise for the training swimmer.

Johnny also recalled his earliest memories after moving to Chicago as a child, as well as his most outstanding swimming records and Olympic triumphs right up through his retirement in 1929. The volume was dedicated: "To William Bachrach, my coach, and to the members of the Illinois Athletic Club."

The book was partially excerpted in two outstanding articles published in the *Saturday Evening Post*, one of the premiere magazines of the era. Part one, "My Methods of Training," was published March 8, 1930, and then subsequently followed on March 29 with part two, "Diet and Breathing to Swim." Both articles were written by Johnny Weissmuller in collaboration with Clarence A. Bush.

A published writer in the *Saturday Evening Post*, author of a new autobiography published by a major publisher, a $500-per-week endorsement contract with B.V.D., his first motion picture role under his belt, and the adulation of the world for his past athletic achievements were impressive accomplishments — especially for a kid who had to drop out of school at an early age to help with the family finances.

Johnny had a wonderful life going for him and an incredible future waiting to unfold, but there was one important ingredient missing: romance, love, and the companionship of an adoring female. Not that there weren't plenty of offers and opportunities for Johnny with the opposite sex. It was just that the right girl hadn't come along just yet.

But that all changed on Valentine's Day, 1931, when Johnny was introduced to Bobbe Arnst, a New York actress who was performing with the Ted Lewis band in Miami. Miss Arnst was one of Ziegfeld's girls, and had featured roles in several Broadway musical comedies, including *Simple Simon* and *Rosalie.* Johnny's friend Pete Desjardins had seen Bobbe perform her club act with Ted Lewis, and was impressed with the talents of the pretty blonde. He thought his friend Johnny should meet the petite Broadway star, and brought them together on Valentine's Day.

The magic of Cupid worked (in this case Desjardins was the angel of love), as Johnny and Bobbe fell head-over-heels in love. It was a classic case of love-at-first-sight, and the young lovers each leaped into the affair without a second thought. Culminating a torrid fortnight of courtship, an eager Johnny popped the question and asked Bobbe to marry him. A trembling Bobbe smiled, said "Yes," and the young lovebirds were married in Fort Lauderdale by a county judge on Saturday, February 28, 1931.

On March 5th, the *New York Times* reported the following which came out of Miami Beach, Florida:

"The secret marriage last Saturday of Bobbe Arnst, Broadway actress, and Johnny Weissmuller, holder of many swimming records, was announced today.

"They said they were married by County Judge Fred Shippey at Fort Lauderdale, after a whirlwind courtship that started when they were introduced on St. Valentine's Day. Both gave their age as 26. George Murphy and Juliel Johnson of New York accompanied them to Fort Lauderdale for the wedding. After a week's honeymoon here, they will go to New York."

The whirlwind courtship spurred on by mutual infatuation had lasted exactly two weeks to the day. When the "why" question was posed by members of the press, Johnny responded with honesty when he said: "We knew we were in love. So we didn't see any point in waiting."

When they married, Bobbe gave up her career as an actress. She had been quite successful in New York, where she was part of a strong supporting cast in *Rosalie*, a Ziegfeld musical starring Marilyn Miller that ran from January 10 to October 27, 1928. Bobbe was also a supporting actress in *Simple Simon*, a musical starring Ed Wynn which ran from February 18 to June 14, 1930. Some of the greatest actresses in Hollywood had gotten a start as a Ziegfeld actress or Follies' showgirl, including Barbara Stanwyck, Paulette Goddard, Irene Dunne, and Marion Davies. Perhaps Bobbe didn't have that level of talent, but she had been successful in New York and showcased her talents with the Ted Lewis band in Miami.

Perhaps a year or so later Johnny would admit that he and Bobbe had little in common and had unwisely rushed into the marriage. With coach Bachrach back in Chicago at the time of the affair, there had been no one for Johnny to turn to for advice in the matter. But for the time being they were newlyweds in love, legally bound by matrimony, and living a carefree life in Florida.

Johnny was 26-years-old, Bobbe was his fair young bride, and for the moment they were able to enjoy the pleasures of marital bliss without concern for the future. Later on, the pressures of living in Johnny's limelight would be a divisive force that would destroy a marriage built like a house of cards — virtually lacking a firm foundation. Nevertheless, Johnny and Bobbe started out as happy as two meadow larks.

★ ★ ★

Shortly after Johnny's marriage to Bobbe, he was offered a transfer to the B.V.D. west coast offices in Los Angeles, which he gladly accepted. Johnny had fostered Hollywood aspirations for several years, and this indeed appeared a golden opportunity to realize these ambitions. Once again it was a matter of fate, and Johnny's timing couldn't have been more fortuitous. Bobbe was also happy with the world-famous Johnny Weissmuller, her new husband, by her side.

Johnny and Bobbe stopped off in Chicago on the way to California, so that Bobbe could be introduced to Mother Weissmuller. Johnny was nervous when he brought his new wife home to meet his mother, hoping for her approval. But he was worried without cause, as Mrs. Weissmuller embraced her new daughter-in-law and welcomed her into the family. Johnny was as proud as a peacock when he introduced Bobbe to his brother Peter, and his coach, William Bachrach, during their short stay in Chicago. Everyone seemed to like Bobbe, so Johnny was sitting on top of the world.

It would never be quite the same for Johnny and coach Bachrach, after Johnny pulled up his roots and moved to Hollywood. Distance and circumstance came between them, and Johnny had to now make all the major decisions in life by himself. A boy had become a man with the separation from his longtime mentor. But they remained good friends through the years, and coach Bachrach was always there for Johnny if he needed some advice.

However when it came to affairs of the heart, like his marriage to Bobbe, he usually just charged ahead. Like many human beings, Johnny let his heart guide his emotions. Whether it was in romance or business, he was a very trusting soul. He just didn't figure that anyone could ever lie to him, or purposely deceive him.

Johnny was like a bighearted kid, without an evil bone in him. He assumed everyone else was the same, until he learned a few lessons through the years. Life would be a continuing education for Johnny, in the "school of hard knocks." But he never lost a goodly portion of that boyish innocence and charm, and that in itself was why Johnny was so internationally loved by the masses. He never let fame and fortune go to his head. Johnny started out broke, and later made millions as Tarzan — but he always remained a simple soul at heart regardless of his financial status.

When they arrived in Hollywood, Johnny and Bobbe took a studio apartment at the La Leyenda Apartment Hotel on Whitley Street between Vine and Highland. This was in the spring of 1931, and other aspiring entertainers that lived in the hotel during that era included character actor William Frawley (who would gain his greatest fame as Fred Mertz on *I Love Lucy*), and a struggling crooner by the name of Bing Crosby. Harry Lillis Crosby made his first Hollywood movie, *King of Jazz*, in 1930 and eventually became a good friend of Johnny's.

One of Johnny's requisite duties for B.V.D. was staying in shape, so he'd look good in their sportswear. Johnny also was compelled to swim almost daily, otherwise he felt like a fish out of water (literally). To that end he migrated to the Hollywood Athletic Club, which was located on Sunset Boulevard. Because of his widespread travels as a competing swimmer, Johnny was familiar with the club. The H.A.C. had a swimming pool that was perfect for his needs, and the club itself reminded him of his own club back in Chicago, the I.A.C. Bobbe would often accompany her husband to the club to work on her own splendid figure. She had taken up swimming after her union with Johnny, and he found her to be an eager and willing pupil.

Since the H.A.C. was in the heart of Hollywood, it catered to many actors and motion picture people including directors, producers, and screenwriters. Those that came to the club came to sweat off a few pounds, tone the muscles, and flatten the stomach. One such individual was Cyril Hume, a screenwriter who often visited the club to work out, swim a few laps and get a massage. At this time Hume had been assigned to write the screenplay for the new Tarzan movie being produced by MGM.

On one of his visits to the H.A.C., Hume would make a discovery that would alter the course of Hollywood history. The Tarzan chapter might have been minor and only a footnote, if not for the alignment of the stars on this particular day. As Hume's path neared the path of a former Olympic swimmer one afternoon, the future of Tarzan the ape-man on screen, a character created by Edgar Rice Burroughs, would soon become indelibly etched in the hearts of all true movie fans.

CHAPTER FIFTEEN

The Hollywood Jungle

This particular story has been told countless times by dozens of story tellers over the years; a true story that always comes out the same. It was late summer, 1931, and Johnny was diving and taking his daily laps in the pool at the Hollywood Athletic Club one morning. As usual, a cast of curious onlookers had gathered to admire the great Johnny Weissmuller. (A young John Wayne, eventually to become a close friend of Johnny's, was one of the regulars at the H.A.C. who enjoyed the daily swimming exhibitions of Weissmuller.)

Johnny was also noticed by Cyril Hume, a top-notch screenwriter for MGM who was also enjoying a workout at the club. Hume was currently assigned to write a script for a new jungle adventure, *Tarzan, the Ape Man*, which might possibly be a loose sequel to a huge current hit for MGM, *Trader Horn*. Now Hume was not a casting agent, but he was well aware that the studio was conducting an exhaustive search for an actor for the

261

lead role of Tarzan, the fictional jungle man created by Edgar Rice Burroughs.

MGM had been testing dozens of actors for the role, but none as of yet had filled the bill. Young stars Clark Gable and Joel McCrea were considered, but weren't really the right type for Tarzan. The studio had tested Neil Hamilton, but found him more suitable for another lead role in the picture. Cowboy hero Tom Tyler and former football star Johnny Mack Brown were two of many young actors who tested for Tarzan — and failed.

What the studio really sought was a young unknown with an athletic background, and so 1928 Olympians like Weissmuller, Buster Crabbe, and Herman Brix were all considered by MGM for the demanding role of Tarzan. Brix, a leading candidate because of his strong masculine looks and athleticism, knocked himself out of the running by breaking a shoulder during the filming of *Touchdown* (1931).

Buster Crabbe was tested for the role, and had been doing some stunt work on other pictures. In the adventure thriller, *The Most Dangerous Game*, Crabbe performed a risky dive from a boat into a river for star Joel McCrea (and picked up $30 for his troubles). Crabbe, however, was preparing for the upcoming 1932 Olympics, and later claimed he might have turned down the role if it was offered to him (which it wasn't). Knowing how badly Buster wanted to win a gold medal, it is certainly believable that he would have passed up the role of Tarzan for his final shot at gold in Los Angeles at the Tenth Olympiad.

Directing the picture would be W. S. "Woody" Van Dyke the director of *Trader Horn,* who had shared his vision of his perfect "ape man" with Hume. "I want a man for Tarzan," said Van Dyke, "who is young, strong, well-built, reasonably attractive, but not necessarily handsome, and a competent actor. I want someone like Jack Dempsey, only younger." This vision echoed in Hume's mind as he watched Weissmuller repeatedly dive into the pool and stroke from end to end with the perfect form of an Olympic champion.

Hume, like most Americans, was familiar with the Olympic feats of Weissmuller. He just didn't realize that the Olympic gold medalist and the man in the pool were one and the same! Hume inquired as to the identity of the swimmer, and was practically dumbstruck when he was informed, "Why, that's Johnny Weissmuller . . . the Olympic champion!"

Immediately, at that moment, Hume realized that here was the man — the perfect man — for the role of Tarzan. He had worked out much of the script in his mind, and he could visualize Weissmuller in the role. "Eureka!"

thought Hume to himself. "The brass at MGM are going to love me when I bring this big fella in to test for Tarzan!" When Johnny finished his swim, he pulled himself out of the pool and was met by an electrified Hume, who stuck out his hand and introduced himself. "Mr. Weissmuller, I'm Cy Hume. I work for MGM, the movie studio."

Johnny smiled and shook his hand, but was hardly impressed at this point. He had met plenty of motion picture people over the years, including the great Douglas Fairbanks, who had invited him to his home back in 1925. Hume's excited mouth was babbling like a brook, and Johnny could hardly make sense of what he was talking about. Suddenly, it all began to click. Hume was asking if Johnny would like to come down to MGM to test for the role of Tarzan!

Johnny could hardly believe his ears! He had been hoping to break into the picture business, and had stated as much in his autobiography. The producer on the aborted Jeanne Eagels project had suggested he move to Hollywood if he was to obtain his goal. Now here was a man who was asking him to come down and test for a role that was coveted by some of the best actors in the business. Mr. Fairbanks himself had suggested that Johnny might make a perfect Tarzan some day; Johnny had laughed at that suggestion but now here was the very same role being offered. It only took Johnny a few minutes to realize that Hume was serious, and he accepted his offer to accompany him down to MGM to meet the producer and director of the picture.

That afternoon Johnny had lunch with Hume at the MGM commissary, as the various contract players came and went over the lunch hour. Some of the faces were familiar to Johnny, but the names escaped him for the most part — he was a little bit in awe of his surroundings. MGM in those days had many of the greatest stars in Hollywood under contract, including: Lionel Barrymore, Norma Shearer, Joan Crawford, Wallace Beery, child-star Jackie Cooper, Marie Dressler, Greta Garbo, and John Gilbert (whose $250,000 per picture deal was unheard-of for the times). Clark Gable and Jean Harlow weren't household names, but on the verge of stardom.

Hume prepped Johnny on what he could expect when he met Hyman and Van Dyke. He impressed upon Johnny that these two men would be making the decision on whom would be named the next Tarzan. Johnny told Hume that he had acted acceptably in the one picture in New York for Flo Ziegfeld, and explained his disappointment with the aborted Jeanne Eagels' project.

Walking the halls of MGM to an executive office, Johnny was introduced by Hume to producer Bernard Hyman, and director Woody Van Dyke. These men were shrewd judges of talent, and after the amenities were exchanged, they began to scrutinize Johnny for any flaws that might exclude him as the next Tarzan. A mop of dark brown hair, intense brown eyes, six-foot three-inches tall, and 190 pounds of lean muscularity that exuded an aura of perfect health.

They asked their guest to strip to his shorts to see how he would look in a loincloth — with a shrug of his shoulders, Johnny obliged. Weissmuller had spent half his life in a swim suit standing, diving, and swimming in front of millions of admirers — to him it was a natural state of being. Try as they might, they couldn't find any physical flaws. Johnny's perfect physique was the envy of many, and Van Dyke could see that this young man had all the physical qualities he was looking for in his Tarzan. Hyman was a born skeptic and a tougher nut to crack, but he conceded to let Johnny test for the role the following day.

"What d'ya say your name was, young fella?"

"Johnny . . . Johnny Weissmuller," answered the young fella.

Hyman's response at this point would bring a smile to the face of Weissmuller every time he would recall the moment the rest of his life. At this precise moment, Johnny couldn't understand what the heck he was talking about!

"Weissmuller?" mused Hyman. "Too long for the marquee. Find him a movie name — something with snazz that is short and exotic."

(It was standard Hollywood practice to change screen names to something more flamboyant. Boris Karloff had been William Pratt and macho star John Wayne started life as Marion Michael Morrison.)

About this time Van Dyke and Hume looked at each other in amazement. Now Hyman lived and breathed the picture business, and didn't care anything at all about the world of sports. Van Dyke jumped in at this point, and said to Hyman:

"Barney, this young man is the world's champion swimmer. He's an Olympic champion and he's known around the world," sputtered an exasperated Van Dyke.

A broad smile slowly came across the face of Hyman, as he realized the million dollars worth of free advertising a famous name would bring to a new picture like Tarzan.

"Weissmuller. Yes, of course. Swimming champion. All right then, no problem. We'll just lengthen the marquee. Woody, set him up for a screen test tomorrow."

And that was the beginning of the Johnny Weissmuller era as Tarzan. The smiles quickly broke into action, and Van Dyke arranged for Johnny's screen test the following day. Shortly after the release of that first Tarzan picture, Johnny told journalist Grace Mack what had happened at the screen test.

"The director sent for me about *Tarzan*," recalled Johnny. "He (Van Dyke) wanted me to make a test. 'But I can't act,' I told him. 'I don't want you to act,' he said. 'Just do as I tell you. Climb that tree and walk on the limb, then drop to the ground.'

"Well, that was easy. When I was a kid I was always climbing trees and walking around on roofs. At the old swimming pool in Chicago I used to walk the narrow bars which were above the water and I had done a lot of trapeze work to strengthen my arms. So I climbed the tree and walked out on the limb. I dropped to the ground as he told me and, luckily, I landed on my feet. The next day I was told that I had been given the role. *I was an actor!* Funny, isn't it?"

Weissmuller in the role of Tarzan and MGM seemed to be a match made in heaven. But there was a major obstacle that had to be overcome — namely Johnny's exclusive contract with B.V.D. Johnny wasn't overly impressed with the studio's offer of $175 a week, considering he was making almost three times that with B.V.D. Johnny's money from B.V.D. was guaranteed, while the MGM contract called for six-month options.

At six-month intervals they could drop the actor and owe nothing beyond the words, "Don't let the door hit you on the way out."

MGM was willing to up Johnny's price, and Johnny wanted to be Tarzan, but B.V.D. didn't want to release their star property without compensation. They also didn't want to stand in Johnny's path to stardom, so a compromise was worked out between the powers-that-be: MGM stars like Greta Garbo, Jean Harlow, and Joan Crawford — the most beautiful women of the era — posed in B.V.D. swim wear for magazine ads and publicity photographs. Weissmuller was now free to sign with the movie studio, and realizing his vast potential, met his salary request without quibbling.

History was made on October 16, 1931, when Johnny signed a seven-year contract with MGM which called for a beginning salary of $500 per week, with built-in raises up to $2000 per week. This was substantial money for a Hollywood newcomer, but MGM realized that if Weissmuller as the new Tarzan was a success, he would be a hot property indeed. (And if by chance he flopped, the studio would terminate his contract after one picture and send him packing. Quite a deal — for MGM.)

Weissmuller would be the sixth screen Tarzan, but the first to make a "talkie." The first movie Tarzan had been Elmo Lincoln, in *Tarzan of the Apes* (1918). Lincoln also made *The Romance of Tarzan* (1918), as well as a 15-chapter serial in 1921, *The Adventures of Tarzan*. Gene Pollar, a former New York City fireman, was the second actor to portray Tarzan in *The Revenge of Tarzan* (1920). Also released in 1920 was *The Son of Tarzan*, a 15-chapter serial with P. Dempsey Tabler as Tarzan. (The real star of this picture was Hawaiian actor Kamuela Searle, in the title role of Korak, son of Tarzan.)

Tarzan took a break from the screen until 1927 when James Pierce, future son-in-law of author Edgar Rice Burroughs, starred in *Tarzan and the Golden Lion*. The fifth screen Tarzan, and the last of the silent era, was Frank Merrill in the 15-chapter serials *Tarzan the Mighty* (1928), and *Tarzan the Tiger* (1929).

Johnny Weissmuller was handed a distinct advantage over his predecessors. The difference between "silent" movies and the new "talkies" was like comparing the beauty of Greta Garbo with that of Marie Dressler — there was no comparison! It was the horse-and-buggy era versus the jet-age.

Suddenly, everything was traveling faster, better, and certainly more exciting in the sound age that included numerous technological advancements that improved the quality of filmmaking. So there is really no fair comparison between Johnny and the Tarzan actors that preceded him on screen.

In terms of movie-making capabilities, the Prehistoric Age had concluded to make way for glamorous new stars and the Golden Age of Hollywood. And thus it was Johnny's turn to bring the heroism of Tarzan to the big screen.

Author Edgar Rice Burroughs had brought Tarzan to the masses on the printed page. Now Weissmuller would turn that popularity into a screen legend that would live forever.

CHAPTER SIXTEEN

"Tarzan, the Ape Man"

Things were looking good for Johnny and Metro-Goldwyn-Mayer. Physically, Weissmuller was the quintessential actor for the screen personification of Tarzan. Tall, muscular, and lithe like one of the big jungle cats — physically he was perfect for the role of an untamed man living in a savage jungle land. When Johnny turned serious before the camera, his deep, brooding countenance and a wild animal expression in his eyes made him extremely believable as Tarzan.

MGM did seek to improve Johnny's voice, and sent him to famed voice instructor Morando to enrich the timbre and lower the pitch of his voice, which at times was quite high and squeaky. Whenever Johnny got excited — up, up, up went his voice! Morando taught Johnny the proper use of his diaphragm, along with numerous vocal exercises designed to lower the tone of his speaking voice, giving the new Tarzan an authoritative growl to his commands.

By this time MGM had their Tarzan, and

they had their story. What they needed now was the female lead for the picture, for the role of Jane. It just so happened that Maureen O'Sullivan had recently been released by Fox Film after her initial six films for the studio were only mildly successful. The 17-year-old Irish beauty had been discovered in 1929 in Ireland by producer Frank Borzage, and subsequently signed to a contract with Fox Film to star in *Song o' My Heart* (1930).

After her dismissal by Fox Film, a disheartened Maureen spent her last $150 on publicity photos she hoped would resurrect her career. Fortunately for Maureen, her agent Tom Conlon got the stunning portfolio of photos to Metro, which in turn asked her to test for the plum role opposite Johnny. Felix Feist conducted her screen test, and the rest is Hollywood history. She was perfect for Jane and was signed to a long-term contract by Irving Thalberg, who personally selected Maureen for the role.

A short history lesson is necessary here to explain MGM's interest in producing a Tarzan picture. In 1929, MGM studio chief Irving Thalberg assigned W. S. "Woody" Van Dyke to direct a jungle picture called *Trader Horn* (based on the journals of Alfred Aloysius Horn, a genuine African adventurer). Filmed on location in Tanganyika, Uganda, Kenya, the Sudan, and the Belgian

Congo, *Trader Horn* achieved an unparalleled level of authenticity and realism in film-making. There were genuine dangers in filming in untamed Africa, and thus a team of professional white hunters escorted the actors and production crew to guard against possible attacks by the indigenous wild beasts.

Midway through the African filming, MGM decided that *Trader Horn* must be a "talkie," resulting in numerous additional headaches and technical problems for an already beleaguered Van Dyke. Further magnifying their technical problems, the jungle and wild animal footage shot by cinematographer Clyde de Vinna was simply not enough to make the motion picture envisioned. And thus it was back to Hollywood with an unfinished project, and a discouraged cast and crew. At this point, Van Dyke was reportedly almost fired by Thalberg and the entire project scrapped. Fortunately, Van Dyke was allowed to complete his exciting jungle adventure in Hollywood that soon became a box office smash around the world. *Trader Horn*, once almost abandoned, became a classic motion picture which was nominated for Best Picture 1930-31.

In *Trader Horn*, a veteran trader (Harry Carey) and his young partner Peru (Duncan Renaldo) discover a beautiful white woman (Edwina Booth) who is the leader of a tribe of savage natives. Eventually the beautiful jungle goddess, Nina, falls in love with the handsome Peru, and the small band narrowly escape the jungle hazards of wild beasts, starvation, and bloodthirsty tribes, to return to civilization. (Portraying the role of Renchero, Horn's faithful gun bearer, was an authentic African chief, Mutia Omoolu, who was brought back to the United States to complete his scenes in the picture.)

Searching for a follow-up to *Trader Horn*, Irving Thalberg negotiated with Edgar Rice Burroughs to produce an MGM picture based on his jungle legend, Tarzan. A contract was signed in April of 1931, and sealed with a check for $20,000 (there was also an option for two additional sequels). MGM's deal with Edgar Rice Burroughs was that the new motion picture would use his characters including Tarzan, but would not be based upon the works of the author. Burroughs was also paid $1,000 per week for five weeks to read the scripts, pointing out any material that conflicted or infringed upon his original stories. Since the studio was unauthorized to use the author's fictional ape language for their movie, new words were invented including the classic "Umgawa," a multipurpose command that directed the beasts to obey by the tone of Tarzan's voice. (During moments of levity, Johnny used to recall that "Umgawa" meant, "Let's get the hell out of here!")

275

With sufficient leftover footage from the *Trader Horn* expedition available (and no desire whatsoever to return to Africa), producer Bernard Hyman assembled basically the same crew that worked on *Trader Horn*, including director Van Dyke, scriptwriter Hume, photographer Clyde de Vinna, editor Ben Lewis, and recording technician Douglas Shearer. The MGM jungle was the Toluca Lake region of North Hollywood, which was complete with its own river. The area west of Hollywood known as Sherwood Forest was also used, and the safari river crossing and the realistic hippo attack were shot at Lake Sherwood. An African landscape was created in Hollywood by bringing in truckloads of tropical fruit trees, plants and other lush vegetation, all planted especially for the jungle production.

The fictional scenario for the MGM Tarzan pictures was beyond a rugged, mountainous barrier — almost a sheer cliff — called the Mutia escarpment. The African escarpment was often represented by gigantic background artworks (called matte paintings), some of which were hauntingly realistic and blended smoothly with the jungle sets. Despite the relatively primitive cinematic techniques of 1931, the film succeeded on a technical as well as artistic basis. Rear projections for the wild animal shots (with the actors moving in the foreground) were realistic enough to be believable, and were also used in some early scenes where Jane is standing close to some beautifully plumed native tribespeople.

The story began as adventurers James Parker (C. Aubrey Smith) and Harry Holt (Neil Hamilton) lead a safari beyond the Mutia escarpment in search of a fabled elephant graveyard, hoping to recover a fortune in ivory tusks.

Jane Parker (Maureen O'Sullivan) arrives to join her father, who has serious reservations about allowing his daughter to join this dangerous expedition. Jane enlists the support of Holt, who is infatuated with the young English beauty — and thus Parker relents.

The safari natives are superstitious of the Mutia, a sheer mountain of dizzying heights; the narrow trail is perilous as one of the bearers falls to his tragic death. A treacherous river crossing becomes deadly when they are attacked first by a herd of hippopotami and then crocodiles, who make a grisly meal of two of the unfortunate safari natives. The hippos are called off by a strange cry that comes from the jungle, and they get first glimpse of a savage white man who leaps through the trees — Tarzan the ape-man!

Jane is the first white woman Tarzan has ever seen, and following a primitive instinct, he abducts her and carries her through the trees to his lofty lair. At first Jane is frightened of Tarzan, who can only mimic her English — but soon she falls in love with the jungle man, who is noble of heart and unafraid of any man or beast.

While Tarzan is away hunting, Parker and Holt discover Jane in the treetops and kill one of the great apes guarding the girl. An enraged Tarzan takes his revenge on the safari, killing them one by one — until the ape-man is wounded in the head by a bullet from the rifle of Holt (who jealously covets Jane for himself). Saved by one of his apes, Tarzan is carried to safety by Timba the elephant — the great apes lead Jane through the jungle, and she nurses him back to health.

When Tarzan recovers, he and Jane discover romance in their viney "garden of Eden" — their playful fun turns into passionate lovemaking. Tarzan is dejected when Jane rejoins her father, who has been desperately searching for his daughter. The Lord of the jungle rejoins his world, and Jane reluctantly rejoins hers.

When the safari is captured by a tribe of barbarian dwarfs, Cheeta races to warn Tarzan of Jane's precarious plight. With his thundering war cry, Tarzan incites his elephant allies to action and together they charge the dwarf village. The diminutive hostiles begin throwing their captives into a pit containing a giant ape, who crushes his victims like toys. When Jane is thrown into the pit, both Holt and her father jump in to save her. They all seem doomed until Tarzan arrives in the nick of time to battle — and kill — the savage brute.

Tarzan's mighty elephants arrive and destroy the village and trample the dwarfs, while Jane, her father, Holt, and the ape-man escape on the backs of two elephants. One of their huge mounts is wounded and dying, and the noble beast leads them through a waterfall to the secret entrance of the sought-after elephant graveyard. They have found their riches, but their jubilance is short-lived as Parker dies of his wounds. Jane is heartbroken at her father's death, and sends Holt back to civilization by himself. Jane remains with Tarzan in the African jungles to share a new life with the man she loves.

When Metro signed Johnny Weissmuller as Tarzan and Maureen O'Sullivan as Jane, the studio's brilliant bit of casting produced an unbeatable team as the jungle man and his mate. Weissmuller and Ms. O'Sullivan had a very special chemistry for each other that worked remarkably well, giving a warmth and genuineness to their roles as Tarzan and Jane. When the advertising came out for the film, MGM didn't miss a trick when it came to playing up the romantic — and sensual — relationship between Tarzan and his new-found love. The advertising catchlines blared out the questions that had to be asked!

"*Are you ready for the thrill of your lifetime!* Unquestionably it is the year's outstanding Dramatic and Romantic experience. You will hail it as the *Trader Horn* of 1932! Metro-Goldwyn-Mayer answers the demand of the nation for another Giant Entertainment of primitive Life and Love. Today this town sees motion picture history made."

"*Girls! Would you live like Eve — if you found the right Adam?* Don't miss the Bath of Love, in the crystal-clear Jungle pool!"

"*Modern Marriages could learn plenty from this drama of Primitive Jungle Mating!* Edgar Rice Burroughs' newest Tarzan thriller gives you a new kind of love-thrill. The Law of the Jungle is Nature's truest Law. When Tarzan saw the woman he adored — he abducted her! *And she loved it!*"

In 1992 Maureen O'Sullivan appeared on the TNT special, "MGM: As the Lion Roars," and recalled the instinctive relationship formed between Tarzan and this woman he had found in the jungle. "He was a man who had never seen a woman before, so it was a fairy tale — and yet it was two real people," said Maureen. "He didn't know what to do with a woman — I guess he found out pretty quick. But he didn't know what it was, when he found her — was it a monkey? She was able to teach him many things that he was unaware of. It was a lovely, innocent concept, and yet very sexy."

Johnny's Tarzan was a little rough on Maureen's Jane at times during filming, but a intuitive roughness that led to their instinctive romance. In one scene Tarzan literally knocks Jane off her feet with a playful chop to her thighs, and she lands on her derriere with a loud plunk (this obviously stung the actress quite a bit). Moments later, the playfulness turns to passion in their eyes. Tarzan lifts Jane in his arms and carries his woman — now submissive — to an obvious treetop romantic interlude. Although only implied as the scene fades, this cinematic romance was extremely effective in its sensuality.

Years after the filming of *Tarzan, the Ape Man*, Maureen O'Sullivan fondly recalled a playful incident between herself and her co-star. "I was deathly afraid of heights," said Maureen with a laugh. "And one day, Johnny Weissmuller and I had to cower in the high branches of a tree for one of our scenes. Johnny was a practical joker — he knew I was afraid of heights. So he began to shake our branch and I screamed. As I shrieked, Johnny smiled."

Johnny responded with a sarcastic wit becoming his mischievous personality, "Me — Tarzan! You — Jane!" Of course, this famous comic variation of the dialogue that was actually spoken in the film: "Tarzan . . . Jane . . ."

(as the ape-man touches first his own chest and then Jane's), broke up cast and crew members alike.

The incredibly conditioned and athletic Weissmuller did many of his own stunts in the Tarzan films, such as riding elephants, climbing trees, swimming and diving, and battling his enemies (both human and animal). One particular stunt that required great strength was Tarzan being pulled by one arm from the giant ape's pit by an elephant, while lifting Jane and Holt (O'Sullivan and Hamilton) out of the pit with his free arm!

Alfredo Codona, a renowned aerialist and member of the aerial trio, "The Flying Codonas," did all the shots of the ape-man swinging through the trees (on specially constructed trapezes). Skilled "lion man" Bert Nelson, animal trainer for the A. G. Barnes circus, did the scenes with Tarzan in a death struggle with a ferocious lion. (This beast was Jackie, a tame lion trained by Nelson that Johnny became very close and familiar with — at least close enough that he didn't get devoured in the close-up scenes that Johnny himself filmed.)

The shots of Codona and Nelson doubling for Weissmuller were not entirely convincing — it was vaguely obvious that it wasn't Johnny in these short scenes. The many dangerous stunts that Weissmuller performed himself gave the Tarzan pictures a trademark realism and believability. Stunt doubles are a necessary evil of action pictures, to save the stars from lengthy periods of recuperation in the hospital. But Johnny's ability (and courage) to perform many difficult and dangerous stunts brought a grim reality to his Tarzan portrayals — in some instances he was literally facing grave danger as the cameras rolled.

Johnny spent two decades in the "saddle," riding the mighty elephants that had the power to crush a man without remorse. (Just such a tragic incident had happened during filming of the silent film, *Son of Tarzan*, in 1920, when star actor Kamuela Searle was fatally injured during production. In one of the final scenes of the film, Searle was strapped to a pole and hauled through the jungle at high speed by an elephant. After completion of the scene, the nervous beast accidentally slammed the pole and Searle to the ground, resulting in injuries that caused his death.)

By 1931, movie producers had learned that Indian elephants were easier to work with than the African species, so the Indian pachyderms were fitted with false ears (covering their own small ears), as well as extended tusks. In *Tarzan, the Ape Man*, the climactic elephant stampede of the dwarf village took five days to orchestrate, and was one of the most thrilling scenes in any Tarzan picture.

Johnny Weissmuller himself originated the

famous yell that became the standard used in most of the Tarzan pictures, including the films made after Johnny retired from the role. Johnny's own yell was overdubbed three times to achieve a resonating sound, and MGM sound technician Douglas Shearer mixed in extremely short clips of unrelated sounds that filled in the "holes" in the recording: a hyena's yowl played backwards; a camel's bleat; the pluck of a violin string; and a soprano's high-C. (They didn't have synthesizers in those days, so they used a group of freak miscellaneous sounds to perfect the Tarzan yell created by Weissmuller.)

Years later in a television interview, Johnny noted the origin of his Tarzan yell. "When I was a kid I used to read all the Tarzan books," he recalled, "and they had kind of a shrill yell for Tarzan. And I never thought I'd ever make Tarzan movies, but when I finally got the role of Tarzan, they were trying to do yells like that. And I remembered when I was a kid I used to yodel at the picnics on Sundays, and I said, 'I know a yell.'" At this point the former Tarzan broke into his famous jungle cry, "Aaahhhhh-eeeeeeeee-aaaahhhh-eeeeeee-aaaahhhh-eeeeeee-aaa ahhhhhh!"

Filming of the jungle classic began on October 31, 1931, and concluded just eight weeks later in time for the Christmas holidays. From the opening credits accompanied by the haunting musical theme, "Voodoo Dance," right down to the final moments when Jane decides to stay with the man she loves (appropriately enough, a clip of Tchaikovsky's "Overture to Romeo and Juliet" played over the final scene), *Tarzan the Ape Man* succeeded unconditionally as both an exciting adventure and a satisfying romance of the heart.

Previewed in February of 1932 and released in late March, fans around the world loved the picture and the excitement created by the electrifying performances of Johnny and Maureen, and stampeded to the box offices to make the film one of the top moneymakers of the year. Johnny's salary from the modest budget of $653,000 would have been four-thousand dollars for the two months of filming — an incredible bargain considering the film eventually made tens of millions of dollars and is still making money in video sales decades after the original release.

A few published comments from movie fans included the following, from fan magazines:

"We who thrilled at seeing Johnny Weissmuller cut through the water were equally as thrilled by his performance in *Tarzan*." Dolly Ashley, Baltimore, Maryland.

"Our local newspapers said that *Tarzan, the Ape Man* was just a lot of hokum and trick photography. But the critics did not see it as the public did — a relief from the average type of picture. It took our minds off our troubles and, for awhile, we were free as *Tarzan* from financial and business worries." Mrs. G. H. John, Cincinnati, Ohio.

"*Tarzan, the Ape Man* is the most interesting picture I have ever seen; Johnny Weissmuller, as *Tarzan*, the most interesting character ever shown on the screen. I think this great swimmer will also become one of our great movie actors." Marion Hemmer, Lockport, N.Y.

Gossip columnist Louella Parsons also noted on May 8th: "The athletic Weissmuller, whose splendid physique was the subject of much discussion after he appeared in *Tarzan, the Ape Man*, has had three stories specially written for him by Edgar Rice Burroughs.

"Looks as if he will soon establish a Gable following, that will make his prowess as a swimmer come second — how that lad does the American crawl!"

Motion picture critics — whose jobs depend on critical analysis — could find little fault with the film and Johnny Weissmuller, and practically stampeded over each other in praise of the star, his lovely co-star Maureen, and every aspect of *Tarzan, the Ape Man*.

"*Tarzan* is a triumphant blend of the qualities of prehistoric hokum, which are bound to be popular with all people at all times. In any event, that unassuming Greek god from the Illinois A.C., Johnny Weissmuller, gives a remarkable performance as the ape man who turns out to be not ferociously African but respectably British. This tribute isn't intended to imply that Mr. Weissmuller is talented in the same sense that George Arliss is talented; indeed, he makes no pretensions whatever to technical histrionic skill. But the quality that sets him apart from other stars of stage or screen is his engaging diffidence, which is so indisputably genuine that it constitutes a constant apology for his Olympian strength and agility." *Richmond Times-Dispatch* (Robert E. Sherwood)

"Fame as a champion swimmer may help Mr. Weissmuller to the eminence he seems bound to achieve, but his acting qualities will also help. A subtle touch of the animal nature in *Tarzan* is indicated in his frequent turning of the head, in his alertness in the presence of danger. It was something shown by Nijinsky in his impersonation of the *Fawn*. Athletically, he competes with exalted predecessors." *Literary Digest*

"*Tarzan* is a frank and exuberant frolic in the imaginative literature of the screen . . . It even has a way now and then of making fun of itself, a ruse so disarming that you are tempted to enjoy the picture most when you are believing it least . . . However credible or interesting Tarzan may be on the printed page, I doubt very much if he emerges in such splendor as he does in the person of Johnny Weissmuller, the swimming champion.

"As Tarzan, Mr. Weissmuller makes his bow to the movie-going public, and as Tarzan he will probably remain bowing through a whole series of these pictures, even though the public may clamor to see him in Clark Gable roles . . . There is no doubt that he possesses all the attributes, both physical and mental, for the complete realization of this son-of-the-jungle role. With his flowing hair, his magnificently proportioned body, his cat-like walk, and his virtuosity in the water, you could hardly ask anything more in the way of perfection. And for the portrayal of Tarzan, nothing short of perfection would be permissible.

"As the English girl who has gone to Africa with her father in search of treasure, Maureen O'Sullivan gives one of her most charming performances. One can understand why Tarzan swings her around that way in the trees, and why he calls out his elephant friends to save her when she is about to be devoured by a horrible gorilla. She helps to make this infatuation of Tarzan's the most plausible thing in the picture." *New York Evening Post* (Thornton Delehanty)

"The most vital statistic of all is the fact

that a lad (Johnny Weissmuller) who had never been in a picture before, who had been interested in nothing but swimming all his life, and who frankly admits he can't act, is the top-notch heart-flutterer of the year." *Photoplay Magazine* (Katherine Albert)

"Johnny Weissmuller is the ideal choice, representing as he does, the movie maiden's prayer for a cave man, ape man, and big fig-leaf-and-bough man. Tall, built like a Greek statue . . . *Tarzan* is a first-rate show." *New York Sun* (John S. Cohen, Jr.)

"JOHNNY WEISSMULLER, CRACK SWIMMER MAKES HIS FILM DEBUT AS A WILD MAN OF THE JUNGLE . . . Youngsters home from school yesterday found the Capitol a lively place, with all sorts of thrills in the picture *Tarzan, the Ape Man,* and Johnny Weissmuller as the hero, a so-called ape man . . . Mr. Weissmuller does good work as Tarzan and Miss O'Sullivan is alert as Jane." *New York Times* (Mordaunt Hall)

After the film was previewed in February of 1932, author Edgar Rice Burroughs sent director Woody Van Dyke a letter thanking him for a screen Tarzan that did justice to his literary creation:

"This is a real Tarzan picture. It breathes the grim mystery of the jungle; the endless, relentless strife for survival; the virility, the

289

cruelty, and the grandeur of Nature in the raw."

Burroughs described Johnny Weissmuller as a "great Tarzan with youth, a marvelous physique, and a magnetic personality." An exalted Burroughs also gushed over Maureen O'Sullivan when he called her ". . . my perfect Jane. I am afraid that I shall never be satisfied with any other heroine for my future pictures . . ."

Maureen O'Sullivan later recalled further memories of her life and the Tarzan movies in her memoirs, which were published in Great Britain in 1994:

"Luckily I was never attracted to my co-stars even though I worked with some of the most glamorous men in the world — Robert Taylor, William Powell, and even Johnny Weissmuller. While the whole of America thought I was having an affair with Johnny, nothing could have been further from the truth. Johnny was an amiable piece of beefcake — a likeable overgrown child who enjoyed childish pranks. There was never a glimmer of a romance between us." (Maureen was speaking of a young Johnny in his late-20s at this time. He DID mature as time went by, although he remained a likeable MAN who enjoyed childish pranks!)

Actually, there would have been little chance for Maureen to fall for Johnny or anyone else, considering she had fallen in love with John Farrow in 1931 before filming ever began on *Tarzan, the Ape Man.* Farrow and O'Sullivan met during the filming of *Payment Deferred* (1932); she was the female lead opposite Charles Laughton and John Farrow was the assistant director and script consultant. Despite the fact that their relationship was on-again, off-again until they married in 1936, there was really never anyone else for Maureen.

Certainly it was for the best that Johnny and Maureen were never romantically involved, as they were able to work together for ten years without the complications of a romantic tryst. Often when a romance ends so does the friendship, but they remained friends throughout their lives. Johnny was married to Bobbe Arnst when the Tarzan series began, and shortly thereafter found his own burning romantic flame: Lupe Velez.

CHAPTER SEVENTEEN

Hollywood's Wild Man

Johnny was on top of the world, and all of the world loved Hollywood's newest heartthrob. In an article entitled "Hollywood's Wild Man," Grace Mack described this stunning newcomer to the silver screen, after Johnny's smash debut in *Tarzan, the Ape Man.*

"In this role he is what Hollywood calls *a natural.* He stands six-feet-three in his bare feet and weighs 190 pounds. His body is hard and supple . . . slim-waisted . . . narrow-flanked. He might have indeed been the original model for Edgar Rice Burroughs' fictional hero. And because so much of his life has been spent in an abbreviated swim suit he is utterly *un*selfconscious. As a matter of fact, he hates clothes, never feels quite at ease in them, and his greatest trial is the business of getting into a Tuxedo and a stiff collar. Also, he confesses that he's always had a mad desire to live in a tree. He never sees one of those tall, swaying coconut palms with the feather-duster tops without wanting to climb it.

"In talking to him you feel the spirit of youth incarnate. He is the personification of radiant good health. Like a bright thread running through the pattern of his life story is the ever-recurrent phrase: *"I loved to swim."* The glory of winning [to Johnny] was never as important as the joy of swimming."

Johnny's flawless physique was also the subject of many a screen story, and one such article's title blared out:

"Is this the World's Most Perfect Male?"

An early publicity photo of Johnny as Tarzan was accompanied by the following paragraph and description:

"The newest bother to boyfriends. The newest wonder-man to make the girls sigh and wish home were like Hollywood. Just as we're beginning to calm down a bit over the Gable charm, Metro goes and springs another sex-appeal boy on us — Johnny Weissmuller, the swimming champ. When as Tarzan, the Ape Man, Johnny begins dragging Maureen O'Sullivan around by her ankles, women audiences just about weep with envy. Here's how this new Adam is built:

"Height — 6 feet, 3 inches; Weight — 190 pounds; Neck — 16 inches; Relaxed upper arm — 13 inches; Flexed upper arm — 14 ½ inches; Forearm — 12 ¼ inches; Wrist — 7 ½ inches; Chest (normal) — 40 ¼ inches; Chest (expanded) — 43 ¾ inches; Waist — 32 inches; Hips — 41 ¼ inches; Thigh —

21 ¾ inches; Knee — 15 ¾ inches; Calf — 14 ½ inches; Ankle — 9 ¼ inches; Reach — 69 ½ inches."

Another article published prior to the release of the second Tarzan feature was equally complimentary, as the headline boldly stated:

"Johnny Weissmuller has World's Finest Physique"

"Many new things are started by motion pictures — fads, styles and building designs — but it remained for Johnny Weissmuller to set a new model in physique for men! The former swimming champion, who scored such a success in *Tarzan, the Ape Man,* is declared by health experts to have the finest proportioned body of any man living. This tremendous physique that enabled Weissmuller to set over 75 national and international records in his years of swimming competition brought gasps of admiration from audiences when they first saw him on the screen."

Unfortunately, Hollywood being the city of "Glitz, Glamor, and Gossip," there was trouble brewing in Paradise for Johnny. The studio got Johnny and Bobbe together to explain that their new star needed to be seen about in public with the stars of the picture, like Maureen, as well as other beautiful young MGM actresses. And Johnny needed to make these public appearances sans his petite wife

Bobbe, who was a virtual unknown in Hollywood (and thus there was no publicity value in them being seen together).

Bobbe said she understood and wanted what was best for her husband, who was suddenly a movie idol in addition to being a famous Olympic champion. Events that transpired as a result of Johnny's new stardom, effectively drove a wedge between the two that would ultimately end their relationship within a few months.

On one such publicity junket to New York City for *Tarzan, the Ape Man*, in March of 1932, Johnny was staying at a small hotel just off Broadway that was popular with MGM players, and was owned by former Ziegfeld star Marion Davies. Also staying at the same hotel was Mexican star Lupe Velez, who was starring on Broadway in the Ziegfeld stage production, *Hot-Cha*, which had opened on March 8th at the Ziegfeld theater. (Interestingly, *Hot-Cha* was financed by gangsters Dutch Schultz and Waxey Gordon, who discovered show business to be a legitimate enterprise to channel their ill-gotten gains. Ziegfeld's recent history of flops dried up his usual money sources, leaving mob money as his only financial hope to produce this show.)

Miss Velez saw the handsome star of the new MGM Tarzan picture in the hotel lobby, and realized that this young Adonis was perhaps the one to allow her to forget the man she couldn't forget — Gary Cooper. She later phoned Johnny in his room and asked him to have a drink with her. Johnny saw no harm in having a cocktail with Lupe, whom he knew to be an actress in the employ of his studio. The only problem here was that Lupe had a stunning 37-26-35 figure, all seductively poured into a five-foot, one-hundred-nine pound package. One glass of champagne led to another, and that was the beginning to the affair between Johnny and Lupe that culminated in their marriage the following year.

Lupe Velez was born as Maria Guadalupe Velez de Villalobos in San Luis de Potosi, a tiny suburb of Mexico City, on July 18, 1908. She inherited her talents from her mother, Josefina, an opera singer who had performed the lead role of *La Boheme* at the Mexico City Opera House. Lupe's father, a colonel in the Mexican regular army, was killed in action while Lupe was a teenager. Lupe had taken dancing lessons as a girl and learned voice training from her mother, and was determined to make a career in show business. When she headed for Hollywood in 1925 at the age of seventeen, she was turned back at the border because she was underage. "All the way back to Mexico City I cried," recalled Lupe "but I'd show them. I *would* get to Hollywood some way. I appealed to the president, to the ministers, to everybody in

Mexico City. After a lot of letter writing between Mexico City and Washington and what you call 'red tape' they said I could cross the border." Eventually Lupe was allowed to enter the United States, and she arrived without a penny to her name; she had been robbed on the train by a friendly man who held her hand and stole her purse.

Miss Velez, exuding a raw natural talent and flamboyancy, finally made her Hollywood debut in 1928 at the age of nineteen. Silent film star Douglas Fairbanks was shooting *The Gaucho*, and approved the choice of Lupe as his gypsy lover, the "Wild Mountain Girl." Velez became a major film star with this role, and the critics raved about this fresh young newcomer. Mordaunt Hall of the *N. Y. Times* said of Lupe: "Miss Velez gives a capital characterization as the Mountain Girl. Whether in rags or lace, she gives blow-for-blow to the men who get in her way."

It wouldn't be telling any tales out of school to note that Velez soon became a very "popular" young woman in Hollywood, and had well-publicized affairs with numerous Hollywood leading men, including Douglas Fairbanks, Sr., Tom Mix, Clark Gable, Charlie Chaplin, Victor Fleming, John Gilbert, Jack Dempsey, and most notably Gary Cooper.

Lupe fell passionately in love with Cooper, whom she met while filming *Wolf Song* in

1929. To indicate how big a star Lupe became practically overnight, she was paid $14,000 for her work in *Wolf Song*, while her male co-star worked for only $2,750. During this period of time Cooper had his own share of affairs with many of the top Hollywood female stars, and he wisely ended the stormy relationship with Lupe in 1931. It is doubtful that Lupe ever completely forgot Gary, her pain and passion so great that she threatened him with a gun when the affair ended.

Lupe lived life with a reckless exuberance and was famous for her notoriously bad temper and outrageous stunts. In the 1972 biography of Florenz Ziegfeld, *Ziegfeld*, author Charles Higham relates the following concerning Lupe's antics during the run of *Hot-Cha*: "Lupe was very hard to handle, and her behavior was very strange. Just after the curtain fell on the sixth night in New York, she took her $2,500 check for her first week's work, ran across the street to the bank, banged on the door, and demanded that it open immediately. A large crowd gathered to gaze at her in astonishment.

"Later she failed to turn up at a matinee performance, and Ziegfeld sent Goldie [Ziegfeld's secretary] to fetch her while the curtain was held for an hour. Goldie arrived at Lupe's hotel and heard a commotion in the room. When the door opened, Goldie was astonished to see Lupe's sister giving the star of

Hot-Cha a high colonic irrigation [enema] on the carpet. 'I've got a hangover!' Lupe said rather shakily. Goldie dragged her to her feet and slapped her in the face. Then she hauled Lupe down the stairs, threw her in a taxi, and drove her to the theater, where she struggled through the performance in her drunken condition."

Elizabeth Dickson of *Collier's* magazine defined Lupe's particular brand of sex appeal in a June 1932 article called "The Girl with One Talent." She noted that Lupe had something that most women don't have: Something defined as *lure*. "It isn't beauty. It isn't brains. It isn't ordinary charm. This thing called 'lure' is a current that goes out from its possessor and brings back to her almost anything she wants. Take Lupe Velez for example. New York at this moment thinks this Mexican whirlwind tops the lure market by several miles. She never acted in her life and that's her secret. Fantastic? Yes, she's all of that and the despair of her agent."

Lupe had "lure" and got what she wanted in life, especially in the "male" department. The saying "deadlier than the male" was never more true than in Lupe's case. And then along came Johnny in the spring of 1932: another "ready-made fool" who fell madly in love with the beautiful and sexy Miss Velez. It wasn't long after Lupe returned to Hollywood in mid-June (after the close of *Hot-Cha*), that Johnny's marriage to Bobbe officially collapsed and he asked her for a divorce. Johnny can't be faulted for making a romantic error with Lupe, as many other men including Gary Cooper had done the same thing.

Hot-tempered Lupe not only had a reputation as a two-fisted drinker and promiscuous lover, but for throwing some of the wildest parties in Hollywood. One such shindig occurred in August of 1932, a few months after she met Johnny. Lupe's 75 guests were reportedly entertained by cockfights and stag movies, and the food and liquor flowed continuously during a nonstop two-day barbecue. Lupe loved to dance at these parties to Latin music, lifting her skirts high above her head — the uninhibited lass wore no undergarments to the amazement of her guests!

When Johnny and Bobbe tied the knot in February of 1931, it was big news in America. He was a national sports hero, and certainly one of the most eligible bachelors in the country. So when his marriage ended so quickly — that was also big news. Compared to philandering Hollywood idols like Gary Cooper and Clark Gable, Johnny was a regular choirboy. America wanted to know what had happened to end the seemingly ideal romance of Johnny and Bobbe. Was it an involvement with Lupe Velez?

Even before he ever met Lupe, the studio strongly suggested that Johnny divorce Bobbe Arnst for the good of his career. This was a suggestion that he refused, pleading that he loved Bobbe. However, the couple had violent arguments over the situation, and finally Bobbe packed her bags and moved home to her mother.

Bobbe Arnst told her story first in a *Screen Book* interview entitled "Tarzan Seeks a Divorce."

"Yes, Johnny and I are finished. He wants a Mexican divorce but I won't have it. We will get an honest-to-goodness California divorce, though, as soon as we can file the papers. Johnny is madly in love with Lupe Velez. I do not know whether or not she loves him or if they will get married but I've known about the affair for some time. I've tried to fight it out. It's no use, the gossips win. Marriage can't be the victor in Hollywood.

"I've lost but I'll try to take it like a man, and if Lupe, or anyone else can make Johnny happier, I want him to have her. I loved him and did what I could but Hollywood was too much for us. It breaks my heart to lose my boy but I'll play the game, no matter what it costs me.

"It happened so suddenly that I was dumbfounded. While Johnny was in New York he wrote me long love letters almost every day and when he returned it was like another honeymoon. We had never been so happy with each other — not even when we were first married.

"One night after returning from a party he said without warning, 'I want a divorce.'

" 'Why, Johnny. There must be a reason.'

" 'No, only that I want to be free.'

"He's such a big baby and so unbelievably naive.

"When I saw a preview of *Tarzan* I knew Johnny would be besieged by millions of women, women who wanted him. I thought that the best way to hold him against them was to give him free rein. I wanted to go to New York with him but I knew I should not, so I stayed at home. I thought I could beat this game which Hollywood plays but now I admit I have lost.

"I have nothing against Lupe. She was very kind to me once, when I was ill in New York. I do not know if she even cares for Johnny in a big way but I am sure he is infatuated with her."

Johnny told his own side of the story, at the behest of MGM, in a published interview entitled "The Weissmuller Divorce." The author of the interview prefaced the article with this paragraph:

"Johnny Weissmuller, who set a new fashion in screen heroes with his 'Tarzan,' groped for a summation of reasons to explain the failure of his marriage to Bobbe Arnst, former Broadway star — a marriage which started glowingly under a glamorous Florida moon — and ended glaringly under the Kleig lights of Hollywood."

"I need freedom to be happy," explained Johnny. "Bobbe wanted a regulation husband. It was impossible to compromise between my need and Bobbe's want, so a divorce was the only solution. Bobbe was dancing in a night club in Miami, and I had come down for a swimming exhibition. We met. Florida was romantic — there was the moon and those beautiful nights — and this sweet girl. We didn't give ourselves a chance to know each other. We fell in love."

"But we should never have married. I realized that a month afterwards. After all, we are entirely different personalities. I've lived in the daytime — I've done simple things all my life like swimming and playing squash and golf. I am accustomed to a lot of action — to starting in the morning and being on the go the entire day. Bobbe's life was at night — that was part of her career. Her routine was sophisticated as compared with mine — house-parties and openings and night clubs. By nine o'clock I was ready for bed. At that time Bobbe was just waking up.

"She gave up her career — not that I asked her to. As a matter of fact, I wanted her to continue on the stage because I felt that she needed an interest of her own — quite apart from me. But she preferred to be my wife only and I appreciated it. I still think she is one of the sweetest girls in the world — but we simply couldn't make the necessary adjustments.

"My life had always been free. I had been accustomed to going around without question or hindrance. I liked to swim with the boys. I liked to play on the beach with kids — and teach them to have fun in the water. Bobbe couldn't understand why I wanted to leave her even for a moment, unless I had ceased to love her. She didn't realize that no two people can be constantly together. And we were together — every minute of the day and night. And no matter how much you care towards a person it gives you a feeling of being tied hand and foot never to be alone — never to be away from that one human being even for a second.

"No marriage can stand up under the strain of incessant association. I had been accustomed to doing everything my way — and to be suddenly asked to give up all other companionships — to meet objections to my occasionally being with the boys I've worked with and played with, seemed unreasonable. It led to trouble.

"Bobbe and I have never had any serious disagreements. They were always little squabbles. But there was a constant round of them. The only times I left her alone was after one of these, when I simply had to get away by myself."

When the Weissmuller divorce was announced, Bobbe moved back to New York. She later admitted that she was given $10,000 from MGM to help make a new start — elsewhere. A generous amount but a small price considering that Metro could now advertise their new mega-star Johnny Weissmuller as a swinging bachelor who was available to all females in the land. In one magazine, a full-page photo of a bare-chested Weissmuller was accompanied by this blurb:

"Johnny Weissmuller, the screen's sleek swimming sheik, recently divorced from Bobbe Arnst, musical comedy star, is reported growing affectionate towards Lupe Velez, Mexican movie star. His next picture is *Tarzan and His Mate*, in which he is co-starred with the fair Maureen O'Sullivan, of MGM."

And that blurb was a perfect example of the MGM strategy in marketing Johnny. In one paragraph, and one handsome profile shot (naked to the waist), the new Tarzan was linked to sexy young star Lupe Velez, as well as the very fair (and single at the time) Maureen O'Sullivan. The marketing strategy was brilliant, and translated into millions of dollars for MGM in receipts from the first several Tarzan pictures.

Speaking of Maureen O'Sullivan, she was

one of Louis B. Mayer's favorite leading ladies during the balance of the 1930s, and always portrayed gentle, romantic, and courageous women. In 1932 alone she had seven pictures in release, as well as the incredibly successful *Tarzan, the Ape Man*. With her warm beauty, fine acting talents, and screen sensuality, there was no danger of Maureen being typecast as the jungle lass, Jane (as Johnny was with his character of Tarzan). In fact, over the next ten years she would make a remarkable 42 motion pictures, including the six MGM Tarzan adventures. (All the more extraordinary when you consider she also gave birth to the first two — Michael and Patrick — of her eventual seven children, all by her husband John Farrow.)

Initially, MGM had similar plans for Johnny Weissmuller and announced that he would be starring in a new adventure to be filmed in the Frozen North, entitled *Eskimo*, which would also be directed by Woody Van Dyke. But the studio had a change of heart, and decided to keep Johnny under wraps until the next Tarzan adventure. (Van Dyke did direct this grim 1933 melodrama filmed in Northern Alaska, which starred genuine Eskimos in the lead roles.)

Meanwhile Johnny, with time on his hands (so to speak), was able to attend the summer Olympics which were held in Los Angeles in

August of 1932. With Weissmuller now retired from swimming competition, the American team was no longer a prohibitive favorite to capture the majority of the medals (as they had done in 1924 and 1928, with Johnny as their star captain). In fact, the American men's swim team would win only a solitary gold medal in this Olympics, and then only by the slimmest of margins.

Leading the American Olympic swimming squad was Buster Crabbe, who was taking a break from his law studies as well as his budding acting career to compete in the 400-meter and 1500-meter events. In one of the closest and most exciting finishes in history, Crabbe won the gold medal in the 400-meter freestyle by one-tenth of a second over the world record holder, Jean Taris of France. (Crabbe's gold medal lessened his disappointment at finishing fifth in the 1500-meter freestyle event.)

Johnny Weissmuller, sitting in the front row, got so excited during the thrilling race that he leaped over a fence to get a closer view of the finish. Johnny also rushed down to be the first to congratulate Crabbe, who finally won his coveted gold medal. In his autobiography, *A Self Portrait*, Crabbe recalled his moment of triumph after his victory:

"Johnny Weissmuller was in the audience and came poolside to congratulate me. My dad came over to where I stood bobbing in the water, leaned over the edge and kissed me on the cheek. That was one of my most cherished moments."

In that instant, Johnny proved what a class individual he really was. He had conceded his position of "King of Swimmers" to Buster Crabbe, and offered his heartfelt congratulations to his friend. Although the two men would continue to be friendly rivals over the duration of their lives, they nevertheless had a strong mutual respect for each other. This was Crabbe's second and final Olympics, and he too would be joining Johnny in the make-believe world of Hollywood. Buster later made his most famous quote, concerning his narrow victory in the 400-meter race:

"That one-tenth of a second changed my life," mused Buster. "It was then that [the Hollywood producers] discovered latent histrionic abilities in me."

Buster's gold medal did indeed lead to his first starring role as Kaspa, the lion-man, in *King of the Jungle* (1933), with co-star Frances Dee. With the immense success of Johnny Weissmuller in *Tarzan, the Ape Man*, other studios like Paramount were attempting to imitate that success. In this story, a child lost in Africa is raised by lions and grows to be Kaspa, lion-man and king of the jungle. This excellent adventure was probably the best motion picture that Crabbe ever made in his long Hollywood career, and led to Crabbe being cast as another "jungle man" soon thereafter.

With MGM taking their time in preparing their next adventure to be called *Tarzan and His Mate*, producer Sol Lesser took advantage of an option he had with Edgar Rice Burroughs to produce his own Tarzan picture independent of the Metro series. He realized that if he hurried to a 1933 release, his Tarzan would find a waiting audience that had paid millions to see Weiss- muller in *Tarzan, the Ape Man*. It would be impossible to get Weissmuller for Lesser's film, since he was in preparation for his own upcoming Tarzan portrayal.

Although Lesser liked Buster Crabbe for the role, the producer had a problem: his contract with Burroughs stipulated that this film must star James Pierce, son-in-law of the author and the star of the 1927 silent feature, *Tarzan and the Golden Lion*. The problem eventually solved itself when Pierce, realizing he was too far out of shape to compete against Weissmuller's image of Tarzan, accepted a $5,000 payment to relinquish his grip on the role.

And thus Crabbe was given the role of the ape-man in *Tarzan the Fearless*, and once again Buster was following in the wake of Johnny Weissmuller. Crabbe had finished a distant second to Johnny in collecting swimming records and gold medals, and once again he would be overshadowed by the immense success of his predecessor. Years later Crabbe put his disappointment in the Tarzan role into words: "The worst Tarzan was me. We had two animals — an elephant that had retired from the circus and a lion with no teeth. But there were a lot of good fights in it, so the kids liked it."

Once again from his autobiography, Crabbe expounded on trying to live up to the level of expectation that had been set by Johnny in the recent mega-success of *Tarzan, the Ape Man*:

"Lesser and the industry got the message that *Tarzan the Fearless* was an inferior product to Weissmuller's *Tarzan, the Ape Man* that had come out earlier. Mine came out on August 11, 1933, and I was asked to tour several key cities to give some publicity to the film. I assumed the identity of Buster 'Tarzan' Crabbe for a month or so, signed autographs, promoted the film on radio and in personal appearances at theaters. But no amount of promotion could save it. I rather enjoyed all the hoopla, but it was a hectic pace being always on the go.

"There was talk that Lesser would exercise his rights to make another Tarzan picture early the following year. But Metro, which still had Weissmuller sitting in dry-dock, made offers to Lesser for his remaining rights to the four films. I knew that if the two parties got together, my chances of continuing as Tarzan were practically nil. Eventually, Lesser sold three of his remaining four rights to MGM for a quarter of a million dollars and Johnny was back in his ready-made role again."

And so that was the end of the role of Tarzan for Crabbe, but their paths would continue to cross for many years to come. Buster would have to play second-fiddle (the villain) in two future Weissmuller films, *Swamp Fire* (1946), and the Jungle Jim adventure *Captive Girl* (1950). But Buster was able to gather his own significant share of fame on the silver screen in his most famous roles of space adventurers Buck Rogers and Flash Gordon, as well as scores of westerns and adventure pictures over a 30-year career.

In 1933, as one of America's most famous sports heroes, Johnny lent his name to one of America's most enduring breakfast cereals, Wheaties! Minneapolis-based General Mills began marketing Wheaties in 1924, and during the Depression a box of the wholesome wheat flakes was priced at eleven cents. Full-page ads in prestigious magazines like *The Saturday Evening Post* and newspaper print ads (in comic strip form) came out in August of 1933, featuring Johnny Weissmuller. (Two other similar ads for Wheaties came out around this time, featuring home run king Babe Ruth and former heavyweight champion Jack Dempsey.)

Johnny's cartoon character promoted Wheaties to youngsters who could fill in a coupon and receive an action photograph of Johnny swimming the "crawl." The photo was signed "Johnny (Tarzan) Weissmuller," as the ad also noted him as the star of the new MGM action thriller, *Tarzan and His Mate*.

"I'll give you a free photograph," said cartoon Johnny, "if you'll eat WHEATIES for breakfast. Because WHEATIES with milk or cream and sugar will help make you strong so you can do the 'crawl' like me."

In the final decade of the 20th century, sports heroes like Michael Jordan and Tiger Woods have promoted Wheaties to the current generation. But in 1933, it was Olympic champion Johnny Weissmuller telling the youth of America to eat their Wheaties for good health and maximum energy. Johnny was a true national hero, and with his fame spreading around the globe because of Tarzan, there were plenty of Wheaties being eaten by the youngsters (and adults) of America.

The free signed photograph was a special bonus for a whole generation who became fans of Johnny, swimmer extraordinaire and motion picture hero as Tarzan. (Another product that was popular in the 1930s was "Tarzan" bread, with a peak of 75 million loaves sold in one year. The bread sold like crazy, because all the kids wanted to be strong like Tarzan!)

Pitching cereal and bread didn't require much of his time, but Johnny wasn't just idly wasting his free hours while he was waiting for his next Tarzan picture to begin production. He loved to swim and go ocean surfing at Santa Monica bay, a sport in which his friend Duke Kahanamoku was a great champion. Riding the surf on his plywood board, awkward and heavy by today's standards, Johnny could catch a strong wave with the wind at his back and feel a freedom that could only come for him when he was on the water. Freedom for Johnny would always be the water — swimming, skindiving, boating, sailing, fishing, and surfing. They were mostly solitary sports, but they brought immense exhilaration to his heart.

That summer of 1933, spending much of his time at the beach, he was appointed to the Santa Monica life guard squad. Johnny took a regular shift each week, on a volunteer basis — in other words, no pay. For Johnny this wasn't a publicity stunt, but MGM did take advantage of the opportunity for some free publicity. The studio sent Maureen O'Sullivan and a photographer down to visit Johnny on one of his lifeguard shifts. Maureen posed for the camera as a swimmer who nearly drowns, and Johnny demonstrated lifesaving techniques, artificial respiration, and first aid for the victim.

This was the real thing for Johnny, who felt a need to put his time to good use and perhaps save a life in the process. The following report from Santa Monica was filed by the Associated Press, and was published in numerous newspapers including the *New York Times* on August 11, 1933. "Johnny Weissmuller, champion swimmer and screen actor, made his first rescue today since he was appointed to the Santa Monica lifeguard squad. Weissmuller saw Bob Wheeler, 12, sinking off the Municipal Pier, and swam to save him."

Johnny was credited with saving eleven lives in 1927 after the disaster of the *Favorite*, the pleasure boat that sank in Lake Michigan. Once again Johnny was a real hero, and saved another life — this time a young boy. Johnny again proved he was not just a motion picture character pretending to do heroic deeds on screen. Weissmuller was as genuine as they come — a real American hero.

CHAPTER EIGHTEEN

Johnny and Lupe
Were Lovers

The tumultuous five-year relationship of Johnny and Lupe officially began on October 8, 1933, when they were secretly married in Las Vegas. Lupe was working on her latest motion picture on location in Nevada, and Johnny went to visit her for the weekend. Johnny was twenty-nine and Lupe a few years younger at age twenty-four — their brief affair had blossomed into passionate love. The time was right for them so they just decided to "tie the knot." Justice of the Peace Ryan performed the simple ceremony at four o'clock early Sunday morning, as Lupe legally became "Mrs. Johnny Weissmuller." However, the marriage was kept secret for three weeks, apparently at the whim of Lupe — the first of many "whims" that Johnny would have to endure from his new bride, the hot-blooded Latin lass who would eventually become famous as the "Mexican Spitfire."

Johnny and Lupe both spoke briefly to the

press on October 29th, as they admitted that the rumors of their marriage were true. "It was my own business," said Lupe. "I felt like saying I wasn't married, and now I feel like saying I am married." In referring to a story scheduled to appear in the November issue of a movie magazine, Johnny explained why they had denied their marriage previously: "We wanted to give the magazine a break."

Meanwhile, there was no time for an extended honeymoon as filming had already begun on the second Tarzan picture for Johnny, *Tarzan and His Mate*, and thus it was back to Hollywood on Monday morning. After the marriage was announced to the public, Johnny moved out of the small house he had been renting and into Lupe's two-story Spanish-style mansion at 732 N. Rodeo Drive in Beverly Hills. The boudoir of Miss Velez was pure Hollywood — an eight-foot by eight-foot low bed in an arena that was painted black, gold and silver, and surrounded with furnishings upholstered with decadent plushness. There was, of course, a swimming pool in the back yard for Johnny, who would have been a fish out of water without his daily swimming regimen.

In addition to a beautiful diamond ring, Johnny gave Lupe a thirty-four foot schooner for a wedding present which he christened the *Santa Guadalupe*. (The boat was named after Lupe, whose legal name was Maria

Guadalupe Velez de Villalobos — later short-ened to her screen name of Lupe Velez.) The boat was moored in L.A. harbor, and the ini-tial voyage was to be to Catalina Island for a picnic, some 20 miles away. They made a splendid looking couple: Johnny in his cap-tain's hat and sailor togs, and Lupe looked equally sharp dressed as the first mate. A Sunday afternoon away from work, and a beautiful day for two young lovers to spend together.

All of Johnny's good intentions turned sour when Lupe became seasick, as the choppy seas turned her stomach upside down. A dis-appointed Johnny had to bring the boat about and return to port, long before the journey was supposed to be completed. The schooner was too lightweight for the rough seas of the Pacific Ocean, which tossed the craft about and also tossed poor Lupe, who was only used to being on solid ground!

Undaunted by this early misadventure, Johnny later traded the *Santa Guadalupe* in on a fifty-foot sailing vessel named the *Allure*. This new two-masted schooner was heavier and more solidly built, and capable of han-dling the rough seas. Lupe eventually came to love sailing on the *Allure* with Johnny, in what would be some of their happiest moments of their mercurial relationship.

The boat would be moored at Catalina Is-land, and the trip from the mainland could be accomplished in 90 minutes by Johnny's speedboat. The anchored *Allure* was a tourist attraction as well as a favorite of photographers, who would snap photos of Johnny and Lupe at Catalina — strolling hand-in-hand, relaxing, shopping, fishing — to peddle to the numerous movie magazines. They were definitely a hot item, and America wanted to read about and see pictures of perhaps the hottest romance in Hollywood. (Taking photographs, incidentally, was also a favorite hobby of Johnny's during the 1930s. He would often have his trusty Kodak box-camera with him to take photos of Lupe and any of his friends that were willing to pose for the amateur shutterbug.)

The *Allure* was a seaworthy craft that slept six people, although normally it would only be Lupe and Johnny aboard. The lovebirds spent their free days sailing the waters around Catalina Island and deep-sea fishing, away from the immense pressures of Hollywood life. Johnny also enjoyed skin diving — exploring the clear ocean waters while Lupe lounged on the decks of the *Allure*. The captain's quarters included a comfortable double-wide bunk that folded into the ship's hull when not in use. The ship's chronometer, a brass nautical clock used for navigation, was Johnny's crown jewel on his cherished boat. It had been a gift from several of the crew members who worked on the Tarzan movies, and was inscribed "To Tarzan" with the names of James McKay, J. Marchant, Len Smith, Art Smith, Willard Vogel, Al Scheving, Chet Davis, Hank Forester, George Lee also engraved. Years after the *Allure* was sold, Johnny kept the chronometer as a memento of the friends that presented him the gift, and the countless hours of relaxation and pleasure aboard the craft. These happy days were probably the highlight of his relationship with Lupe.

Johnny was now the proud owner of an automobile for the first time in his life — a 1932 Chevrolet Six two-door roadster. This sharp-looking convertible sold for the sum of $475 for the basic model, direct from the factory in Flint, Michigan. He never could afford a car during his years as an amateur swimmer, and had traveled too much to need an automobile until landing in Hollywood in 1931. In fact, no one in his family had ever even owned a car simply because it was a luxury that was out of reach.

Barely two weeks after the announcement of the Weissmuller union, Gary Cooper announced his own engagement on November 6, 1933 to wealthy debutante Veronica Balfe. Cooper officially ended his bachelorhood on December 15, 1933 when he married the 20-year-old aspiring actress — who was called "Rocky" by her friends — in a private ceremony. The affair of Cooper and Lupe was now ancient history, and each had now married and buried the past. But Lupe always felt like the "woman scorned," and whenever her path was crossed by Cooper, she often made a scene.

The Weissmullers and the Coopers seemed to inexplicably run into each other from time to time, and often with disastrous results. Once the couples arrived simultaneously at the Newark airport, where a photographer asked the newlyweds to pose for a photograph together. Johnny and Cooper were fine with the notion, but Lupe angrily refused. "I'm happily married and so is he. I wouldn't pose with him. Besides, he's no oil painting, that one."

Johnny could keep Lupe in line, but another time she was on the town without her husband and ran into Gary and Rocky at the Trocadero Cafe in Hollywood. The new Mrs. Cooper refused to acknowledge the presence of Lupe, who made Rocky very aware of her presence by tossing a drink in her face! Lupe made an awful scene, kicking and screaming as Cooper tried to calm her down. Johnny was undoubtedly relieved that he missed this particular "catfight" between Lupe and Rocky, leaving "Coop" to put out the fireworks between the two females.

The marriage of Johnny and Lupe started out smoothly enough, and they seemed to be genuinely in love with each other. Lupe's favorite activities included the boxing matches, and Johnny was a willing escort. (Weissmuller had done some amateur boxing as a teenager back in Chicago, and had made friends with heavyweight kings Dempsey and Tunney during his own rise to fame.)

Lupe reveled in the noise, the excited crowds, and the anticipation of two fighters battling for supremacy in the ring. Lupe loved to make an entrance, especially at the boxing matches with Johnny. The stadium lights would dim especially for their entrance, as a murmur would arise from the crowd: "Tarzan and Lupe are coming!" Johnny could only smile and wave to the crowd as Lupe took her bows and then her front row seat.

One writer noted the presence of "the tempestuous Lupe in the front row at the Hollywood Legion Stadium, pounding on the bloodstained canvas of the ring and screaming profane Mexican incantations at brown-skinned countrymen who were failing to live up to her high standards of combat . . . '*Hijo!* Get up, you son-of a-beetch!' "

Lupe's infatuation with pugilism stretched to giving Johnny a pair of boxing gloves one year as a Christmas gift, on which she had inscribed: "Darling, so you can punch me if I ever leave you." Lupe was quite an athlete in addition to being a marvelous dancer, and included among her hobbies roller skating, bicycling, and was an adept and quick-fisted boxer! She was also a big fan of stock car racing, cock fighting, and bullfighting back in her native Mexico.

Back in Hollywood, they were both working on pictures for MGM: Johnny on *Tarzan and His Mate* and Lupe's busy schedule had her acting in four films that would be released in 1934. Lupe had a new contract with MGM and her films for the year included *Laughing Boy* with Ramon Novarro (and directed by Woody Van Dyke); *Palooka* with Jimmy Durante; *Strictly Dynamite* with Durante; and *Hollywood Party*. This very funny Hollywood spoof had a top-notch cast that included comedy legends Jimmy Durante (once again), The Three Stooges, Laurel and Hardy, and of course, Lupe, herself blessed with a comedic genius that brought her far more screen roles than her beauty or inherent sexuality.

Two sequences stand out in *Hollywood Party* as memorable: Jimmy Durante satirizing the Tarzan character with his outrageous "Schnarzan" (and Lupe as his jungle woman "Jaguar Girl"); and Lupe in an hilarious egg-breaking skit with Laurel and Hardy, a battle of one-upmanship with Stan and Ollie, and Lupe, taking turns cracking eggs over each others' heads. Originally the cast of

Hollywood Party was to include Clark Gable, Joan Crawford, Jean Harlow, and also Johnny Weissmuller in cameo roles; however, they were simply too "big" for this parody of Hollywood.

In her seventeen years as a motion picture star, Lupe portrayed many women of exotic extraction, from her Mexican heritage to American Indians, Eskimos, Hindus, and Chinese. One magazine writer described Lupe as a talented, enigmatic force to be reckoned with: "Her cinematic blend of passionate nature, bustling activity, and mercurial reversals of mood established her as the foremost example of the generously endowed and correspondingly fickle female of her race."

When Christmas 1933 arrived, Johnny bought Lupe two Mexican Chihuahua puppies that Lupe named "Mr. Kelly" and "Mrs. Murphy." Another gift for Lupe, who loved to be adorned in expensive jewelry and exotic perfumes, was a wristwatch with a ruby bracelet.

Although their fights would be legendary in Hollywood during the five years of their stormy marriage, it was never gentle Johnny beating up Lupe — it was the other way around. Fortunately, Johnny was strong enough to keep the damage caused to his person by his wild woman to a minimum. The petite Lupe, precisely five-feet and one-half inches and a potent 109 pounds, was a regular hell-cat and was willing to stand up to any man, including her six-foot three-inch husband.

The hot-tempered Lupe was also quick to defend her man, who was usually smart enough not to brawl with any troublemaker who might try to pick a fight with "Tarzan." One evening a customer at Ciro's, a popular dance club in Hollywood, took umbrage to Johnny's shoulder-length locks (for the Tarzan role) — also apparently the man's girlfriend had been flirting with Johnny. The fiery Lupe jumped to her feet and punched the interloper in the nose, and shouted: "You big ape! You leave my man alone! If he ever picks on you, there will not be enough for minced pie!"

By this time Johnny was steamed up, and asked the rude ruffian if he cared to settle the argument outside the club. "No thanks!" retorted the man, who grabbed his girl and headed for the exit. "I've had plenty from one of the family!" Lupe and Johnny embraced and could only laugh at what turned out to be an unusual public display of unity and affection.

According to Velez' biographer, Floyd Conner, in the book *Lupe Velez and Her Lovers*, the Mexican Spitfire also took her toll on Johnny in the bedroom, inflicting more wounds than the jungle animals he fought on the sets of Tarzan:

"Weissmuller fared little better during their lovemaking. Lupe's was so ferocious that Johnny looked like a wildcat had attacked him. He arrived on the Tarzan set, his magnificent body covered with strawberry-size hickeys, scratches, and annular bites on his pecs. The studio had to use extensive body makeup before he was ready to shoot."

Through the years there would be a great deal of publicity concerning the fights of the couple, but Lupe defended their marriage as typical of Hollywood: "Fight? We all do. Johnny and I may fight, but no more than the rest of Hollywood. They call each other 'Darling' in public, and then go home and smack each other in private. When Johnny and I get sore, we get sore no matter where we are! The way to be happy through marriage is to fight once a week, maybe more."

While Lupe defended their public battling as promoting harmony in the relationship, it also brought much publicity to the famous motion picture couple. One fan magazine published a photo of Johnny and Lupe, smiling at each other with the "look of love" at a table in the Hawaiian Paradise Club, a popular night club frequented by celebrities. The caption asked the question: "What's wrong with this picture? Usually blows and angry words were flying between the movies' handsome Tarzan, Johnny Weissmuller, and his off-and-on-again wife, Lupe Velez."

Johnny and Lupe had a classic "love-slash-hate" relationship. When they loved, they were happy. But when they hated, they fought long and loud in battles that echoed throughout Hollywood. On January 24, 1934, after less than four months of alternating marital bliss and disharmony, Lupe announced an immediate trial separation. She didn't bother to tell Johnny, who was "astonished" to read of the separation the following morning. Lupe was quoted as saying: "We will try a separation for eight days, and then if we can no longer stand each other I will sue for a divorce. I love Johnny, and he loves me, but we have two terrible tempers. We fight all the time. There is no other man — and no other woman."

When Johnny divorced Bobbe Arnst in 1932, one of his stated reasons was incompatibility: Bobbe was a nightowl and he was a day person. However, the exact same situation existed with Lupe, who was ready to howl at night while Johnny preferred to stay home and unwind after a hard day on the Tarzan set. Their physical attraction for each other aside, they began as a classic case of incompatible life-styles (although eventually Johnny learned to love the night life that was Lupe's life blood). They often fought like

dogs and cats, and this dangerous cat —
Lupe — had sharp claws. (Lupe was also
known to brandish a knife in her fits of anger
— she used it on Gary Cooper once and drew
blood, leaving a scar on his arm.)

For each separation, though, there would
be a reconciliation. After this first separation,
they kissed and made up. Until the next time,
and there were many next times over the five
years of their marriage. Lupe also filed for divorce on July 10, 1934, and this report was
published by the Associated Press:

"The Lupe Velez-Johnny Weissmuller
marriage is headed for the divorce courts, the
little Mexican actress said today. She asserted she would file suit against the former
Olympic swimming star immediately, and
would charge 'mental cruelty.'

"Miss Velez said she and her husband separated finally yesterday after several previous
estrangements."

Again this was a short-lived separation.
Despite their fights, Lupe truly loved her
"John-ee." She would run back to his arms
after each separation, never fully realizing
that one day she would lose him forever.

Later in the summer Johnny had a chance
to stand up for his beloved Lupe when she became a target of Sacramento District Attor-
ney Neil McAllister, who was conducting an
investigation of the Communist influence on
the motion picture industry. Numerous Hol-

lywood stars were questioned including movie tough guy James Cagney, as well as Mexican stars Ramon Novarro, Dolores Del Rio, and Lupe Velez. (Apparently the only "evidence" that linked these people to the investigation was a slip of paper that had their handwritten names upon it that was found in the effects of Caroline Decker, a secretary for a Communist farm workers union. Hell, it was probably a list of her favorite actors and actresses!)

When Lupe's name was added to the list in this 1934 investigation, Johnny came to the defense of his wife and spoke out on her behalf. "Any attempt to link Lupe with radicalism is silly and ridiculous," protested an angry Johnny to the press.

Lupe herself said to the press, "Me a Communist? Ho, I don't even know what the blazes a Communist is." And of course she didn't, and the investigation died away. This probe foreshadowed the Communist witch-hunt of 1947 when "The Hollywood Ten," a group of famous writers, directors, and producers, refused to tell the Un-American Activities Committee whether or not they were Communists. All served short prison terms and were "blacklisted" in Hollywood for many years.

In August of 1934, Lupe and Johnny attended a formal dinner dance at the Little Club in the Ambassador Hotel; also attending were Gary and Veronica "Rocky" Cooper. This time a photographer succeeded in coaxing the two couples to pose for a group photograph. Johnny and Lupe smiled, and Rocky beamed for the photographer. The laconic Cooper, however, couldn't bring himself to smile, realizing he was sitting on a powder keg! On this particular night the keg — Lupe — did not explode and there was no trouble of note.

Lupe received a personal blow in 1934 when MGM declined to pick up the next option on her contract, leaving her "high and dry" and virtually unemployed. Although the studio claimed they no longer had an interest in making films targeted at the Spanish-speaking market, this seemed to be an empty excuse for dumping Lupe. Indeed, she had a broad fan base that wasn't really based on her ethnic background. Lupe's best films were her comedies, which everyone loved.

It is more likely and logical that MGM was weary of the Velez' antics, and the negative publicity created for her husband — and one of their most marketable stars, Johnny Weissmuller. It is also very probable that Lupe was jealous of her husband's success, especially after her contract was terminated by the studio that employed them both. Lupe did not like to be scorned, and after her dismissal by MGM (the ultimate act of scorn), she took her rage out on the one person who truly loved her — Johnny.

The saga of Lupe and Johnny would continue for several more years, as their fights, separations, and reconciliations would become part of Hollywood folklore. But for now a more important story was the fabulous success of the second collaboration of Johnny and Maureen O'Sullivan in *Tarzan and His Mate*, which was released in the spring of 1934. Johnny's personal life at this time was in chaos, but his professional life was a smashing success.

CHAPTER NINETEEN
"Tarzan and His Mate"

Tarzan fans the world over were clamoring for their hero, Johnny Weissmuller, and their heroine, Maureen O'Sullivan, to return to the screen with a new jungle adventure. After the immense success and worldwide popularity of *Tarzan, the Ape Man*, a sequel was inevitable. The disappointment of the ill-fated 1933 release, *Tarzan the Fearless* starring Buster Crabbe, had only served to whet the appetites for all true Tarzan fans for the long awaited reunion of Weissmuller and O'Sullivan. *Tarzan and His Mate*, delayed for many months because of production problems, was finally ready for release in the spring of 1934.

Of the more than forty Tarzan films that have been produced over the years, *Tarzan and His Mate* is arguably the greatest Tarzan picture ever produced. There is hardly a moment in this story that doesn't qualify as cinematic poetry in motion, as the core romance between Tarzan and Jane is threatened to be torn asunder by greedy interlopers from the outside world. The second screen collaboration of Johnny Weissmuller and Maureen O'Sullivan is simply the definition of a classic romantic adventure.

With Johnny Weissmuller in the midst of all of the electrifying action, the character he had created in his first starring role now became his virtual persona. With his second portrayal, Johnny now became the ape-man to all Tarzan fans forevermore. Weissmuller's dark-haired, virile image and the perfect symmetry of his physique helped to form the definitive Tarzan. Johnny didn't have a way with women as did Gable or Cooper, nor did he have their acting talents, but he did have his own unique charisma and a powerful aura of masculinity that made him ideal in the role of Tarzan.

In over one-hundred publicity stills photographed for this picture by MGM photographer Clarence Bull, Johnny is pictured in his loincloth and Maureen in her skimpy antelope-skin two-piece outfit. In many of the photos Tarzan has Jane slung over his shoulder, ready to carry her off to the tree-tops for an assumed primitive romantic interlude.

There probably have never been a sexier set of photographs taken for any other legitimate film in history. It was pleasant work posing with Maureen and Johnny loved it. (It also provided him many opportunities to play the little tricks and jokes on her that were his stock in trade.) More importantly the fans were enthralled by this jungle romance between the ape-man and his mate, and the many photographs taken for this picture thoroughly enhanced the beauty of the event.

Once again the catch lines from a massive advertising campaign blared out the return of Tarzan in an all new jungle thriller, *Tarzan and His Mate*:

"HE'S BACK AGAIN! JOHNNY WEISS-MULLER — the one and only TARZAN — again battles the terrors of the jungle for his bride!"

"HE DARED JUNGLE TERRORS FOR HER LOVE! Ruler of a wild domain, sharing his throne with a White Goddess who defies the laws of society for the thrill of being carried away in the arms of her mate!"

"WHITE GODDESS of the JUNGLE! She traded civilization for the love of Tarzan, her mate! While Tarzan's brawny arms held her close . . . the jungle's furies meant nothing to the White Goddess of wild Africa."

"THE ORIGINAL TARZAN — JOHNNY WEISSMULLER! Primitive lovers in a Paradise of Peril! America's Adam and Eve return to thrill you as the Adonis of the jungle battles man and beast — for his bride — in the greatest romantic adventure of them all!"

★ ★ ★

Tarzan, the Ape Man concluded with Jane remaining in the jungle with Tarzan, presumably to live their lives together. In this 1934 sequel, *Tarzan and His Mate,* the character of Harry Holt (Neil Hamilton) returns to Tarzan's jungle a year later in hopes of harvesting a fortune in ivory tusks from the elephant burial ground. Holt and his new partner Arlington (Paul Cavanagh) intend to steal the ivory, as well as bring Jane back to civilization. Both of the men lust after the beautiful Jane, who of course only has eyes for her jungle man and has no intention of ever leaving him. Tarzan sees the two men as they are: immoral interlopers who will break all the rules to cash in on the riches of the ivory.

Realizing Tarzan's death is the only avenue to the coveted ivory and Jane, the cowardly Arlington shoots Tarzan from ambush and leaves him for dead. When they trick Jane into believing that Tarzan has been killed by a monstrous crocodile, her remorse clouds her judgment and she agrees to lead them to the burial ground. The ivory becomes secondary when the safari is captured by the fierce Giboni tribe, and the only escape route is blocked by a pride of man-eating lions. Holt and the safari leader Saidi (Nathan Curry) die honorable deaths in acts of bravery, and the coward Arlington meets his deserved fate. Jane is the last survivor clinging to her life as the lions surround her — only a small fire she has started between her and the lions. With Tarzan dead — she thinks — there is little hope that she will survive.

Although Tarzan's head wound is grievous, his apes nurse him back to health and he leads his elephants on a triumphant charge to save his mate and crush all of his enemies. In the final scene, Tarzan gathers Jane in his arms, as she tells her beloved mate, "Tarzan, always is just beginning for us." Together they ride one of Tarzan's mighty elephants back to the sanctity of their jungle home.

Whereas Johnny's early career in the movie business would be exclusively as the Tarzan character, Maureen O'Sullivan had been kept extremely busy by MGM in the two years since the release of *Tarzan, the Ape Man*. Maureen would always be known for her convincing portrayals of gentle women, and her own unique beauty made her a legend in an era of unforgettable female movie stars. But the scanty outfit that she wore in *Tarzan and His Mate* also brought her a certain amount of notoriety when the film was released. A leather halter top and matching loincloth were Jane's basic wardrobe, and for taking a swim with Tarzan she wore nothing at all! (Naturally, this scene caused a furor with the censorship people.)

In March of 1992 Maureen O'Sullivan

shared her thoughts on the sexuality of the characters in *Tarzan and His Mate*. (From her appearance on the TNT special, "MGM: *When the Lion Roars*.")

"They tried different things to make Jane look pretty sexy," said Miss O'Sullivan. "And first off they had the idea of having Jane wearing no bra — no brassiere at all — and she would always be covered with a branch, and they tried that and it didn't work. So then, they made a costume and it wasn't that bad at all. There was a little leather bra and a loincloth with thongs on the side. But it started such a furor, that the letters just came in. So it added up to thousands of women who were objecting to my costume. And I think that was one of the things that started the Legion of Decency.

"Now in those days," continued Maureen, "they took those things very seriously, the public did. Do you know I was offered land in San Francisco, I was offered all kinds of places where I could go in my shame — to hide from the cruel public who were ready to throw stones at me. It's funny you know — we were unreal people and yet we were real."

As screen characters Johnny and Maureen breathed life into the story book players of Edgar Rice Burroughs, capturing the essence of a primeval man and his mate. The playfulness between Tarzan and Jane on-screen was often endearing, and finally provocative. In one scene Jane receives gifts of an evening gown, stockings and French perfume, and dresses to impress Tarzan. He approves of this new look with a lusty gleam in his eye, and scoops up his mate and carries her away to their lofty love-nest, with hardly a protest from Jane.

Sol Lesser, who tried in vain to coax Maureen out of retirement when he became producer of the Tarzan series in 1943, offered his retrospective viewpoint of Miss O'Sullivan as Jane:

"Maureen O'Sullivan was an ideal Jane with a figure that is greatly revealed in the second Metro picture — but done so beautifully that it couldn't be criticized. As I recall the situation she is standing on a tree limb with Tarzan. He tugs at her garment, dives in the water and she dives in after him. Then she comes up from the swimming scene with her breast exposed. It was done in such good taste — I think that a kind of snobbishness developed afterwards with Miss O'Sullivan from her role as Jane. Maybe the public kidded her too much — or maybe she thought it wasn't good acting, I don't know. But I do know the movie audiences worshiped her."

The controversial underwater swimming sequence that followed Jane (Maureen) being tossed into the river by Tarzan was in actuality, Weissmuller and Josephine McKim, a petite Olympic swimmer who doubled for Miss

O'Sullivan. This underwater "ballet" is memorable for its graceful choreography and again the playful love between Tarzan and Jane. The ape-man kissing his beloved mate underwater is one of filmdom's most memorable love scenes.

Johnny's Tarzan wears his loincloth during the scene, but Jane (Miss McKim) is *au naturel;* this particular sequence was unacceptable to the Production Code Office which previewed the picture. After getting the thumbs down from the censors, MGM appeased the Code Office by reshooting the scene with Jane in her basic halter and loincloth. However, three different versions (one included the original nude sequence) were released to different areas of the country, depending on local censorship codes. When the first three MGM Tarzan pictures were released on videocassette in 1991, the nude swimming sequence was included in all its splendor. Fortunately for real film fans, this scene — tasteful rather than lewd — was not lost in the previous half-century.

A great deal of publicity after the release of *Tarzan, the Ape Man* announced the probability that Johnny Weissmuller's next Tarzan film would be filmed on location in Africa, seeking the reality of *Trader Horn*. That scenario never happened, and instead the Tarzan pictures were filmed in Hollywood for many years. The excessive costs and problems of the *Trader Horn* expedition scared off the money men at MGM, which sacrificed some realism for a greater profit. Johnny would have welcomed the challenge of filming in Africa, but Maureen might have balked at the proposition of living in the primitive conditions for an extended period. (As it was, she lost 45 days of the filming schedule when she was sidelined by an appendectomy.)

Woody Van Dyke, director of *Trader Horn* and *Tarzan, the Ape Man* was unavailable to direct *Tarzan and His Mate*. Initially taking the helm was Cedric Gibbons, who worked as art director on most of the MGM Tarzan adventures.

Filming began on the MGM back lots on August 2, 1933 under the direction of Gibbons and with a secondary cast that included Neil Hamilton returning in the role of Harry Holt, and Rod LaRocque as Martin Arlington, the corrupt partner of Holt.

Near the end of August, shock waves hit the set as Gibbons was replaced as director by Conway, JackJack Conway, a versatile director who worked for MGM for many years. Also seeking a chemistry change in the cast, Rod LaRocque was replaced by Paul Cavanagh in the second lead role of Arlington. (Cedric Gibbons is given full director's credit, but he was obviously in over his head in his first and only shot at directing a picture at MGM.) When filming resumed in early September, Conway directed the dialogue segments of the film while a trio of assistant directors — James McKay, Errol Taggart and Nick Grinde — worked with the second units. Once again Sherwood Forest and Lake Sherwood were the basic shooting scenarios, plus the swamp lands of Woodland Park, as well as Big Tujunga and China Flats.

One of the most realistic scenes ever filmed for a Tarzan picture was Weissmuller's underwater river battle with a giant crocodile, a classic scene that was reused several times in the MGM series. In this scene, a desperate Tarzan must swim at full speed to intercept a monster-sized crocodile that is about to devour Jane. Calling upon his every ounce of strength just to hang on and also elude the powerful tail, Tarzan struggles with the mighty amphibian and finally manages to knife it to death.

This fierce watery battle lasted several minutes, with Johnny spending many strenuous hours in the tank to accomplish a few minutes of screen action. Working in approximately eighteen feet of water in a tank on Lot 1, Johnny grappled with the huge mechanical reptile, stabbing it repeatedly with his knife. The simulated death was accomplished when dye sacks in the neck of the creature were cut open by Johnny's knife, and fake blood gushed out from the fatal wounds. (Josephine

McKim doubled as Jane with the crocodile thrashing in the water and trying to flatten her with its wildly spinning tail.) Although this beast was a mechanical creation, a number of times in the Tarzan movies Johnny wrestled with live 'gators that were imported from a local California alligator farm. Although this was dangerous work for Johnny, the risk was minimized by working in a tank of frigid ice water — which made the reptiles lethargic and turned Johnny a shade of pale blue!

On the set in August of 1933 as a guest of MGM was author Edgar Rice Burroughs, who was paid $45,000 by MGM for the rights to produce *Tarzan and His Mate.* He later wrote a letter to his son Hulbert, and among his observations he noted that "the underwater shot of Weissmuller fighting the croc" was going to be "very thrilling." Shortly after signing to be Tarzan, Johnny was invited by Burroughs to his estate in the San Fernando Valley, which he dubbed "Tarzana" in honor of his most famous literary character. Johnny later recalled that Mr. Burroughs would often visit the set during the seventeen years of his run as Tarzan, and the author seemed to be amazed at his ability to work with the various wild animals that were used in each picture.

One of the most exciting and perilous scenes ever filmed for any Tarzan picture was

Johnny riding on the back of an African rhinoceros named Mary, and finally killing the runaway beast with his knife. MGM animal trainer Emerson, GeorgeGeorge Emerson imported the beast from Germany, and rode Mary in the most dangerous scenes shot in the rhino corral on Lot #2. (This rhino was not actually killed nor were any of the wild creatures that did battle with Tarzan in the studio settings. Collapsing knives and fake blood spewed out cinematic illusion, but nevertheless there was genuine danger for the actors who worked with the animals.)

Historical accounts of the filming relate that Weissmuller also rode Mary during part of the scene, despite the pleadings of his wife, Lupe Velez, not to do so. Johnny was never afraid to try dangerous stunts, and he simply told Lupe that riding Mary would be great fun that he didn't intend to pass up! This particular rhino was indeed a dangerous beast, and at one point charged and smashed into a heavy metal cage that enclosed a camera crew and their equipment. (During his many years of battling lions, rhinos and alligators, Johnny received more than his share of cuts, bruises, scrapes, cracked ribs, and even a broken nose at least twice. Johnny didn't flinch when asked to try a risky stunt during his years as Tarzan — he enjoyed the challenge and it was all part of the job description.)

Newsweek magazine noted the following

about this famous scene in the picture: "The most daring feat of all is the hero's dangerous act on the back of a bona fide rhinoceros. George Emerson, former big animal man of Ringling Brothers, declared that he had never heard of anyone, trainer or actor, who had ridden on the back of this fierce animal . . . Johnny Weissmuller, as well as Tarzan, must have been born under a lucky star."

In another memorable scene, Tarzan is enraged when the heartless Arlington shoots one of the elephants so they can follow the dying beast to the elephant graveyard. Tarzan picks up the coward and lifts him over his head like he were merely a rag doll, postponing his death only at the frantic request of Jane. (There was no trick photography involved here, just the brute strength of one of filmdom's earliest strongmen, Johnny Weissmuller.)

Alfredo Codona once again doubled for Johnny in the treetops, and the Flying Codonas performed the scene where Tarzan, Jane and Big Cheeta do their own jungle "trapeze" act. An adagio team executed the stunt of Jane diving from a high branch into Tarzan's waiting arms below. (Johnny and Maureen also did the stunt themselves, but her leap was from a much lower platform; the effect being that it looked very much like they had executed the high dive themselves.)

Bert Nelson again doubled for Weissmuller

in battles with first a lion and then a lioness, but Johnny did grapple with Jackie the lion in the climactic scene before Nelson took over the balance of the sequence. The courageous Betty Roth, wife of lion trainer Louis Roth, doubled for Miss O'Sullivan in the dramatic scene where two snarling lions have Jane trapped on a narrow ledge.

The heart-pounding finale with Tarzan backing slowly through dozens of the killer beasts was actually Weissmuller on a sound stage in front of the rear projection of the lions. This classic scene with Johnny giving off his thunderous call for help to his faithful elephant friends is certainly a cinematic masterpiece. The sequence was so ingeniously conceived and edited that it raises the hackles on your neck, even with the vague realization of the viewer that this was some of the earliest conceptions of "trick" photography.

Perhaps the most magnificent scene in this picture is of Weissmuller astride the lead elephant of the herd called by Tarzan to surround the elephant graveyard, while his savage female counterpart (Maureen) rides on the head and trunk of a smaller pachyderm. This portrait was both primitive and majestic, watching two wild creatures themselves riding to the rescue on the majestic beasts that were the friends of Tarzan. There were some very genuine risks involved for Johnny and Maureen in working with the many dangerous animals used in the Tarzan pictures.

The elaborate production of *Tarzan and His Mate* was more than a year in the planning stage and took approximately eight months to complete the filming. The final cost of $1.3 million dollars was an enormous sum for the Depression and almost double the cost of filming *Tarzan, the Ape Man*. In the United States and abroad, the film was a smashing, resounding success which played to massive audiences (especially in foreign markets, punctuating the international appeal of Tarzan). When the picture opened in New York in mid-April of 1934, it was received with thunderous applause and appreciation by fans across the nation.

Meanwhile the critics were even more lavish in their praise than they had been for *Tarzan, the Ape Man*. At this point in time Johnny could do no wrong, at least when it came to his role of Tarzan. Weissmuller was truly "King of the Jungle," as noted in these samples of critical reviews of *Tarzan and His Mate*, the crown jewel of the long-running Tarzan adventure series.

"When a film such as *Tarzan and His Mate* comes along, the writer breathes a sigh of relief. The decision is simple. If you like romance and adventure, and have enough imagination to shut off your analytical mental machinery for a couple of hours, you will have a perfectly swell time watching Tarzan and his animal pals weave the sort of heroic drama that our fondest childhood dreams were made of. What boy hasn't dreamed of himself as the jungle knight created by Johnny Weissmuller — and what girl hasn't imagined herself a Maureen O'Sullivan, being rescued every 15 or 20 minutes by her primitive sweetheart?

"And another thing: Goodness knows there are few enough films that are suitable for children. Even in this one there are one or two scenes and a few lines of dialogue without which the picture would have been more acceptable juvenile entertainment. But taken as a whole, it is an exceptionally fine thing for your youngsters to see, and the best part of it is that you can go along with them and get just as much kick out of it as they do. When a film like that comes along, it's news.

"Mr. Weissmuller, as Tarzan, is more at home before the camera than in his first film, but fortunately the producers have seen fit to keep him in his wild state, and we find that his knowledge of the English language has not been allowed to grow to the point where he has much talking to do. In his athletic activities — such as diving and swimming, and scrapping with the critters — he is everything that could be desired. I doubt if there is any kind of motion picture entertainment more enjoyable to the average fan than the spectacle of a well built athlete in action.

"Miss O'Sullivan as Tarzan's wife (yes sir, his wife, in case you've been wondering) continues to be one of the most delightfully natural and naive of the screen's young ladies.

"All of which has probably given you the impression that this reporter thinks you should see *Tarzan and His Mate*. And I might add that you should take the children, but the advice would be superfluous. Every youngster in the country will probably want to see it — and I don't blame them." *Family Circle* (Harry Evans)

"Having apparently dwelt in the jungle since they met in *Tarzan, the Ape Man*, Johnny Weissmuller, the swimming ace, and the comely Irish colleen, Maureen O'Sullivan, are now to be seen at the Capitol in a sequel to their first adventure. The current offering, which is hailed as *Tarzan and His Mate*, is, if anything, even more fantastic than its predecessor . . . Aside from the wild tale, this film is a marvel from a photographic standpoint. Tarzan has his hand-to-hand encounters with leopards, hippopotamuses, and other beasts, and Jane has anything but a merry time with several lions . . . Needless to say that Miss O'Sullivan and Mr. Weissmuller acquit themselves in the same favorable fashion they did in their former hectic experiences." *New York Times*

(Mordaunt Hall)

"There are just as many yodels, just as many lions, just as many elephants, just as much of Cheeta and just as much excitement in *Tarzan and His Mate* as there was in *Tarzan, the Ape Man*. With the result that this sequel in the adventures of the jungle-hero is every bit as entertaining as its predecessor... The cast plays capably, including an amazingly competent crocodile (mechanical) which puts plenty of vim and vigor into its scene! The picture is liable to leave you limp — but it provides a generous amount of thrilling and diverting adventure." *Daily Times* (Doris Arden)

"*Tarzan and His Mate* is the mild name Metro-Goldwyn-Mayer have chosen for the most exciting movie of the season. So exciting is it that even in the most ludicrously impossible scenes, the audience sits on the edge of the seats, cheering lustily and praying for the safety of the agile ape-man (Weissmuller) ..." *Newsweek*

"*Tarzan and His Mate*, happens, it is true, to be much the best directed and best photographed film in the entire Tarzan cycle. With an admirable sense of delicacy, the producers have refrained from intruding for too long at a stretch on the tropical intimacies of Tarzan (Weissmuller) and his noble English-born mate (Maureen O'Sullivan)." *The Nation* (William Troy)

348

It was obvious now that the Tarzan series would continue for many years to come, although no one could have predicted that Johnny would last seventeen years in the title role. Author Edgar Rice Burroughs even suggested that a new Tarzan picture should be produced each and every year, and be released in the spring to coincide with the arrival of the circus.

To this end Mr. Burroughs decided to produce his own Tarzan film independent of the MGM series, and intended to film on location in the jungles of Guatemala. Planning a 1935 release, Burroughs' request to borrow Johnny Weissmuller for his production was flatly turned down by MGM. With his number one choice for Tarzan (Weissmuller) basking in the limelight of success, Herman Brix was chosen to star in *The New Adventures of Tarzan*. (The handsome and athletic Brix, a teammate of Weissmuller's on the 1928 Olympic squad, won a silver medal in the shot put in the Ninth Olympiad.)

After weeks of filming under difficult conditions in the jungles of Guatemala, the finished product was decidedly inferior to the exciting brand of Tarzan action that Johnny Weissmuller had brought to the screen in his first two portrayals. Burroughs was the first to agree that their film was virtually a disaster, as he recorded in a memorandum

349

dated March 5, 1935:

"MGM, with little or no story, made two successful pictures because of the tremendous amount of action injected. We must face the fact that we have little or no action in our picture; and what impressed me last night was the fact that we had sacrificed both the story and the scenic shots in an effort to achieve action that was either not there or not worthwhile, and what action there is, is not particularly thrilling."

Sparse audiences checked out this new Tarzan picture upon its release in 1935, and agreeing with Burroughs' own evaluation of the lackluster film, movie fans decided to wait for the next Weissmuller adventure coming in 1936, *Tarzan Escapes*.

Burroughs had challenged the mighty forces of nature with his Guatemalan expedition, and unfortunately failed. A sequel released in 1938 was entitled *Tarzan and the Green Goddess*, and attempted to recoup the money invested in the original motion picture. (This was an even weaker film that was simply a remix of *The New Adventures of Tarzan*, with some added footage.)

Burroughs learned a hard lesson that he was an author and not a Hollywood producer, and went back to writing stories about his jungle hero, Tarzan. Burroughs admired Johnny Weissmuller as the greatest Tarzan, and for making his fictional character even more famous and successful than even he imagined was possible.

In the aftermath of this jungle disaster, erstwhile Tarzan Herman Brix, in order to distance himself from his former career as an athlete and the Tarzan role, changed his name to Bruce Bennett. The former Tarzan went on to a long and successful career as both a leading man and supporting actor in numerous dramatic films including *Sahara* (1943), *Dark Passage* (1947), *Treasure of the Sierra Madre* (1947), *Sudden Fear* (1952), and *Three Violent People* (1957).

*Johnny Weissmuller, Johnny Sheffield, and
Maureen O'Sullivan*

A classic pose of
Johnny Weissmuller as Tarzan

Reproduced below (in three parts) is a single entry from the parish register, Volume VII, p.24, for the town of Freidorf. Johnny's date of birth was June 2, 1904, and the baptism was performed on June 5, 1904. (The photocopy of this document was sent by the mayor of Freidorf to a friend of the author in Germany, Carolin Kopplin, and forwarded to the author in 1995.)

Date of birth / Baptism   Name   Sex / Birth

#39 June 2nd / 5th   Janos (Johann) male / legit.

Parents and profession   Religion   Residence

Weissmuller, Peter (day laborer from Varjas)
Kersch, Elizabeth   (from Freidorf)

Borstner, Janos   Oschsenfelder, Wendel
Zerbesz, Katharina

*William "Big Bill" Bachrach and
his prize student, Johnny*

Johnny and Peter at ages three and two,
respectively

Mrs. and Mrs. Weissmuller with sons
Johnny and Peter

Johnny and his brother Petey . . .
I.A.C. teammates, January 1923

357

*Johnny always loved the children . . . and
they adored him (circa 1922)*

1924 Paris Olympics . . .
after winning 400-meter semifinal

*Johnny and "Duke" Kahanamoku at the
1924 Paris Olympics . . . a gold medal for
Weissmuller and the silver for his American
teammate in the 100-meter freestyle*

*A happy young man at the 1928
Amsterdam Olympics . . . double gold medal
winner in the 100-meter freestyle and
4x200-meter relay event*

At the Midwick Country Club, Pasadena, California (August 25, 1925). Johnny won numerous pro-am tournaments during 50 years of golfing . . . also had five holes-in-one during his lifetime.

*Johnny preparing to do live radio drama
for B.V.D. The dapper fellow next to him is
Ed Sullivan . . . future television star.*

Buster Crabbe on the left, Johnny on the right . . . 1927 swim meet

Johnny proudly representing the United States at the opening ceremonies of the 1928 Amsterdam Olympics (Bud Houser is behind Johnny with the American flag)

The "King of Swimmers" and his trophies

Director Woody Van Dyke with
Edgar Rice Burroughs and Johnny

Johnny and his new bride, Bobbe Arnst,
pose affectionately in Miami Beach
The couple met on Valentine's Day, 1931,
and were married two weeks later

Bobbe Arnst is flanked by her husband Johnny, and his good pal and partner in the comedy diving team, Stubby Kruger. Dressed in their B.V.D.s, they are performing at the Ambassador Hotel Pool, Los Angeles (Sept. 11, 1931)

1932 Olympic backstroke champion Eleanor Holm and Johnny pose for B.V.D.

A million dollar smile . . . after signing his new contract with MGM, 1931

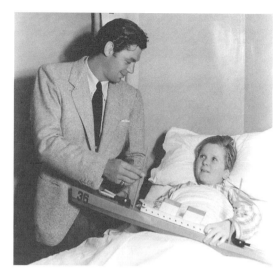

Johnny presents a toy boat to MGM child star Jackie Cooper at the Hollywood Hospital after an appendix operation

Two of MGM's "biggest" stars . . . Johnny Weissmuller and Spanky Mc-Farland of "Our Gang"

Johnny showing off his brawn . . .
how long can he hold this pose?

*Johnny's first car: 1932 Chevrolet Six
two-door roadster convertible*

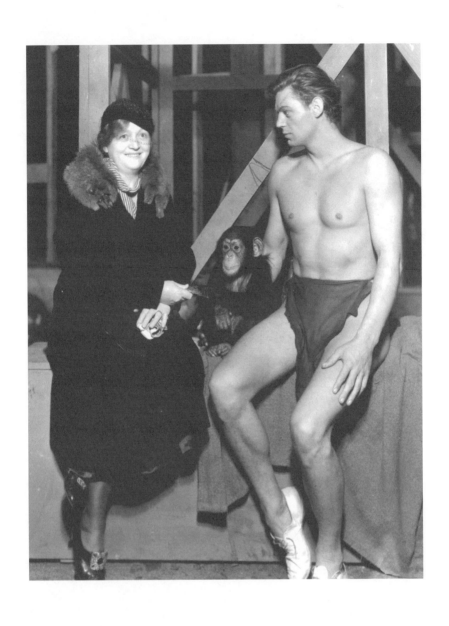

*Johnny with his mother, Elizabeth,
and a favorite chimp*

*Happy days for Johnny and Lupe at the
Trocadero cafe*

*Johnny and Lupe at the Little Club with
Adrienne Ames and Bruce Cabot*

*Johnny and Lupe at Paddington Station in
London, October 5, 1934*

Johnny and his two favorite girls . . .
Mother Elizabeth and wife, Lupe Velez

Johnny and Lupe aboard the Santa
Guadalupe, Catalina Island, 1935

*Johnny takes his unofficial turn at July,
1938 swim meet*

*The quintessential Johnny . . . super sailor
prepares for an ocean voyage*

*"Johnny Weissmuller has
World's Finest Physique"*

Johnny with his "Tarzan" speedboat and lifeguard uniform, Santa Monica, 1933

Lupe and Johnny at Catalina Island for the Bobby Jones Tournament (1937)

*Wartime photo of wet Johnny . . . he signed
thousands of these for veterans*

The stars of the show . . . Johnny, Maureen and Cheeta in "Tarzan, the Ape Man"

"Tarzan, the Ape Man" (1932)

The elephant graveyard . . . "Tarzan and His Mate" (1934)

The jungle lovers of "Tarzan and His Mate" (1934)

*The famous cage rescue from
"Tarzan Escapes" (1936)*

*Tarzan and Boy at the grave site of Jane
. . . this scene doesn't exist in the picture*

A classic pose from "Tarzan's Secret Treasure" (1941)

The three stars of "Tarzan's New York Adventure" plus Cheeta

"Now . . . Tarzan Make War!"
Johnny with Frances Gifford in "Tarzan
Triumphs" (1943)

Acquanetta as the savage priestess of
"Tarzan and the Leopard Woman" (1946)

Linda Christian with Johnny in "Tarzan
and the Mermaids" (1948)

Wedding day photo
Johnny and Beryl August 20, 1939

Johnny with son John Scott on the set of
"Tarzan's New York Adventure"

The four stars of "Swamp Fire" (1946)
Buster Crabbe, Carol Thurston,
Virginia Grey, and Johnny Weissmuller

A happy Johnny as "Jungle Jim"

The wedding day of Johnny and
Allene Gates . . . January 29, 1948
The happy couple tied the knot at the
Donner Trail Dude Ranch

*Johnny receives his Hall of Fame Award in
1950 for being named
"Greatest Swimmer of the Half-Century"
(Duke Kahanamoku is crouched next to
Johnny . . . Allene is behind her husband)*

Jungle Jim and his pet crow . . .
"Mark of the Gorilla" (1950)

Jungle Jim springs into action!

Johnny and Maria in Kingston, Jamaica
enjoying a belated honeymoon

Johnny is twice blessed here . . . wife and stepdaughter Lisa

Johnny enjoying the pool action at the Swimming Hall of Fame

Johnny receives thousands of get-well cards from his fans while recuperating at the Motion Picture Hospital after his 1977 stroke

Swimming to glory . . . Johnny Weissmuller, World's Greatest Swimmer

The marble stone marker of Johnny Weissmuller . . . Valley of the Light cemetery, Acapulco, Mexico

CHAPTER TWENTY

Not Quite Heaven

With the immense success of the first two Tarzan pictures, one would assume that Johnny would be guaranteed all the happiness that heaven would allow. However, Lupe's emotional state was always unstable — at best — her entire life. She was deeply afraid that her home would be robbed, and thus had iron bars installed on all the windows. Further evidence of her paranoia involved a tear-gas container installed in the Weissmuller automobile that was supposed to be a deterrent against theft. Her convoluted statements to the press concerning Johnny, as well as the unfounded accusations against her husband, also confirmed her emotional instability.

With their relationship in the usual state of romantic chaos, Lupe headed for England in October of 1934 to star in *The Morals of Marcus* (1935), a melodrama with Ian Hunter. On October 5th, Lupe and Johnny arrived together at Paddington Station on the Ile de France boat-train. Johnny had finished his promotional work for *Tarzan and His Mate*, and wanted to be with his wife while she worked in Twickenham on her new movie.

Lupe was still a marketable star in Great Britain, and made two additional British films in 1936: *Gypsy Melody*, and *Mad About Money* (which wasn't released in the U.S. until 1938). During the four-year period 1935 to 1938, Lupe appeared in only a single American film, an RKO comedy called *High Flyers*, in which she was billed third to the team of Bert Wheeler and Robert Woolsey.

Marital troubles between Johnny and Lupe continued unabated, and on the second day of January, 1935, she once again filed a petition for divorce. Lupe's imagination was running as wild as her own spirit, as she charged that Johnny during the last six months "had continued his practice of cursing and swearing at her and throwing furniture around, parts of which at times struck her, cutting and bruising her."

Beginning to weary of Lupe's antics and delusions, Johnny agreed to a divorce through his own statement to the press on January 7, 1935. He vehemently denied, however, that he had ever hit her with pieces of furniture, as she had charged. (If Johnny ever threw any furniture, it was probably at her parrot: an annoying little bird that included in its incessant Spanish squawking a simple phrase in English, "Hi, Gary! Hi, Gary! Pretty boy . . ." The parrot had been a present from Gary Cooper to Lupe, during their high-voltage relationship at the beginning of the decade.)

To be fair to Lupe, she was under the stress of being unemployed after her contract was terminated by MGM. Although the marriage seemed doomed, Johnny and Lupe reconciled once again when she dropped her divorce suit and all the charges. Getting back to work would be the best thing for Lupe, but unfortunately Miss Velez was "dead" in Hollywood for the time being. The few offers that came her way quickly dissipated into motes of dust, further frustrating her.

This was a lady who had been very "hot" in Hollywood for the previous six years; suddenly she was considered "poison" by Tinseltown producers. One would have to consider the theory that Lupe was indeed "blackballed" from the American film industry for the next several years, after the 1934 investigation into the Communist influence in Hollywood. Credibility isn't stretched too far to see a possible connection between Lupe being named in the investigation, and the fact that she couldn't find a job in Hollywood for the next several years (with one minor exception).

Johnny knew that to save his marriage to Lupe, he would have to help her career. In

1936, Johnny and Lupe signed to do a vaudeville tour, in which they were paid $5,500 per week as a team. Together they performed a "Tarzan and Jane" skit, capitalizing on the popularity of Johnny's screen character. Lupe Velez did what she did best on stage: singing, dancing, and clowning around. She also revealed a marvelous talent to impersonate some of the top actresses of the day, including Gloria Swanson, Dolores Del Rio, Katharine Hepburn, as well as French silent film star, Jetta Goudal. Lupe also brought her stage act to London in the fall of 1936, for an Adelphi Theatre revue, but returned on Christmas Day to join her husband for the holidays.

The long separations with Lupe working in England seemed to stabilize their relationship, and thus the marriage continued on its rocky course. Meanwhile, Johnny garnered some further negative press from a smear article written by a Chicago writer, which was titled, "Johnny, the Man-Monkey."

This piece of tripe penned by a hack writer accused Johnny of living the high life in Hollywood, while his mother was still working her job as a cook for the Turn-Verein Society in Chicago, and in essence living in "poverty." This was the depths of the Depression, of course, and there was plenty of poverty in every city of America.

But Johnny was wrongfully accused in this situation. He had been sending his mother a generous allowance each month that paid her bills, and in fact had offered to buy her a house in Los Angeles if she wished to move to the West Coast. Mrs. Weissmuller didn't have to work unless she chose to — which she did. She enjoyed her life in Chicago's North Town, her job, her friends, and her beloved St. Michael's church, the center of many of her activities. Her younger son Peter, who turned 30-years-old in 1935, still shared the Cleveland Avenue family home with his mother.

Elizabeth Weissmuller was proud of all of her eldest son's accomplishments, first as a champion swimmer and now as the famed Tarzan of the movies. (Now of course he was the "defamed" Tarzan of the movies.) MGM released a statement declaring the slanderous article to be completely unfounded, and demanded (and received) a retraction from the paper that had printed the original article. This was necessary damage control, but most of Johnny's fans recognized the article as it was — a biased pack of lies from an unknown writer seeking a name for himself.

Eventually Mother Weissmuller did accede to Johnny's wishes to move to Los Angeles. It was with considerable remorse that she left her home of 25 years — the North Town neighborhood of Chicago — and all of her memories behind. Johnny bought a house for his mother and Peter, who also pulled up his roots to join his famous brother in Hollywood. (Peter became a stunt man and earned a solid reputation while working for MGM and other studios.)

Meanwhile, amidst the commotion of his personal life, Johnny had a job to do — Tarzan of the movies. It was pretty clear by now that Johnny was going to be Tarzan, and that he would not be acting in other motion pictures as originally predicted.

Johnny's star as Tarzan was shining so brightly that MGM didn't want to take a chance and put him in another film that might bomb, and thus tarnish his screen image as the heroic jungle man. For better or for worse, Johnny was typecast as Tarzan the ape-man forevermore.

Johnny's next assignment would eventually be titled *Tarzan Escapes*, and again he was teamed with Maureen O'Sullivan, who was a major cog in the MGM film factory. The busy actress was featured in no less than eight films during the two years (1935-36) that *Tarzan Escapes* went through its various stages of chaos, and finally, completion.

This troubled production required fourteen months to complete and underwent almost a complete metamorphosis before finally being released in November of 1936.

Actually two Tarzan pictures were produced, with the initial version relegated to a dungeon somewhere in the bowels of MGM. They then started over with a new director, producer, scriptwriter, a drastically altered story line, revised cast and a substantially altered crew.

The original production staff had included James McKay as director, and Karl Brown authored a script tentatively titled *Tarzan Returns*. Contributing to the screenplay was John Farrow (who was engaged to Maureen O'Sullivan).

Tarzan and His Mate had been released in the spring of 1934, and MGM had fully expected that the new Tarzan adventure would be ready for release by Christmas of 1935. Production was underway by July, and concluded after 95 days of shooting in October. Perhaps feeling that they needed to rush *Tarzan Returns* to compete with Edgar Rice Burroughs' 1935 release of *The New Adventures of Tarzan*, MGM had shot itself in the foot and created a substandard motion picture. After screening *Tarzan Returns*, the MGM decision makers decreed the picture in its present form was unacceptable for various reasons, including the lack of a central plot menace.

After the Burroughs' film failed at the box office, MGM was determined not to make the same mistake by releasing a bomb. By January of 1936, the pink slips were handed out; it was necessary to bite the financial bullet and practically start from scratch, with numerous changes including a new title: *Tarzan Escapes.*

Richard Thorpe took over as director, and worked from a new script written by Cyril Hume. Thorpe was famous in Hollywood for only needing one take to complete a scene; he was a skilled craftsman who directed well over 100 films during his long career. (He would also direct the final three MGM Tarzan pictures, *Tarzan Finds A Son, Tarzan's Secret Treasure,* and *Tarzan's New York Adventure.*) The newly titled *Tarzan Escapes* went back into production in July of 1936 and concluded in September, with the final cost ballooning to well over one million dollars.

Significant cast changes included Darby Jones replacing Everett Brown as Bomba, and the bumbling character of Rawlins (Herbert Mundin) was added. Rawlins provided comic relief but also proved to be a true friend of Tarzan's, and risks his own life to warn him of mortal danger. Initially terrified of the ape-man when he drops from the trees like the wild man of Borneo, Rawlins develops a potent respect for Tarzan when he gets to know him. "Mr. Tarzan is the finest gentleman I've ever known," confides Rawlins to Jane.

Tarzan Escapes had Rita and Eric Parker

(Benita Hume and William Henry) seeking out their cousin Jane in Africa, to inform her of a large inheritance that she must return to England to claim. Their safari is guided by the unscrupulous Captain Fry (John Buckler), who secretly schemes to cage Tarzan and exhibit him around the world like a sideshow freak.

When Jane is reunited with Rita and Eric, she offers her life in the jungle with Tarzan as proof she doesn't desire the money waiting for her in England. However, when Jane discovers that they have financed the expedition with their last savings, she decides to return to England to sign the documents and then let them have all of the money. Tarzan is dejected when he learns that Jane is leaving their home, if only temporarily.

As the safari departs, Rawlins suspects that Captain Fry is planning to lure Tarzan into his cage, and doubles back to warn his friend. Fry catches up with Rawlins in the jungle, and in cold blood shoots the little man in the back. Fry then tricks Tarzan into his cage with the false story that Jane has left him forever for a new life in England.

Meanwhile, the safari is captured by a savage tribe who also claim the caged ape-man as their prize. Desperate to help Jane, Tarzan escapes with the aid of his loyal elephants, who rip open the bars of his cage. Tarzan rescues Jane and her friends, who narrowly escape through a cave permeated with smoke and slimy creatures. Fry is the last to emerge from the cave, and Tarzan orders the cold-blooded killer back into the bog, knowing he will die — this is his death sentence for murdering Rawlins. Jane is reunited with Tarzan, and she vows never to leave his side again.

(Originally filmed was a terrifying scene with the safari attempting to traverse a creepy, haze-shrouded swamp that was infested with deadly vampire bats and hostile pygmies. This exciting vampire bat scene was regrettably lost on the cutting room floor, and perhaps was considered too horrifying for the juvenile audiences expected to view the film.)

To pacify the censors and the rigid Production Code of 1934, Maureen O'Sullivan's revealing outfit from *Tarzan and His Mate* was replaced in *Tarzan Escapes* with a ragged jungle shift that displayed a lot less "skin" and toned down her sexuality. An underwater swimming "ballet" similar to the one in the previous film was used; however, this time they kept the basic jungle attire on the couple. After their playful swim, Jane responds in kind to Tarzan's "look of love." Her expression melts into submissive sensuality, and she releases the orchid in her hand into the slow river current. The scene fades to black, with the obvious implication that Tarzan and his mate will consummate their love for each other. Back in the 1930s, they knew how to do a love scene with class. This was an era of romance, rather than blatant sex in the cinema.

Johnny did an excellent job of portraying remorse and desolation at the thought of Jane leaving him to return to England. Weissmuller never claimed to be a great actor, and the restrictions put on his character didn't give him much latitude for artistic expression. Nevertheless you could always feel genuine heartfelt emotion coming from his Tarzan.

Once again the love scenes of Weissmuller and Miss O'Sullivan were tender and touching, giving the story clearly a memorable romantic theme as well as being a thrilling jungle escapade. Although not a true classic in the sense as the first two films of the series, *Tarzan Escapes* succeeded as a first-rate adventure that enraptured audiences worldwide once again. It took two tries to get it right, but the result was well worth the extra effort.

Throughout the years, Johnny always enjoyed telling the story of one of his most harrowing experiences while filming *Tarzan Escapes*. On one particular day a thrilling scene was to be filmed with Johnny in a steel cage, that was to be thrown off of a cliff into the river by his antagonists in the story. Tarzan's elephants would then come to his rescue and extricate him from his watery grave, and pull apart the bars on the locked cage so Tarzan could escape. (And thus the title of the film!)

Johnny was testing the cage during rehearsals and the lock jammed. Suddenly one of the elephants that were his would-be rescuers accidentally knocked the cage into the tank that served as the river, with Johnny locked inside! Panic struck the set, as the star of the show was locked in a steel cage submerged in a tank of water! Rushing to the scene of the accident was director Richard Thorpe, cameraman Clyde de Vinnade Vinna, animal trainer Emerson, GeorgeGeorge Emerson, and everyone else close enough to help.

Johnny knew that he could hold his breath for at least three minutes, perhaps longer. Now he was trapped in a cage submerged underwater, and all he could do was hold his breath until he was rescued. A few anxious minutes later the cage was hoisted out of the tank, and Johnny was found in undamaged condition. In his years of playing water polo he learned how to hold his breath and stay underwater for several minutes. In this instance, that unusual ability probably saved his life.

The conclusion of filming on *Tarzan Es-*

capes signaled a new beginning for Maureen O'Sullivan, who married John Villiers Farrow on September 12, 1936 when she was 25-years-old. To Maureen, the dashing Australian was the most exciting man in Hollywood — anywhere, for that matter. From the beginning of their life together, Maureen wanted to have a lot of children. To that end, she succeeded — Maureen and John Farrow produced a total of seven children. Farrow was just beginning his career as a director and wasn't making a lot of money, so Maureen had to keep making movies. Thankfully, she was able to find the time to make three more excellent Tarzan adventures with Johnny, before she retired from the screen for several years to raise her children.

Johnny was happy for Maureen when she married Farrow, whom he had known for several years. Maureen was one of Johnny's closest friends in Hollywood and the object of many of his practical jokes, often on the set of the Tarzan movies. In 1991, Maureen admitted her affection for Johnny, as she fondly remembered:

"We were dear friends. He was simple, unpretentious, without conceit — a wonderful big kid."

Meanwhile, Johnny's relationship with Lupe was remarkably stable for the time being. After their brief separation in January of 1935, the waters of their marriage remained relatively calm through all of 1936 and 1937. It did seem to Johnny that everything in their home was Lupe's, including the pet Chihuahuas that he had given her their first Christmas together. To help balance this situation, Johnny brought home a dog one day that he rescued from the animal pound. The large dog was only a mutt, and mutts in those days were "put to sleep" (euthanized) if they went unclaimed after a short stay at the pound. Johnny called the dog "Otto," and he now had an ally in the household — a canine friend to take for walks and for company when Lupe was working out of town.

Although Johnny and Lupe managed to stay out of the headlines, Mr. Weissmuller caught some negative press twice in a 30-day period in the fall of 1936 while he was in New York to promote *Tarzan Escapes*. In the first instance, a patently absurd rumor started that had baseball player Lou Gehrig replacing Johnny as the next Tarzan. B. R. Crisler of the *New York Times*, apparently bitter that he couldn't get an interview with Johnny about this rumor, wrote the following bit of nonsense in his *Times* column "Film Gossip of the Week," dated October 25, 1936:

"Apology: This space was reserved for a story about Tarzan till a very late hour. First we tried to get in touch with Johnny Weissmuller, the discontinued Tarzan, who was said to be sulking like Achilles, in the Hotel Lombardy, but were assured by the switchboard girl that he had just sailed for England, probably to brood. Then we called Lou Gehrig, the home run king and Tarzan-apparent, at his New Rochelle home and learned that, tired but happy, he had gone fishing to recuperate from his session the day before with the New York press.

"We wanted a statement from Mr. Weiss-muller because we felt that his case is a peculiarly poignant one, as the most promi-nent living ex-Tarzan — MGM having sold its rights to the handsome and titled pithecanthrope without selling its rights to Mr. Weissmuller. Our reasons for wanting to get a statement from Lou Gehrig, on the other hand, should be apparent to any red-blooded sports-loving American. But always ready to give up at the first hint of difficulty, we decided just to drop the matter till Lou and his dimples definitely get on the screen — a place where, it seems to us, they have al-ways belonged — home runs or no home runs."

The rumor had got its start a few days ear-lier when the Associated Press reported that Christy Walsh, business manager for Gehrig, said that his client was interested in starring as Tarzan should Johnny Weissmuller decide to abdicate his throne. Walsh contacted Sol Lesser, who was currently searching for an actor to portray Tarzan in his upcoming *Tar-*

zan's Revenge, and indicated that Gehrig would be interested in the lead role (a role that eventually went to Glenn Morris). When Gehrig was asked about the possibility of starring as Tarzan, he responded in a glib manner. "Maybe they'll have an ape slinging coconuts at me and give me an old-fashioned war club to belt them back," said Lou with a smile.

Gehrig never did play Tarzan in the movies, but he did sign a contract with Sol Lesser to make movies. The 1938 contemporary western, *Rawhide*, was the only film role for Gehrig — he portrayed a baseball player who hangs up his mitt to take up a peaceful existence on a ranch. Lou Gehrig, "The Iron Horse," was the most beloved baseball player in America at this time (after the 1934 retirement of Babe Ruth), and as of yet had not developed any symptoms of the disease that would force his early retirement in 1939 and sadly end his life just two years later. (Gary Cooper, who played a minor role in the life of Johnny Weissmuller, would portray Gehrig in the 1942 film biography, *Pride of the Yankees*.)

Johnny was still at his peak as Tarzan, and Gehrig continued to do what he did best — hit home runs and play first base for the New York Yankees. But a month later Johnny got some additional unwanted publicity from the following headline in the November

25th *New York Times*:

"FILM TARZAN IRKED BY NIGHT CLUB ROW — Weissmuller Denies It Was He Who Punched Naval Officer in Disputed Melee." The *Times* article added: "Different versions were current yesterday of a fist fight that enlivened the Stork Club early yesterday morning and revolved around Johnny Weissmuller, the screen Tarzan and former swimming champion, and Lieutenant Cameron Winslow Jr., U.S.N., son of the late Rear Admiral Winslow.

"There is no doubt that Lieutenant Winslow was punched in the left eye, which was discolored and useless all day. But the mystery of who hit the lieutenant remained unsolved. Mr. Weissmuller, who admitted he was at the club and witnessed the sparring, emphatically denied that he struck the naval officer."

Weissmuller told his side of the story to the press from his room at the Hotel Essex: "I was not the guy who hit him," said Johnny. "When I fight, I certainly know who I hit. After the disturbance started, I walked away, and now I get the blame. I never saw this guy in my life before, and I don't want to be known as a nightclub fighter. I have to depend on my reputation."

Apparently Johnny and his guests were partaking in a joke and were all wearing sunglasses, with the first person to remove the glasses paying off a $50 bet to the rest of the group. When Johnny passed the Winslow table, the lieutenant asked, "Why don't you take off those glasses?"

Johnny didn't take the man seriously and replied, "It's just a gag." Winslow then got out of line and provoked the situation when he said, "Well then, why don't you get a haircut?"

Weissmuller was contractually obligated by MGM to wear his hair long for his Tarzan role and to keep it long all the time for his numerous publicity junkets. Nevertheless, Johnny took offense and responded, "Why don't you come outside."

At this point Johnny's companions stepped into the middle of the discussion and started a fight with Winslow, while Johnny was pushed away from the fray by Stork Club waiters. Mr. McBain, a spokesman for the club, dismissed the encounter as "a quiet, simple affair, the flurry of punches lasting less than five minutes, in which Mr. Weissmuller did not participate. It was not a brawl, just a bit of an argument."

The next day a small headline in the *Times* noted:

"TARZAN IS ABSOLVED OF STRIKING OFFICER."

Lieutenant Winslow issued a statement concerning the fiasco at the Stork Club on Tuesday morning, absolving Johnny of any part of the fracas: "Reports that Mr. Weissmuller struck while his gang held me are simply misquotations," said the lieutenant. "I don't believe he got in any punches himself."

At six-foot three-inches and over 200 pounds of muscle during his Tarzan years, there weren't many nightclub patrons who wanted to step outside with Johnny Weissmuller. From time to time a drunk might attempt to impress his lady friend, but Johnny had the ability to laugh off most of these situations. For the most part he avoided nightclub confrontations, and his friends (or club waiters, also his friends) would step in and stop altercations before anything — such as a fist fight — could happen. Johnny was easygoing and it was rare when he lost his temper, but it did happen occasionally during the "Lupe" years. Fortunately he escaped from this Stork Club row with his reputation as a gentleman intact.

Because of the protracted shooting schedule for *Tarzan Escapes*, Johnny was unable to attend the 1936 Olympics held in Berlin, Germany. He had won his five gold medals between the 1924 and 1928 Games, and been an interested spectator at the 1932 Olympics held in Los Angeles. While Johnny was finishing his work on *Tarzan Escapes*, Adolph Hitler's Nazi Germany hosted the

Eleventh Olympiad, an Olympics that brought fame to American track star James Owens, "Jesse" Owens. Also gaining fame at these Games was American track athlete Glenn Morris, who won the decathlon by a wide margin over his closest rival.

Morris is mentioned here because after winning the gold medal in the decathlon, he was the next athlete tabbed for Hollywood stardom. Or at least so thought Sol Lesser, who still owned the rights to produce a Tarzan picture, and planned to release his *Tarzan's Revenge* (1938) during the lull before the next Weissmuller picture, *Tarzan Finds A Son!*, which would be released in the summer of 1939.

Teamed with Morris as Tarzan's love interest was Eleanor Holm, the 1932 gold medal winner in the 100-meter backstroke event. Holm was also a teammate of Glenn Morris on the 1936 Olympic team, and as defending champion in the backstroke event was the prohibitive favorite to triumph again. However, she was expelled from the American Olympic swim team by Avery Brundage, president of the I.O.C., for breaking training during the nine-day ocean voyage to Germany. The specific charges against Miss Holm were for "excessive drinking and shooting craps," which she did not deny. (Miss Holm also had been a teammate of Johnny Weissmuller on the 1928 American swim team, as the 14-year-old schoolgirl from Brooklyn placed fifth in the 100-meter backstroke.)

Portraying Tarzan was Glenn Morris' only starring role in the movies, and in fact a supporting role to John Barrymore and Joan Davis in *Hold That Coed* (1938) was his only other motion picture credit. *Tarzan's Revenge* was also the solitary motion picture role for Eleanor Holm, who did a nice job as the sharp-witted "Eleanor" (who falls in love with a very subdued Tarzan).

Miss Holm did stay in the entertainment business though, and went from Tarzan's jungle to Billy Rose's Aquacade. Eleanor signed to be the star attraction of the Aquacade in 1937, and then married her boss, impresario Billy Rose, in November of 1939. (Eleanor Holm and Johnny Weissmuller would be the stars of Billy Rose's Aquacade at the 1937 Cleveland Exposition, and the 1939 New York World's Fair.)

Sol Lesser had a fascination with Edgar Rice Burroughs' Tarzan character his entire life, but it wasn't until he signed Johnny Weissmuller to star in the RKO films beginning in 1943, that he would find success in producing the Tarzan pictures. To that end, *Tarzan's Revenge* was an entertaining little B-picture, but there was absolutely no comparison between Glenn Morris as Tarzan, and Johnny Weissmuller. It's hardly a fair comparison for Morris, who was only given four words of dialogue in the entire picture and approximately ten minutes of screen time.

But with each Tarzan imitator that came along — and departed quietly — the status of Weissmuller as the greatest Tarzan of them all, grew and grew. The three pretenders to Tarzan's throne during the 1930s — Crabbe, Brix, and Morris — barely put a dent in Johnny's armor, which was as thick as an elephant's prickly hide.

Johnny's relationship with Lupe had cascaded along its charted course like a runaway truck barreling down a mountain road. Bear in mind that there were no brakes on this truck, so a destructive crash was the inevitable fate awaiting the vehicle. They seemed to be back on the road to love in April of 1937 when the newspapers published a photograph of the couple that was captioned, "Lupe Velez and Johnny Weissmuller have again found romance at Santa Catalina Island. Johnny is here to compete in the famous Bobby Jones Trophy Tournament." It was a blissful weekend for Lupe and Johnny, who had become a top amateur golfer and consistently placed high in the standings of these celebrity tournaments.

In the early months of 1938, however, the

marriage of Johnny and Lupe began to enter the final stage before disintegration. After one of their little rows, Johnny had gone out and rented himself a small apartment as a sanctuary when he and Lupe weren't getting along. As noted before, when they loved each other it was great times and marital ecstasy for the couple. But when they fought — and they were legendary Hollywood fighters — it could have been another rematch of Jack Dempsey and Gene Tunney, the hallowed heavyweights of the 1920s.

To temporarily escape his fights with Lupe, Johnny headed for New York to attend the June 22, 1938 heavyweight battle between current champion Joe Louis, and German champion Max Schmeling. Among the 70,000 boxing fans that gathered at Yankee Stadium to witness one of the most ballyhooed boxing matches of all-time, were numerous Hollywood celebrities to include Bob Hope, Gary Cooper, Douglas Fairbanks, Clark Gable, and Weissmuller. Schmeling had knocked out Joe Louis in 1936 in a nontitle fight, and the former champ had designs on regaining the crown that he held from 1930 to 1932. But Louis was determined to defeat the only man who had ever beaten him in the ring, and pounded his opponent into a first round knockout, less than two minutes into the fight. For Johnny, both the fight and the respite were too short — it was soon back to Hollywood and his own boxing partner, Lupe.

One of the final public appearances for Johnny with Lupe was at the Tailwaggers Ball, a gala event held at the Hollywood Hotel. The event was held to raise money for a new animal hospital in Hollywood, and to train seeing-eye dogs for the blind. Hosting the Ball was Bette Davis, a notorious animal lover, and among the guests were some of Hollywood's biggest names: Errol Flynn, James Stewart, Joel McCrea, Norma Shearer, and the wealthy eccentric Howard Hughes (long before he earned his deserved reputation as "reclusive").

According to Velez' biographer Floyd Conner, the final straw for Lupe and Johnny may have come during an evening out at Ciro's nightclub, a popular dance hotspot on the Sunset Strip. During dinner this particular evening, Johnny finally ran out of patience with his beloved Lupe, who raised the ire of her husband with another of her patented public displays of disharmony. From the book, *Lupe Velez and Her Lovers*:

"Lupe and Johnny argued all evening, which was not unusual. She was always throwing fits in public and he usually was able to restrain himself. The strain of the marriage finally took its toll on his patience. Without warning, Johnny grabbed his salad and dumped it on Lupe's head. For once,

Lupe Velez was speechless."

Lupe was no longer speechless on July 20, 1938, when she filed her third divorce suit against Johnny. There had been reconciliations after the 1934 and 1935 divorce actions filed by Lupe, but this time it would be final. In divorce court on August 15, Lupe testified in Superior Court that her husband was "very insulting," went into rages in front of her guests, broke a lamp, called her "dirty names" and threatened to kill her little dog.

"Your Honor," she said to Judge Burnell, "I tried so hard, but it got so I couldn't stand it." Lupe complained to the court that her husband didn't want her to go places, even to a beauty parlor.

"He probably thought you didn't need beauty treatments," commented a sympathetic Judge Burnell.

Johnny did not contest the proceeding, and agreed to pay Lupe $200 per week for 156 weeks (except when she was working). Lupe started working a great deal in 1938 after the divorce, so it was a favorable out-of-court settlement for Johnny. Lupe also got the house in Beverly Hills and the furniture, and Johnny kept his schooner, the *Allure*, and his "Tarzan" speedboat.

After the divorce proceeding, Lupe offered her own version of why the marriage to Johnny finally ended after five explosive years: "Because I am supposed to be nuts everyone blames me entirely for the divorce. In some of my movies I am crazy, sure. That's all right for my work, but offstage I am not temperamental. I am easy to get along with, yes?"

The rhetorical question she asked went unanswered, although Johnny certainly would have had a different viewpoint than Lupe. But Johnny was a gentleman and didn't air his dirty laundry in the press. He was also ready to get back to work, and pre-production had already started on his next Tarzan adventure, *Tarzan Finds A Son!*, which would begin filming in a few short months. The best thing for Johnny — to clear his troubled head — was to get back to work on the Tarzan set.

After the divorce, Lupe and Johnny went their separate ways without any further sparring. Lupe's career, stagnated the past few years, suddenly bloomed to her highest popularity with the succession of "Mexican Spitfire" comedies she starred in for RKO. Hollywood finally found a way to showcase her talents, and she made nine films in the very successful series, beginning with *The Girl From Mexico* (1939) and concluding with *Mexican Spitfire's Blessed Event* (1943).

Sometime after the divorce, Lupe was asked by the press to name the ten "most interesting" men she had ever met in her life. Included on her impressive list were Clark

Gable, boxer Jack Dempsey, President Franklin D. Roosevelt, author Ernest Hemingway, composer George S. Kaufman, her Broadway co-star Ed Wynn, Metropolitan opera singer Laurence Tibbett, composer George Enesco, and labor leader John L. Lewis. Proving Lupe still cared for Johnny, he headed her special list of celebrities and famous Americans. There was no Gary Cooper on the list, while Johnny — her one and only husband in her life — was number one.

Lupe had added more than a few grey hairs to Tarzan's temples during their five-year roller coaster ride of wedlock. There's only one "Lupe" in a man's life, and it's doubtful that Johnny ever completely forgot her. But there was no more Johnny and Lupe. For the time being, it was just Johnny and his mutt dog, Otto.

(Sadly, the faithful Otto died by poisoning when Johnny was in Florida filming segments of his next Tarzan picture. The killer of the mutt was never discovered, and the loss of his pet only further amplified the heartache he had experienced in his years with Lupe Velez.)

CHAPTER TWENTY-ONE

Big John & Little John

MGM knew they had a winning team in Johnny Weissmuller and Maureen O'Sullivan as Tarzan and Jane. They also realized they could make this team even stronger by giving Tarzan and Jane a son — and thus creating new situations to further endear the public to the "family" of Tarzan. The latest Tarzan adventure would be called *Tarzan Finds A Son!*, and what MGM wanted was a miniature Johnny Weissmuller to portray the jungle foundling who becomes their son. The ideal choice would be an athletic boy who could swim, climb trees, and also become an effective actor.

The hunt for the son of Tarzan began with an MGM ad in the *Hollywood Reporter*, seeking a *"Tarzan Jr."* Literally hundreds of young boys were screened for the enviable role, questing a lad who not only looked the part of a boy raised in the jungle, but with the physical stamina to handle the role of Tarzan's son. The winner of the sweepstakes turned out to be seven-year-old Johnny Sheffield, who not only physically filled the bill but was a talented child actor with Broadway stage experience. Johnny was born in Pasadena, California on April 11, 1931, and was your quintessential "All- American" boy.

When English-born actor Reginald Sheffield saw the ad seeking the son of Tarzan, he knew his young son would be perfect for the role. Young Johnny had just finished working in the Broadway play, *On Borrowed Time*, in which he portrayed the grandson of star Dudley Digges. Johnny Sheffield had been a frail and underweight child, and had weighed only four pounds at birth. But his father designed and administered a program of healthy food and vigorous exercise for his son, who blossomed into the picture of perfect health by age five. After his father responded to the ad, Sheffield was interviewed by the MGM hierarchy, by author Edgar Rice Burroughs, and by the star of the show, Johnny Weissmuller.

Weissmuller personally gave the final "OK" on the selection of Sheffield as "Boy," and gave his movie son swimming lessons before and during the production of their first film. Big John developed a strong affection for Little John (as he would be called), and they were very close during the decade that they filmed their eight Tarzan pictures together.

In 1999, John Sheffield was kind enough to allow me to publish his memories of sixty years in the past, when he first met Johnny Weissmuller and gained the role of "Boy." Herewith are Mr. Sheffield's own recollections of what for him was the biggest break in his young life. The year was 1938, and the city was Hollywood, California, where dreams are born.

"Father read an article in the *Hollywood Reporter* which asked: 'Have you a Tarzan Jr. in your backyard?' He thought he did and set up an interview. I was told there were more than 300 boys applying for the job of 'Boy.' Although I didn't know it at the time, the audition was to have two parts: first the 'Screen Test' and then the 'Swimming Test.' Had I known about the latter, I might have entered the former with a bit more trepidation.

"The screen test wasn't going to be too difficult as my acting training came in the Theater, first on the west coast and then on the east coast, with my name 'up in lights' on Broadway in the play *On Borrowed Time*. I had 'paid my dues' as an actor and all that was involved was getting used to working before a camera and the crew rather than a theater audience. My father coached me for the screen test as he had done for the Theater.

"Johnny Weissmuller liked me. It was decided that he should give me a swimming test as part of the selection process. Well, I could

433

not swim a stroke at the time, but Big John said he would give me the test anyway! Someone 'up there' liked me! It was time to get in the water with Tarzan.

"I'll never forget going with one of the world's all-time greatest swimmers to the Hollywood Athletic Club for the test. I went into the locker room with this undefeated Olympic champion and we suited up! Big John knew I couldn't swim; that didn't make any difference to him. He knew Tarzan would have to teach Boy how to swim anyway. Big John was really a super guy, full of life and fun to be with, and he was always kind and attentive to me. As it turned out Big John only wanted to be sure that I wasn't afraid of the water and that I was willing to try to swim. He and Tarzan could handle the rest.

"We arrived poolside (Weissmuller always called it the 'Tank'), Big John dove in the deep end and positioned himself about ten feet from the edge. He told me to jump in and come to him. I took a big jump and when I reached him he had his knee up to form a bench for me to sit on. When I sat on his knee, it was like a concrete abutment and I knew I was safe even though we were in the DEEP end of that BIG WATER FILLED TANK! I was secure even though he was treading water! Johnny was smiling at me. He told me to take a deep breath and hold on.

We went under and he swam back to the side of the tank with me holding on. We later did the same thing on film at Silver Springs. (So you can see a portion of my swim test with Weissmuller today!) It reminds me of the Athletic Club and my first swim with this Olympic champion; we enjoyed many more swims together.

"When we got out of the water and toweled off, Big John announced: 'This kid can swim just fine.' That was it! Tarzan, the Ape Man who swings through the trees and lives way 'up there' on the Escarpment, liked ME!

"So you see it was my father who answered the 'call' and Johnny Weissmuller liked me and picked me to be his son, Boy! It pays to have someone 'up there' who likes you. I have been fortunate that way."

With the critical cast selection of Sheffield as Boy completed, it was now up to screenwriter Cyril Hume to find a way around the Hays Code (the censorship people) in giving Tarzan and Jane a son in *Tarzan Finds A Son!* (They had never been formally married, so the character of Jane would not be allowed to have a baby.) This dilemma was resolved as the story begins with Tarzan finding a baby in the jungle, after the child's parents are killed in a small plane crash. This helpless lost child could not survive in the jungle alone, so he is adopted by Tarzan and Jane and becomes their son. He is a welcome addition to the family of Tarzan, and the proud new daddy — simplistic in his language skills — calls his son "Boy."

A few years later, relatives of the lost boy journey into central Africa to search for traces of the plane crash and any survivors. Sir Thomas Lancing (Henry Stephenson) hopes to find his nephew and his wife and infant son alive, while the unscrupulous Lancings (Ian Hunter, Frieda Inescort) seek proof of their cousin's death — and therefore a claim on the substantial estate. Eventually, the searchers come upon Tarzan and Jane in the jungle, and their young son with the singular name. When the Lancings discover that Boy is the sole survivor of the plane crash, they plot his ultimate demise so they can steal his rightful inheritance. A moral issue is raised between Tarzan and Jane, over what is the best interest for their son. Should he remain in the jungle with his adoptive parents, or return to England with virtual strangers to claim his heritage?

Jane is fooled by the clever Lancings, and agrees to let them take Boy back to London for his education. Of course, Tarzan refuses to listen to any plan that would take his son away from him. Torn between her loyalty to Tarzan and her love for the boy, Jane feels she does the right thing when she traps her mate in a deep grotto so that the Lancings can take her son back to England. The dastardly plot becomes secondary when the safari is captured by the savage Zambeli tribe, and certain death awaits them all. The only man who can save Tarzan's mate is Tarzan, who overcomes insurmountable odds and is reunited once again with Jane and Boy.

Filming began on January 9, 1939, with Richard Thorpe as director and a potentially traumatic experience to all movie fans written into the script: Maureen O'Sullivan's character of Jane was to die at the end of the film, the victim of a Zambeli spear! (Miss O'Sullivan was pregnant as production began on *Tarzan Finds A Son!*, and had asked to be written out of the series so she could concentrate on raising a family with husband John Farrow.)

However, an alternate ending was also filmed about a month after the close of production in which Jane did indeed survive her spear wound. Fortunately after previewing the picture, the MGM brass realized that negative audience reaction to the death of the character of Jane might easily have doomed the series. The studio executives made whatever concessions were necessary to Maureen — the new mother — in order to insure her return to the series. (In the latter stages of her pregnancy, Maureen was photographed from the waist-up, or partially hidden behind tables and other props, to camouflage her condition.) MGM was willing to bend over backwards to keep the successful team of Johnny, Maureen, and Johnny Sheffield together for as many Tarzan adventures as possible.

The stellar cast also included Ian Hunter as the immoral Austin Lancing; Henry Wilcoxon as the shady safari guide; Laraine Day in a small role as Boy's natural mother; and veteran actor Henry Stephenson as Sir Thomas Lancing. Stephenson lent a measure of class to all of his portrayals, and was superb in this story as a man of principle who is murdered for warning his new friends Tarzan and Jane of the evil plot of the Lancings.

Some of the finest underwater swimming scenes in any Tarzan picture were photographed for *Tarzan Finds A Son!* at Silver Springs, Florida near the end of the shooting schedule. The crystal clear water of Silver Springs was the perfect playground for Big John and Little John, who frolicked and splashed underwater for approximately four minutes; at first swimming with a baby elephant named Baby Bea, then playing below-surface hide-and-seek, and then "hitching" a ride behind a huge sea turtle who pulled the ape-man and son along behind like he barely knew they were there.

The playful acts of cavorting, swimming

and diving were so genuine that it was obvious there was a real affection between the screen father and son, and the extended underwater sequence was absorbing and enchanting. The final three minutes of the seven-minute scene had Boy lounging on a giant lily pad, then floating downstream in the swift current towards the waterfalls; a thrilling moment ensued with Weissmuller showing his best Olympic champion swimming form in speeding to rescue Boy. (The MGM river back in Hollywood was the scenario for Boy's near tragic mishap, with a "dump tank" on lot 1 creating the waterfall effect.)

As in previous Tarzan films, a fascinating collection of wild animal footage (mostly reclaimed from *Trader Horn*) was skillfully edited in, including great flocks of birds, crocodiles hungrily gulping their dinners, roaring lions, a herd of elephants, and hippos yawning, exposing cavernous mouths. There was also a vicious battle royal between a leopard and several baboons, and then a wild free-for-all between a black panther, a spotted leopard, and a pack of hyenas. Thanks to the extensive use of stock footage from the previous Tarzan adventures, the cost of producing *Tarzan Finds A Son!* was less than one million dollars ($880,000).

Various working titles had been bantered about by the MGM executives during production, including *Tarzan in Exile* and *Son of Tarzan*, but the final title was perhaps the most appropriate: *Tarzan Finds A Son!* Released in June of 1939, the movie-going public had waited almost three years for the genuine article of a Weissmuller and O'Sullivan Tarzan picture. Movie fans certainly weren't disappointed, as the new adventure was one of the very best of the long-running series. Audiences were also treated to a new process that produced an effective aqua hue to the film print, derived from mixing a sepia tone and a platinum tint; not Technicolor by any means, but it did give a more lifelike quality to the film texture.

Johnny Sheffield as Boy was effectively cast, and was indeed an athletic, miniature version of his mentor, Big John. The lad did most of his own stunt work and portrayed his role beyond the highest expectations. Weissmuller later stated with admiration that young Sheffield was "the greatest child athlete he had ever seen."

In 1998, Johnny Sheffield recalled more of his memories of making this film with Johnny Weissmuller as his mentor:

"It was both scary and great fun when I first went to work at MGM to film *Tarzan Finds a Son*. Scary because it was all new; it was my introduction to 'Hollywood,' and movie making. It was great fun because I was surrounded by the best in the 'Business' at

Metro-Goldwyn-Mayor and I had Johnny Weissmuller as my friend and Jungle Father. This film was my introduction to Tarzan and my jungle family. As soon as I could get around Tarzan (Big John), he taught me to swim and showed me the ropes (uh, vines).

"The soundstage was fitted out with all kind of vine-covered ropes and rigging and I, for the first time in my life, got to swing on vines with the World Champion vine swinger. Tarzan showed me the Vines/Ropes. Big John would say 'hold it this way' . . . 'Push with your legs' . . . 'Watch where you are going!' Many fans report that the minute they got home from the movie theater they were swinging all over the place, too! Tarzan taught me to eat when I was hungry and sleep when I was tired. There weren't any arguments; I did what Tarzan told me to. He gave me values. He taught me to tell the truth; Tarzan hated a liar.

"Jane blew it big time for a while in this one. She was truly sorry so Tarzan forgave her, on the spot! Repentance and forgiveness were part of my training. Tarzan taught me to love and respect the animals and how to communicate with them.

"*Tarzan Finds a Son!* also produced some of my favorite scenes. Like the tarantula scene. The property men showed them to me long before the scene was filmed so I wouldn't be too frightened. Nice try. They scared the you know what out of me. I'll never forget them coming at me. Man, did I yell! When Dick Thorpe said, 'Action,' it all became REAL. Big John told me not to fear the spiders; he said that as soon as I CALLED he would come and rescue me and he did! Tarzan was always there for me."

Sheffield developed his own version of the mighty cry that was used whenever Boy was in trouble and needed Tarzan's help — which was often! Doubling and stunt work that was done for Sheffield was performed by a 32-year-old midget named Harry Monty, who was known professionally as the "Midget Strong Man with the most muscular perfect physique of any small person in the world." Johnny Weissmuller once again showed his great physical strength and athleticism, twice lifting full-grown men cast as African warriors over his head like they were lightweight toys!

Maureen O'Sullivan portrayed her role of Jane with the same depth and sensitivity that was now inherent in her character. The scenes in which she struggles with her own conscience and must decide what's best for her son — and what's best for Tarzan — are extremely heartwarming. Maureen truly was a marvelous actress who made her Jane, the mate of Tarzan, a woman who was believable and courageous — as well as simply beautiful. Her near-fatal confrontation with a hostile spear produced the touching, emotion-evoking reunion of Tarzan and Jane near the picture's conclusion.

The ape-man's tears were genuine, and there wasn't a dry eye in the house as Tarzan gathered his love in his arms with grateful joy when Jane opens her eyes and says, "Darling, everything's all right." Limited by the vocabulary that his Tarzan character was allowed to use, Weissmuller was confined as an actor with very little latitude for artistic expression. However, Johnny was always able to show strong emotion that welled up from his soul, and as Tarzan he continued to be a natural.

After making it big as Tarzan of the movies, Johnny always wanted to expand his horizons and portray other characters on screen. And other studios came calling, asking MGM to loan Weissmuller for their adventure or dramatic picture-in-the-works. But of course these other dramatic roles never came his way, because of MGM's steadfast refusal to allow Johnny to portray any character other than Tarzan. They felt he was too valuable a property, and perhaps his Tarzan image too easily damaged, to take a big risk for perhaps a small financial gain. It had been Thalberg, IrvingIrving Thalberg's policy for several years, NOT to loan out the MGM galaxy of stars to other studios. If movie fans wanted to see Gable, Crawford, or Weissmuller, they could only see them in MGM pictures. Even after Thalberg died in 1936, the policy stayed the same for the time being.

MGM was paying Weissmuller's hefty salary — which was $2,500 per week at this time — and they had complete control over his screen destiny. It was this type of control that had caused progressive-thinking actors Douglas Fairbanks and Mary Pickford (along with their partners Charlie Chaplin and D. W. Griffith), to form their own production company (United Artist's Film Corp.) in 1919 to produce their own films. But Johnny had no such choice — he was under contract to MGM and could only work when they had another Tarzan movie ready to roll into production.

The studio did, however, allow Johnny to participate in swimming exhibitions and major water shows (Aquacades, as they were called). And thus when Billy Rose came calling after the completion of *Tarzan Finds A Son!*, MGM was more than willing to loan Johnny out to Rose for the 1939 New York World's Fair. The executives at MGM were shrewd businessmen and charged Rose $5,000 per week for Johnny's services, while he only received his normal $2,500 per week salary from the studio. Of course this wasn't fair to Johnny, but he was working again at what he loved — swimming and diving — so it wasn't his style to complain. (Complaints fell on deaf ears anyway — it was simply called power.)

Co-starring with Johnny as his fellow headliner was 25-year-old Eleanor Holm, the soon-to-be wife of Billy Rose. Johnny had been friends with Miss Holm since the 1928 Olympics, and on numerous occasions he and Lupe had been dinner companions of Eleanor and her first husband, orchestra leader Art Jarrett. Johnny had also worked with Eleanor at the 1937 Great Lakes Exposition with the city of Cleveland hosting Billy Rose's Aquacade. The dynamic duo had been paid $30,000 for starring together in this particular show, which opened on May 29, 1937 and ran through the summer. Johnny and Eleanor were immensely popular with the fans, and Saturday afternoon crowds of 10,000 people paid $1.50 each to watch the Olympic champions cavort (along with 60 other performers) — executing aquatic stunts in a three-million-gallon stage.

Impresario Billy Rose was a well-known songwriter, night club owner, and Broadway producer in the 1930s who had formerly been married to Fanny Brice. His 1935 Broadway production of "Billy Rose's Jumbo" was later brought to the big screen in 1962. But he is perhaps most famous for his brilliantly-staged Aquacades, and the 1939 World's Fair would be the site of his most spectacular water show ever. Rose was investing

$300,000 of his own money into the show, and he felt he knew what the public wanted — pretty girls! "I won't have much nudity in my Aquacade," Rose told reporters, "but the girls will wear tiny wet bathing suits . . . Listen, I'm no moralist. If I could get results with naked women, I'd put on naked women."

Under the guidance of Rose, a colossal outdoor theater was constructed with a 275-foot pool as the centerpiece of the show. The massive stage on the water's edge — 200-feet deep by 311-feet wide — had 75-foot diving towers on both ends, while a water curtain across the proscenium squirted water 40-feet high. There would be dozens upon dozens (72 to be exact) of lovely young women along with numerous handsome young men — singers, dancers, synchronized swimmers, and divers. Musical entertainment for the gala productions was provided by the Fred Waring Glee Club, and conducted by Vincent Travers. In all there were 220 performers in the company, including the "Last of the Red Hot Mamas," Sophie Tucker, opera star Everett Marshall, and a Morton Downey chorus also entertained the fervent crowds.

Huge audiences would attend the Aquacade shows, which were the most popular event of the New York's World Fair. Several million people attended the Aquacade that summer, including a full house of 8,500

446

on opening night, May 1, 1939. On that day President Roosevelt gave a speech at Flushing Meadows for the opening ceremony, which was also attended by special guest Albert Einstein.

Billy Rose became a millionaire as a result of the immense success and popularity of the Aquacade at the 1939 World's Fair. From the book, *Billy Rose: Manhattan Primitive*, author Earl Conrad notes the following: "The entertainment provided by the swimming spectacle of the approaching Aquacade, featuring Eleanor Holm, Johnny Weissmuller, and later, Buster Crabbe — that was a notch above what most fairs had to offer. It was talent, choreography, pageantry, beauty, and human physical perfection. This Billy organized, even though others provided the art and the performance."

When you as a spectator could watch Johnny "Tarzan" Weissmuller, along with the divine Eleanor Holm, performing feats of skill and grace, with scores of beautiful performers adding to the majesty of the production — well, it was a sight to behold and remember. Headlining the extravaganza were Johnny and Eleanor — other stars included Gertrude Ederle, the first woman to swim the English Channel in 1926, and Pete Desjardins, the two-time gold medal diver from the 1928 Olympics (and a very close friend of Johnny's). Stubby Kruger, "The

King of Comedy Diving," was also there to perform his renowned comedy-diving act with his partner, Johnny Weissmuller.

Another young performer who auditioned but failed to gain a job as a comedy diver was 23-year-old Jackie Gleason, long before he gained his great fame as a TV and motion picture star. Johnny later recalled that Gleason's hilarious "belly-flop" dive from the high board was deemed too dangerous for the show by Billy Rose, who sent the young man packing.

1937 to 1940 were Gleason's lean years, in which the young comic and emcee worked for $75 per week, often bouncing around the country looking for the next gig and meager paycheck. The Aquacade didn't work out for Gleason, but it was the start of a long friendship for Johnny and Jackie, as the tandem often met on the golf course in later years.

Wearing golden swim trunks to highlight his magnificent physique, Johnny performed numerous show dives and aqua "dances" with Eleanor Holm. The highlight of these aqua ballets was a swimming waltz to the music of the Fred Waring orchestra, with Johnny and Eleanor gracefully performing their trademark strokes: the American crawl for him and the backstroke for her. As the waltz became more intimate, Eleanor would have her legs around Johnny's hips, as his powerful stroke propelled them both through the water to the delight of the audience.

Johnny was in such superb physical condition for the Aquacade that he beat the current national freestyle champion, Walter Spence, in a practice 100-yard race at the New York Athletic Club. Weissmuller's time was 48.5 seconds, which was faster than his best time for that race during his amateur career that had ended in 1929. Johnny was helping to train Spence (a future Hall-of-Famer) for the coming national championships when this remarkable moment occurred. The fastest time Johnny had ever posted in the 100-yard freestyle was an American record of 49.8 seconds in 1927. A dozen years after his retirement from amateur swimming, Johnny was faster than he ever was!

A visitor at the 1939 World's Fair was Bing Crosby, who was traveling back from Meadowbrook after a round of golf with his close friend Harvey Shaeffer. Crosby fancied himself a diver, and Bing said to Harvey, "Weissmuller is an old pal of mine. Why don't we go in and catch the show?"

After watching the initial diving show, Crosby bragged to Harvey that he could perform those kind of stunt dives — especially if he had an incentive. A one-hundred dollar bet turned out to be Bing's incentive, who figured he could talk his buddy Johnny into allowing him to do one dive during the next show.

From his 1953 autobiography, *Call Me Lucky*, here's Bing's remembrance of the funny incident that he pulled off with the help of his cohort-in-gags, Johnny:

"A hundred dollars absolutely fascinates me," said Bing, who agreed to go off the board during the second show. "After the first show we went back stage and visited Weissmuller and Kruger and the other boys we knew in the swimming dodge. I revealed my plan to Weissmuller, but to no one else.

"Johnny got me one of Stubby Kruger's comedy suits, one of those early 1900 bathing suits with the bloomers and the full sleeves and the guimpe-effect for a blouse, and a hat to match. I hid out backstage until I heard him call my name. Weissmuller simply announced: 'Bing Crosby of Hollywood, next diver.'

"I sprang blithely out on that board with my pipe in my mouth and took off. I had planned to do a plain front jackknife but just as I left the board I fell to wondering what would happen to the pipe in my mouth — maybe when I hit the water the impact would drive it right through the back of my head — so I switched my plans in midair and went in feet first. I lost my pipe, however.

"When I swam out I beat it back to Weissmuller's dressing room, where I was confronted by Billy Rose, the producer, who was in a positive snit. I imagine he had visions of me getting hurt, Paramount suing him, unfavorable publicity, and other things of like nature.

"I managed to calm him and I went on my way with Harvey, but he wouldn't pay me the hundred. He made the point that in his opinion, going in feet first didn't represent a dive, so he cut me down to sixty-five dollars. How he arrived at that precise figure I've never been able to figure out."

Despite all the good times of the Aquacade, Johnny was experiencing a recurrence of an old problem: an ear infection that had plagued him going back to his days as a competitive swimmer with the I.A.C. Johnny had been signed for the six-month run of the Fair, doing four shows per day, seven days a week. In each show he appeared twice, including the "Grand Finale" with Eleanor Holm and the full company of performers.

Johnny had been able to cure this problem in the past by dousing his inner ears with pure alcohol, which effectively dried up the troubling ailment. Even though he was advised by a doctor that he could lose his hearing if the chronic infection wasn't allowed to heal itself, Johnny decided to "tough it out" for the time being. The only cure would be to stop swimming, which was an impossibility unless he quit the show. And Johnny wouldn't consider that option unless the problem worsened.

The star of the show also noted to reporters that the Aquacade was not all fun and games, but was a stressful seven-day a week job. "There's quite a difference," conceded Johnny, "between swimming in a show and swimming for the fun of it. At the beach you can relax, mentally and physically. But when you're swimming for exhibition, you have to be alert all the time and that's a definite strain."

Johnny and Eleanor also were asked to do some writing themselves during the Fair, as they co-wrote a series of magazine articles covering basic swimming and diving techniques. The articles were entitled "GET IN THE SWIM . . . and build a beautiful body while you're doing it!"

Johnny's philosophy was unchanged since the publication of his 1929 autobiography, *Swimming the American Crawl.* He was a strong advocate that every child should be able to perform basic swimming skills, at least enough to save one's own life in the event of a boating or pool accident.

Fitness guru Weissmuller also firmly believed that swimming was the best exercise available for youngsters and the elderly as well. It required no special equipment, and there were lakes and pools in every city of America. His entire life Johnny advocated that swimming should be included in every school's basic physical education program, and that every student should partake in these rudimentary lessons. Johnny espoused these basic principles in the articles that he co-wrote with Eleanor Holm.

Back at the Aquacade, it was on with the show.

CHAPTER TWENTY-TWO

A Precious Gem Called Beryl

During the calendar year 1939, Johnny's personal life had taken a turn for the better. The final months of his marriage to Lupe had been a tremendous emotional strain for him, and he wasn't sure if he would ever consider matrimony again. In the spring of 1938, Johnny met an attractive young woman, Beryl Scott, during a golf tournament at the famed Pebble Beach golf club near Monterey, California.

At first it seemed that these two were unlikely compatibles — more like oil and water. 21-year-old Beryl had been born in Toronto, and now was recognized as a San Francisco "socialite." Her parents were affluent and listed on the Social Register — her father Arthur was a dealer in Oriental rugs in the Golden Gate City. Beryl was refined, educated, fashionable and perhaps a bit overwhelmed by the attention that movie star Johnny Weissmuller heaped upon her after their introduction.

Johnny, raised on the North Side of Chicago, was hardly a socialite. He was probably more well-known for spatting in public with Lupe Velez, and his name would never make the Social Register. But Johnny was smitten with Beryl, and in time he would win her over with his own brand of gentleness and romantic chivalry. It also didn't hurt that he was a famous athlete and actor, and certainly still one of the handsomest Hollywood heroes this side of Clark Gable.

In 1939, Johnny Weissmuller was easily one of the most admired men on the entire planet. There were millions of women who wanted to be the next Mrs. Weissmuller, but Beryl was the lucky gal chosen by Johnny to be his subsequent mate. More than anything, Johnny wanted to have children and to be a father. Beryl also shared this passion for parenthood, so this would be their common bond. (Beryl, by the way, is the name for a family of precious stones. A green beryl is better known as an emerald.)

On February 21, 1939, it was announced by MGM that Johnny would wed Miss Scott as soon as his divorce from Lupe was final — which would be in two months when the necessary red tape was completed. Before joining the Aquacade in mid-April, Johnny purchased a large corner lot in the upscale suburb of Brentwood. Beryl visited the exclusive neighborhood with Johnny, and they discussed the architect's plans to build their new home on Bristol Avenue. (This house was next to the mansion of Joan Crawford, who had known Johnny since his early years with MGM.) The following announcement appeared in the *New York Times* on May 28, 1939:

"Johnny Weissmuller, the swimmer, who is appearing in Billy Rose's Aquacade production at the World's Fair, announced yesterday that he and Beryl Scott, San Francisco society girl, would be married on July 11th somewhere in New Jersey. The marriage will take place twenty-four hours after Weissmuller's divorce decree from Lupe Velez, film actress, becomes final."

Johnny obviously was "chomping at the bit" to marry Beryl, but the final divorce decree with Lupe hit a few snags regarding the settlement, and the wedding had to be postponed past the July 11th date. Finally, on August 16, 1939, a California judge handed down the final divorce decree that would allow Johnny to marry Beryl. And they didn't waste a great deal of time, either. At one o'clock early Sunday morning, August 20th, Johnny and Beryl became "man and wife" in the town of Garfield, New Jersey.

The ceremony took place at the home of City Councilman Henry L. Janowski, who was a friend of Johnny's, and they were married by Mayor John Gabriel of Garfield. The "best man" was Sherman Billingsley, who operated the famed Stork Club in New York. A group of friends of Johnny and the new Mrs. Weissmuller also attended, having motored in from New York for the ceremony and late wedding party. They were now legally married, but there was no time for a honeymoon. Johnny had less than twelve hours before his next water show at the New York World's Fair!

Meanwhile back at the Aquacade, the problem with Johnny's ear infection had escalated. He was still doing four shows a day, and on weekends there were five shows squeezed into each day. Johnny was beginning to worry that he would go deaf from the ear ailment (and the only treatment was to get out of the water for several months). The star didn't want to let the show down, but after serious discussions with both MGM and Billy Rose, it was decided that Buster Crabbe would fill in for Johnny during the final weeks of the 1939 season at the Aquacade. (Crabbe would also return to headline the Aquacade at the New York World's Fair for the 1940 season, with Johnny becoming the star of the new Aquacade at the San Francisco World's Fair.)

Johnny was relieved to be able to return to

California, where his troublesome inner ears were allowed to dry out and return to a semblance of normalcy. He was also between Tarzan pictures, and thus had time to spend with Beryl and begin planning their new home and family. By the spring of 1940, Johnny was feeling as healthy as a war-horse and his ears were no longer giving him a problem.

With the United States on the verge of entering into World War II, Weissmuller wrestled with the notion of joining the army to serve his country. He was past the mandatory draft age maximum of thirty-five, but he could still enlist if he so chose. There were some big Hollywood stars who would be serving in the military, including James Stewart, Clark Gable, Robert Montgomery, and Henry Fonda. But as a new husband and a father-to-be, Johnny knew that discretion would be the better part of valor. He could serve his country from stateside, and still be close to his pregnant wife. (Beryl became pregnant approximately Christmas of 1939.)

It was also back to work for Johnny, who would this time be the headliner of the San Francisco World's Fair Aquacade, which would open on Treasure Island in San Francisco Bay in the spring of 1940. This spectacular water show was another brainchild of Billy Rose, who was always willing to reap another fortune after the colossal success at the New York World's Fair.

Johnny needed a new swimming partner, as Eleanor Holm had remained with the New York World's Fair (which would open for a second season in May of 1940). Seventy-five young women were selected for an audition for a chance to star in the Aquacade opposite Johnny Weissmuller. One of the hopefuls for the choice position as female star of the Aquacade was a 17-year-old swimming champion by the name of Esther Williams.

Miss Williams had won her first A.A.U. championship gold medal in the 100-meter freestyle in 1939, representing the Los Angeles Athletic Club. (Her winning time of one minute and nine seconds compared favorably to Johnny's 1924 world record in the same event, with his brilliant time of 57.4 seconds — a record that lasted more than ten years.) Williams would have been a favorite at the 1940 Olympics, which were canceled due to World War II.

The choice for his new partner was strictly up to Johnny, who selected Esther Williams from a group of five finalists. It was really no contest, as Esther won the job as Johnny's partner and later won the hearts of movie fans as she swam her way through a number of entertaining romantic comedies over the next decade.

It would be fair to give some credit to Johnny for "discovering" Esther Williams, whom he chose to be his co-star in the Aquacade. Johnny also knew of her interest in becoming a movie star, and later called his bosses at MGM to draw their attention to his young aquatic discovery. Esther soon found the doors of Hollywood wide open after starring with Johnny in the Aquacade. It's also not a coincidence that her first screen role was with Johnny's studio, MGM, as she portrayed the sexy new girlfriend of Mickey Rooney's girl crazy Andy Hardy, in *Andy Hardy's Double Life* (1942).

In 1999 Esther Williams recalled some memories of working with Johnny in the Aquacade. "In the show, I performed the solo number first, and then Johnny and I swam the duet," said Esther. "We looked good together, because we both had powerful kicks and could lift ourselves high in the water and swim in unison to the music. Weissmuller and I both had what swimmers call 'balance in the water,' the ability to hold your balance and be able to rise out of the water while swimming. I learned to swim in tandem with him, swimming backstroke while he was swimming crawl. I touched my toes on each side of his waist to be propelled forward (and to hold him back) as he swam toward me as if in a race. Johnny Weissmuller had the most powerful crawl stroke, and swimming with him was like traveling in the wake of an ocean liner."

And indeed the show was a huge success, as Louella Parsons wrote in her nationally syndicated column: "Johnny Weissmuller, Esther Williams, and Morton Downey are the biggest forty cents worth of entertainment I ever saw."

The Golden Gate International Exposition, or San Francisco World's Fair as it was known, was a great success due in large part to the popularity of the Aquacade. Johnny and Esther Williams, as the stars of the show, were hugely popular. Johnny also commanded an additional audience with his comedy diving act, now with his new California partner Bill Lewin.

Johnny had a lot on his mind these days. His role as Tarzan was only temporarily dormant, but his job with the San Francisco Fair kept him constantly in demand. His marriage to Beryl looked to be a solid relationship, and he would soon be a father for the first time. It was an exciting time for Johnny, who would celebrate his 36th birthday in the summer of 1940. He was still a relatively young man, and really looked much younger that his chronological age. Father Time had yet to catch up to Johnny Weissmuller.

With Johnny working in San Francisco it was a natural for Beryl to live in the city with her parents, while she awaited the birth of their first child (which was due at the end of the summer). On September 23, 1940, Johnny became a proud papa for the first time when his son John Scott Weissmuller was born at the Stanford hospital in San Francisco.

Johnny's diving partner, Bill Lewin, brought word to Johnny that he was the father of a healthy baby boy. In those days, it was unheard of for the father to be anywhere near the delivery room; and thus he was doing his nervous duty in a nearby bar when Lewin brought the happy news. Johnny passed out the cigars and rushed to the hospital to be with Beryl, and to get his first glimpse of his very own son. (The San Francisco Fair ended on September 27th, and thus Johnny was able to spend most of his time with his wife and new baby.)

Johnny had finally realized the dream of his lifetime: to be the father of a newborn child. But, inexplicably, there were already cracks in his relationship with Beryl. On the morning of December 10, 1940, less than three months after the birth of their first child, Beryl asked her lawyer to sue Johnny for divorce on the grounds of "extreme cruelty." Later in the very same day, Beryl further instructed her lawyer to delay action until she had a chance to talk to Johnny, who was out of town at the time.

However, this was an early indication that the union was not on solid footing. Their only area of true compatibility was the common desire to have children, and that would not be enough to hold the relationship together. Johnny had been working seven days a week at this time with the Aquacade during Beryl's pregnancy, as well as preparing for his upcoming portrayal in *Tarzan's Secret Treasure*. Beryl — the society girl — might have come a little unglued with the stress of a new child to care for 24 hours a day, and her famous husband literally working all the time. But for the moment, things were patched up and tranquility returned to the household.

Johnny went back to the jungle vines on June 14, 1941 with director Richard Thorpe behind the reins of the 10-week shooting schedule for *Tarzan's Secret Treasure*. Screenwriter Cyril Hume once again wanted to eliminate the character of Jane, making Tarzan a bachelor open to new romantic situations. Hume's early outlines included a beautiful "glamour girl" hunting big game in Africa, where she encounters Tarzan, who has a wounded heart after the death of his mate, Jane. Hume had drafted a script called *Tarzan and America's No. One Glamour Girl*, which featured a character called "Sylvia Starke, International Glamour Girl No. 1." (It is interesting to note that Brenda Joyce had recently starred in a 1940 film called *Public Deb No. 1*, about a young socialite who is constantly in the newspapers because of her glamorous doings. It would be pure speculation that Hume had Miss Joyce in mind to replace Maureen O'Sullivan, although Brenda was indeed hired as the new Jane a few years later.)

This plot line was rejected by the MGM brass, who refused to write Maureen O'Sullivan out of the Tarzan pictures. After all, they'd managed to talk Maureen into staying for at least two more pictures as Johnny's co-star. At this point a disgruntled Hume asked to be relieved and script responsibility was turned over to Myles Connolly and Paul Gangelin.

In their story, Boy is saved from a certain death by a safari that is seeking a lost city and perhaps a fortune in lost gold. Tarzan owes a debt of gratitude to the men for saving Boy, so he offers to lead them to the lost city. Boy also is grateful to his saviors, and he lets it slip that Tarzan knows of a "secret treasure" — a whole mountain of gold.

Gripped by "gold fever," decent men become criminals and kill one of their own — the Professor, the leader of the safari. They then kidnap Jane and Boy and force Tarzan to lead them to the mountain of gold. Without remorse, they cut Tarzan's vine and he falls to the bottom of a deep ravine where he lies unconscious. Of course, as in any good Tarzan picture, the men of evil die in a climactic finish as Tarzan and his thundering herd of elephants come to the rescue of Jane and Boy.

The only survivor from the safari was a whiskey-drinking Irishman by the name of O'Doul, portrayed superbly by Barry Fitzgerald. His character of O'Doul developed a strong affection and loyalty to Tarzan, and was rewarded in the final scene with a basket of gold and the thanks of Tarzan and his family. (Fitzgerald appeared in many classic films during his career — usually as a warm-hearted bumbler — including an Academy Award winning role in 1944 for *Going My Way*.)

Tom Conway portrayed the number one villain of Medford, who dies a grisly — but deserved — death in a crocodile infested river. (Conway, the brother of actor George Sanders, was well known as the "Falcon" during the 1940s in a highly successful series of detective thrillers.) Cheeta the chimp began playing a larger role in each successive Tarzan adventure, and getting into more and more mischief; this time the chimp took a liking to Mr. O'Doul's Irish whiskey and gets monkey inebriated.

Johnny the animal lover got along extremely well with the various chimpanzees that worked in the Tarzan pictures. This mutual affection was so strong that he seemed to have a natural affinity for the apes that were always nipping the other actors — especially Maureen — behind the scenes.

Underwater filming in Wakulla Springs, Florida produced the scene with Tarzan, Jane and Boy frolicking and cavorting underwater with Baby Bea the elephant, and also a giant sea turtle. (Johnny as Tarzan even caught a large fish with his bare hands for the jungle family's dinner.) Also photographed in Florida were the underwater portions of Tarzan's rescue of Boy and Jane from the film's grand finale. The final battle royal in the river with scores of hungry crocodiles threatening the lives of Jane and Boy — with Tarzan's ever-faithful elephants to the rescue — was a thrilling and fitting climax.

Years later, Johnny Sheffield delved back into his memory banks and recalled some highlights of working with Johnny and Maureen on *Tarzan's Secret Treasure*.

"Many scenes in this movie were filmed on location in Florida," noted Sheffield. "Almost all the swimming scenes were done there. The 'high dive' was taken down river from Silver Springs. Ross Allen would go ahead of us and search the bank for alligators and cottonmouth water moccasins. He found a few too. I remember one time he got a water moccasin on the bank and put it in his mouth and swam it back to the boat. A few minutes later Big John and I were working right there on the bank where Ross captured that aquatic pit viper.

"No, I didn't make the dive; they said I was too young and didn't want to take a chance on injury. In the swimming scenes there is an under water shot of Happy which happened by accident and I believe it to be the only underwater shot of a young elephant swimming or any elephant for that matter. My three elephants, Sally, Happy and Queeny were on this raft near the beach at the Spring when Happy fell off. The assistant cameraman was in the 'Camera Bell' at the time and alertly started rolling as soon as he saw what was happening. What a shot! And it was an accident! [The Camera Bell was a specially designed metal drum attached to a barge and set several feet below the surface, with an optical glass window for the camera port.]

"Swimming with Johnny Weissmuller was a real pleasure. There were some good shots of us there at the Spring and some really good shots of us at the climax of the movie when Tarzan swam down river and rescued Jane and me from the Joconi. Big John was like a motor boat in the water. There is one cut during the rescue of me motoring along just like Tarzan that I really like."

One pint-sized addition to the standard plot formula was a native boy named Tumbo (Cordell Hickman), who becomes friends with Boy (Sheffield). The two jungle young-sters took turns saving each other from dan-ger and the innocence of their friendship was really rather endearing. Child actor Hickman was well cast as a native lad who is suddenly orphaned, and thus becomes a member of the Tarzan family for this particular story. Johnny Sheffield fondly remembered that "Cordell Hickman as Tumbo was a pal both on and off the screen."

There were a scarcity of outstanding roles for black actors during the first few decades of the motion picture era, but the Tarzan ad-ventures provided a few rare exceptions. While it is true that the African natives and porters were stereotyped characters, the oc-casional opportunity for a splendid charac-terization proved to be the exception to the rule.

In *Tarzan's Secret Treasure*, Cordell Hickman portrayed a courageous young lad who is friends with the son of Tarzan on an equal basis. (Meanwhile, the role of Saidi in *Tarzan and His Mate* was a fine portrayal by Nathan Curry, and perhaps the supreme example was Mutia Omoolu's brave and loyal Renchero in the earlier film, *Trader Horn*. In fact, Horn and Renchero were like brothers in this compelling story. There was dignity and heroism in these particular roles, a stark departure from Hollywood's stereotyping of black actors into less than complimentary cubbyholes.)

One of the warmest scenes in any Tarzan picture had Johnny and Maureen as the jungle couple discussing their son Boy, and how easily he is impressed by the outsiders from civilization. Johnny's Tarzan feels these interlopers are mostly fools, with little comprehension of the values of the jungle people. "None of them have what we have," says Jane tenderly. "Tarzan have Jane," replies the ape-man with conviction. "Has it seemed a long time, Tarzan?" asks Jane romantically. "Sun make one safari for Jane and Tarzan," answers Tarzan matter-of-factly. "Oh Tarzan, a poet couldn't have said that more beautifully," responds Jane.

This was a lovely romantic scene that was the hallmark of the MGM Tarzan movies: a true romantic relationship between Tarzan and Jane that often wasn't present in later Tarzan pictures. After a swim together, there's more romantic love talk as Tarzan and Jane lie together on the riverbank, and then kiss sensually. In 1934 the Hays Office eliminated the sexy outfits of Maureen O'Sullivan and the eroticism of a nearly naked jungle couple, unmarried lovers living in a virtual Garden of Eden.

But even in the latter films there was always that lovely romantic relationship between Tarzan and Jane, portrayed with such perfect screen chemistry by Johnny and Maureen.

More than sixty years after the release of the initial MGM Tarzan pictures, Johnny Weissmuller and Maureen O'Sullivan are still symbols of a savage — yet romantic — relationship. The photographs of Johnny and Maureen together from these early films are still published in magazines on a regular basis, because no amount of years passing by could dull their romantic appeal to the masses. The photographs are admittedly sexy, but they also convey a once-in-a-lifetime love affair that everyone would like to embrace just once in a lifetime.

The death of Irving Thalberg in 1936, MGM's boy wonder of the 1930s, had caused a shift of direction by the studio. Thalberg favored a literary basis for many of the studio's great films, and the Tarzan films based on the works of Edgar Rice Burroughs were a stellar example. The Tarzan series at MGM was beginning to wear thin after a full decade, as the formula plots, the stock footage used repeatedly in each successive film, and the studio's waning interest in Tarzan pictures signaled the coming end. Budget-cutting also resulted in the films becoming shorter in length, relegating them to the lower half of twin-bills at the theaters.

When *Tarzan's Secret Treasure* was released to movie-going audiences at Christmas of 1941, the United States and Japan had engaged in war after the attack on Pearl Harbor, and Johnny Weissmuller had been portraying Tarzan for a full decade. A maturing Weissmuller was a few pounds heavier than his competitive days as a swimmer, but this was his only visible concession to age. Johnny was still powerfully built and presented a commanding figure as the heroic Tarzan, and would still have several good years to come in his signature role.

Maureen O'Sullivan, at age thirty probably was at her peak in all the feminine ways — Maureen as Jane was still the ultimate match for Weissmuller's Tarzan. But she was also a young mother now, and contemplating a larger family. It would only be a matter of time till she would be forced to give up the role of Jane, and make her family her number one priority. A final portrayal in *Tarzan's New York Adventure* would be the swan song for her as Jane.

Meanwhile, Johnny's personal life was holding together and his own little family was expanding. Beryl gave birth to their first daughter, Wendy Ann, on June 1, 1942 in Los Angeles. Now the family was four, with baby Wendy joining two-year-old John Scott as the centerpieces of the family. Johnny was on break between Tarzan pictures, and it would be two months before the publicity junket would begin for *Tarzan's New York Adventure*. And thus he was able to relish the delights of a brand new baby in the household, as well as the tasks of feeding and changing diapers.

To accommodate a growing family, Johnny and Beryl purchased a larger home in Brentwood on Rockingham Avenue, which overlooked scenic Mandeville Canyon. The Spanish-Mediterranean villa had originally been built by actress Helen Twelvetrees, and was subsequently owned by Charles Laughton and his wife, Elsa Lanchester. This was certainly the finest home that Johnny had ever owned in his lifetime, and it seemed the perfect scenario to raise a family. In addition to the requisite swimming pool for Johnny's daily workout, there was a badminton court, a small guest house, and the property was shaded year-round by majestic avocado trees. (The smaller Bristol Avenue home owned by Johnny and Beryl was sold to rugged actor Robert Preston, who had become a big Hollywood star after the 1939 release of the desert classic, *Beau Geste*.)

This setting had the makings of an idyllic life for Johnny, Beryl, and their children. When Johnny found out from Beryl in the fall of 1942 that he was going to be a father once again the following summer, he could only smile at the thought of his expanding family. But there were small cracks in the foundation, and the current happiness they were experiencing would be the highlight of their relationship together. Johnny's world was his Tarzan role, his motion picture buddies, and his regular physical fitness routine which included swimming, golfing, and tennis, among other sports.

Beryl's life was her children, her own circle of friends, and her husband. Unfortunately, with the busy schedule of a Hollywood star, Johnny was never around enough to keep Beryl happy. Slowly, the cracks in the foundation were widening, and the two principals were becoming more and more distant to each other.

CHAPTER TWENTY-THREE

MGM Swan Song

Seeking to give the Tarzan series a new direction and perhaps a new look for Weissmuller, the scenario for the final MGM adventure was shifted to New York City — a drastic change considering the story of Tarzan is about a jungle man who lives in the wilds of Africa. In the original 1912 Tarzan story by Edgar Rice Burroughs, *Tarzan of the Apes*, the ape-man follows the woman he loves — Jane — back to America to capture her heart. However it took a full decade to get Johnny Weissmuller out of the jungle and into a suit, in *Tarzan's New York Adventure*.

This story is really one of the most heart-warming of the entire series, as Tarzan must travel halfway around the world to find his son (Johnny Sheffield), who has been stolen from his African home. At times this lovely little film brings tears to your eyes, as Tarzan fights for Boy in the courtroom against heartless lawyers, and also against insurmountable odds in the steel and concrete of an alien jungle called New York City. Once again Johnny

Weissmuller did his best acting with his superhuman actions, in one death-defying stunt after another to save Boy.

With his loincloth left behind in the jungle, Weissmuller cut an imposing figure in a 1940s double-breasted suit, which highlighted his broad shoulders. Maureen O'Sullivan also looked stylish clothed in the latest female fashions of the civilized world, her antelope-skin apparel left behind in the jungle. But film fans were accustomed to seeing Maureen dressed like a lady, as a vast majority of her films were non-jungle roles. But Johnny in a suit? There was no guarantee that this concept would work, and yet this film was one of the most popular of the MGM Tarzan films.

Tarzan's New York Adventure begins in Africa, where an unscrupulous animal trapper, Buck Rand, observes Boy and his trio of baby elephants performing a series of circus tricks. Boy is befriended by Jimmy Shields, who halts Rand's plan to kidnap Boy and sell him to a circus. After a tragic accident befalls Tarzan and Jane in which they are presumed to be dead, Rand indeed kidnaps Boy and brings him to New York to star in Colonel Sargent's circus.

When Tarzan discovers that Boy has been taken away in an "iron bird," he uses gold nuggets to charter a plane for Jane and himself to travel to America. After arriving in

New York City, Tarzan and Jane track Boy to a circus run by Rand and Colonel Sargent, who somehow has gained legal custody of the jungle lad.

A determined Tarzan arrives at the circus ready for action, but he is convinced by Jimmy Shields to go to court to regain Boy's custody. A day in court fails to get Boy back to Tarzan and Jane, so the ape-man takes the law into his own hands! Tarzan evades the police by diving from the Brooklyn Bridge into New York harbor, while Jane and Shields travel by car to the circus.

When Tarzan arrives, the kidnappers are retreating with Boy as their hostage. Tarzan, overpowered and caged by Rand's men, calls the circus elephants to his aid, as they bend the bars and free him. Leaping into the speeding car, Tarzan saves Boy as Rand and Sargent are killed in a spectacular car crash. Back in court the judge is compassionate and returns Boy to Tarzan and Jane, who are anxious to return to their African home.

Tarzan's New York Adventure was decidedly different from the previous MGM Tarzan pictures, and for the most part a refreshing change of pace. Tarzan battling lawyers and crooks in the concrete jungle of New York City still contained plenty of action and adventure, and Tarzan's willingness to risk his own life for Boy was the ultimate display of courage.

A top-notch cast included Charles Bickford as the lion trapper who kidnaps Boy, Paul Kelly as the pilot who aids Tarzan in finding his son, and Virginia Grey as the torch singer, Connie. Hollywood veteran Chill Wills portrayed the good guy who befriends Boy, and then gets murdered despite his heroism. (This plot device allowed for the villains Rand and Sargent to die at the end of the picture, thus receiving just retribution for their cold act of murder).

The original screen Tarzan, Elmo Lincoln, appeared in a bit part as a roustabout (circus laborer). Lincoln, the star of the 1918 silent feature *Tarzan of the Apes*, had bounced around Hollywood for years finding small roles and working as an extra. After starring in a number of action serials in the 1920s — including Tarzan — there were no major roles for Lincoln after talking pictures arrived around 1929. Years later Johnny Weissmuller recalled that he would bump into Lincoln from time to time, most often on the beaches around the Santa Monica pier.

Johnny Weissmuller did plenty of stunts in the picture, including the exciting studio scenes of Tarzan climbing on the exterior of a New York skyscraper, as well as location shots on the real Brooklyn Bridge. Johnny later recalled that they had to get permission from the city of New York to block off both ends of the bridge, so they could film this scene. "It was easy to climb up there," said Johnny matter-of-factly. "I didn't do the dive because it was over 300 feet high." (Tarzan's classic dive off the Brooklyn Bridge into the murky waters below was actually a weighted dummy captured on film by cameraman Jack Smith, himself perched at the top of the scenic tower on the MGM backlots.)

Johnny had theater patrons in fits of laughter when his Tarzan takes a shower with his clothes on, and then gives his mighty war cry to Jane's utter disbelief! Then the ape-man shows his savvy goes beyond the jungles and has the gallery in stitches, when he makes a monkey out of the opposing lawyer in the courtroom battle over Boy's custody.

Perhaps the most classic scene from any Tarzan picture was used once again in *Tarzan's New York Adventure*. Johnny and Maureen reenacted the famous "Me Tarzan, you Jane" scene on the veranda of their treehouse, as Jane confides to her mate, "You're my goodness, darling — my strength." Tarzan responds to Jane's romantic admission and gently taps Jane's bosom and then his own, and says with tenderness, "Tarzan — Jane."

At this moment Tarzan is aroused by passion and kisses Jane, then scoops up his mate and carries her away to a presumed romantic encounter — the scene fades leaving the rest to the imaginations of the audience. (It's a good thing that Maureen was a petite 115 pounds, because Johnny was always picking her up and carrying her off into the trees!)

Johnny Sheffield remembered this particular film as a favorite of all of the Tarzan family: Big John, Maureen, and Little John.

"Drama, suspense, comedy, excitement, education, adventure, and plot — this Tarzan has them all," noted Sheffield. "The others don't even come close! I still get excited watching this intercontinental adventure. It is a thrill looking up there and realizing I was part of it!

"What makes this Tarzan a 'Classic' is the family oriented plot and freedom of choice. Tarzan operates from emotion, principles and acts through freedom of choice. He is not confined to the escarpment; he is bringing up his family there by choice. No one in their heart takes exception to Tarzan's motives.

"In a 'Classic' there can be no unrest over the plot; the audience must be 100% behind the hero and 100% against the villain. Period! Who can argue against a man fighting for the survival of his family?

"Who can forget the courtroom scene when Tarzan and Jane see that the system won't get Boy back and they hold a 'family conference' right there in the courtroom to decide upon a family plan of action! 'Jane say, Tarzan go?' 'Yes, Tarzan,' she replies. Tarzan states, 'Tarzan get Boy back' and it's on! Cheetah cheers and Tarzan is 'out of there' with the 'City's Finest' right after him.

"He went along with civilization on a legal and political level until his instincts for family preservation required him to take direct action. We see that action explode as Tarzan swings over Manhattan and heads for Brooklyn! What could be more cosmopolitan than to dive off the Brooklyn Bridge? Is that a show stopper or what? If that doesn't stop your heart, you are already dead.

"There is plenty of comedy, too. What about the tailor scene in Nairobi where Tarzan is fitted out for safari to civilization or Cheetah and the cosmetics? Cheetah learned a lot on the adventure. I smile when I remember how well she uses the gavel to maintain order in the court. That's not easy to do with young chimpanzees! There is comedy in the movie and it changes and improves with the years.

"*Tarzan's New York Adventure* involves the resourcefulness, and humanity of Tarzan; family and responsibility as the nucleus for human growth and happiness; the vulnerability of the family to outside influences of evil. When circumstances compelled Tarzan to venture out across this world, he demonstrated his values by action and was willing to risk it all for his family. The movie clearly demonstrates family values."

★ ★ ★

Around this time MGM made a cold business decision — they felt that with the war expected to last for an indeterminate length, the lost revenue of the European market made the Tarzan series less financially attractive to the studio than in years past. Rather than negotiate for the rights to produce new Tarzan pictures, they simply bowed out and allowed Sol Lesser to take over the series. The enterprising Lesser purchased all rights from Edgar Rice Burroughs to produce future Tarzan pictures (with RKO distribution).

Maureen O'Sullivan's loyalty to MGM — and to Johnny — kept her doing the Tarzan films three years beyond when she wanted to quit to be a full-time mother. (By this time Maureen was pregnant with her second son, Patrick, and now she was completely serious about retiring from acting. *Tarzan's New York Adventure* was her last role until 1948, when she starred with Charles Laughton and Ray Milland in the taut thriller, *The Big Clock*, which was directed by her husband, John Farrow.)

When the series switched to Lesser/RKO, Maureen was no longer bound by any such loyalty to her studio. (Misplaced loyalty, perhaps, considering the big studios could drop you like a stone if your usefulness to them had dried up.) Unfortunately, this was the case with Johnny — who was never offered another starring role for MGM despite the millions of dollars he had made for the studio the previous decade.

Sentimentalists they were not, and it was without any particular remorse that MGM unloaded the rights to the Tarzan series as well as Johnny Weissmuller's contract for "unspecified considerations." Lesser, who had Buster Crabbe and Glenn Morris as stars of his two Tarzan pictures during the 1930s, finally had what he wanted more than anything: Johnny Weissmuller as his Tarzan. Years later, longtime Tarzan producer Sol Lesser succinctly described his favorite Tarzan actor:

"Weissmuller not only had the physique but he had that kind of face — sensual, animalistic, and good-looking — that gave the impression of jungle . . . outdoor life. Undoubtedly, Johnny was the greatest of all Tarzans."

Although Johnny had a contract with Lesser to do several Tarzan pictures, he also had the option to take other roles for other studios. Having been frustrated the past ten years by the ironclad MGM contract that didn't allow him to portray any character except Tarzan, Johnny managed to find a loophole in the system that kept actors tied to a particular studio like indentured servants (albeit in the case of Johnny, a highly paid indentured servant).

To this end, Pine-Thomas Productions, which was a company affiliated with Paramount, negotiated a deal with Weissmuller to make three non-Tarzan pictures: a war movie as an army flyer; a second wartime role as a war correspondent; and a cowboy picture. Former Tarzan Buster Crabbe at this time was doing "B" cowboy pictures by the dozen, so Johnny figured that he could do the same and be successful. Of the three ideas, the melodrama tentatively titled *Combat Correspondent* sounded the most promising for a challenging role. Johnny would have been in the title role, in the story of a combat reporter who gets into the thick of the action behind the lines in Europe.

"Swimming gave me my start, but my pal Tarzan did the real work. He set me up nicely," noted Johnny to reporters. "I feel I'm now in a position to risk a change. With clothes on, I may not even have to starve myself all the time. I've nothing against the loincloth, but this constant diet [to stay trim for the role of Tarzan] is murdering me!

"I've no fixed idea about shedding my jungle role entirely," added Johnny when asked if he was giving up the role of Tarzan. "I've still got a contract with Lesser. But I'd like to move into the Douglas Fairbanks type of action pictures. I'm no great actor, but my fans like me, so why shouldn't I give it a whirl?"

Unfortunately for Johnny, World War II greatly compromised the motion picture industry, as well as the more obvious and severe repercussions to the entire country. As the war years went by, the proposed roles for Johnny gathered dust and then finally were shelved indefinitely. (This 1943 agreement with Pine-Thomas went unfulfilled until 1946, when *Swamp Fire* would be Johnny's first starring role outside of his Tarzan character.)

RKO was a much smaller studio than MGM, and accordingly had a smaller budget for the Tarzan pictures. The area chosen to replace the MGM jungle was the Los Angeles State and County Arboretum at Arcadia, California, about fifteen miles northeast from downtown Los Angeles.

The Arboretum was complete with a lagoon and naturally lush vegetation, making it the perfect backdrop for all the studio Tarzan films produced by Sol Lesser. Exterior location settings also included Lake Sherwood, with city scenes photographed at the RKO Encino Ranch, and interiors were shot at RKO Pathe in Culver City.

The first feature without longtime mate Maureen O'Sullivan would be the war propaganda picture, *Tarzan Triumphs*. With Weissmuller set as Tarzan, and Johnny Sheffield returning as Boy, Sol Lesser needed an actress for Jane. Lesser greatly admired Miss O'Sullivan, not only for her beauty but for her considerable acting talents. (Holding out hope that Maureen would return to the series eventually, Lesser refused to recast the character of Jane. Instead, an absentee Jane would be in London caring for her sick mother, and her letters to a lonely Tarzan and Boy would keep alive her character.)

For the role of his heroine, a jungle beauty called Zandra, Sol Lesser conducted extensive screen tests before deciding on 21-year-old Frances Gifford, whom had previously starred in the 1941 Republic serial, *Jungle Girl*. Miss Gifford was under contract to Paramount at the time and opposed doing the film, preferring to seek a variety of roles away from the jungle. Holding all the cards, all-powerful Paramount would not relent and loaned her to Lesser despite her lack of enthusiasm for another jungle portrayal.

Seeking to ease her resistance to the role, Lesser presented Miss Gifford with an orchid on the first morning of shooting. After meeting her friendly co-stars, Big John and Little John, she succumbed to the jungle charm of Tarzan and Boy and became a willing accomplice to the project. Frances Gifford as Zandra the Palandrian was a stunning beauty, and a competent actress. While she wasn't a romantic replacement for Jane, she most definitely was a capable heroine who worked very well with Weissmuller and Sheffield in this picture.

In this story, Zandra and her people live in the hidden city of Palandria, and she becomes friends with Tarzan and Boy in an unforgettable manner: Zandra saves Boy's life when he falls to a treacherous ledge, and then Tarzan arrives to save them both in the nick of time. Later, a Nazi safari arrives in Palandria and repays their kindness and hospitality by conquering the city and enslaving the inhabitants. Only one man can save the people of Palandria, and Zandra flees through the jungle to find Tarzan.

When the Nazis kidnap Boy, it is an enraged Tarzan who declares: "Now, Tarzan make war!" Although captured himself by the enemy, Tarzan frees himself with his knife slipped to him by his faithful friend, Cheeta the chimp. After recruiting an army of Palandrians to fight the Nazis, Tarzan takes to the jungle in pursuit of the cowardly Colonel von Reichart. The evil Nazi is tricked by Tarzan into falling into a lion pit, as Tarzan speaks this ironic epitaph: "In jungle, strong always survive . . ."

Tarzan triumphs once again as Zandra and her people are saved from the tyranny of the Nazi invaders.

Tarzan Triumphs, an American propaganda film targeted at Hitler's Nazi regime, was directed by William Thiele, who had come to Hollywood in the 1930s from his homeland of Germany. The German soldiers were all portrayed as either evil or ignorant; in this particular picture the Nazis represented the bad guys usually embodied by greedy white men who invade Tarzan's jungle. (The clever screenplay by Roy Chanslor and Carroll Young managed to stay on course despite the heavy propaganda message.)

British actor Stanley Ridges effectively portrayed the role of the vile Colonel von Reichart, a character so evil he literally dripped with venom. A memorable scene had Tarzan toying with von Reichart in the jungle: a game of cat and mouse with the rattled Nazi stumbling in perpetual circles. Tarzan taunts his enemy and repeats, "Nazi — Nazi — Nazi — Nazi," until his opponent's weapon is empty, depleted of bullets fired at the elusive shadow of Tarzan. He then maneuvers von Reichart into falling into a pit occupied by a starving lion, where the Nazi dies a most gruesome death.

In another classic scene, Tarzan is wounded by the German soldiers — Zandra revives him and warns that the Nazis have seized his son. "Took away? Boy?" cries out an anguished Tarzan. Then in an unforgettable moment, grabbing his knife in his hand and gritting his teeth, the ape-man pronounces with fierce emotion:

"NOW! TARZAN MAKE WAR!" It's a true fact that patriotic American audiences actually got to their feet and cheered after Weissmuller growled his immortal lines.

Johnny Weissmuller had added a few extra pounds since his last portrayal, but his great physical strength carried him through the role with the dignity of an ancient lion. At age thirty-eight he still looked capable enough to take on a whole army by himself. The action is almost nonstop as Tarzan takes on the German army — and wins! Johnny's locks were also longer and shaggier than in any previous Tarzan picture, and a new (slightly modified) Tarzan yell was recorded for the RKO series.

Johnny's forte was ACTION — not rambling discourse — in the RKO Tarzan films, and years later Sol Lesser explained his philosophy for the minimized dialogue: "Tarzan is an international character and about 75 per cent of the film grosses came from foreign countries during the period I was producing the films. Their demands were for action, not words. Too much dialogue would only serve to slow up a Tarzan picture and weaken its strongest appeal to the foreign theatergoer — the universal understanding of action and pantomime." Released in February of 1943, *Tarzan Triumphs* was Lesser's biggest money-maker of all his Tarzan films.

★ ★ ★

Things appeared to be looking good for Johnny career-wise, as well as in his personal life. When a second daughter, Heidi Elizabeth, was born on July 20, 1943, it was beginning to look like the Weissmuller clan would someday take on epic proportions. John Scott, now approaching three-years-old, and his two baby sisters provided plenty of family activity around the house for Johnny and Beryl. They also had two dogs as pets, terriers named Dinny and Shep. It seemed to be all the ingredients for an All-American happy family. Unfortunately, it simply wasn't to be and within months it would all begin to unravel.

Meanwhile, *Tarzan's Desert Mystery* was once again a Tarzan movie without a Jane, leaving the ape-man and Boy as two bachelors in their jungle paradise. Sol Lesser still had hopes of persuading Maureen O'Sullivan to return to the series, so in this story Jane was still in London; she's nursing wounded soldiers in a British hospital, as her letter to her beloved Tarzan and Boy explains. She also sends an urgent request to Tarzan to journey to a distant jungle to collect fever medicine for wounded British troops. William Thiele had collaborated with Weissmuller to create a classic film and major success with *Tarzan Triumphs*, but this effort was second-rate.

489

For the female lead, Lesser chose 22-year-old Nancy Kelly, an RKO contract player who later received her best roles on the Broadway stage. Miss Kelly was a gifted dramatic artist for whom Hollywood couldn't seem to find a proper niche. (The exception being an Academy Award nomination for *The Bad Seed* {1956}, in which Nancy Kelly recreated her stage role.)

In *Tarzan's Desert Mystery*, Miss Kelly played Connie Bryce, a lady magician who mysteriously becomes the secret emissary to a troubled sheik. Connie collides with Tarzan and Boy in the desert and forms an alliance with the dynamic jungle duo, who are traversing the desert to collect the fever medicine. It is Connie's mission to expose the villainous Paul Hendrix (Otto Kruger) to a rather naive Prince Selim (Robert Lowery). Hendrix is a profiteer who has conned the Prince into allowing him to take charge of the city's industries and oppress the people. He also imprisons Tarzan on a trumped-up charge of horse theft for releasing a beautiful wild stallion from the clutches of Hendrix's men. After the Prince is murdered by Hendrix, Connie is framed and sentenced to die by hanging. It is up to Tarzan to escape his prison and save Connie, as the fugitives take flight into the desert on the back of the wild stallion. A final confrontation between Tarzan and Hendrix in a mysterious cave, results in the blackheart becoming the bitter dinner of a man-eating spider.

Released in December of 1943, *Tarzan's Desert Mystery* was certainly the poorest of the twelve Johnny Weissmuller Tarzan pictures. Regrettably, it was exceedingly long on desert (photographed at the Olancha sand dunes near Lone Pine), and desperately short on anything one could truly call a "mystery." A standard programmer at only 70 minutes in length, it could have been called a desert "horse opera," rather than a true "Tarzan" picture.

Johnny Weissmuller must have felt like the Forgotten Man; his dialogue consisted of about forty words for the whole picture, and he spent much of his time locked in a prison away from all the action. The most dangerous creature Tarzan had to fight was a man-eating plant; he even needed his elephant friends to get him out of the trap. Meanwhile, Miss Kelly carried the lead and cavorted with Boy and Cheeta, as well as matching wits with the rather despicable Otto Kruger as Herr Hendrix. Easily the best action scene in the film is when Weissmuller mounts the wild stallion Jana, frees dozens of other wild horses, and escapes into the desert with Boy, Connie and Cheeta. Although this was a milder propaganda film than *Tarzan Triumphs*, the evil-doers once again were those contemptible

Nazis waging a war against the world.

Tarzan's Desert Mystery ultimately failed as an action/adventure picture — and with Jane missing from the story as well, there was no romance to rescue it. By the time the next Tarzan picture was released in April of 1945, the world war would be nearing its end and a new Jane — Brenda Joyce — would be back in the ape-man's arms in *Tarzan and the Amazons*. Admittedly, Johnny had let himself get out of shape for this picture; at age thirty-nine the years and a few too many pounds were starting to show. But the reasons for Johnny's weight gain went way beyond these obvious factors.

Behind the scenes, sadly, Johnny's marriage to Beryl was failing. It was a classic case of Johnny being so unhappy at home that he practically ate himself out of his role as Tarzan. (This would be one of the few times in his life that Johnny would be out of shape. He peaked at 35 pounds over his ideal weight during this period of turmoil in his personal life, and was dangerously close to burnout in everything he loved dearly — including his Tarzan role.) Johnny knew that in order to clear his mind of troubles, he needed to be in top physical condition. So he began a serious regimen in the gym and the pool for several weeks near the end of 1943, and was soon back in his normal superlative physical shape.

Part of their problems had arisen when Beryl sold their beautiful home on Rockingham, citing an inability to get enough domestic help during the war to take care of the sprawling mansion. Johnny didn't want to sell the property but was overruled by Beryl, who purchased a smaller home on Latimer Road. Further exacerbating Johnny's unhappiness was the lack of a swimming pool on this new property. A daily swim at home was part of his ritual, and now suddenly there was no pool as he gradually lost his muscle tone and gained weight. (No pool at home for Weissmuller — the world's greatest swimmer — equalled an unhappy Johnny. The closest pool for an occasional swim was at the nearby Will Rogers Polo Club.)

On October 21, 1943, Beryl and Johnny filed for a legal separation to try to resolve their differences. Beryl stated that "incompatibility" was the primary cause of their marital difficulties. Their third child, Heidi, had been born just four months prior to the separation, adding to the tragedy of the situation. This wasn't the end of their relationship entirely, but the separation would last for several years.

The moment the Christmas holidays were over, on December 28, 1943, Beryl sued for divorce, alleging the tried and true "grievous cruelty." Mrs. Weissmuller requested all of their community property (valued at

$200,000), plus $1,650 monthly alimony and the custody of their three children, John Scott, Wendy Ann, and Heidi Elizabeth. It would be 1948 before Johnny and Beryl would be legally divorced, but for all practical purposes the marriage was over. For the sake of the children, they looked for solutions to keep the family together. But unfortunately there were no easy answers or remedies — they were simply incompatible in every important aspect of life.

CHAPTER TWENTY-FOUR

The Patriotic Johnny

While many of the bachelors of the Hollywood industry entered the military and served Uncle Sam during the war years, Johnny was exempt because of his age and his status as husband and father. But he was still determined to serve his country and he started with the Hollywood Canteen, which opened in October of 1942.

Hollywood Canteen was an enlisted man's club on a grandiose scale, and the entertainment included a constant parade of many of the biggest stars of stage and screen. Only "dogfaces" were allowed in the Canteen, as the officers had their own clubs. The Canteen became such a legendary part of Hollywood that they made a movie about it in 1944 called *Hollywood Canteen*, from which the proceeds helped to fund the organization and others like it around the country. (Other clubs around America were called Stage Door Canteens, with the flagship location being on West 44th Street in Manhattan. Another movie, *Stage Door Canteen*, had among its many famous stars, *our hero,* Johnny Weissmuller.)

The Hollywood Canteen — a redwood planked structure resembling a large double barn — was located on Cahuenga just off Sunset Boulevard in the heart of Hollywood. The friendly atmosphere on the inside was an oasis for those men home on leave, or waiting to ship out to one of the combat arenas. This was the "Big Daddy" of all U.S.O. clubs, with a stage for the entertainers, a large dance floor, tables and chairs for the G.I.s to sit and gawk at the many stars who came each night to entertain these stateside troops. Fire regulations allowed for only 500 men to be in the building at one time, but on most nights as many as 2,500 soldiers would spend an hour or so in the club for a cold drink or two, and then move on so that others could take their turn inside the club. The Canteen was open seven days a week: Monday through Saturday evenings from seven till midnight, and Sunday afternoons from two until eight p.m. Hundreds of attractive young women volunteered as hostesses, serving up sandwiches and beverages from the snack bar with their warmest smiles for America's soldiers-in-waiting.

The Canteen was a phenomenon that was unrivaled in history in terms of the "stars" fraternizing with the common man. On any given night the biggest stars in Hollywood could be seen sitting and talking with G.I.s, including Bette Davis and John Garfield, the co-founders of the organization. The stars included Joan Crawford, Buster Keaton, Bob Hope, Bing Crosby, famed ventriloquist Edgar Bergen (and his "partner" Charlie McCarthy), Ray Bolger, Harpo Marx, Katharine Hepburn, Ida Lupino, Eddie Cantor, Barbara Stanwyck, Peter Lorre, Jack Benny, Roy Rogers, and too many more to even list. There was entertainment as part of the agenda, and the various orchestras played so the men could dance with the volunteer hostesses. In her autobiography, *Portrait of Joan*, Joan Crawford recalled spending Monday nights at the Canteen serving behind the snack bar and writing postcards — "hundreds of postcards" — to soldiers overseas. She also worked for Allied Relief, the Red Cross, and made numerous "poetry recordings for the boys overseas." These were typical contributions from America's celebrities, who all pitched in to do their part for the cause.

Johnny's forte was neither singing nor dancing, and certainly not reading poetry, so he often washed dishes at the Canteen to do his fair share. He would sit with the soldiers for hours and converse about his Olympic adventures and his Tarzan role, sharing a cup of coffee with men who would soon be marching off to war. Johnny's Tarzan yell was a popular request, and he could rarely resist an opportunity to entertain a crowd with his trademark "yodel." And these particular audiences were so enthralled with Johnny and his genuinely down-to-earth persona, that he was more than willing to grant the numerous requests to hear the Tarzan war cry.

Although Johnny never charged for his Tarzan call, in one instance a Texas oil tycoon paid $5,000 to America's service charities to hear the famous Tarzan yell just once. Johnny would always break into a big smile after the Tarzan yell (partly out of embarrassment that a grown man was still playing what amounted to children's games). But for $5,000 for a worthy cause, Johnny would be willing to give his Tarzan yell any time and any place!

If you've never seen *Stage Door Canteen* (1943), this wonderful musical-and-comedic salute to American patriotism is a must-see if you love old movies and all the great stars of yesteryear. The story itself is several interwoven vignettes about young soldiers who all fall in love with the Canteen hostesses on the day before they ship out for distant shores. There are so many stars in cameo roles that they go by in a blur, including Johnny Weissmuller. Johnny's short bit was memorable and hilarious, to say the least.

There were more than 50 big stars in this

picture, and movie patrons would sit in their chairs and nudge each other and smile as the parade of celebrities continued for the two hours of the picture. The stars all worked on a "favored nations" clause, and 90 percent of the profits went back to the American Theatre Wing, which used the money to pay operating expenses of the Canteens around the nation.

Stage Door Canteen was produced by Johnny's new partner in the Tarzan series, Sol Lesser, and directed by Frank Borzage (who indirectly had a great deal to do with Johnny's career success — he was the man who discovered Maureen O'Sullivan in her home country of Ireland in 1929). Besides Johnny's cameo bit, other stars included: George Raft is seen as a dishwasher; Harpo Marx clowns around and chases after pretty girls; George Jessel reprises his famous phone call to "Mama"; Ray Bolger shows off his incredible talents as a song and dance man; famed stage actress Katherine Cornell does a snippet from her stage version of *Romeo and Juliet*, with a young soldier who is a big admirer of Miss Cornell; and Katharine Hepburn in a short dramatic scene with the young female star of the picture, Cheryl Walker.

Johnny's short bit was as a dishwasher (well, he's actually drying), along with his partner, comedian Franklin Pangborn, who's doing the plate washing. Stage actress Lynn

Fontanne calls out, "Oh Johnny . . . bring some more plates, please." Johnny replies, "All right, Miss Fontanne." At this point things get funny, as his partner says, "It's beastly hot in here — I'm suffocating." Johnny says, "That's what I say!" and takes off his shirt! "Now . . . I feel natural!" In reality, Johnny now looks just like his famous character of Tarzan — drying dishes! (Franklin Pangborn was in scores of films beginning in the 1920s; one to remember was as the frustrated photographer who tries in vain to get Spanky McFarland to sit still to have his photo taken in *Wild Poses,* an "Our Gang" comedy from 1933.)

The admiring partner says of Johnny, "Wow! What a chest!" With Johnny wearing a broad smile, his washing partner (Pangborn) gives his own comedic Tarzan yell and practically knocks himself out as the real Tarzan catches him in his arms. Johnny could only smile as the story moves on to the next star and the next sequence.

The music in this picture is well worth the price of admission, including Ethyl Merman belting out "Marching Through Berlin"; "Bombshell From Brooklyn" performed by Xavier Cugat and his orchestra; "Quick Sands" sung by Ethyl Waters; Gracie Fields sang "The Machine Gun Song"; and Benny Goodman played "Why Don't You Do Right?" (This number was sung by a young Peggy Lee, who was unbilled in the picture.) Other orchestras that performed included Kay Kyser, Freddie Martin, Guy Lombardo, and Count Basie. All in all, *Stage Door Canteen* was a heartwarming story and a great show for the noblest patriotic cause.

The Hollywood community made major contributions of themselves towards raising money for the war effort, and Johnny did more than his fair share in the various fund-raising endeavors. Johnny had started golfing back in the 1920s when he was a member of the Illinois Athletic Club, and he was one of the top celebrity golfers in the country. Wartime exhibition golf matches raised money for America, as celebrities and top golf professionals teamed up to collect dollars for the war effort. (In the case of female golfers, they were all amateurs. There was no professional golf tour for women until several years after the war ended.)

The best lady golfer of this era — probably any era for that matter — was Babe Didrikson Zaharias. In her 1955 autobiography, *This Life I've Led*, she recalled that Bob Hope and Bing Crosby were the two best celebrity golfers, with Johnny Weissmuller and Mickey Rooney not far behind in the talent department. (Johnny was also close pals with these three great comedians, and played golf with them many times in his lifetime.)

"Bing was the best player of all the Holly-wood actors, but Bob was coming right along. It was a scream, playing with those two," said Babe. "Bob is funnier than Bing, because Bing is a little more conservative and a little more concerned with his golf. But there wasn't a minute Bob Hope was on the golf course that he wasn't clowning. The people really enjoyed it.

"I played benefits for the different armed-service charities with other Hollywood celeb-rities who were pretty good golfers, like Mickey Rooney and Johnny Weissmuller. My idea still was that the more I got to play with the men, the better it would be for my golf game."

Johnny was friends with Babe Didrikson Zaharias, who was voted "Greatest Female Athlete of the Half-Century" by the Associ-ated Press in 1950, at the same time Johnny was named "Greatest Swimmer of the Half-Century." (When Babe was diagnosed with cancer in 1953 and subsequently under-went surgery, Johnny was one of her many friends in the sports world who sent her a message of encouragement that she could beat the cancer and continue her career. Johnny had lost a dear friend in Sybil Bauer in 1927, when she succumbed to cancer at the young age of 22. The Babe did win this particular battle and was able to continue her career, winning several tournaments after her cancer surgery. Sadly, a recurrence of the cancer ended the life of Babe Didrikson Zaharias in 1956 at the age of 45. Despite a valiant battle, Johnny and the world would lose another friend to cancer.)

As the war progressed, Johnny spent much of his time visiting with wounded and disabled veterans at VA hospitals. A chat with Tarzan, a signed photograph, a handshake and smile from Johnny Weissmuller — whatever it took to help the morale of the troops was what he was willing to give. Along with many other stars, Johnny visited military bases and participated in shows for the troops. Of course, Bob Hope was the all-time king at performing for soldiers during every war or conflict that involved Americans. Johnny was always willing to be upstaged by Hope, who had plenty of gags in his bag of tricks about Johnny and his Tarzan role. "Hey, did you hear the one about Weissmuller and Maureen O'Sullivan in the jungle . . ." Johnny could only smile!

At Camp Pendleton in Kentucky, Johnny performed his comedy diving act to the absolute delight of the troops. The recruits were also being trained to dive from a 30-foot tower, a daunting assignment that would be necessary if they became part of any landing force. Some of the young men could barely even swim, but after watching Johnny demonstrate how easily the dive could be made they were able to accomplish the task themselves. Somebody invented a slogan that became the battle cry for this training event: "If Tarzan can dive into a tank of cold water, then so can a marine!" Johnny always led by example, and as usual his example was superlative.

Johnny was also involved in some more serious and dangerous aspects of training at the Long Beach Naval Academy in California. Twice a month for two years he instructed trainees how to swim out from under water covered with flaming oil or gasoline, an absolute certainty if any type of military craft was struck by enemy fire. Johnny even demonstrated a dangerous dive into burning gasoline from a 15-foot platform, proving to the most skeptical soldier that this could be accomplished without serious injury. (Although Johnny did complain of singeing his eyebrows!) When the trainees saw that Weissmuller had the courage to perform a dangerous feat, it gave them the inspiration to accomplish what they had previously feared to even attempt. Courage was something that Johnny was able to call upon in times of crisis, and he displayed his courage time and time again in his lifetime.

Since his divorce from Lupe Velez in 1939, Johnny had occasionally crossed paths with the former Mrs. Weissmuller. When he was planning to wed Beryl and only awaiting his final divorce decree, he had bumped into Lupe at Toots Shor's famous restaurant in New York. Lupe had advised her soon-to-be ex-husband that Beryl wouldn't be right for him because she was not an actress. (Undoubtedly feeling a little jealous that Johnny had a new lady in his life, Lupe probably would have found wrong in any woman that Johnny chose as her successor.)

But their sporadic meetings over the ensuing years were always cordial, and Lupe even included the Weissmullers on her guest list for an occasional cocktail party that she held at her home, which she called "Casas Felicitas" (Happy Home). It was with some surprise that Johnny read in the newspapers on November 27, 1944, that Lupe had announced she was going to marry Harald Ramond, a French actor who was being considered for the lead role in the screen biography of Rudolph Valentino. Johnny was surprised only because Lupe had never remarried after their divorce, and now she was engaged to a man whom she had been dating for only a few months and was a virtual Hollywood unknown. (Ramond was also eight years younger than Lupe.)

Lupe remained in the news when she telephoned her close friend Louella Parsons on December 11th and announced that the engagement to Ramond was terminated. It was later revealed that Lupe was four months pregnant, and Ramond had agreed to marry her only to give the baby a name. The heartless Ramond further stipulated that Lupe would have to sign an agreement that the marriage was solely for that purpose. And thus Lupe ended the engagement, too deeply wounded by this situation with Ramond to proceed with a loveless marriage. To Louella Parsons the fiery Lupe said, "I told him to get out! I like my dogs better!"

Two days later, on December 13th, Lupe attended the premiere of her latest film, *Nana*, a drama set in 1870s Paris about a prostitute with a heart of gold. (It was later agreed that Lupe had given the best dramatic performance of her life in *Nana*, her final film.) Lupe attended the premiere with her best friend, Estelle Taylor, along with Mrs. Jack Oakie. During the course of the evening, Lupe told Estelle: "I am getting to the place where the only thing I am afraid of is life itself . . . I am just weary with the whole world. People think that I like to fight. I have to fight for everything. I'm so tired of it all. Ever since I was a baby I've been fighting. I've never met a man with whom I didn't have to fight to exist."

Perhaps this private conversation with Estelle Taylor — in retrospect — explained her legendary fights with Johnny. With Lupe, her fighting was simply a matter of survival. She just didn't know any other way to exist. But now, apparently, she no longer had a reason to fight against the odds.

The next morning, December 14th, all of the Hollywood community was shocked when it was reported that Lupe had committed suicide the previous evening. Johnny Weissmuller was probably more shocked than anyone, and his grief was deeper than he had ever experienced. He had known Lupe as a fighter, not someone who would give in to the world and take her own life.

The official police report had determined that Lupe returned from the premiere the previous evening to her Laurel Canyon mansion that she shared with her two sisters, her dogs, and 75 canaries. (According to the eccentric Miss Velez, she knew the names of each bird.) Her family was not home and thus she proceeded to dress herself in her favorite blue silk pajamas, reclined on her oversized silk-sheeted bed, and took a fatal overdose of sleeping pills at approximately three a.m. The following morning, secretary Beulah Kinder was unable to waken Lupe from her fatal sleep, and frantically called for a doctor and the police. At first thinking Lupe was just asleep on her bed, Miss Kinder later told police, "She looked so peaceful."

When the doctor arrived at the house, Lupe was immediately pronounced deceased. One of the policemen at the tragic scene related, "She looked so small on that out-sized bed that we thought at first she was just a doll."

An obviously distraught Lupe had left behind two notes by her bed, in her own handwriting. The first note was written to Harald Ramond, the father of her unborn child who had apparently driven her to this act of desperation:

"May God forgive you and forgive me, too. But I prefer to take my life away and our baby's before I bring him shame or kill him. How could you, Harald, fake such a great love for me and our baby when all the time you didn't want us? I see no other way out for me, so good-bye and good luck to you. Love, Lupe."

The second note was to Lupe's companion and secretary of ten years, Beulah Kinder:

"My faithful friend, you and only you know the fact for the reason I am taking my life. May God forgive me, and don't think bad of me. I love you many. Take care of your mother, so good-bye and try to forgive me. Say good-bye to all my friends and the American press that were always so nice to me." A postscript that was written on the back of this note said: "Take care of Chips and Chops." (They were Lupe's pet dogs.)

There is also another account of Lupe's death, a sordid version that has never been officially confirmed or denied. Every story that has ever been written about Lupe offers this alternate scenario, as follows: After Lupe had made her decision to end her life, she swallowed an overdose of Seconal tablets and reclined on her bed, crossing her hands across her abdomen. She imagined how lovely she would be when she was discovered the next morning in her silk pajamas, in the beautiful surroundings of her bedroom.

But here the story veers dramatically, into a macabre tale perhaps more bizarre than in any Hollywood movie. As Lupe began to drift off into her eternal sleep, her spicy Mexican dinner reacted with the Seconal tablets, causing a violent stomach sickness. Stumbling to the bathroom in a semiconscious state, and perhaps now regretting her fatal decision, Lupe died on the bathroom floor.

According to this rather imaginative, perhaps fictional account of her death scene, this is where Lupe was found the next morning. (Both the statements of the police on the scene and that of Beulah Kinder contradict this story, leaving it dubious at best.)

Whichever version one cares to believe, it was nevertheless the sad end of Lupe Velez. Her body lay in state for three hours on December 21, 1944 at the Church of the Recessional, Forest Lawn Memorial Park in Glendale, before a nondenominational service was held.

Johnny Weissmuller, still deeply saddened

by the self-destruction of his former wife, was one of the pallbearers that also included her close friends, Gilbert Roland and Arturo de Cordova. More than 4,000 fans and admirers filed by her open casket to say a final good-bye to the "Mexican Spitfire," one of Hollywood's most popular and vibrant personalities.

After the California service, Lupe's body was flown to Mexico City for religious rites and final interment. She was buried on December 27, 1944 at the Pateon de Dolores Cemetery (graveyard of sorrows). Jorge Negrete, popular screen tenor, spoke for ten minutes over the grave. "Lupe, our friend, you are being lowered into the ground of your homeland." Police were unable to control the crowd of thousands, who pressed close for vantage points to view the ceremony for their beloved Lupe.

Bo Roos, who was business manager for both Lupe and Johnny Weissmuller, estimated her estate at close to $200,000. Half of the estate was left to Beulah Kinder, her faithful friend and secretary. The remainder was to be paid monthly to her family — two sisters, a brother, and her mother — through a trust fund. Lupe's possessions — at one time shared with Johnny — were auctioned off on June 22, 1945. Her home in Beverly Hills, the Casa Felicitas, was sold for $41,750 to Mrs. Virginia Kuppinger, the wife of a United States naval officer. Her prized jewelry collection brought over $100,000, and her two fur coats (chinchilla and sable) sold for close to $50,000. The silver, gold, and ebony headboard of her oversized bed was sold for a mere $45.

Over the years there have been many cruel jokes about the death of Lupe Velez, in regard to the second version of her death scene. But it was no joke to Johnny and the rest of the Hollywood community — rather it was the saddest of all events. Harald Ramond was ostracized in Hollywood for his influence on Lupe's suicide, and dropped out of sight to be heard from nevermore.

For Johnny, these were simply the saddest of times. Despite the frequent fights during their marriage, Johnny had truly loved Lupe. And they became better friends after the divorce, than when they were married. The death of Lupe added an additional burden to his shoulders, already weighted from his legal separation from Beryl and his children. A divorce was imminent for Johnny and Beryl, but the inability to negotiate a property settlement was standing in the way of the legal proceedings.

But with the conclusion of World War II, there was a new hope in the air. For his volunteer service to his country, Johnny received a scroll from the Treasury Department which noted:

"In recognition of distinguished and patriotic service to the Cause of Freedom, rendered in behalf of the War Finance Program of the United States Government, this citation is awarded to Johnny Weissmuller." (The document was signed by Henry Morgenthau, Jr., who was the Secretary of the Treasury under President Franklin Delano Roosevelt.)

It was also time for a new beginning for Johnny, as he went back to work in 1945 on his latest picture, *Tarzan and the Amazons*. It was a new day, a fresh start, and a new Jane for Johnny — Brenda Joyce.

CHAPTER TWENTY-FIVE

Old Tarzan Gets New Jane

The 1945 entry, *Tarzan and the Amazons*, introduced a new female co-star for Johnny in the person of 27-year-old Brenda Joyce. The character of Jane had been absent from the Tarzan family the previous two pictures, as Sol Lesser had held on to a thread of hope that Maureen O'Sullivan would end her retirement and resume her role. On December 3rd of 1943, Louella Parsons had noted in her Hearst gossip column that the original Jane would be returning: "Maureen O'Sullivan to resume her job as Tarzan's mate . . . Maureen and John Weissmuller will co-star in *Tarzan and the Amazons* for RKO and Sol Lesser." However, Miss O'Sullivan was pregnant again (with daughter Mia Farrow), and the rumors of her return were finally put to rest in 1944 with the signing of blonde and gorgeous Brenda Joyce as the new Jane. Johnny later joked: "I'm not sure what my young fans will think when they find out that Tarzan has a new blonde Jane in his treehouse!"

Brenda Joyce had been discovered by Darryl Zanuck while she was a student at U.C.L.A., and made her memorable film debut as Fern Simon in the spectacular 20th Century-Fox production of *The Rains Came* (1939). She was a Cinderella girl for Fox, gaining roles in the 1940s that required a fresh face and her specific outdoorsy beauty. Her co-star in *The Rains Came*, Tyrone Power, once called her "the girl with the undazzled charm." Brenda had recently starred in *The Enchanted Forest* (1945), the story of a young boy who learns about life from an old hermit who lives in the splendor of nature's forest. Brenda was also at the peak of her popularity when she teamed with Johnny to star in the Tarzan series, appearing in a total of five films for the year.

Born in Kansas City, Missouri as Betty Leabo in 1918, Brenda was married and had two children of her own when she accepted the role of Jane in *Tarzan and the Amazons*. As the new Jane, Brenda Joyce had a tough act to follow — Maureen O'Sullivan was internationally adored in her role as Johnny Weissmuller's Tarzan mate. However, Brenda seemed to fit in rather nicely with the Tarzan family of Weissmuller and Sheffield, and thus she made an ideal screen mother for Boy and jungle wife for Tarzan. 14-year-old

Johnny Sheffield as Boy was beginning to grow out of his name, but for the time being he was still fine for the son of Tarzan.

Johnny Weissmuller at age 40 had really worked hard to get himself into shape, and Tarzan appeared much closer to his championship form of yesteryear. Johnny was also back to his original forte in *Tarzan and the Amazons*: swimming the American crawl. An exciting scene had Tarzan slicing through the river water at breakneck speed to rescue Boy from a crocodile — killing the man-made beast in a savage battle as he had done many times before in the MGM pictures.

The story began as Jane is returning to Tarzan and Boy after spending many months in England during the war. A heroic Tarzan saves the life of a young woman from the claws of a panther, and then returns Athena (Shirley O'Hara) to her people — a lost race of beautiful Amazon women. Tarzan is the lone outsider who is allowed to enter or leave Palmeria, and he is a friend of the wise old queen of the Amazons (Maria Ouspenskaya). Also arriving in Africa at the same time as Jane are a group of archaeologists led by Sir Guy Henderson (Henry Stephenson), who is fascinated by the premise of a lost culture of Amazon women. (Especially since the Amazon river and the legend both belong in South America!) Protecting the land of his friends, Tarzan rightfully refuses to help the expedition, which is guided by fortune hunter and Tarzan nemesis Ballister (Barton MacLane).

Temporarily misplacing his loyalty, Boy leads the expedition to Palmeria. After entering the forbidden land, they are all sentenced to a life at hard labor. The deaths begin to mount in the quest for the priceless sacred symbols of the Amazons, as Athena and Sir Guy are murdered by the ruthless Ballister. Tarzan arrives in time to save Jane from the jaws of a lion, and turn the tables on Ballister (who sinks into quicksand for his final resting place). A final act of heroism by Tarzan saves his son from a death sentence and returns the stolen sacred symbols to the Queen.

Johnny and new mate Brenda Joyce were given a strong supporting cast in *Tarzan and the Amazons*, including Maria Ouspenskaya as the queen of the Amazons. She was twice nominated for supporting Oscars (*Dodsworth* and *Love Affair*), but perhaps her most memorable role was as the gypsy woman whose werewolf son bites Lon Chaney, Jr. in *The Wolf Man* (1941). Classy gentleman actor Henry Stephenson spoke in irony when he is introduced to Tarzan as Sir Guy Henderson: "I'm very glad to meet you Tarzan. Jane has told me so much about you, I almost feel I know you." (Stephenson had a twinkle in his eye when he spoke this line to Weissmuller, as the veteran character actor had appeared in *Tarzan Finds A Son!* in a similar role.)

Director Kurt Neumann was well in command directing action thrillers, and kept Johnny in the middle of a plenitude of fast-paced excitement and adventure. There was also no pause in the action for any real romance between Tarzan and the new Jane. (There was a little playful fun, perhaps, but nothing resembling the steamy love affair that was the trademark of the early years of the classic Weissmuller and O'Sullivan relationship.)

Brenda Joyce had successfully stepped into the jungle clogs of Maureen, and would continue on with the role of Jane even beyond Johnny's years as Tarzan. Miss Joyce brought her own brand of warmth to the role, and indeed was a special Jane who rivaled Maureen as a favorite of the fans. Brenda would make a total of five Tarzan pictures, second only to Miss O'Sullivan's six. Certainly Maureen was the most popular Jane, but Brenda Joyce was a close second and brought a popularity back to the Tarzan pictures that had been missing during the two films that the character of Jane was written out of the story.

Weissmuller himself was never more popular as Tarzan, and was receiving thousands of letters each week from fans around the globe. At a 1946 personal appearance in Galveston, Texas, hundreds of fans crowded onto a pier hoping to get close to Johnny for an autograph from their hero. As the pier became dangerously overloaded, the wooden structure collapsed 17 feet to the beach and surf, injuring 37 people. Johnny, who had seen his share of water tragedies in his lifetime, was not injured in the mishap.

Johnny continued his physical reincarnation and really looked his best in years for his role as the ape-man in *Tarzan and the Leopard Woman*. The former world champion swimmer would turn 42-years-old in the summer of '46, but the trimmed-down Johnny looked like he could continue on as Tarzan indefinitely. In an early scene, Tarzan enters into a wrestling match with one of the local strongmen (played by pro wrestler "King Kong Kashey"). Weissmuller easily hoisted the burly 200-pound Kashey over his head like a bale of hay, and tossed him aside like a stuffed doll.

Brenda Joyce was proving to be a popular choice as the new Jane, while still finding time to appear in three additional films in 1946. Little John Sheffield (who wasn't quite so little anymore), engaged in serious battle for the first time on screen in defending Jane from the young killer Kimba (Tommy Cook), who had plans to cut her heart out. Portraying Lea, the High Priestess, was an actress who had chosen an unusual moniker to replace her legal name of Burnu Davenport: "Acquanetta." The exotic looks of Acquanetta made her an exquisite choice as the villainess, Lea, the ruler of the deadly cult of leopard worshipers.

In this story a jungle caravan is annihilated, and a survivor tells Tarzan of being attacked by leopards. The jungle-wise Tarzan realizes that these leopards are a deadly cult of men who worship a leopard god and claw their victims to death, and cut out their hearts to prove their manhood. Tarzan leads a safari to investigate and they are savagely attacked by leopards, but the ape-man is hardly fooled by the ruse. Behind the evil doings is the High Priestess Lea (Acquanetta), who is aided by the diabolical Dr. Lazar (Edgar Barrier), a native doctor who resolves to destroy the men who invade his country to plunder their resources. Lea sends her demented little brother Kimba to spy on the jungle man, who poses a threat to her cult.

Meanwhile Tarzan, Jane and Boy are all captured in attempting to free four young school teachers who are kidnaped by the leopard men — all are sentenced to die by sacrifice in a cult ceremony of the leopard people. Cheeta cuts the bonds of the captives at Tarzan's order — when they are safely away, the ape-man explodes! As Tarzan pulls down the pillars that support their underground temple, the leopard worshipers are crushed lifeless. Dr. Lazar and Kimba die at each other's hands in a bitter struggle fueled by their mutual hate. The mystery is solved and Tarzan has destroyed the leopard woman and her strange evil cult.

Tarzan and the Leopard Woman was mostly nonstop action and thrilling drama, with Tarzan usually right in the middle of it all. The ape-man fighting the leopard men in the crocodile infested river, and again in the jungle, were exciting battles. Another graphic scene showed Tarzan's safari being attacked by real leopards, with the ape-man in the middle of the fray. Although Johnny fought with a trained leopard, the real leopard footage edited in made the entire scene very realistic. Tarzan's next battle against the forces of evil would be in the bayous of Louisiana against a name from the past, Buster Crabbe, in *Swamp Fire*.

Johnny Weissmuller and Buster Crabbe had a long (and mostly friendly) rivalry in the swimming pool and on the screen. After they both climbed out of the pool for good, they competed for the role of Tarzan and Johnny was triumphant. It seemed Crabbe was always following in the footsteps and rather tall shadow of Weissmuller. Escaping Johnny's shadow was a formidable task for Buster, a daunting assignment that seemed to haunt him his entire life. The comparisons were inevitable, and Crabbe never achieved the stature of Johnny or the immense public adulation. But he tried extremely hard and had a successful career that many would envy.

When they teamed up for the movie *Swamp Fire* in 1946, the pecking order was status quo: Johnny was the hero, Johnny Duval, while Crabbe was the villain, a bayou trapper named Mike Kalavich. In this story Johnny was a local hero who comes home from the war to reclaim his girlfriend Toni (Carol Thurston), who is also coveted by Mike. Johnny Duval is a war-shocked veteran who lost a ship during the war and blames himself for the loss of his men. Back home in Louisiana he soon regains his job as a Coast Guard bar pilot, and saves the life of rich society girl Janet Hilton (Virginia Grey) after her yacht is stranded in the Gulf.

By this time Johnny has two girls in love with him, and a river swamp rat who hates him. The girls fight (literally) over Johnny, and then get thrown in the river to cool off. It all comes down to a final showdown between Johnny and Mike, who has set the swamp on fire to gain vengeance against his rival. Toni gets caught in the fire, is subsequently saved by Johnny, and then catches a bullet meant for her lover from the scoundrel Mike. The two men battle into the swamp, where Mike tries to end Johnny's life with his razor-sharp knife. They struggle to the death, but Johnny is victorious! Johnny and Toni decide to get married and he goes back to work as a Coast Guard captain.

Crabbe portrayed a quintessential villain in *Swamp Fire* — heavy foreign accent, pencil-thin mustache, and a hatred for the hero of the story, the clean-cut war veteran Johnny Duval. In his autobiography, *A Self Portrait*, Buster recalled filming the climactic fight scene with Johnny. According to Crabbe, Johnny had taken a couple of shots of brandy to warm his insides when they went into the frigid tank to film the scene:

"*Swamp Fire* was the first picture I made with Johnny Weissmuller. I played the part of a mean villain who preyed on the inhabitants of the Louisiana Bayou, while Johnny starred as the hero who gives me my comeuppance at the end. Besides fighting alligators, Johnny and I had a long fight scene in the end of the movie, requiring that we stay underwater for most of the battle, rolling and turning in locked combat until he eventually comes up the winner.

"Well, Johnny had trouble staying down during the filming of the scene. The water was cold in the tank — purposely cold because whenever actors went into water with live alligators the alligators weren't doped up for the fight scenes, they were numbed in the cold water, making them lethargic. Johnny had spent much of his idle time that day sip-

522

ping brandy to keep warm, so when our fight scene time came, he ruined several takes by bobbing prematurely to the surface. We were supposed to remain submerged for 30 to 45 seconds, thrashing water, until I would send a burst of bubbles to the surface to indicate the fight was over.

"I could never drink hard liquor while swimming, especially if the water was cold. It made me sick to my stomach. It wasn't my place to preach to Weissmuller, but his continual blowing of the scene was keeping me in frigid water longer than I cared to be, so I was determined that the next time the cameras rolled, we'd complete the scene. The tank was about four and a half feet deep, with windows in the walls for the camera to film through. Weissmuller and I ducked under and began our make-believe struggle to the death, but this time I got a headlock on him and rolled over and over, keeping him down by force. He jerked and struggled to break my hold — which only made the battle seem more realistic, which, in his case, it was — but I held on. When I felt we'd been down long enough, I let out a burst of air and released old John and he popped to the surface.

" 'What the hell you trying to do?' he gasped, 'drown me?'

"I wasn't worried about drowning him. Even though he'd let himself get out of condition, I knew he had enough reserve to stay down much longer if he had to. He just needed someone to persuade him to give a little extra."

It seemed to be kind of a mean-spirited thing for Crabbe to do — holding Johnny underwater when he was expecting his fellow actor to just complete the scene as rehearsed. Crabbe was four years younger than Johnny's 42 years, and maybe was in a little better shape at this point in time. But Johnny saw the humor in it and never held a grudge, and later had his own version of this story, which was completely different!

"They co-starred Buster and me in a turkey called *Swamp Fire*," recalled Johnny, "and the big scene was a fight in a lake. Well, the lake wasn't ready for us, it was 59 degrees and Buster wasn't ready for the lake, either. He got his foot wet and howled and sent somebody for brandy. He took a big slug of it and then we started wading in and before we were up to our knees he belted me a good one and said, 'That's for Honolulu,' — he meant one of the times I beat him swimming.

"Then he gave me another roundhouse and said that was for somewhere else and about then I decided he had quite a list to run through — I ducked and Buster went right over in the water and lay there and I had to fish him out. The director thought it was great and when I got Buster back on land he said, 'Thank heavens I got that out of my system.' "

Well, you can believe whichever of these two stories you wish . . . it's easy to see that there are two sides to every story, especially between two old friendly rivals. Crabbe never managed to beat Johnny in a swimming contest, and in their two films together he was stuck as the villain to Johnny's hero. But there was friendship as well as respect between the two men, despite the fact that the green-eyed monster — jealousy — occasionally tainted Crabbe's words and actions towards Johnny.

In one scene Johnny must race to rescue Toni (Carol Thurston) from a bayou 'gator, and wrestle and knife the beast into submission. This was awfully reminiscent of Johnny doing the same thing in his Tarzan pictures. Johnny had more dialogue than his Tarzan character, but action was his forte and there was plenty in this Louisiana bayou swamp adventure.

Swamp Fire was Johnny's first picture for producers William Pine and William Thomas, and it would also be his last. He was paid $75,000 for starring in the melodrama, but the rest of his three-picture contract went unfulfilled. The cowboy picture they had envisioned for Johnny had fallen by the wayside, and with World War II concluded war pictures were also out of vogue for the time being. When *Swamp Fire* opened in New York in late August of 1946 at the Gotham theater, other pictures that opened that same week included Humphrey Bogart in *The Big Sleep* (at the Strand), and Burt Lancaster in the crime thriller *The Killers* (at the Winter Garden). With these classic *films noir* on the menu, most movie fans decided to wait for Weissmuller to resume his Tarzan role. Johnny later said, "I took one look at that picture and went back to the jungle!"

Johnny indeed went back to the jungle for his next portrayal, *Tarzan and the Huntress*, and stayed there virtually for the rest of his career. As Johnny noted many times, "There was swimming in the Tarzan pictures, and my fans forgave the fact that I wasn't a great actor." Johnny wasn't belittling himself, just giving an honest appraisal of his acting abilities. In actuality, he was more than a decent actor who was highly believable on screen. For Johnny's fans, it was really more than that: They admired and adored him for all his heroic action in his twelve Tarzan pictures and the later Jungle Jim portrayals. And they certainly forgave him for his forgettable foray into the Louisiana bayou country in *Swamp Fire*.

Tarzan and the Huntress commenced as the birthday of King Farrod is being celebrated by all his subjects and close friends, including

Tarzan, Jane, and Boy. Meanwhile, Tanya Rawlins (Patricia Morison) and Karl Marley (John Warburton) have come to Africa to capture wild animals for zoos. Limited by the king's quota of two animals per species, the king's corrupt nephew Ozira (Ted Hecht) enters into a secret pact with the greedy hunters and has the king murdered. Meanwhile, Prince Suli (Maurice Tauzen) narrowly escapes death himself but lies unconscious in the jungle. When Tarzan discovers the hunters trapping without quota, he orders them to stay on the far side of the river and then calls all the animals to his side of the river with his mighty jungle cry. Chief hunter Paul Weir (Barton MacLane) ignores Tarzan's order and crosses the river to trap animals (but Cheeta warns his master).

Tarzan and Boy stealthily enter the hunters' camp at night and steal all their guns, and release the caged animals — they also discover the wounded Suli in an animal trap and save his life. Tarzan single-handedly eliminates three hunters who track him into the jungle, and Ozira and Karl are killed under the crush of Tarzan's mighty pachyderms. Paul Weir dies a grisly death when he falls into an occupied lion trap, but Tanya manages to escape Africa in her plane. Tarzan saves Jane and Boy from a perilous trap in a hunter's net, and Prince Suli takes the throne as the rightful king.

The "huntress" of the title of *Tarzan and the Huntress* was sultry Patricia Morison, who was hired by Sol Lesser to confront Tarzan in this adventure about ruthless big-game hunters who invade the ape-man's domain. Miss Morison's character of Tanya Rawlins was more honorable than her male counterparts who die in the story (Barton MacLane and John Warburton), and is allowed to "escape with her life" by plane at the end of the picture; justice seemed to have been served without killing off the misguided Tanya. (Miss Morison's motion picture career began with a bang in 1939 with the lead role of the merciless heroine in *Persons in Hiding*, a gangster picture in which she becomes a public enemy. Her 1940s portrayals included the title role in the "B" picture, *Danger Woman*, which also starred Brenda Joyce.)

As a change of pace, producer Sol Lesser allowed a measure of romance into the story, as Johnny Weissmuller and Brenda Joyce engaged in a little serious smooching as well as some playful fun between Tarzan and Jane. (This wasn't Johnny and Maureen steaming up the vines, but it was some genuine affection between the jungle couple.) A nice touch was a smoothly choreographed swimming scene, with Tarzan, Jane and Boy performing some synchronized swimming: crawl, backstroke, crawl, backstroke — all in perfect rhythm and coordinated grace. *Tarzan and the Huntress* was one of the better RKO Tarzan adventures because of the excellent use of that time-tested formula plot: greedy foreigners come to Africa to brazenly plunder, and Tarzan takes exception and rises to battle the forces of evil.

Johnny Weissmuller never did get to film a Tarzan picture in Africa — instead they brought Africa to Johnny. In this particular adventure a great deal of fascinating wild animal footage was used to exceptional advantage: aerial shots of huge herds of zebras and elephants, and great flocks of birds; terrestrial shots of savage lions and leopards; and roiling rivers infested with reptiles and hippopotami. The native big game hunt was an exciting segment, culminating with an almost grotesque pool of dozens of snapping crocodiles (hungrily awaiting the next unfortunate victim). The climactic scene where Tarzan's elephants come charging to the rescue, used some well conceived rear projections to maximum effect. (And with the thrilling musical score pounding in the background, it was indeed memorable.)

Johnny Sheffield, who as a seven-year-old had made his debut as Boy in the 1939 classic *Tarzan Finds A Son!*, was now a solidly built 15-year-old lad who was approaching six-feet in height; this would be Sheffield's final Tarzan picture, as he had simply outgrown the role of Boy. (Sheffield went on to star in his own series of jungle adventures, beginning with *Bomba, the Jungle Boy* in 1948; there were eleven additional *Bomba* sequels through 1955. Having had enough of the jungles by the end of the *Bomba* series, Johnny Sheffield retired from films and entered college at U.C.L.A., eventually gaining a degree in Business Administration.)

Although their paths went separately at this junction, Big John and Little John remained friends the rest of their lives. As the years moved by in a blinding blur, they carried with them many fond memories of the Tarzan years. For Johnny Weissmuller, his long and illustrious career as the cinema Tarzan would conclude after his role in the next Tarzan adventure, *Tarzan and the Mermaids*, which would be filmed in Acapulco, Mexico.

CHAPTER TWENTY-SIX

Adventures in Paradise ... Acapulco

Tarzan and the Mermaids would be Johnny Weissmuller's final portrayal as Tarzan, ending his seventeen-year reign as the King of the Jungle. Johnny had visited the famed vacation land of Acapulco many times, starting with a short holiday that he took after retiring from swimming in 1929. Johnny also owned a piece of the cliff-top Los Flamingos Hotel, an investment orchestrated by his business manager, Bo Roos. The classic old hotel had been built during the Depression, and was situated on top of the highest cliffs of Acapulco some 450-feet above sea level.

The spectacular open view of the ocean was only one of the attractions, as the famed Acapulco cliff divers performed daily at the nearby "La Quebrada" cliffs. Located within five minutes of the hotel was the bull ring where the brave matadors and bulls fought to the death, as well as the "Caleta" and "Caletilla" beaches where Johnny would take his daily swim in the ocean.

Several other Hollywood stars (all clients of Roos') also owned a share of the 28-room luxury hotel, including Johnny's old friend John Wayne. Johnny had been close pals with Duke Wayne going back to the early 1930s at the Hollywood Athletic Club, where they both were members. Wayne would often invite Johnny to spend a few days in Acapulco aboard his yacht, *The Wild Goose,* along with other Wayne cronies and drinking buddies. Other members of the famed "Hollywood Gang" that were part-owners of the Los Flamingos included Red Skelton and Fred MacMurray (as well as Bo Roos himself). Johnny actually owned about 17% of the hotel, as did John Wayne and Red Skelton, while the remaining shares in the hotel were split between Roos and MacMurray (who wound up a multimillionaire when he retired from acting).

Filming on *Tarzan and the Mermaids* began in the spring of 1947 and was supposed to last only three months. However, various delays ranging from minor to catastrophic, stretched the production schedule out to nine months. (Eventually, Johnny's new fiancee Allene Gates got lonely during the protracted shooting calendar, and came down to Acapulco to spend some precious time with her husband-to-be.) A young lad named Mike Oliver, who would grow up to be the editor of the *Acapulco News* and Johnny's close friend for 35 years, was at this time a young Tarzan fan who was thrilled to hang around the filming locations and run errands for an American movie icon, Johnny Weissmuller.

"Johnny was my hero," recalled Oliver, "and as a kid I got up every morning at five-thirty to collect his lunch from the Casablanca Hotel and go with him on location at the lagoon out at Pie de la Cuesta where filming started at sunrise and lasted until sunset. Johnny and I were inseparable. He would take me to Caleta Beach where we paddled around on a paddle board and he kept giving me swimming instructions. I already knew how to swim but not nearly as well as when he was through with me. In the evenings I would sit next to him at the hotel bar while he had his drink and for me he would order a Shirley Temple, a soft cherry drink. I was in seventh heaven with Johnny and my heart would jump with joy every time the filming was postponed another month."

The Acapulco scenery was enormously breathtaking throughout the movie, and the high dives photographed from overhead angles and from the beaches below were magnificent. In previous accounts of the filming of this picture it was reported that a tragic accident occurred when Angel Garcia was killed making Tarzan's climactic dive from the highest cliffs, his body crushed on the rocks after making the dive. According to Mike Oliver, this was a completely erroneous anecdote. Two separate incidents occurred to account for the mistaken report, as Oliver recalled in a 1999 letter.

During production of the picture there was a tragic death, but it was not the diver named Raul Garcia, who was doubling for Johnny. A wooden bridge was being built for a scene filmed on the tiny El Farallon Island, where George Zucco as the villainous high priest would climb to the top of the mound in conducting one of his bizarre religious rituals. During filming, two speed boats would carry the lumber and carpenters to the island, so the workers could construct a walkway to the top of El Farallon.

In the words of Mike Oliver: "One of the carpenters fell in the water and just as he came to the surface, two speed boats which were floating there, slammed together and crushed the man's skull. Sol Lesser, in Hollywood, was informed of what happened and shut down the filming for one day in respect of the man who had been killed."

A second incident, which did involve the diver Raul Garcia, is again explained by Mike Oliver in an excerpt from his book, *Mike Oliver's Acapulco*: "One night during the filming of *Tarzan and the Mermaids*, Johnny decided to go to La Perla and watch the cliff divers, as in the movie there was a scene where Johnny dives from the cliff top. It was Raul Garcia's turn and being the leader of fourteen divers, he dedicated his special performance to Johnny. With all the lights off in the gorge below, it was complete darkness except for two lighted torches Raul held in each hand while waiting for the precise wave to dive into — that wave giving the diver the added depth needed to survive the plunge.

"Raul was the only diver who spoke English and when he came to the top of the stairs at La Perla to wave to the customers, they gave him a thunderous applause. Then in English and in front of everybody he challenged Johnny to do the dive. Johnny was deeply embarrassed but rose to meet the challenge, but the RKO executives in the club immediately stopped him (claiming that if anything happened, hundreds of people would be out of work, the movie could not be finished and the insurance company would not cover any accident of this sort). Johnny, who really had no desire to dive off this very high cliff, sat down quite relieved. Johnny and I remained friends for the rest of his life. He would entertain me at his home in Beverly Hills or Las Vegas, and I him on his return visits to Acapulco."

Throughout his years as Tarzan, Johnny had a risky habit that produced many grey hairs on the head of his producer, Sol Lesser.

Even when a stunt double was used for a very dangerous stunt, Weissmuller would attempt the stunt after the scene was filmed to see if he could actually do it. In the case of the perilous high dive from the cliff, Johnny was willing but fortunately he was talked out of performing a dive higher than he had ever attempted before. In this case, a dare from diver Raul Garcia could have been a tragic ending for Johnny.

Weissmuller at age 43 was still powerfully built, and a scene where he fights a half-dozen men was awe-inspiring as he hoisted one man over his head like a child. True, he didn't have the lean physique of his younger days, but this veteran Tarzan still fought his enemies with the heart of a lion and the strength of three men. The swimming and underwater scenes, always Johnny's forte, were exciting and demanding sequences.

The role of the maiden Mara went to the relatively unknown Linda Christian, a stunning 24-year-old Mexican actress who had made her film debut in *Up In Arms* (1944). The beautiful Miss Christian later became the wife of Tyrone Power, and was destined to eventually marry into European nobility.

Brenda Joyce was by now a fixture in the Tarzan pictures as Jane, but missing was Johnny Sheffield as Boy (who was now "Bomba, the Jungle Boy"). Boy's absence from the story was explained by a letter from

England, where their son had gone to pursue a formal education. British actor George Zucco invariably made a diabolical villain (as he did in the Sherlock Holmes films pitted against Basil Rathbone). Zucco's sinister high priest Palanth was no exception, although his evil presence was overcome by Tarzan.

Photographed on location in Acapulco, the story takes place on a mysterious island protected by the impenetrable jungles of Tarzan's Africa. The people that inhabit this land are known as Aquaticans, and they live in constant terror of the sinister high priest Palanth (George Zucco), and his fake pagan god, Baloo (Fernando Wagner). The diabolical tyrant intends to force the beautiful maiden Mara (Linda Christian) to marry the false deity, who in reality is a cohort of Palanth called Varga. Preferring death to this marriage, Mara flees Aquatania to find her banished lover, Tiko (Gustav Rojo).

Meanwhile, Tarzan is surprised to find a runaway girl — Mara — hooked in his fishing net. Mara tells her story to Tarzan and Jane, who are sympathetic and offer to help her in a crusade against the evil forces in her village. But the cult-followers of Baloo overpower Tarzan and kidnap Mara, forcing her back to a marriage that would be worse than death. A grim Tarzan tracks them back to Aquatania, while Jane summons the Commissioner to investigate the virtual slavery overseen by the high priest. In Aquatania, Tarzan's life is threatened by Palanth, while Varga intends to murder Jane before she can uncover his racket of stealing pearls from the natives. A heroic Tarzan makes a perilous dive from the high cliffs to do battle with Palanth's cult-followers and a deadly giant octopus. He survives against these great odds, and climbs back to the top of the cliff as Jane is about to be thrown to her death by the evil ones. Tarzan unmasks Varga to reveal an ordinary mortal, and hurls the false deity to his deserved demise on the rocks below.

The powerful climax orchestrated by director Robert Florey, with Tarzan battling underwater with first a horde of divers and next a giant octopus, and then hurling the evil Baloo onto the rocks below, was a fitting ending for Weissmuller's nearly two decades of action as Tarzan. The musical score for *Tarzan and the Mermaids* was composed and directed by noted composer Dimitri Tiomkin (who would eventually win several Academy Awards for his music). Tiomkin's score was at times haunting and powerful, especially the savage vocal choral chants to the false god, Baloo.

The *Motion Picture Guide*, praising Weissmuller's final Tarzan portrayal, said: "The film is aided by Florey's fine direction, Draper's superb camera work, and

Tiomkin's score."

It really had seemed that the end would never come, but Weissmuller was finally stepping down from his role of Tarzan as he would reach his 44th birthday in June of 1948. For the first time in nearly two decades, Johnny Weissmuller would not be the screen Tarzan. The new ape-man would be Lex Barker, who had what is required of all Tarzans: perpetual youth. Brenda Joyce would join Barker in *Tarzan's Magic Fountain* (1949), her final portrayal as Jane before retiring to devote herself to her husband, children, and a life outside of Hollywood's land of make-believe.

There are four precepts that Tarzan — embodied by Johnny Weissmuller — must follow, according to the creator of Tarzan, Edgar Rice Burroughs: (1) Tarzan must not kill, except in self-defense or for food; (2) he must never drink or smoke, and must always remain pure in mind and body; (3) he must never fight except in defense of the oppressed; (4) and Tarzan, pure at heart, must never cast a romantic eye towards any woman but his Jane.

Perhaps oversimplifying his own concept of Tarzan, Weissmuller once said (with a twinkle in his eyes): "Tarzan is just a big-muscled guy who is sharp about jungles." He was never worried about his acting, or how the reviewers felt about his histrionic abilities. He was, however, concerned about his young audiences enjoying his films, as he asked: "Will the kids like this?" Johnny accepted the burden of role model to the young generations, and if he ever failed to live up to the expectations of his adoring public, he would be greatly disappointed in himself. He always tried to live up to the screen persona of Tarzan, but of course only a literary figure — or a celluloid image — could actually do that which is truly impossible.

In January of 1948, several weeks before the spring release of *Tarzan and the Mermaids*, writer Thomas Brady of the *New York Times*, offered his own interpretation of the great success and appeal of Weissmuller's Tarzan pictures:

"Tarzan's appeal to audiences is fundamental. He invariably demonstrates that a simple, righteous man can take care of himself and his family, a dictum that most people nowadays wish desperately to believe. His appeal goes even further than that of the screen's cowboy heroes and crook-chasers. The ape-man abandons civilization completely and relies on himself alone. He is above and beyond plumbing, automobiles, and taxes. The atavism to which he appeals is an escapist desire. There are other reasons for Tarzan's popularity, too: he combines the excitement of a wild-animal act with an acrobatic performance; he puts on some fine swimming exhibitions; and he operates against a background of lush jungle scenery. Add all of these things together and you begin to see why nearly 140,000,000 people see every Tarzan picture, from New York to Bombay. The foreign audience is far greater than the American. The overseas life of a Tarzan film is from five to ten years, during which time it attracts about 100,000,000 people to the box office.

"In 1932 Johnny Weissmuller, an Olympic swimmer, was introduced as the jungle king and, ever since has dominated the field despite the appearance from time to time of minor incarnations. Weissmuller, who lives modestly in Beverly Hills between the annual Tarzan pictures, believes he has as good a life as any Hollywood actor. He works only twelve weeks out of the year and has an annual income in excess of $50,000. Weissmuller is no more a typical actor than Tarzan is a typical character. The only concession he has made to Hollywood is to marry three times. He still retains his simple and athletic tastes. He plays a great deal of golf, and in the summer spends his days at Newport Bay, where he operates a small business renting pedal-driven boats." (This indeed sounds like Johnny — a simple venture that kept him close to people and to water, things most dear to his heart.)

You will notice that Mr. Brady stated that each of Johnny's Tarzan movies were seen by approximately 140 million moviegoers worldwide. Today, if a picture brings in over 100 million dollars it is considered very successful, and as the totals go up it becomes a blockbuster. The average price to see a movie today is at least six dollars, while back in 1930s and 1940s it was approximately twenty-five cents or less. Translated into today's dollars, a Weissmuller Tarzan film shown worldwide to 140 million customers might gross in the vicinity of 840 million dollars!

Even though he retired his loincloth in 1948, Johnny's Tarzan pictures would be playing first-run in foreign theaters for many years to come and making money for MGM and RKO. And then of course there was his new series of action movies, "Jungle Jim," which would also become immensely popular in all four corners of the world. Johnny Weissmuller's movie heroes made millions of dollars for the studios — at twenty-five cents per satisfied customer.

CHAPTER TWENTY-SEVEN

Johnny + Allene = L-o-v-e

With his Tarzan role behind him, it was time for Johnny to move on in life. The first order of business was to complete his divorce from Beryl so he could marry his new flame, Allene Gates. Johnny and Allene first met at the California Country Club, a luxury golf course in which he was an investor. Miss Gates, 18-years-old when she was introduced to Johnny during the war, was the daughter of golf celebrity Ward "Three- Iron" Gates, and the great-granddaughter of Heber Kimball, Brigham Young's Mormon aide. Johnny was more than twenty years older than Allene, a stunningly beautiful lass who was very mature-looking for her age.

Allene was extremely attractive in a Nordic sort of look: fair skin and blonde hair, tall and "leggy," and she could easily have worked as a fashion model. Allene, a nonswimmer, was purported to have said on occasion, "I'm known as the bathing suit that never got wet." This athletic young woman was an accomplished amateur golfer who practiced at the California Country Club, where her path often crossed with the movies' Tarzan during their practice sessions. She soon became friends with Johnny, and friendship quickly moved towards romantic captivation.

Knowing his divorce from Beryl was imminent, Johnny too began to fall in love with Allene (despite the difference in their ages). They seemed to enjoy the same activities, they both loved the sport of golf, and for Johnny this new and exciting relationship began to fill the massive void in his heart after his separation from Beryl. (Certainly, Johnny had accepted the fact that his marriage to Beryl was over, but the loss of his children through the separation was especially painful for him. Although he was able to see John Scott, Wendy, and Heidi on occasion, it was a far cry from the happiness of being surrounded by the love of his three children in his own home.)

When Johnny headed down to Acapulco in the spring of 1947 to film *Tarzan and the Mermaids*, it was supposed to be a short separation for the two lovers to sort out their feelings. Eventually, Allene joined Johnny in Acapulco for the balance of the production schedule, and when they returned to California at the end of 1947, they were both ready for the commitment of marriage (pending

Johnny's divorce).

Meanwhile, back in 1946 financial advisor Bo Roos had put Johnny on a tight budget, expecting that the divorce from Beryl was going to be a costly one for his client. Johnny questioned why it was necessary to pinch pennies, when he had made millions from his role of Tarzan the previous fifteen years. (It is true that Johnny was naive when it came to financial matters, and he placed his trust in Roos to properly handle his earnings. Little did Johnny know — but he would find out a few years later — that Bo Roos had made many unwise investments that left Johnny very close to being broke.)

In fact, this minuscule weekly stipend of $50 was publicized in an October 26, 1946 *Evening Gazette* article by Bob Thomas, entitled "Tarzan Earns 50 G's a Year But Gets Only $50 a Week." Thomas went on to say in the article, including quotes from interviewing Johnny:

"As a result of his wives, and the income tax department, Weissmuller finds himself on a very strict financial diet set by his business manager. Johnny gets all of $50 a week for himself. Such a financial situation might drive some of Hollywood's more temperamental stars to all sorts of strange pastimes. But Johnny just keeps making 'Tarzans.'

"When I visited him on the set of his latest opus, *Tarzan and the Huntress*, I found him sitting in the shade, clad in his trusty loin-cloth, playing gin rummy (a passion of Johnny's) with one of his jungle cohorts. Very disillusioning, but I drew closer to kibitz in my best jungle fashion. Stopping the game momentarily, Johnny told me about his status. 'Yup, it's true,' he laughed. 'I get $50 a week from my pay check. So I have to go out and play golf to make some money.' (Apparently his gin rummy isn't too successful.) I suggested he might make more money in pursuits other than Tarzan. 'Nah,' he said, 'I have too much fun making these. Besides, I like having to stay in good shape for them.' "

Certainly Johnny saw the humor in his own situation, and the article by Bob Thomas was mostly in good fun. While he could laugh at himself, his impending divorce was no laughing matter. It kept going around and around in circles, as the months went by without a resolution. And since Johnny really wanted to get back to actually spending some of the money he earned, he was willing to be more than fair when it came to providing in the future for Beryl and his kids.

When the squabbles over the divorce settlement hit the gossip columns, Louella Parsons spilled all the dirt: "If Johnny Weissmuller is willing to pay a minimum of $600 a month and 25% of his earnings he can have his divorce from Mrs. Beryl Scott Weissmuller, from whom he has been separated almost two years. But yesterday, Johnny refused to sign. He thought Mrs. Weissmuller's demands too exorbitant, but her attorney, Charles Katz, is holding out firmly for that amount, while Frank Belcher, representing Johnny, said the demands are out of all reason.

"According to Bo Roos, who manages Johnny, Mrs. Weissmuller has been given a counteroffer of 25% of his earnings with all doctor bills for the children taken care of, and the house and furniture. Johnny hasn't a job, said Bo, so how can he pay $600 a month?

"Johnny wants the divorce so he'll be free to marry Allene Gates, but Mrs. Weissmuller said yesterday, 'I won't give him his freedom unless he supports the children and me.' "

Naturally, Johnny had every intention of supporting his children and Beryl, but the small fortune he had made as Tarzan had been piddled away by the mismanagement of his funds by his business manager. Roos — without any plausible answers — rationalized to Johnny that his previous divorces and his style of high living, had devoured all of his cash assets. However, these reasons from Roos were simply empty alibis, as Johnny's modest payments to Bobbe Arnst and Lupe Velez had ended years ago.

Contrary to Roos' assertion, Johnny was certainly not a "high liver" and lived well within his substantial means. Johnny really didn't have any expensive hobbies or extravagances; these all belonged to Roos, one of the all-time great mis-managers of other people's money. Also, Roos' statement that Johnny didn't have a job was an oversimplification; although Johnny was retired from his role as Tarzan, he was only temporarily unemployed — and Bo Roos was well aware of the situation. (There was a deal in the works for Weissmuller to be "Jungle Jim" for producer Sam Katzman, but that wouldn't be announced until a later date.)

Eventually an acceptable divorce settlement was hammered out by the respective lawyers, and Johnny would soon be free to marry Allene. On January 29, 1948, Johnny received his divorce in Reno, Nevada, affixing his signature to the papers that ended his eight-year marriage to Beryl. Five hours later, with his bride-to-be on his arm, Johnny "strolled down the aisle" at the Donner Trail Ranch in California and took Allene Gates to be his lawfully wedded wife. It was Johnny's fourth marriage, and Allene's first shot at holy matrimony. A rejuvenated Weissmuller was 43, and Allene was 22-years-old when they became man and wife. Having a beautiful young wife was a fountain of youth for Johnny, who had suffered an uneasy loneliness the past few years during his separation.

After the wedding reception at the dude

ranch, Mr. and Mrs. Weissmuller left for a honeymoon in London, where Johnny would be starring in a spectacular new British "Aquashow" from February 23rd through March 27th. That meant that they would have three weeks for their honeymoon (prior to the beginning of the Aquashow), although Johnny had to spend some of his time in rehearsals. Johnny had been to London previously during the war, when he starred in an aquatic show at the Blackpool Tower Circus, which included a performing elephant troupe.

Forsaking the major hotels for a quiet flat overlooking Hyde Park in London, the newlyweds spent their days in leisure taking in the sights and sounds of London. Hyde Park occupies nearly one square mile and includes the Serpentine Lake, as well as the adjoining Kensington Gardens and Kensington Palace. Points of interest within Hyde Park for the honeymooners included: Rotten Row (horse riding trail); Speakers Corner (where anyone can get up on a soapbox and speak on any subject); and Marble Arch, the site of the Tyburn gallows which stood at the west end of Oxford St. from the 12th-century until 1783. (Many martyrs were publicly hanged at Tyburn due to their "controversial" religious beliefs.)

During the daytimes they would explore the historic streets of London, enjoying the

Tower of London, Tower Bridge, Big Ben, the Houses of Parliament, and Trafalgar Square (Nelson's Column — which leads down to the Mall and Buckingham Palace). The lovebirds would stop by the Dorchester Hotel on Park Lane to enjoy an English cream tea, and for lunch they could choose between the Savoy Hotel's Grill as well as Simpson's Restaurant in Piccadilly. Johnny would also take a daily dip (weather permitting) in the Valentines Pool in Redbridge, an open air swimming pool that was a favorite cooling off spot for locals and visitors alike. (When this famous pool closed in 1995, the headline in the *Redbridge Post* said: "Last dip in the pool where Tarzan swam . . . The open air pool where screen Tarzan Johnny Weissmuller swam is to close down. Weissmuller, an Olympic swimmer, is said to have always taken a dip in the Valentines Park Pool when visiting London in the 1940s.")

Each evening Johnny and Allene dined in the finest restaurants, toasting each other with glasses filled with champagne like any typical young couple in love. Their romantic evenings included boat rides along the Thames to either Kew Gardens or Hampton Court Palace. It was a wonderful honeymoon vacation for both of them, but finally it was back to work for Johnny when the Aquashow opened on February 23rd. Henry Seff's Aquashow was to be held at the Earls Court exhibition grounds in London, and was billed as the "Health and Holidays Exhibition 1948."

Sharing the spotlight with Johnny as his co-headliner was 23-year-old "Belita," whose full name was Belita Jepson-Turner. In addition to her superb skills as a swimmer, the lovely blonde Belita first became famous as an ice skater and at age twelve had represented Britain at the 1936 Olympic Games in Berlin. The talented Belita was a professional ballet dancer, a gifted painter, and an accomplished pianist and violinist. She had made her Hollywood debut in *Lady Let's Dance* (1944), and appeared in films such as *Suspense* (1946), *The Gangster* (1947), and *The Hunted* (1948). She was also the star of the "Ice Capades" during the war for two years, and after the close of this latest Aquashow was due to return to New York to headline a new production of the Ziegfeld Follies.

Obviously, Belita had the credentials and talents to share the spotlight with Weissmuller, who was a huge star in Great Britain and all of Europe because of his Tarzan movies. Johnny had starred in numerous Aquashows the past two decades such as the Aquacades in 1939 and 1940. Also revived once again was the diving partnership of Johnny and Stubby Kruger, who had first performed their world famous comedic diving act a quarter-century in the past at the

551

1924 Paris Olympics.

Johnny and Stubby had been close friends for many years, as well as partners in this famed diving act that was loved by every audience lucky enough to see them perform. While Johnny was making his fame and fortune in Hollywood, Stubby — billed as the "King of Comedy Diving" — toured the world with various partners including Johnny and Buster Crabbe. (Kruger also did stunt work in movies and had small roles in numerous pictures such as *Huckleberry Finn* with Mickey Rooney, and *Mutiny on the Bounty* with Charles Laughton.)

Johnny was top-billed and opened the main program with Belita, in a stunning water show in the tradition of Billy Rose's Aquacade. Following acts included Harry Lester and his Hayseeds in a skit called "Way Out West"; Bob Bradborn in "Antics on a Log"; Joe Loss and his Augmented Dance Orchestra; and "Aqua-Romance in Dance Time," which featured a bevy of performing "Aquamaids" and "Aquamen."

Belita then rendered a solo exhibition, and Johnny and Stubby closed out the main entertainment with their comedic diving act. Other musical and dance numbers included "An Old Time Beach" skit, as well as "A Modern Beach" which included the classic song, "Got A Date with the Sun."

The program also announced that heavyweight boxing champion Joe Louis was "In Person . . . In Action," and giving boxing exhibitions in the Arena of Sport. Johnny had known Louis since before the war, and had attended some of his championship boxing fights. (Years later, when the two champions had retired from the spotlight, they both worked at Caesar's Palace in Las Vegas as public relations ambassadors-at-large.)

When the Aquashow concluded on March 27, 1948, it was back to Hollywood for Johnny and Allene to begin a new life together. While he was in London with the dual responsibilities of a honeymoon and the Aquashow, the following announcement had appeared in various newspapers including the *New York Times*:

"Johnny Weissmuller, whose screen activities have for the most part been confined to Tarzan films, has formed a new producing company in partnership with Sam Katzman and William Berke to make jungle and adventure pictures for release by Columbia.

"Weissmuller's contract with his own company and Columbia is for five years and calls for the production of four films in the first two years with minimum budgets of $350,000 each."

During his years of working for Sol Lesser and making Tarzan pictures, Johnny had asked to be a partner and thus receive a share of the profits for his lion's share of the work. But Lesser — holding all the cards because Johnny was under contract — refused that offer from his star and instead kept most of the millions from the Tarzan movies for his greedy little self. Now Johnny was older, wiser, and smarter, and he also was a partner in the new "Jungle Jim" venture with Katzman and Berke.

Johnny knew he had been getting the shaft from Lesser the producer, as well as Bo Roos when the latter put him on that $50 per week allowance (which was hardly enough to keep Tarzan in fresh loincloths). But now, as a partner rather than employee, he felt he would have more control of his financial future and reap a larger share of the profits. Although this was true, with Bo Roos still in charge of his business affairs, even these increased monies would continue to be dribbled away through the sieve-like hands of the slippery Roos.

Sadly, with a lifetime of hard work that earned millions for others, Johnny himself would never be a rich man. He deserved to be, but perhaps he really didn't care. After all, it was only money.

CHAPTER TWENTY-EIGHT

A New Hero: The Intrepid Jungle Jim

Johnny's return to the United States after his London honeymoon with Allene (and the Aquashow), coincided with the release of his final Tarzan film, *Tarzan and the Mermaids*, which opened in New York in late March, 1948. But the Tarzan role was now past history, and his new "Jungle Jim" character would be his primary occupation and financial pipeline for the next eight years. His two partners in the production company would be Sam Katzman and William Berke, who would serve as producer and director, respectively. (Johnny was with the famed William Morris agency at this time, which handled all of his share of the legal machinations.) Katzman's reputation was that of a second-feature producer, and was known in Hollywood as the "King of the Quickies." Similarly, Berke was well known as a director of low-budget films (second features that primarily were the lower half of twin-bills).

The "Jungle Jim" adventures were B-programmers that were targeted at a young audience who went to the Saturday matinees to see action movies and serials, as well as adults who were hard-core Weissmuller fans who were drawn to the screen magic of their hero. (It didn't matter to these millions of fans that the former Tarzan was older, had gained a few pounds, and the Jungle Jim features were pure "pulp-fiction" — it was still Weissmuller "kicking some butt" and they loved it.) Over the next eight-year stretch, Johnny would star in sixteen of the Jungle Jim adventures, all of which were immensely popular and financially successful. Although these would be budget films, there was always a message conveyed by the trials and tribulations of Jungle Jim: "Good triumphs over evil."

Meanwhile, marketing genius Sol Lesser re-released *Tarzan and the Amazons* (1944), and *Tarzan and the Leopard Woman* (1945), in the latter part of 1948. The second time around for these two Weissmuller classics brought in twice the box office receipts as they did when they were originally released. Lesser also noted why Weissmuller had been so popular as Tarzan, as he rolled wheelbarrows of cash to the bank from the re-release of these two films:

"Tarzan is pure escapist entertainment," drawled Lesser. "He is the original superman fighting for the rights of the downtrodden and the persecuted against all villains, be they human or beast. He rules with a minimum of words — hence, he is understood by all. Rarely does Tarzan get gooey with Jane. Thus, the kids love him, and so do the old folks."

While Lesser and RKO were making millions once again on the popularity of Johnny Weissmuller, the greatest Tarzan of them all didn't make a dime when his old films were shown again in re-release. This disparity was before the actors got smart and began receiving residuals and/or a percentage for their work along with a salary. This inequity was extremely unfair to stars such as Johnny, who literally brought the patrons to the theaters. But in many cases these same stars wound up broke in their old age while their films continued to make money for the producers and movie studios.

To close the book on Tarzan, a joke was going around Hollywood prior to the release of the first Barker Tarzan adventure, which was tentatively titled *Tarzan and the Fountain of Youth*. (It was officially released as *Tarzan's Magic Fountain*.)

"Tarzan and the fountain of youth?" the boys snickered. "Yeah, Johnny dives in — and out comes Lex Barker!"

The "Jungle Jim" comic strip was created

in 1934 by cartoonist Alex Raymond, on the very same day he also developed the equally famous "Flash Gordon" strip. The popular King Features Syndicate comic strip first went to the big screen in 1936 in the form of a 12-chapter serial, *Jungle Jim*, starring Grant Withers and Betty Jane Rhodes. Then in 1948, along came Johnny in a role that seemed tailor-made for him to replace his Tarzan role.

Johnny's "Jim" was a combination super safari guide, white hunter (although he never killed for sport), and genuine jungle hero who jumped at every opportunity to leap into any fray, as long as there was someone to be saved (from treacherous man or killer beast). Jim dressed in tailored jungle khakis that showed off his broad shoulders and narrow waist, and completed the outfit with a wide-brimmed safari hat and his trusty knife, sheathed on his belt. In the Tarzan series, Johnny had Cheeta the chimp as his animal companion. Jungle Jim, however, went one step further and had two trusty critters who were always playing little tricks on him — a crow called Caw-Caw, and a lovable dog named Skipper. (After the first few films the dog and crow were dropped in favor of a chimp named Tamba, a descendant of the original Cheeta from the early Tarzan movies.)

Jungle Jim's right-hand man in the first adventure was played by Rick Valin as Kolu, and Valin appeared in several of the succeeding films in a variety of characters. Cast as the rather sexy sister of Kolu was Lita Baron as Zia, who has a massive crush on the tall jungle hero. (Jim humors Zia and other lasses who swoon in his direction, as just simple cases of "puppy love." Jim's a "real man" and willing to flirt and admire, but he's just too darn busy saving lives and busting heads of the nefarious scoundrels for any serious romance.)

Portraying lady scientist Hilary Parker was Virginia Grey, who knew Johnny well and had appeared in *Swamp Fire* and *Tarzan's New York Adventure*. Miss Parker looks all business doing a tough job in a man's world, but she also has a romantic eye for the dashing Jim, who saves her life once or twice during the course of things.

Last but far from least in our cast of characters was the backstabbing villain, Bruce Edwards, portrayed by none other than future Superman, George Reeves. At this time Reeves was just another struggling young actor, but his TV series *Superman* would make him one of the most famous and successful television actors of the 1950s. Earning a few dollars as a treacherous fortune hunter pitted against Jungle Jim, assisted Reeves to survive until his ship arrived in 1951 on the powerful wings of Superman. Reeves portrayed his character in an early "Clark Kent" fashion (pretending to be someone other than his real self), a smarmy entrepreneur who figures the best way to earn a buck is to steal it. Reeves is a smart-alecky type who asks the commissioner in an early scene, "Where's Jungle James? I need to hit him up for another loan."

The initial adventure, aptly named *Jungle Jim*, was penned by Carroll Young, a veteran Hollywood writer who had written the script for several of the Tarzan series, and would write many of the future Jungle Jim stories. Columbia Pictures would be distributing the films in a general partnership with Weissmuller, producer Katzman, and director Berke. The Jungle Jim adventures all began with the rather ominous and dramatic theme by Mischa Bakaleinikoff, which became very familiar in time as it was used at the opening of every film.

The story begins as Jungle Jim attempts to save the life of a native, who dies at the claws of a leopard (killed by Jim, but too late to save the man). In the dead man's clenched fist is a golden vile — Jim retrieves it and brings it to the local commissioner (Holmes Herbert). Jim realizes the vile contains poison used by jungle "devil doctors," but later learns that the potion in a reduced state could be used as a cure for polio. Arriving on the scene is the headstrong lady scientist Hilary Parker (Grey), who hires Jim to lead an expedition to the lost temple of Zimbalu to acquire a quan-

560

tity of the precious medicine. The denizens of Zimbalu are a witch doctor cult who perform human sacrifices, their victims stunned by small doses of the poison.

Tagging along is jungle photographer Bruce Edwards (Reeves), who hopes to steal the fortune in golden artifacts from the temple of Zimbalu. Jim becomes suspicious that several near-fatal mishaps along the trail were caused by Edwards, and warns Hilary (who is temporarily fooled by the suave con artist). When they reach Zimbalu, Edwards manages to impress the temple dwellers with the "big magic" of his camera, which captures their images in photographic splendor.

Meanwhile, Jim's safari men have been captured and are hanging by their heels (literally), waiting their inevitable death by poisoned spear. As Edwards gathers the golden artifacts for his hasty exit, Jungle Jim explodes into action. Jim and Kolu release their cohorts and do battle with the devil doctors, many of whom die in the fiery pit of sacrifice. Edwards himself falls to a flaming death, as Jungle Jim leads his companions safely from the temple of doom. Their reward for risking their lives is a giant vat of the polio medicine, as Hilary thanks Jim for his heroics.

Producer Sam Katzman used every trick in the book to flesh out the 70-minute programmers, including using a great deal of stock footage from the vaults of Columbia Pictures. Especially effective was an extensive use of footage from the old Frank Buck travel documentaries, such as *Jungle Menace* (1937). While this jungle and wild animal footage was entertaining and exciting, it often had nothing to do with the somewhat far-fetched plots of the "Jungle Jim" stories. The intrepid Jungle Jim would be leading a safari through the jungle and suddenly the screen would be filled with cute monkeys cavorting in tall trees, or savage beasts that reared up as denizens of danger to Jim and his companions. Sometimes Jim would have to fight a lion, a leopard, or even a tiger — to save the life of a comrade or a damsel in distress (and these stock scenes were used over and over whenever possible). A few minutes later, the stock footage safely stored away, Jim and friends would arrive at their scheduled destination.

Although the plots were mostly serious and involved everything from foreign agents to lost cities and hidden treasures, the Jungle Jim films would probably be called "high camp" by today's standards. Even the kids in the theaters knew that the giant apes who were Jim's friends, were nothing more than men in shaggy suits and ape masks. Jungle Jim's pet crow and dog, Skipper, also were constantly involved in humorous situations, and they often managed to pull Jim out of a tough scrape.

Jungle Jim engaged in many battles and confrontations with the wild creatures of Africa, but in one scene in order to save Hilary (Virginia Grey) from a hungry crocodile, he pulls out his revolver and pumps several shots into the beast. You never saw Tarzan do that! (However, the gun was never used after this episode. It represented the wrong image for the fearless Jungle Jim, who henceforth did all of his fighting with his knife and his fists.)

Johnny performed numerous underwater fight scenes in every picture — many sequences of one minute duration or longer of tough underwater work like battles with crocodiles, sharks, sea serpents, and of course the deadliest of all predators — MAN! Johnny never used a stunt double for any of his water fights, because he was the best in the business — how could you double for the King?

Weissmuller was finally allowed to use standard dialogue as Jungle Jim, although he remained low-key and did most of his talking with his heroic actions and mighty fists. Like Tarzan, he was not given to meandering conversations and chose his words carefully. But still, Weissmuller proved that he could use dialogue as well as the big name dramatic actors — rather than a hack, he was believable as an actor.

When *Jungle Jim* was released at Christmas of 1948, it was greeted with cheers from movie fans who realized they were getting added mileage from their old hero, Johnny Weissmuller, now performing his heroics in tailored jungle fatigues. Admittedly, Johnny had gained some poundage during his honeymoon that he couldn't conceal during one swimming scene with Lita Baron and Virginia Grey. Before long, however, Johnny had worked and sweated himself back into shape — for the balance of the Jungle Jim series he looked like he was in trim condition and didn't have to embarrass himself in the swimming scenes with pretty young women.

The original *Jungle Jim* was quickly followed by the 1949 entry, *The Lost Tribe*, which once again had Johnny battling the unwelcome forces of evil as only he could do. The citizens of the lost land of Dzamm are wealthy beyond belief with diamonds, but only care for their privacy. When local boss Calhoun (Joseph Vitale) and Captain Rawling (Ralph Dunn) discover their hidden sanctuary, the ruler of Dzamm asks Jungle Jim to offer a pouch of diamonds to the outsiders to leave them alone forever.

Not satisfied with this token of wealth, the greedy strangers capture the beautiful maiden Li Wanna (Elena Verdugo) and force Jim to take them to her village so they can steal all of the diamonds and golden artifacts. Once within the boundaries of the lost city, Jim's gorilla friends come to his aid and crush the band of outsiders who had come to plunder and kill. Jim is thanked by his new friends, including the lovely Li Wanna, for his heroic role in defeating the interlopers from the outside world.

Also starring in *The Lost Tribe* was Myrna Dell as Lorina, the sexy girlfriend of the low-life Calhoun. Lorina is attracted to Jim, who sees through her attempt to seduce and trick him into revealing the location of the hidden city. Later, Lorina tries to warn Jim of the danger and to save himself, but she is killed by Calhoun for her disloyalty. (Jim was hog-tied at that moment and was forced to watch her death — later he avenges her murder when Calhoun meets his own grisly fate.)

There were several new action scenes filmed for this picture, including Johnny wrestling with a real alligator in the river; grappling with a lion (tame lion, that is) in the jungle; and even fighting a shark in an underwater rescue mission. Many of these same scenes of Johnny battling real jungle creatures would be used in future Jungle Jim features, to save wear and tear on the star of the show. Weissmuller probably received more cuts, bruises, and abrasions than any other star actor in history, in filming the realistic fight scenes with wild animals. But Johnny wanted to go the extra mile so that his fans — especially the children — knew that he was more than just a cardboard hero who had stuntmen performing all the tough stuff. And these films were primarily for the youngsters, as the *Motion Picture Guide* noted about *The Lost Tribe*: "Kids will enjoy this pre-Raiders of the Lost Ark adventure."

After their marriage the newlyweds were living in an apartment building owned by Johnny, on Almont in Beverly Hills. Around this time Allene was able to bask in the limelight for a few minutes herself, when she won the Lakeside Women's Golf Championship. As a prize, Allene was presented with a cocker spaniel named Lucky, in addition to the first-place trophy. Allene was one of the better lady amateur golfers, in an era when women were just forming their own professional circuit, named the LPGA. But many women preferred to keep the prestige of their amateur status, rather than turning pro. As long as Johnny was making money as Jungle Jim, there was no need for Allene to gamble for the small purses on the early ladies pro circuit.

Meanwhile, Allene and Johnny had drawn up plans for a new home of their own, that was to be built by a construction company owned by the omnipresent Bo Roos. The new Weissmuller palace was located on Lorenzo Drive in West Los Angeles, near the Rancho Country Club. Johnny made sure that this house had an Olympic-sized swimming pool for his daily swimming workouts, and also for his three children when they were able to visit their father and Allene for a weekend. All of Johnny's friends were welcome at his home, including John Wayne, who had been pals with Tarzan's alter-ego ever since their early days in Hollywood.

Also visiting Johnny at the new home was Duke Kahanamoku, who had come to Hollywood for a supporting role in Wayne's *Wake of the Red Witch*, which was released the same week as the first *Jungle Jim* feature. Kahanamoku had carved out his own niche in Hollywood, ever since leaving the amateur swimming ranks after his defeat at the hands of Weissmuller in the 1924 Olympics in Paris. Duke had acted in numerous films (estimated at over 100) beginning in the silent era, in a range of mostly Polynesian roles from kings to warriors. (Coincidentally, his credits included *Where East Is East* {1929}, a starring vehicle for Lupe Velez long before she met her future husband, Johnny.)

1950 was a busy year for Johnny, as he completed three Jungle Jim films amongst his other endeavors. *Captive Girl* once again reunited Johnny with his old friendly rival, Buster Crabbe, for the second time in their careers. Buster portrayed Barton, a ruthless treasure hunter who would stop at nothing — including murder — to steal the lost treasure beneath the "Lagoon of the Dead." When the two men meet face to face in the swampy jungle, Barton smiles a villain's smile and says, "I know you — you're Jim . . . Jungle Jim." Barton then introduces himself as a treasure hunter, and a wary Jim holds this particular jungle vermin in obvious disdain. The stage is now set for a final confrontation between these two rivals, an underwater death fight in the treacherous lagoon.

This excellent story by Carroll Young was not exactly original: a wild orphaned girl (Anita Lhoest) grows up in the jungle after her missionary parents are killed by savage witch doctor Hakim (John Dehner), who performs human sacrifices at the lagoon. Several years later, Jungle Jim is sent into the jungle to find the lost girl, Joan, who lives in the jungle near the village of his friend, Mahala (Rick Valin). Besides the evil witch doctor, Jungle Jim encounters a second deadly adversary in his quest to locate the girl, the ruthless Barton (Buster Crabbe), who plans to steal the gold and jade relics that lie at the bottom of the Lagoon of the Dead.

Jim tracks the girl through the jungle, and saves her from a deadly quicksand bog. The girl and Mahala are captured and sentenced to death by Hakim, as Jim is knocked into a steep ravine (presumably dead). Jim's chimp, Tamba, throws down a vine for his escape, and he rushes to the rescue of his friends. He must first battle Barton in the lagoon, who after struggling with Jim gets caught in his own safety rope and drowns amidst his "priceless" treasure. Jim then joins the melee against the witch doctor, who also sinks into the oblivion of the Lagoon of the Dead. Joan, the former wild girl, is returned to civilization by her new friend, Jungle Jim.

During the 1950s, Johnny and Buster cashed in on their popularity with youngsters and their legendary status as Olympic swimmers, by endorsing swimming gear by Healthways, a Los Angeles based sporting goods company. The "Aqua-Pro Swimming Goggles" were for teens and adults; the "Jr. Goggles" were for the younger swimmers; and the "Standard Web Feet" were swim fins for various ages of swimmers. Both Johnny and Buster had their photographs on the product packages, along with their authorized signatures. The paths of the two men would continue to cross throughout their lives: swimming rivals, Olympic teammates, comparisons as Tarzan, two films together, and numerous personal appearances and collaborations.

Mark of the Gorilla had Jungle Jim going up against a gang headed by Brandt (Onslow Stevens), who disguise themselves as gorillas to recover a fortune in buried Nazi loot from the war. Jim receives an urgent message for help from Warden Bentley, who is in charge of a large African game preserve. During his journey, Jim joins forces with Nyobi (Suzanne Dalbert), who is the Princess of Shalakari and seeks to recover the treasure stolen from her people. After Jim's arrival, Bentley is murdered by Brandt, leaving his niece Barbara (Trudy Marshall) in charge of the game preserve. It looks like curtains for Jim, Barbara, and Nyobi, after they are captured by Brandt's gorilla men and taken to the hidden cave where the gold has been stored since the war. Jim overpowers his captors and stalks Brandt up a treacherous cliff face — the villain makes a fateful slip and falls to his death surrounded by his precious gold bars.

This film was loaded with action, and in the final scenes a gun battle rages outside the cave between Brandt's men and the native rangers. Meanwhile, inside the grotto Jim battles with his knife and fists, and overpowers the men who had been ordered to kill the jungle man and the two women. The *Motion Picture Guide* rated this one of the better Jungle Jim adventures, noting: "Performances are convincing, with good production values considering the modest budget."

Pygmy Island involved Jim searching the jungle for a missing army captain, who just happens to be a beautiful W.A.C. on a secret mission for her government. Captain Ann Kingsley (Ann Savage) travels to pygmy land to gather Nagoma plants, which yield a resilient substance used for developing strategic war materials. Also seeking the rare plants are Marko (Steven Geray) and Kruger (William Tannen), agents for a rival foreign country. Marko's gang of cutthroats disguise themselves as "Bush Devils" to scare off the little warriors, but they don't fool Jungle Jim, who leads an army expedition to rescue Ann and recover the plants for the United States. Jim rescues Ann, but in turn is captured and held hostage to insure safe passage for Marko and his villainous cohorts. But Makuba and his men ambush the caravan and swarm over Marko and Kruger, as the little warriors are the heroes. (The pygmies of the title were none other than Hollywood little people — dwarfs and midgets — led by Billy Curtis as Makuba and Billy Barty as Tembo.)

CHAPTER TWENTY-NINE

The Greatest Swimmer Award

Although every knowledgeable sports expert in the world put Johnny Weissmuller at the top of the list as the best swimmer of all-time, it became official the first week of February, 1950. An Associated Press poll of sports writers and broadcasters from around the nation voted Johnny to be the "Greatest Swimmer of the Half Century, 1900-1950."

Weissmuller received 132 votes, 30 more than the combined votes of all the other candidates, and 112 more than the second-place finisher. Johnny's close friend and rival from the old days, Duke Kahanamoku, finished in fourth place with ten votes.

The Associated Press news release of February 7, 1950, said of Johnny: "There was no doubt that the tall, panther-like Weissmuller, a product of the public pools of Chicago, was to speed swimming what Jack Dempsey was to boxing, Bob Jones to golf, or Bill Tilden to tennis. He shone in his field with the same brilliance and power as these and the other polished performers in sports' dizzy, giddy and golden era of the tremendous Twenties.

"Physically, Weissmuller has changed little since his amateur days, or since he embarked on a pro career and came to Hollywood in 1931. This is truly remarkable because Weissmuller, now crowding the mid-40s mark [in age], has tried and traversed most of the treacherous, tiring trails of this somewhat exacting place called Hollywood.

"Golf now is his devotion, and has been for years. He shoots in the 70's consistently, and was second low amateur in the recent Bing Crosby tournament. Once he shot a 65 at Lakeside. Johnny, in swimming, was most proud of the sixty-seven world records he set, some fifty of which were of major importance. He said he's lost track of them to some extent 'but they held up for a long time.' "

Johnny was in good company when the "Greatest Athletes" selections were made, which included Babe Ruth as the greatest baseball player; Jack Dempsey was judged the best boxer; Bobby Jones and Bill Tilden were winners in the golf and tennis categories, respectively; Jesse Owens was rated number one in track and field; Babe Didrikson Zaharias was voted the greatest female athlete of all time; George Mikan was tops in basketball; and Jim Thorpe, an American Indian from the Sac and Fox tribe, was voted the dual honors of greatest football player and also the greatest athlete from amongst all the champions of the half-century.

(This great sports honor renewed Johnny's popularity as a champion athlete, and a "Johnny Weissmuller" bubble gum trading card was among the novelties that sprouted during the 1950s featuring the former Olympic gold medal winner.)

After his selection as the greatest swimmer of all-time, a host of invitations came Johnny's way in the form of testimonial banquets, awards, and further accolades. A testimonial "roast" was held to honor Johnny on March 8, 1950, at the California Country Club, and was attended by his actor friends and sports heroes from the past several decades. Hollywood director Frank Borzage, Johnny's close friend and golfing pal, organized the Weissmuller tribute. At the speaker's table were many sports legends, including boxer Jack Dempsey, golfer Ben Hogan, manager Leo Durocher, quarterback Bob Waterfield, U.S.C. swim coach Fred Cady, shortstop Luke Appling, college football star Tom Harmon, and numerous others. Telegrams arrived by the dozens from absentee friends from the sports fraternity who wished they could be there on Johnny's big night, as well as the countless friends he had made over the past twenty years in the entertainment business.

A visibly emotional Johnny spoke briefly to those who had gathered to honor him, and clutched in his hand a solid gold watch that was engraved:

"To JOHNNY WEISSMULLER, World's Greatest Swimmer, 1900-1950. From his Friends, March 8, 1950." He gave most of the credit for his success to his coach from the Illinois Athletic Club, Bill Bachrach, for having faith in him those many years before. (Bachrach had telephoned Johnny earlier in the day to offer his congratulations, as well as his apologies that his health didn't allow him to attend in person.)

While performing in a water show at the Duquesne Gardens in Pittsburgh, Weissmuller was invited to a ceremony at his "hometown" of Windber, Pennsylvania. The "Welcome Home Testimonial Luncheon" was held at the New Palace Hotel in Windber, where Johnny was toasted as their favorite son and for his recent honor from the Associated Press.

Johnny was also honored by the Helms Athletic Foundation, which was founded in 1936 by sportsman and philanthropist Paul H. Helms, and whose purpose was serving the interest of wholesome athletics and honoring those deserving of special recognition. Helms Hall on Venice Boulevard in Los Angeles offered shrines and memorials to all the major sports including swimming, baseball, football, golf, tennis, boxing, track and field, basketball, and auto racing. A comprehensive reference library was also organized for the general public to research the history of all these great sports.

The "Swimming Hall of Fame Trophy" was created to honor the greatest swimmers of the half-century, included the name of Johnny Weissmuller for the first full year of his amateur competition, 1922. (This particular award was presented only a single time, otherwise Johnny would have won the award seven years running, 1922-1928.)

Winners during that period of time were all friends and rivals of Johnny's, including Stubby Kruger in 1923; Robert Skelton in 1924; Harry Glancy in 1925; Walter Spence in 1926; George Kojac in 1927; Walter Laufer in 1928. Other winners included Buster Crabbe in 1929, and Duke Kahanamoku for the year 1912.

(Another award that came Johnny's way from the Helms organization was the "Athlete of the Year in North America" for the year 1923. Once again this was a prestigious lifetime award that was presented to Johnny for one of the greatest years of his career.)

All these awards also meant extra money for Johnny, who received a contract from Pabst Blue Ribbon beer to advertise their product. Johnny was featured in several full-page ads in major magazines toasting a cold Pabst Blue Ribbon.

Photographed poolside with a pretty young woman, the ad boasted that "*Johnny Weissmuller*... voted greatest swimmer of the past fifty years — makes the three-way 'experts' test with Pabst Blue Ribbon . . . *Johnny's eyes are pleased* by the creamy head — the brilliant amber color. *Johnny's nose is teased* by the delicate and inviting fragrance of finest malt and hops. *Johnny's taste agrees* Pabst Blue Ribbon has that smoother taste no other beer can touch." (And Johnny's pocketbook was also pleased, as he profited handsomely for the ads as he relaxed by the pool with a cold beer and a pretty girl. What a life!)

With all the wonderful things that happened to Johnny concerning his selection as the "Greatest Swimmer of the Half-Century," he and Allene averted a near tragedy when the car in which they were passengers went out of control and was wrecked one evening the first week of October. An evening out on the town turned sour, and resulted in a trip to the hospital for the occupants of the vehicle. Fortunately for Johnny and his wife, their injuries were only minor with the exception of some lacerations to Allene's face which were more painful than serious.

The following news release was issued by the United Press on October 3, 1950:

"Johnny Weissmuller, swimming star and the 'Tarzan' of the movies, his wife and a Los Angeles couple were injured in an automobile accident near here tonight. Mr. Weissmuller and the couple, Mr. and Mrs. H. J. Long, were not seriously injured, suffering only minor cuts and bruises. Mrs. Weissmuller suffered painful cuts on the face. The car in which they were riding was being driven by Mrs. Long when it went out of control on a sharp curve of the seventeen-mile drive leading to the Del Monte Lodge. As it straightened out, it hit a tree and was demolished."

With his three 1950 Jungle Jim adventures completed, Johnny took a break from films and starred in the latest water show of his career, called the *"JOHNNY WEISSMULLER WATERCADE."*

Johnny's Jungle Jim films proved that he was in great shape during his current mid-life, and he continued to bring his popularity to his fans in water shows throughout the 1950s. Johnny was one of the few movie stars in the business who regularly mingled with the fans, and he signed thousands of autographs each year at water shows and other personal appearances. And it was mixing with his adoring public that motivated Johnny, not the money — he was making plenty from his Jungle Jim films.

During the run of this latest watercade,

Johnny related a story to *Male* magazine entitled MY GREATEST SPORT THRILL, for the January 1951 issue. Johnny told a tale of playing water "chicken" with a shark that would have enjoyed having him for lunch, and he told it with a touch of humor: "The greatest thing that ever happened to me during my swimming career also turned out to be my biggest disappointment. The whole thing was over and done with in less than a half hour, yet in that short space of time I came just about as close to death as a man can get and still come out breathing. The place was Mexico; it was not long after I'd done pretty well for myself copping a couple of championships at the '28 Olympics.

"I was enjoying a vacation at a seashore resort and was taking a swim off a raft not far from shore when a fin suddenly popped out of the water. I just stared at the fin for a couple of seconds and then, before I knew it, a huge, man-eating shark was staring me right in the eye.

"This was no Tarzan picture and no make-believe shark. This was for real, and I don't mind telling you I was nearly frozen — not from the cold water, but from fright. The shark kind of played with me for a little bit. He began to edge around to the right of me, then to the left of me. I was afraid to move, and I thought if I just didn't bother him he'd go play somewhere else.

"The plan seemed to work — for a while. The shark kept his eye on me, paddled around me in sort of a circle, but made no sign that he was getting ready to finish me off. Suddenly, and with a great splash, he disappeared underwater and I figured he'd decided to pass me by and resume his swim. But no such luck. In an instant, there was an upheaval of water behind me and my friend the shark was back again.

"It went on like this for more than 20 minutes. The man-eater had decided to play games, and I was willing to go along with him. I sensed that if I made a sudden break for it, he'd stop being friendly and start being nasty. I couldn't take a chance on that. So the two of us paddled around, each one with an eye fixed on the other. Then, just to change the pace, I ducked my head underwater and swam for a few feet under the surface. That did it! As soon as my head popped up again, the shark, suddenly angered, lashed out at me with a vicious lunge. The lightning-like thrust missed by a hair's breadth — and then there was no longer any choice for me.

"What does a man think about when he's on the threshold of death? All I could keep thinking was, 'Weissmuller, if you've ever set speed records before, set one now!' I thrashed through the water like a man possessed; my arms and legs ploughed through waves as if they were galvanized by a bolt of electricity. A bucket-full of water sloshed down my throat. I swallowed it without a second thought; my sense of taste had been so dulled by the fear that the salt in the water didn't even bother me. I could feel the shark breathing down my neck. He was gaining on me! I could imagine his touch on my shoulder, his massive jaws opening wide, and then tearing my flesh apart. Maybe it was the appalling fear that gave me that extra energy. At any rate, that final shot-in-the-arm catapulted me out of his reach and I was heading into shore, my arms flailing through the water like oars on a racing shell. When I dragged myself up on the beach, I felt like a man who'd just finished a mile swim instead of one that covered not much more than 100 meters.

"The disappointment was this: that swim for life was unquestionably the fastest swim ever made by me or any other man at that distance. I had broken all world's records for the 100-meter swim and yet there wasn't an official timer for miles around! It's a swim that will never go down in the record books — unless my friend the shark learns to talk and vouch for my time."

Considering Johnny's love of swimming in the ocean, this story seems entirely plausible. A shark stalking a swimmer is perhaps a rare happening, mainly because few would live to tell about such an adventure. If anyone could outswim a shark, it would be Johnny. Fortunately he was close enough to shore to outsprint the oceanic killer, otherwise it might have been Johnny for dinner!

Johnny was now averaging two Jungle Jim pictures each year, and 1951 fare included *Fury of the Congo,* which featured Sherry Moreland as Leta, the leader of the female warriors. This adventure sent Jim deep into the Congo in search of professor Dunham (Joel Friedkin) who has been kidnaped by a cast of drug traffickers, led by Cameron (William Henry) and his henchman Grant (Lyle Talbot). Cameron befriends Jungle Jim by posing as a police inspector searching for the lost professor, but in reality seeks to locate a primitive tribe and the sacred animals they call the Okongo, a rare crossbreed of zebra and wild pony.

By the time Jim locates the land of the Okongo, he realizes that Cameron is part of the gang that has enslaved the natives to capture the ponies (which produce a powerful narcotic through the glands). Cameron and Grant force their captives to round up the whole herd of Okongo ponies, planning to kill them all for the narcotics. Meanwhile, Leta leads her warriors against Grant and his men, who all die beneath the spears and arrows of the inspired natives. Jim tracks Cameron into the mountains and as they battle on the treacherous cliffs, Cameron falls and is trampled to death by the stampeding Okongos. Leta thanks Jim for his help, who promises to return for a celebration after escorting the professor back to Cairo.

Jungle Manhunt (1951) had a lovely lady photographer seeking a pro football star in the jungle, where his plane had been shot down during the war. Ann Lawrence (Sheila Ryan) enlists the aid of Jungle Jim, and they discover Miller (Bob Waterfield) living among the natives that saved his life nine years before. Meanwhile, ruthless chemical engineer Heller (Lyle Talbot) has developed a process for producing synthetic diamonds, using local natives as slaves in his mining operation. When members of Miller's tribe are enslaved by Heller's "skeleton men," Bob joins up with Jungle Jim to end the oppression of Heller.

Although they are captured, Jim escapes with the help of his trusty chimp, Tamba, and sets off a dynamite charge to blow up the mining operation. After freeing Bob, Ann, and the rest of the slaves, Jim tracks Heller into the mountains, where he falls to his death clutching his precious chest of diamonds. Ann has fallen in love with Bob, and decides to stay in the jungle with her heroic football star. (Bob Waterfield was a pro football star of the era, and gained his fame as a quarterback for the Rams.)

1952 saw Johnny starring in *Jungle Jim in the Forbidden Land*, a land "forbidden" because the people are peaceful giants that are killers outside their own environment. Lady anthropologist Linda Roberts (Angela Greene) tries to convince Jungle Jim to lead her to the land of the Giant People, so she can study these primitive "missing links." Meanwhile, unscrupulous ivory traders Doc Edwards (William Tannen) and Denise (Jean Willes) plot with the warrior chief Zulu (Fredric Berest) to stampede a huge herd of elephants through a canyon near the land of the Giant People, and slaughter the noble beasts for the ivory. Commissioner Kingston (Lester Matthews) is tricked into thinking that Jungle Jim is a murderer, and plans to take him to Wasabi for trial.

Jim escapes and starts a landslide to reverse the elephants before they reach the pass, and clears himself with the commissioner when Zulu is forced by Jim to expose the real killers — Doc and Denise. In the finale Jim captures Doc and saves Linda from a berserk Giant Man, who grabs Denise and hurls them both from a cliff to their deaths in the canyon below.

Johnny as Jungle Jim must have had fun with this one, as the "Giant People" were wild looking creatures similar to the wolf man makeup of Lon Chaney, Jr. Our favorite hero was busy saving the lovely lady scientist from a hungry hippo, a snarling black panther, a near-tragic fall from a cliff, and the afore-mentioned Giant Man (portrayed by Clem Erickson). Johnny also added a set of bolas to his arsenal, and used them to subdue both man and beast in true Jungle Jim fashion.

The convoluted plot of *Voodoo Tiger* (1952) entails Jungle Jim leading a rescue party for the survivors of a plane lost in the jungle. The lost passengers include night club entertainer Shalimar (Jeanne Dean), and her trained — but deadly — tiger. Jim's rescue party includes Phyllis (Jean Byron) and Major Green (Robert Bray), who are seeking to recover a lost art treasure stolen from France by the Nazis during the war. The treasure was hidden in Africa by ex-Nazi Werner (Michael Fox), who is joined by a gang of American thugs who will stop at nothing to recover the two-million dollar prize. Eventually everyone is captured by a tribe of voodoo headhunters, who are tempo-rarily thwarted by the tiger of Shalimar, which they consider to be the source of their voodoo power.

Jungle Jim must fight a lion to the death to save his friends, and leads their escape through the jungles barely ahead of the voodoo headhunters (who settle for the thugs as vic-tims instead). The happy ending finds Phyllis and the Major falling in love, and Werner confessing the location of the stolen art.

As noted earlier, Johnny spent a great deal of his free time playing golf, especially in celebrity tournaments. Finishing as the second low amateur at the prestigious Bing Crosby National Pro-Am at Pebble Beach one year was certainly one of the highlights of his amateur golf "career." He participated in as many pro-am tournaments as possible, specifically events close to home including the World Entertainment Golf Championships at Long Beach; the Celebrity Pro-Amateur Tournament of Champions at Las Vegas; the Frank Borzage Motion Picture Golf Tournament; the Golden Gate Open; and the occasional out-of-town event, such as the 500 Festival Indianapolis Pro-Celebrity Tournament (in conjunction with the Indy 500 auto race).

Meanwhile, Allene usually accompanied her husband and also competed if there was a ladies tournament in conjunction with the men's. They even journeyed together to countries as exotic and distant as Egypt for golfing exhibitions. Allene continued to have her share of success in the amateur golf world, winning the Los Angeles City Championships that were held at Griffith Park.

Johnny was a fan favorite at any celebrity golf tournament, and often could be coaxed to perform his world famous Tarzan yell. He was also a heck of a golfer, who usually shot in the mid-70's but on occasion cracked the magic "70" mark (including the aforementioned 65, probably the best round of his life). Golf would always be a large part of Johnny's life, and it kept him in the public eye to a certain degree even after his motion picture career ended.

1953 brought *Savage Mutiny* to the screen, in which Jungle Jim is called upon by the U.S. government to help evacuate the inhabitants of a small island that is to be used as testing site for an atom bomb. Jim goes to the island of Tulonga to visit the chief, and he brings along Joan (Angela Stevens), a nurse from the World Health Organization. Meanwhile, foreign spies Bruno and Kroman are intent on sabotaging the evacuation, which would result in the massacre of the natives and the United States being labeled as ruthless murderers in the eyes of the world. The spies stir up the natives to halt the evacuation, and nurse Joan is taken as a hostage to ensure safe passage back to the island.

Jungle Jim leaps into action to thwart the evil plan, but is attacked by Bruno and Kroman in his canoe en route to his mission of mercy. It is an ill-advised attack by the spies on the jungle man — they both die in the river. Jim arrives at the camp of the natives and halts their migration back to the island, just in the nick of time. The bomb explodes and Jungle Jim is called a hero for saving the islanders and Joan.

The next Jungle Jim adventure was *Valley of the Headhunters* (1953), in which government agent Bradley (Nelson Leigh) asks Jim to negotiate mineral rights leases with the local village chiefs, who are friendly with Jungle Jim. Assisting Jim in his mission is headstrong police lieutenant Barry (Steven Ritch), and comely interpreter Ellen Shaw (Christine Larson). Also seeking the valuable mineral rights are jungle crooks Arco and Church, who join forces with evil chief M'Gono, who is under indictment for murder. The corrupt triumvirate impersonate a long dead headhunter tribe, scaring the local villagers and turning them against Jungle Jim.

In an action packed finale, Jim squares off with M'Gono in a knife fight to the death — Jim is the victor! As the battle rages between the loyal villagers and Arco's men, Jim rescues Ellen and knocks Arco unconscious (with an assist from Tamba, the chimp). The mission is triumphant as the mineral leases are signed and peace restored — also a happy ending as Ellen and Lt. Barry fall in love.

Killer Ape (1953) featured a real-life giant, seven-footer Max Palmer, in the role of a mutant beast that is half-man and half-ape. Jungle Jim is called upon to investigate why the indigenous animals have been acting so strangely docile, unwilling to fight back. The cause is evil scientist Andrews (Nestor

Paiva), who has developed a powerful drug that his men are testing on the animals. The chemical warfare agent could be sold to the highest bidder, and used to make an opposing army surrender without a fight.

Meanwhile, fiery village girl Shari (Carol Thurston) accuses Jungle Jim of murdering her brother, who in fact was killed by a giant man-ape who is running amuck in the jungle. When Jim saves the life of Shari's fiancee Ramada (Burt Wenland), his reputation is restored but he himself is captured by the band of outlaw scientists. Jungle Jim escapes and goes after the giant man-ape, who has taken Shari hostage in the cave of death. Jim battles the beast-man, and starts a roaring blaze that exterminates the killer creature. Jim is thankful that the outsiders were all crushed by the so-called missing link, thus destroying the secret of the deadly formula.

Some of Johnny's happiest times during the Jungle Jim years were when his three children came to the set to visit, and watch the on-screen heroics of their father. Allene would often be on the set with Johnny, as she played the role of "step-mom" with dedication and enjoyment when the kids were spending time with them. John Scott turned thirteen in September of 1953, while Wendy and Heidi were eleven and ten, respectively. It was tough on Johnny being a part-time father, but he realized that was the price to be paid for his broken marriage with Beryl.

Johnny had come from a broken family, his father gone by the time he was a teenager, and thus he did his best to be a real father to his own three children. He had survived when his own father deserted the family, but Johnny wanted his youngsters to have the things — especially fatherly love — that he had been denied. Financially, his son and two daughters never wanted for anything. Emotionally, Johnny gave everything of himself that he had to give.

CHAPTER THIRTY

The Return of Tarzan and the Legend of Bo Roos

During the calendar year of 1954, the only Tarzan on the big screen was Johnny Weissmuller. Two of his greatest MGM Tarzan adventures, *Tarzan the Ape Man* (1932) and *Tarzan Escapes* (1936), were re-released to great success — a whole new generation who had only seen Johnny as Jungle Jim now saw him in his prime as the greatest jungle hero of them all. Many of Johnny's Tarzan pictures were re-released over the years, including the wartime thrillers *Tarzan's Secret Treasure* and *Tarzan's New York Adventure* (which were both re-leased again in 1948 to capitalize on the publicity of Johnny's retirement from the role). But in 1954 he was temporarily "top dog" once again, as Lex Barker had retired after five years as the ape-man, and future Tarzan Gordon Scott would not assume the mantle of Edgar Rice Burroughs' hero until

591

the 1955 release, *Tarzan's Hidden Jungle*.

Johnny was still starring in the occasional water show, such as the "Aqua Fair" at the Desert Inn of Las Vegas. Also appearing at the Inn was Red Skelton, who was doing his comedy act of lovable characters, from bums to drunks to the man on the street. Skelton had been friends with Johnny for many years in Hollywood, and on opening night Red paid a visit to Johnny in his dressing room to plan a little gag for the evening's entertainment. Red explained his plan to Johnny, who was always ready, willing and able to inject some humor into any situation involving a crowd of people.

When the lights came up for the aqua show, Johnny was introduced and so was Skelton, who came running over to shake hands with the man best known as Tarzan. At that point the demure dinner crowd went wild with laughter as Skelton missed Johnny's outstretched hand on purpose and lurched into the pool, drenching the fully dressed comedian including his smoking cigar! And no one laughed harder than Johnny, whose high-pitched laughter rang out and could be heard throughout the pool area. Johnny offered Red his hand and pulled his fellow gagster from the pool so the show could go on. Of course, tremendous applause followed for the duo who had once performed the famous comedy diving act together at the California Cabana Club in Santa Monica.

Johnny also reached a personal milestone, when he reached the "half-century" mark on June 2, 1954 — 50-years-old. He had been making action movies for more than twenty years, and he was still going strong. The Jungle Jim pictures were making a great deal of money at the box office, and as of yet were not threatened by the new medium of television (which was slowly gaining headway).

Despite being fifty, Johnny wasn't ready to slow down to catch his breath. He was swimming every day, playing several rounds of golf each week, and starring in the requisite two Jungle Jims each year. Each picture only required a few weeks to produce, although Johnny more than earned his money in the strenuous action scenes.

Jungle Man-Eaters was the initial release for 1954, and this time Jungle Jim was pitted against a murderous diamond smuggler, Laroux, and his evil tribal counterpart, Zulu. When a new diamond field is discovered by three government inspectors, Laroux and his gang are responsible for their deaths. Jungle Jim is asked by the commissioner to stop Laroux and Zulu, who have forced the Kambesi tribe to vacate their homeland so that the diamonds can be mined. The young Kambesi chief (Bernie Hamilton) is a friend of Jungle Jim, who brings in lady doctor

Bonnie Crandall (Karin Booth) to help with the birth of Zuwaba's son. Meanwhile, Laroux kidnaps Bonnie and the new baby to hold as hostages. Laroux plans to smuggle the diamonds out of Africa in a plane stolen from Jim and diamond inspector Bernard (Richard Stapley), who has fallen for the lady doctor, Bonnie.

In a thrilling climax, Jungle Jim frees the hostages and chases Laroux and his satchel of stolen diamonds into the mountains. Jim and Laroux battle on a rocky cliff, and the murderous villain falls to his deserved death on the rocks below. Simultaneously, an explosive charge set by Jungle Jim buries Zulu and his evil tribe, freeing the Kambesi people from oppression. (There's plenty of romance in this one, as the lady doctor and Bernard fall in love and even Tamba the chimp has a girlfriend.)

At this point in time things got a little crazy for the producers of the Jungle Jim series, as the rights had been sold to Screen Gems (a subsidiary of Columbia Pictures), which intended to produce a television show of the same name. Johnny was going to be a busy guy, as he was planning to star in the TV series for Screen Gems, while his partner Sam Katzman still had three stories that were supposed to be Jungle Jim films. A solution to the dilemma simply had Johnny portraying himself in these final three films, and in effect he was "Jungle Johnny."

In Cannibal Attack, Johnny was brought in by the commissioner to investigate the disappearance of several shipments of the valuable mineral cobalt, as well as the murder of one of the mining supervisors. Johnny is introduced to Luora (Judy Walsh), a beautiful native woman who has secret aspirations to build a jungle empire with her partner John King (Steve Darrell), the leader of the mining colony. Luora is a descendant of the Shenzi tribe of cannibals, who hijack the cobalt shipments and place the blame on the river teeming with crocodiles.

After Johnny smells out the crooked plot to sell the cobalt to a foreign government, he and Arnold (David Bruce) set a trap to reel in the whole gang during a final hijack attempt. Luora and King have a falling out, and she murders her former partner with a knife in the back. After the commissioner pays Luora back with a bullet to her evil heart, Jungle Johnny battles the brawn of the outfit, Rovak (Bruce Cowling), in an underwater struggle for supremacy — Johnny wins!

This was one of the better Jungle Jim films, and featured perhaps the most beautiful lady villain that Johnny ever had to confront — Judy Walsh as the duplicitous jungle queen, Luora. As usual there were plenty of chimpanzee shenanigans, this time featuring a new pet for Johnny, Kimba, who replaced the aging Tamba.

After the completion of his latest jungle saga, Johnny was approached at the studio by a mysterious visitor, a Russian, who was accompanied by an interpreter to compensate for the former's lack of the English language. The mysterious stranger was an emissary for the Russian government, who stunned Johnny with an offer to be the coach of the Soviet Olympic swimming team. Although Johnny was honored by such an offer, he also realized that he could never be a coach for any team but the Americans. As diplomatically as possible, Johnny replied:

"I'm an American. I've seen our flag in the place of honor atop Olympic arenas. I believe in fair contests and sportsmanship, but also in national pride. I'd train our boys anytime, but I couldn't train their opponents. It's against my nature."

Although the Russians had been allies of the United States during World War II, the Cold War was now fully in effect and the threat of Communism was a constant barrier between the two world powers. It was an affront to Johnny to even ask him to accept a position working for a Communist nation, and he never gave any serious consideration to the offer. After the 1928 Olympics, Johnny was tendered a similar offer to coach the Japanese swimming team, a proposition he also politely turned down. In the swimming world, Johnny was considered the best there ever was in the field. The Russians at the time were intending to dominate amateur sports including the Olympics, and the offer to Johnny was simply part of their master plan. Johnny turned them down flat, an unequivocal "Sorry, not interested," and the Russians never did come close to their dream of dominating the swimming world.

Meanwhile, part of the reason for Johnny's popularity in Russia was revealed in the Moscow newspaper *Komsomolskaya Pravda*, which was special to the *New York Times* of May 15, 1954. The article noted that four of his old Tarzan films had played in the country recently, and that "postcards of Johnny Weissmuller in the role of Tarzan have become an under-the-counter item in the market of Yakutsk."

The article went on to tell of a woman in the market who kept a fat handbag under her coat stuffed with "art" postcards of Mr. Weissmuller and other fast-selling items, which eager youths snatched up. The cards apparently were also popular with women purchasers.

The "Jungle Johnny" films continued in 1955 with *Jungle Moon Men*, which had

Johnny and lady author Ellen Marston (Jean Byron) seeking a story deep in the jungle, where a tribe of moon-worshiping pygmies are ruled by mysterious High Priestess Oma (Helen Stanton). Joining the expedition are Ellen's boyfriend Bob (Bill Henry), and Santo (Myron Healey), a crook who has his sights set on the lost diamond treasure of Baku, the temple of the "moon men." Oma has the power of eternal life, and she chooses Bob to be her high priest, and places him in a trance.

The jungle man breaks the spell and Oma instead chooses the reluctant Johnny to be her next high priest. When Oma discovers they are all planning to escape, she sentences everyone including Johnny to death — they are tied in a cave as killer lions are unleashed. Diamond thief Santo dies under the claws of the lions, but with the help of Kimba, Johnny and his friends escape and force Oma to show them the secret exit out of the land of Baku. Once on the outside, Oma is "vaporized" by the sun god, freeing the little people from her corrupt power and restoring peace to the valley.

The sixteenth and final adventure in the series was *Devil Goddess*, as Johnny leads Professor Blakely (Selmer Jackson) and his daughter Nora (Angela Stevens) into the interior of Africa to locate a lost professor, who appears to have gone mad and lives at the mouth of an active volcano. But there is method in the old man's madness, as Johnny and Nora discover that he is really saving the girls who are about to be sacrificed in ancient tribal rituals. It is up to Johnny to rescue Saraba (Vera Francis), who is the fiancee of his friend, Teinusi (Abel Fernandez), before she can be sacrificed at the fire mountain. Complicating matters are treasure seekers Leopold and Comstock, who have discovered the lost treasure of King Solomon and plan to steal it from the natives.

Though wounded himself, Johnny manages to get all of his friends including the somewhat looney professor off the mountain just before the volcano erupts. Leopold and Comstock are victims of their own greed and die as the volcano explodes, and in the end the treasure is awarded to the professor and his lovely daughter Nora to take back to their museum.

Of course this was another happy ending in the jungle, as there was always a happy ending culminated by a funny scene with Johnny's chimp getting into some quintessential monkey mischief. Even though the Jungle Jim films would be considered "hokey" by today's standards, they nevertheless were enjoyable fare and were extremely popular with movie fans around the world.

Although the Jungle Jim movie series had

finally run its course, Johnny was moving on to be the star of his one and only television series, appropriately named *Jungle Jim*. After Screen Gems acquired the rights to the Alex Raymond comic strip in October of 1954, they signed Johnny to be the star of the new venture. Pre-broadcast anticipation for TV *Jungle Jim* was so lofty, that by the time the show was available for syndication in September of 1955, the show had already earned $250,000. (And a quarter-million dollars wasn't hay back in 1955!)

There were 26 half-hour shows filmed for the syndicated series, which followed the same concept and format as the *Jungle Jim* films. Johnny starred as Jungle Jim, and a son was penciled into the stories, played by Martin Huston as Skipper. The son of Jungle Jim had a favorite phrase of exclamation, "Holy Toledo," as he and his dog Trader attempted to be more help to Jungle Jim than hindrance. Portraying Kaseem, the Hindu assistant of Jungle Jim, was Frederick Norman, and the jungle ensemble was completed with Tamba, the faithful chimpanzee.

Producing the show was Harold Greene, who stayed with the tried and true formula of using stock jungle and wild animal footage to keep the costs as low as possible. The show went on the air on September 17, 1955 and the 26 first-run episodes aired through the early months of 1956. The television version of *Jungle Jim* lasted only one season, but remained in syndication for several years and continued to make money for Screen Gems. A typical episode was "Striped Fury," airdate October 22, 1955, which saw Jim, Skipper, and Kaseem travel to the distant land of India, where a fierce man-eating tiger is menacing the local natives. Jungle Jim pits his skills against the tiger as well as a terrorist band, who are more deadly than the striped beast of prey.

The highly successful *Jungle Jim* films had been targeted at the Saturday matinee audience, but television at this time was targeting the adult audience, rather than towards children. The TV western was also rapidly gaining popularity, and by the 1958-1959 season twelve of the top 21 shows would be westerns. And so Johnny retired from the Jungle Jim role after one season on television, and also effectively ended his acting career.

Johnny was open to new roles in the movies and television, but he had always been a star. Unfortunately, middle-aged actors in their fifties no longer commanded starring roles and Johnny had no interest in accepting supporting roles as a "heavy." Buster Crabbe had portrayed a number of "heavies" in recent years to keep his career alive, but Johnny would have none of that. He retired from swimming when he was the best in the world and undefeated, and really, he was unde-

feated as Tarzan and Jungle Jim. If Hollywood had no further use for him, he would
find a new career. However, at the moment
he was willing to take any guest starring roles
that came along.

One of the few television appearances of
Johnny's career came on *You Bet Your Life*,
which starred the inimitable Groucho Marx
as the host of a quiz show that really was a
showcase for the spontaneous wit of
Groucho. The show was on the air from 1950
through 1961, and Johnny's appearance was
in the mid-1950s around the end of the Jungle Jim years. Each show Groucho would interview pairs of contestants, asking questions
about their jobs and personal lives, and using
his rapier-like wit to get laughs from both the
guests and audience. Celebrity guests such as
Johnny were rare, and brought much appreciative applause from the audience when he
was introduced. After the interview segment,
the contestants had a chance to answer questions about history, sports, or current events,
and to win a moderate amount of prize
money. Of the three couples, the winner of
the most money got a chance to win a larger
prize by answering a single difficult question
at the conclusion of the show.

Weissmuller was paired with a lovely
young woman, and Groucho's questions
delved into their personal lives and produced
the usual quota of laughter and embarrass-

ment — especially from Marx's classic sarcastic asides, such as: "Say Johnny, what really happened between you and Jane up in that treehouse when you were all alone?" Naturally, Groucho asked Johnny to do his Tarzan yell. After some coaxing, Johnny complied with a prodigious rendition of the famous Tarzan call, which mightily impressed his pretty female co-contestant. It was all in great fun, and the contestants and audience wholly enjoyed the participation of Johnny.

Weissmuller also did a guest bit on *Masquerade Party*, along with Buster Crabbe, in which well-known celebrities were disguised in elaborate costumes and makeup (which in turn were supposed to be a clue to their identities). The panelists, which included people like comedian Jonathan Winters, poet Ogden Nash, and actress Audrey Meadows, questioned the contestants in an attempt to reveal their real identities behind the costumes. Any prize money won by the contestants was donated to the favorite charity of the celebrity. Johnny's distinctive voice was also disguised through the use of a special microphone, that altered the voice patterns. This was simply another collaboration between Johnny and Buster Crabbe — lifelong friendly rivals — that was loads of fun and earned a few bucks for charity.

Johnny was doing his best to supplement

his income during this period of time, including giving swimming lessons to young Olympic candidates at a swimming school in San Diego. He had taught his own son John Scott to swim his famed American crawl, and the younger Weissmuller, had even won the city championships in 1953. But Johnny's son was faced with the inevitable comparisons between himself and his father, the greatest swimmer of them all. He even had to deal with the same name: Johnny Weissmuller. It was a great name, but still it was impossible to get out of his father's shadow in the swimming world.

The elder Weissmuller was disappointed when his son stopped swimming, but he understood; his brother Peter had done the same thing back in the 1920s, leaving the I.A.C. swim team because of the immense pressure of measuring up to a living legend. John Scott eventually did follow in his father's footsteps, but in the acting trade rather than swimming. (His first screen role was in 1958 in Mickey Rooney's final Andy Hardy film, *Andy Hardy Comes Home*, in which young Weissmuller played "Jimmy.")

Around 1961 at age twenty, Johnny Jr. moved up to San Francisco to live with his maternal grandfather. Although it seemed that a Hollywood career was in the offing, he was more greatly interested in stage work and joined a small theater ensemble to learn the ropes of the legitimate stage.

In 1998, John Scott Weissmuller noted that besides the occasional film and stunt work that came his way, such as *American Graffiti* and *Magnum Force*, he portrayed the Indian role in a long run of *One Flew Over the Cuckoo's Nest* in San Francisco. Weissmuller, at six-foot six-inches, was as tall as Will Sampson, who was cast as the Indian in Jack Nicholson's 1975 Oscar-winning motion picture. (Weissmuller also appeared in numerous episodes of the San Francisco-based *Streets of San Francisco* television drama, which starred Karl Malden and Michael Douglas.)

Johnny had high hopes for an adventure series featuring himself and his own son, a TV relationship that would bring great success to Chuck Connors and Johnny Crawford as father and son in the acclaimed western drama, *The Rifleman*. Network executives passed on this idea, and also spurned Johnny's willingness to resurrect the *Jungle Jim* series. Johnny was far from ready to be put out to pasture; he'd keep pitching the ideas in hopes that something would work out. One such idea was a daytime TV program where Johnny — world's greatest swimmer — would demonstrate the art of swimming to Americans of all ages. Johnny figured, "If fitness guru Jack LaLanne can do it, so can I!" Unfortunately, his agency couldn't sell the idea to the networks. Johnny would keep pitching.

Johnny took advantage of his "unemployment" to get in some serious rest and recuperation after *Jungle Jim* ended in 1956 — it was really the first time since his retirement from swimming in 1929 that he didn't have a job that was paying him a lot of money. He was picking up a few bucks here and a few bucks there . . . *Muscle Power* magazine paid him for an article they did on Johnny's training and physical fitness routines. One photo in the October 1956 issue showed a trim and muscular Weissmuller hoisting a barbell over his head, as the caption noted: "Johnny Weissmuller, former movie Tarzan, is enthusiastic bodybuilding fan. He works out regularly, has very fine build."

His income for 1955 was close to $100,000, a substantial amount mostly generated by the Jungle Jim films and his partnership with Sam Katzman. But by 1956 his income dropped to less than $40,000, with only his one season as the TV Jungle Jim on the plus side of the ledger. But Johnny didn't even consider the notion that he might have money problems, and thus bought a $4,000 star-sapphire ring for Allene to commemorate their eighth wedding anniversary on January 29, 1956.

He really felt that with all the millions of

dollars that he had made since entering the movie business in 1931, that he would be set for life in the financial department. After all, hadn't he had Bo Roos managing his money and investments all these years? When Johnny was sued for back-alimony by his ex-wife Beryl Scott (who had since remarried), he was devastated by this unexpected turn of events. The amount was less than six-thousand dollars, a mere pittance compared to all the income he had generated over the years. Johnny stormed down to see Roos at his office, demanding an explanation for the lack of payments to the former Mrs. Weissmuller, money that went to the support of his children.

Johnny assumed it had to be a mistake of some sort, but he was hot under the collar when he confronted Roos face-to-face. Roos squirmed, sweated, and finally confessed to Johnny that all the millions he had earned were gone! For the most part, except for investments that weren't making any money, Johnny and Allene were broke. They owned their home and personal possessions, but precious little else. And of course there was the matter of the back-alimony.

The former actor was stunned, and now could fully empathize with how Tarzan felt when the interlopers came to his jungle to steal, plunder, and devastate the sanctity of his world; without warning, Weissmuller's real world had been rocked. He thought back to when he had first met Roos in the mid-1930s, when both he and Lupe Velez became his clients. All these years Roos had told Johnny he was his friend, and that he had been wisely investing his money. But it all turned out to be a pipe dream. At this particular moment, Johnny felt like throwing Roos right out the window. Roos was through as Johnny's business manager, but it really didn't matter because there was no money left to manage.

Bo (pronounced Boo) Christian Roos, was not an agent but rather a financial manager. From the mid-1930s through the 1960s, Roos represented many of the biggest stars of Hollywood as financial advisor through his Beverly Management Corporation. His list of clients included John Wayne, Marlene Dietrich, Joan Crawford, Red Skelton, Fred MacMurray, Ray Milland, Ward Bond, Merle Oberon, George Brent, and the Andrews Sisters. One person who knew Roos closely, described him as "the sort of man that once you shook his hand you wanted to take a shower."

In the 1995 biography, *John Wayne: American*, authors Randy Roberts and James S. Olson describe Bo Roos as a stereotyped character from a cheap B-movie: "With his hair slicked straight back, his pencil-thin Errol Flynn mustache, his mouth full of straight white teeth, and his perfect tan, Roos was pure Hollywood. He was groomed to please, quick to smile, and make a new friend . . . Certainly, even some of his own clients did not trust the husky, blue-eyed, cigar-smoking Roos."

Around the time that Johnny got the bleak news about his financial picture, John Wayne also asked Bo Roos to give him an accounting of his investments for purposes of financing one of his most cherished projects, *The Alamo*, the story of Texas's fight for independence in 1836. Wayne had long dreamed of producing the historical saga of the Alamo, and he intended on financing the picture through his Batjac production company. The Duke told Roos to let him know how much cash he could raise on his investments, knowing he had made millions from his motion pictures the past two decades.

Roos stalled Wayne for a couple of weeks, and then gave him the same bad news he had given Johnny Weissmuller: the greatest movie star in Hollywood was virtually broke, owning only his house, personal possessions, and his Batjac production company. Wayne fired Roos for the gross mismanagement of his funds, and held him in contempt until Roos' death years later. Wayne had Roos investigated, but no clear-cut evidence of fraud was discovered, only his obscene mismanagement of his various clients' funds.

Johnny Weissmuller had been close friends with John Wayne since the early 1930s, and now they could share a common misery over a drink. (And Duke Wayne really enjoyed his drinking!) The Duke's final wife, Pilar Wayne, recalled in a biography of her late husband, *My Life with the Duke*, that Weissmuller was part of the select inner circle of the Duke's friends, and was always welcome at their home: "In private," said Pilar, "our home served as a club for Duke's friends, who included John Ford, Ward Bond, Grant Withers, Victor McLaglen and his son Andrew, Charlie Feldman (Duke's agent), Johnny Weissmuller (of Tarzan fame), Yakima Canutt, and Jimmy Grant (Duke's favorite screenwriter). I made sure all felt welcome . . ."

Red Skelton was another client of Roos' who also lost his shirt — $10 million dollars of Skelton's money washed down the drain through bad investments, plus Roos' standard ten-percent management fees and ten-percent "accountancy fees." Johnny and Red were friends throughout their careers, and they could also commiserate when they got together in later years over the loss of their individual fortunes — courtesy of Bo Roos.

The Los Flamingos Hotel was one of Roos' investments for his clients, and all the stars would stay at the hotel during their visits to Acapulco. The Los Flamingos became known as "The Hotel of the Stars," but most of these stars (and all of their friends) stayed at the hotel for free, running up expensive tabs. (It's easy to run deep into the red when many of your guests are nonpaying customers, who order the best of everything including champagne and the finest meals.)

The California Cabana Club in Santa Monica was a luxury club with every amenity including an indoor pool, that was owned by Roos' clients including: Weissmuller, John Wayne, Joan Crawford, Robert Walker, George Seaton, Frank Borzage, and Red Skelton. In the afternoons customers could bask in the sun by the outdoor pool with a cold drink, followed by a steam bath and a shave and haircut at the barber shop. There were bars and restaurants as well as a fancy ballroom, where some of the biggest name orchestras in the business provided the nightly entertainment. Many of the same stars that were investors also performed at the club, including Johnny and Red Skelton, who carried on the tradition of Johnny's comedy diving act. (Johnny was the "straight" man, while Red did the comedy routine made famous by Stubby Kruger.)

Once again, this turned out to be a losing proposition for all the investors. Extravagant expenditures caused the club to continually operate in the red, and thus the Cabana Club eventually went out of business, despite the great appeal of all the stars as owners. Johnny and his fellow investors — all clients of Roos' — took a heavy financial loss that was explained by Roos as just so much bad luck. Another turkey which gobbled up the investors' cash was the Pirate's Den Night Club in Hollywood, with partners such as Bob Hope, Bing Crosby, Tony Martin — and of course, Johnny. Unfortunately, most (but not all) of Roos' investments were equally disastrous.

Meanwhile, the California Country Club was a blue-chip investment that Johnny was advised by Roos to sell when he divorced Beryl, because of the California community property laws. Johnny was forced to sell off his shares because all of his other investments were losing money, and this beautiful and popular golf country club would later be valued at millions of dollars. If his other investments hadn't all been in the tank, Johnny could have kept his shares of the California Country Club, a genuine gold mine as well as the place where he had met and fallen in love with Allene.

Besides the numerous insolvent real estate deals, there were dry oil wells, empty natural gas leases, Panama shrimp, wild Hollywood parties for all of Roos' clients, and of course the inflated expense accounts of Bo Roos and his Beverly Management Company. When

John Wayne considered suing Roos to recover some of his losses, the Duke was told by mediator Howard Meacham of CBS Television: "There's nothing left and it's all your fault. How the hell could you give a guy millions and not ask any questions, never follow up on him? If you go to court it's going to make Bo Roos look like a fool and you like a complete ignoramus. Just forget about it and start over."

This statement of beratement and advice from Meacham could just as easily have been directed to Johnny Weissmuller, who was in the same boat as John Wayne. Johnny had no more income from the movie business (except for small residuals from *Jungle Jim*), and so he had to turn to the business world to forge a living to support his wife Allene and pay his alimony and child-support to Beryl (which was cut in half by the court, reflecting his expected lower level of income).

One such business opportunity came from a swimming pool company that offered to make him a partner in exchange for using the name "Johnny Weissmuller" in their promotions. Johnny was to be a spokesman for the portable pools that were constructed on-site, and made of a supertough material called "Bakelite Krene." When the pools proved to be faulty and troublesome, Weissmuller withdrew his endorsement of the company. Johnny had truly believed in the company, but when his fans began complaining about the quality of the product they had purchased, it was time to disassociate himself before his reputation was sullied. Also, the money Johnny had been promised didn't come close to what he actually was paid — it turned out to be another red herring.

Johnny was playing a lot of golf in his retirement, and was consistently winning or finishing near the top of pro-amateur tournaments. One year he lost a close match in a playoff for the World Entertainment Golf Championship to actor Robert Sterling. In 1958 Johnny was invited to a pro-celebrity tournament in Cuba, which during this period of history was in the throes of revolution. Fidel Castro was fighting a guerilla war against the regime of President Batista, and the guerilla troops of Castro were making monkeys of the government soldiers — snipers killing the enemy from trees in a classic example of guerilla warfare. (By 1959, Batista would be forced into exile and Castro would assume the leadership of Cuba as Prime Minister.)

Weissmuller's party of celebrity golfers included songwriter Hoagy Carmichael, bandleader Bob Crosby, and actors Buddy Rogers, Robert Sterling, and Bill Gargan, among other luminaries. They would be commuting to the Villa Real golf course, site of the tournament, accompanied by bodyguards assigned by President Batista to protect the visiting Americans. The party was traveling in an open touring car along a dirt highway, when suddenly they were surrounded by the guerilla soldiers of Castro — brandishing machine guns that warned the bodyguards to throw aside their weapons and raise their hands in compliance.

It was at this point of immense tension and genuine danger that Johnny took the matter into his own hands. Realizing the gravity of their situation, he raised himself up in the vehicle, as the guerillas watched this tall man with the broad shoulders make himself the center of attention. He raised his hands to his face, and then let loose with perhaps the most powerful Tarzan yell of his life! The guerilla soldiers were amazed at this display, and temporarily stunned. When they suddenly recognized this bold "Americano" as none other than Johnny Weissmuller, the famed Tarzan of the movies, the soldiers reacted with unbridled enthusiasm: "Tarzan! Tarzan! Bienvenido! Ah, Juanito! Welcome to Cuba!"

Johnny leaped down from the vehicle to shake hands with the hero-worshiping rebels, and answer their myriad questions about Tarzan, Jane and Boy. Johnny completed his military coup by handing out autographed Tarzan photographs that had been brought along for distribution at the golf tournament. When Johnny explained to his Cuban admirers that the party of golfers was overdue at the golf tournament, they sent Tarzan and his friends along to the Villa Real with an escort to ensure their safety.

Johnny was the toast of the tournament after his heroic stunt, and even Errol Flynn approached him to shake his hand with admiration. Flynn was in Cuba to make a movie called *Cuban Rebel Girls*, his final film before his death in 1959. Flynn's "wicked, wicked ways" (the title of his autobiography) finally caught up with him, and he would die at the young age of fifty years.

In the late 1950s, Johnny recounted an interesting vignette about an accident that endangered his life, here directly quoted:

"One night my wife, Allene, her parents and I were cruising to Catalina Island for a weekend of fishing. We were heading for a cabin on the isthmus toward the northern end of the island.

"Soon after passing the middle of the channel we ran into a squall. The others were in the forward cabin, and I was aft, at the wheel. I got up to batten down the hatch, and a sudden pitch of the boat caught me unaware. I went right over the side, yelling, but when I came to the surface, the stern light was disappearing in the darkness. No one had heard me.

"At first I panicked. I knew my absence would soon be discovered, and they would start circling. But in the darkness, the odds of their finding me were pretty slim.

"I trod water for I don't know how many minutes. In my jumbled thoughts, the word 'lifeline' came through — and instantly contracted to 'line.' I calmed down and began to think. I took a mental bearing on Catalina. The island is about 25 miles long, and I figured if I could set a straight line in my mind, and follow it, I had a pretty good chance of making shore. With more confidence than I had any right to feel, I struck out.

"Three hours later the lights of the island broke through the darkness, and I could have wept. I dragged myself ashore, less than a mile south of the cabin. It was a terrifying experience, but it solidified the philosophy that has kept me afloat in more ways than one."

In 1959, at age 55, Johnny recalled how wonderful his life had been, despite the flaws that marred the perfection of it. "I've had about as perfect a fifty-five years as any human could have," said Johnny. "I started out as a scrawny kid in Chicago and even that was lucky. It got me to swimming and then all the good breaks in the world happened — and kept on happening."

Johnny and the movie-going public got a few laughs in 1959, when MGM released a new version of his classic debut film, *Tarzan, the Ape Man* (1932). The laughs came about because the new adventure, which starred Denny Miller as Tarzan, contained clips of Johnny fighting the monster-sized crocodile that was a classic scene from *Tarzan and His Mate* (1934). MGM also used Johnny's original Tarzan yell, as well as numerous scenes from the 1932 film including Tarzan swinging (with the greatest of ease) through the jungle vines, and the elephant stampede of the pygmy village. The Tarzan films have always been produced with deadly seriousness, with only the chimpanzees providing moments of levity. But this *Tarzan, the Ape Man* — 1959 style — was strictly "high camp." MGM spoofed their own classic film, and gave Johnny some screen time years after his retirement from the Tarzan role.

In the scene where Johnny battled the giant reptile, you can clearly see the face of the original Tarzan several times. That must have been a surprise to the audience members, who had expected to see a new version of an old classic — instead they brought back Weissmuller. Johnny later recalled seeing Denny Miller's version of the film, and noted that he spotted himself several times in the great crocodile fight. "When I saw it, I thought, 'He's a pretty good swimmer.' " Johnny of course was talking about himself, and yes, he was a pretty good swimmer.

Johnny later became friends with Miller and noted, "Denny's one helluva nice guy, but can you imagine — a blonde Tarzan?"

An important link to the past was broken when the man who taught Johnny his swimming skills, Bill Bachrach, died at the age of 80 in 1959. Even in the years after Johnny had bowed out of the Hollywood scene, Bachrach was only a phone call away. "Big Bill," a tough guy as a coach but a kindly old Jewish gentleman in his retirement, was always ready with advice and consolation for Johnny during the toughest of times.

As a young man he had been Bachrach's protégé and had accomplished swimming feats way beyond the coach's wildest expectations; throughout the years he still felt about Johnny like a father loves a son. Johnny never talked about his own father, but he would tell Bachrach stories for hours whenever he was in a mood to reminisce about the good old days. Johnny recalled that Bachrach would carry a small fortune around his waist in a money belt, and thus was always ready to accept a wager against Johnny. Of course Bachrach would collect on any such foolish bets against Johnny, and the money belt just got fatter.

In Johnny's 1930 autobiography, *Swimming the American Crawl*, which was dedicated to his mentor, William Bachrach, he recalled that his coach often had to drive him hard to overcome a tendency towards laziness.

Coach Bachrach demanded that Johnny become a champion, and his word was always final: "In the first year or two I was in the water most of the time, of course. But after the first dozen or two of world's records, it began to be an old story. Many times Bachrach had to drive me into the pool. I'd drift down to the club pool in the afternoon after school, sit around and read the papers while Bachrach finished his siesta.

"When the Big Boy came out of his hibernation and spied me, he'd say, 'Hey, what are you doing here? Get into that pool!'

" 'Don't feel like it,' I'd come back, yawning.

" 'Get undressed and get in there,' Bachrach would say, without batting an eyelash.

" 'Oh, I've just ordered something to eat,' I'd say. 'I'm getting a club sandwich.'

" 'Never mind that club sandwich,' Bachrach would reply. 'I'll take charge of it. You get *OUT* of those clothes and *IN* that water.'

"It is hardly necessary to say that I'd get 'out' and 'in' for various reasons. Maybe I wanted to go to Buffalo for a meet next week, or I was figuring on going to Cincinnati two weeks later, where they always made a big fuss over me. So Bachrach, who could say whether I would go or not, didn't need to threaten; his word was always law with me."

Johnny also later recalled the impact of the

fatherly "Bach" during the course of his entire life: "William Bachrach, swimming coach of the I.A.C., first took an interest in me when I was 15-years-old. Not long after he began coaching me, he gave me some advice that I have used, wet or dry, ever since.

"Bach had been working with me, day after day, in the club pool — on my stroke, my breathing, my starts, my turns. He was teaching me to keep my body high, to swim *over* the water, not through it. And we were progressing. I got so I could do 100 yards, freestyle, in 52 seconds. But there was one catch. All of my training was in that same pool.

"The I.A.C. pool was one of the finest in the country. The bottom was laid out in lanes, with heavy black tile stripes to guide swimmers in competition. I didn't realize it, but subconsciously I had come to depend on those lines to keep me on a straight course.

"Bach didn't realize it either, until he clocked me one day in an unmarked pool. My time had dropped a full fifth of a second. He made me swim a length against the stop watch, and another. Then he exploded. 'Johnny!' he roared. 'You aren't swimming straight! You don't have that black guide line, and you're wobbling all over the pool!'

"He slammed his hat down on a kickboard at one end of the pool, and sent me to the other. 'All right now,' he ordered. 'That hat

621

is your goal. Fix it in your mind, draw a mental line to it, and swim for it. Follow your *own* line, and you'll get there fastest.'

"That advice led me through two Olympic Games and to five Olympic medals. I never again depended on a marked line. I set my own goal and hit out for it. Shortly before the 1928 Games I pulled a tendon in my right leg. Fearing the coach would not let me race if he found out about it, I went around in agony for two days, forcing myself to walk without a limp. My leg simply got worse. Then I realized I had lost sight of my goal. My object shouldn't be to cover up my injury so I could compete, but to get it healed so I could win. I reported to the trainer; heat lamps and other treatments were immediately applied and by the time my event came up, I was able to beat the field. It was a close call, and more than ever I realized the value of Bachrach's insistence on my keeping my eyes on the goal and not merely on the path to it.

"It was an exciting time for me when Tarzan was to be brought to the screen and I was considered for the part. The studio was confident of my athletic ability but doubtful about my ability to act. I was told to take acting lessons. I did. My dramatic coach thought that my swimming style should be changed, to make each stroke more pronounced and photogenic. I tried doing that, and the resulting screen test was terrible. I looked exactly like what I was — a swimmer who couldn't act, and an actor who couldn't swim.

"Completely discouraged, I called Bachrach. 'It's no good,' I said. 'I'll never be an actor.'

"There was a long pause. 'Johnny,' the coach finally said, 'you've lost your mental line. You're veering. You want to be Tarzan. All right. Tarzan was great in the water. So are you. Stop worrying about acting. Be yourself. Set that line in your mind, and follow it.'

"I did just that, and the studio heads were elated over my second test. They even congratulated me on having learned to act. Actually, I was merely doing what I knew how to do, and not worrying about how I might photograph. I was following my own line.

"That mental line has guided me through 18 years of Tarzan, and seven as Jungle Jim. I've had a lucky life. I've been able to make my living doing the thing I most love to do — swim."

CHAPTER THIRTY-ONE

A Final Love:
Johnny and Maria

The winds of change were blowing for Johnny as the new decade opened, and the most serious disruption of his life at the moment was a growing disharmony in his relationship with Allene. This was Johnny's most successful marriage in terms of longevity, reaching a dozen years on their anniversary on January 29, 1960. However, slowly but undeniably his relationship with Allene began to crumble as their affection for each other began to dissolve. Perhaps it was the difference in their ages, or perhaps the fact that Johnny was no longer wealthy and wasn't likely to ever earn the kind of income that went hand-in-hand with his fame as Tarzan and Jungle Jim. When two people begin to fall out of love with each other, invariably there is someone else who enters the picture to further complicate things.

For Johnny, this someone else was Maria Bauman, who was born in Germany and arrived in the United States in 1949. Johnny became friends with Maria during the period of tumult in his marriage to Allene, as Maria threw Johnny a lifeline to keep him from drowning in the sorrow of yet another failing relationship. They crossed paths at a charity luncheon that was held at the famed Luau Restaurant, and in fact were introduced to each other by bandleader Bob Crosby (brother of Johnny's good pal, Bing). Their introduction on this particular day was innocent, but eventually their partnership would become the final love affair of each other's lives.

Maria was born in February of 1922 and was married in the late 1930s, just prior to the outbreak of World War II in Europe. Her husband, Werner Prauss, was drafted and sent to the Russian front, leaving behind his teenaged bride who was now pregnant. This was a story told thousands of times during this chapter of history: The soldier was killed in action leaving Maria a widow with a newborn baby girl, Lisa.

Maria was also arrested by the Nazis during the war, and suspected of being part of the underground resistance movement which involved freedom fighters who wanted no part of the tyrannical Hitler's evil regime. Maria was questioned and later released for a lack of evidence, but a close friend of the family — a lawyer who would often visit Maria and young Lisa — was hanged along with all of his relatives for being part of the underground resistance.

During the war years Maria met a man named Karl Brock who was with the C.I.C., and she worked with him as a translator (making use of her fluent skills in French and English). After the war she came to the United States on a visitor's visa, and soon married Karl Brock.

The war was a series of horrible memories for Maria, and she was grateful to be able to come to the United States and eventually become an American citizen. After her marriage to Karl Brock ended, Maria married Nate Mandell, a self-made millionaire who earned his fortune by inventing and manufacturing the convertible couch.

After years of romantic trials and tribulations, Maria finally met the love of her life, Johnny Weissmuller. She had been married three times and Johnny had four tries at marriage, and this was the real deal — they were soul mates. A romantic relationship between Johnny and Maria began in earnest sometime after his separation from Allene on July 28, 1961.

At that time Johnny packed his personal possessions and moved out of their home on Lorenzo Drive, and took a room at the Bryson Hotel on Wilshire Boulevard. They had been married for thirteen years at this point, but number "13" was an unlucky number. The usual charges were made of "mental cruelty" by the lawyers, and eventually a meager settlement was agreed upon that reflected Johnny's current state of financial affairs: $2,000 cash payable in two years, and a $10,000 life insurance policy on Johnny with Allene as the beneficiary. (This was of course after splitting their community assets, which after paying their community debts, probably didn't amount to a hill of beans.)

Bo Roos had really done a number on Johnny's finances, which was evident by Allene's willingness to accept the paltry sum of $2,000 (and even that money was a promissory note payable two years down the road). Allene wouldn't have any financial problems, though, as she married a manufacturing magnate within a few days after the final decree of her divorce from Johnny. They didn't have any children, so the split was final with no need to look back — another page completed in the Weissmuller biography.

Johnny never spoke an ill word about Allene, who brought him thirteen years of mostly happiness. With a new relationship beginning to develop with Maria, Johnny would be all right after his latest divorce. It took its toll, but the dissolution of any marriage has a share of pain for all parties concerned.

★ ★ ★

Things did become tougher for Johnny, and it had nothing to do with the troubled waters of romance. A sad but expected loss for Johnny was the death of his mother in 1963, who was in her 80s and had lived a full life. Johnny's brother Peter had lived with Elizabeth Weissmuller in the house Johnny had bought for their mother, until the time of her death.

In 1964 Johnny recalled that his mother had never wanted to leave Chicago, her home of many years: "I used to ask her to come out here, but she didn't want to leave her old friends and her work. I always sent her money. Because of the scandals, I convinced her she had to come. She was never happy here. She died last year." (After moving to Hollywood with his mother in the mid-1930s, Peter had married and then divorced. Over the years he worked regularly as a film extra and stuntman, often with his brother's studio of MGM. Although he never achieved the fame of his older brother, Peter Weissmuller earned his living and a solid reputation in Hollywood as a stuntman.)

The most difficult loss of all, and easily the most tragic, was the death of Johnny's 19-year-old daughter Heidi, on November 19, 1962. Johnny's youngest daughter had recently married and was pregnant by her new husband, Michael Husa. Heidi and Michael

628

were traveling by automobile on the way to the San Diego naval base after visiting with her mother, Beryl, in San Francisco, when the tragedy occurred.

According to the California Highway Patrol, Heidi was driving and fell asleep behind the wheel, causing the vehicle to overturn near Laguna Beach on Highway 101. Michael Husa was thrown from the vehicle, while their passenger in the back seat was uninjured. Heidi Weissmuller Husa and her unborn child were both pronounced dead at the hospital, where they had been rushed by ambulance after the accident.

At this particular time Johnny was in Chicago on business, and was staying at a hotel with Maria. When the call came in concerning Heidi, it was Maria who accepted the tragic news over the telephone. When Johnny returned to their room from his business meeting, Maria sat him down and compassionately delivered the report of Heidi's untimely death. Like any father who was told of the death of a child, he was shattered. His remorse was deeper than he had ever felt before; it was a mind-numbing sorrow for the loss of Heidi, and also for his unborn grandchild. The passage of time would lessen the grief, but losing a child who was still a teenager would leave a scar on Johnny that time would never erase.

There were many cards and letters of condolence for the Weissmuller family, after the death of Heidi. One such conveyance to Johnny came from Buster Crabbe, one of his oldest friends and now more than ever a friend rather than a rival. Buster related to Johnny how his own daughter Sande had died in 1957 of *anorexia nervosa,* an eating disorder that caused her death by malnutrition at the young age of 20-years-old. There were many parallels in the lives of Buster and Johnny, and this particular one was the saddest: Each had lost a daughter who was just blooming into womanhood.

On March 22, 1963, Johnny made a guest appearance on the NBC panel show, *First Impressions,* which was hosted by Bill Leyden. Johnny's identity was concealed, and a panel of three (of the usual game show suspects) asked the celebrity a number of questions which needed to be completed by the guest. For example, the question was posed: "It's a mistake not to teach children . . ." Johnny's answer was ". . . to swim." After the eleven questions were asked and answered, the panelists agreed that their mystery celebrity was the world famous swimmer and Tarzan, Johnny Weissmuller.

Optimistically feeling his fortunes were on the rise, Johnny decided to pop the proverbial question to Maria: "Will you marry me?" After a pregnant pause, the stunned Maria's answer was an emphatic "Yes!" Johnny called his old friend Major Riddle at the Dunes Hotel, to make arrangements for the bridal suite and for the ceremony which would take place at the Dunes. This would be Johnny's final stroll down the aisle, and he was determined to do it right this time, all the way down the line.

The Weissmuller home on Roscomare Road was bustling with activity on the Tuesday morning of April 23, 1963, as preparations were being made for the nuptials of Johnny and Maria. Soon the family Oldsmobile was packed for the 265-mile trip through the desert to the Dunes in Las Vegas, where Judge David Zenoff would be performing the wedding ceremony for the happy couple. The best man would be veteran actor Forrest Tucker, who had asked Johnny to assume the same ceremonial duty at his own wedding.

Maria's daughter Lisa was flying in for the afternoon ceremony along with her infant baby daughter from her home in Indianapolis. This would be the first opportunity for Maria and her new husband to see their grandchild, Lisa Maria, who was only eight-weeks-old. (Lisa was married to prominent criminal judge Richard Salb, who was a friend of President John F. Kennedy.)

When Johnny and Maria pulled up at the main entrance to the Dunes Hotel after their four-hour drive from Los Angeles, they were greeted by scores of well-wishers who were waiting to congratulate their favorite hero and his betrothed on their wedding day. Photographers' bulbs popped for the daily edition, as a smiling Johnny and Maria made their way into the Dunes to register for the bridal suite reserved in the name of "Mr. and Mrs. Weissmuller."

A trip to the Las Vegas city hall produced the marriage license for Johnny and Maria, as the out-of-town guests continued to arrive for the wedding. Some of the old gang were there, but many were committed to film locations or were just simply expired. Errol Flynn was gone, as was Ward Bond, Grant Withers, and other cronies of Weissmuller's from the old days. Duke Wayne was always making a movie (it seemed), and at this time was filming his cameo role in *The Greatest Story Ever Told*.

Picking up the entire tab for the wedding reception and the bridal suite was Dunes' owner Major Riddle, who wouldn't hear of letting Johnny pay a nickel for all the expensive accommodations. Comedian Phil Harris was expected to attend, and thus invited Johnny and Maria to be his special guests that evening at the Desert Inn, where he was performing his nightclub act.

Finally, at six o'clock sharp the moment of truth arrived as Johnny and Maria recited their vows before the judge and the wedding guests, and pronounced the "I do's." Moments later, the happy couple kissed and mugged for the photographers. Immediately after the ceremony the reception was held downstairs at the Sultan's Table, as the newlyweds were toasted with champagne and serenaded with violins during the bridal dinner.

As Johnny raised a glass of champagne and toasted his bride, he hoped that his time had come for true happiness. Maria was bride number five, and he dreamed that this would be a love that would last forever (after four marriages of varying degrees of success but all ultimately ending in failure). He didn't know it at the time, but this particular dream would come true. He and Maria would be married for over twenty years, and would fulfil the sacred vow, "Till death do us part."

The final entertainment for the evening was at the Desert Inn, as old buddy Phil Harris gave Johnny the full treatment during his comedy routine. Harris lampooned everything sacred about Weissmuller, including his name, his great swimming career, his seventeen years as Tarzan the ape-man, and even the coming evening of passion for the newlyweds at the bridal suite of the Dunes. It was all in fun and Johnny and Maria knew what to expect, so their laughter was as loud as the rest of the audience.

Johnny even did his Tarzan call on a prearranged cue during a dramatic pause in one of Phil's songs. The audience, stunned at the thundering rendition unique to one man on earth, rose in unison to applaud their long-time hero in a standing ovation that brought tears of pride to Weissmuller. The spotlight was on Johnny, broad-shouldered and still remarkably handsome with his full head of dark hair at age 58. Wearing a smile seen only rarely in his movies, he took his bows as the approval of the audience continued in a thundering final applause. Once again he was standing on the hero's podium to receive the accolades of a champion.

Johnny Weissmuller had visited Chicago numerous times after making Hollywood his home in 1931, but he returned to his Chicago roots with Maria to live not long after their marriage. They resided in Elk Grove Village for two years, as Johnny became vice president in charge of public relations for General Pool Corporation of Addison. By this time, Johnny's insecure financial situation was beginning to stabilize, and he reached a new partnership agreement with the Chicago-based swimming pool company headed by Kurt L. Stier.

They hoped that within a few years the "Johnny Weissmuller All-American Pool" would be found in backyards across America. Johnny once again hammered home the point how important swimming was to the youth of America: "With so much interest in aquatic sports, backyard pools and boating these days, it's a crime for every kid not to know how to swim. Every time I hear of a child drowning, I think how unnecessary it was."

Maria and Johnny weren't wealthy when they moved back to Beverly Hills in late 1964, but they were happy as he recalled in a 1965 interview: "Maria's a wonderful girl," said Johnny. "Everyone who knows her likes her. When you've been married as many times as we have, you look at things a little differently. We try to accept what we've had and lost in the past, and what we have and don't have now." (After marrying Maria, Johnny became very close to Maria's daughter, Lisa, who was the same age as his own daughter, Heidi, who had died in the car crash in 1962. And Johnny was also devoted to her baby, Lisa Maria, who took the place of Heidi's unborn child who also died in the accident.)

Johnny also noted that he was feeling great and still felt very optimistic about the future. "I'm past sixty and I feel like I'm about forty," he said. "I'm in good shape. I don't run around much. I found out how bad it is for a guy like me to get tanked up in public. I've got excess weight, but I could lose it easy. I could still play Tarzan, maybe. You know, my son's six-six and weighs two-twenty and he looks just like I used to. I used to think he'd make a good Tarzan. I been thinking he could play Tarzan's son. And I could play his old man, Tarzan. He could get in jams and I could get him out. That'd be cute — two Johnny Weissmullers. It'd make a pretty good movie or TV series, don't you think?"

The man known as Tarzan made a tremendous number of personal appearances during his lifetime, and this was true especially in the 1960s when his only income often came from signing autographs and shaking hands with the fans that still remembered him as Tarzan and Jungle Jim. An example of these appearances came on December 4, 1964, after the *State Times* in Baton Rouge announced in a full-page ad that "The Original Tarzan — Johnny Weissmuller" would be appearing the following afternoon at the grand opening of a furniture store in this Louisiana city. The ad promised a free autograph and souvenir from "Tarzan," and of course Johnny signed his name, and shook hands, and told his Tarzan stories for an entire eight-Africa, U.S.A.hour day. If Johnny didn't sign a million autographs in his lifetime, it would be surprising. And you could always read a "Johnny Weissmuller" autograph, as each and every letter would be clear and legible.

He also began doing television commercials for the first time in the 1960s, and his first ever was for the Opel Cadet automobile.

The spot was filmed at Africa, U.S.A. (a California jungle and wild animal compound where TV shows and movies were filmed).

"It was like the old times when I saw those elephants," said Johnny with a boyish enthusiasm. "I wish we had a setup as good when I was doing Tarzan. We could have made the films much faster at Africa, U.S.A. We spent too much time building sets in the old days and the pictures took at least four months to make." (Johnny received a new Buick as partial compensation for his work, which was complete with a fake "leopard-skin" top.)

Writer Don Page waxed nostalgically as he prepared for his interview with Johnny, who was his boyhood hero. "It was jolting to suddenly remember how great it was to be a kid when Tarzan walked through the bar at the Brown Derby. As Johnny Weissmuller (the only real Tarzan of them all) loped across the room — minus loincloth, of course — you noticed the shoulders were still wide and square, the chest deep, body military straight. His hair was dark and the smile was white and broad. Unmistakably, it was Tarzan.

"Even in his early 60s, Weissmuller looks 15 years younger. The star of 12 Tarzan films was back in Hollywood after a too-long absence to appear before the cameras again — not as the legendary ape-man, but in a television commercial for Gerald J. Schnitzer Productions. As memories warmed and nostalgia became thicker than jungle underbrush, Tarzan recalled the days of the ape man."

"Grab a vine and let's swing along," wrote Page in his column "Lively Arts: The Personality."

"I didn't have much dialogue as Tarzan, but I know I can play character parts," said Johnny. "There is some talk of me playing a role as the father of Ron Ely [TV's new Tarzan] in an episode this year. I'd love it. Can't you hear me saying: 'Me Tarzan — you Tarzan?' (He laughed heartily.)

"I was on my way to a career as an executive of a swimming suit company when a writer, Cyril Hume, spotted me one day walking through the Hollywood Athletic Club. 'Why don't you do a test for Tarzan,' he said. And I said, 'Me? Tarzan?' I didn't realize then what those words would mean to me.

"The first Tarzan picture made $40 million on its first showing around the world . . . You know, I've just started getting fan mail from Red China and Russia. The movies never stop showing."

Even today (2000), more than 30 years after this statement by Johnny, it is still true. American Movie Classics (AMC) has shown all of Johnny's Tarzan and Jungle Jim films on a regular basis over the past few years, and his six MGM Tarzan adventures are still popular on video with serious film buffs and lovers of great adventure films. Some things never change, including the popularity of Johnny Weissmuller as Tarzan.

CHAPTER THIRTY-TWO

Swimming Hall-of-Famer

In 1965 Johnny received one of the greatest tributes of his life when he was selected as the first honoree to the newly created Swimming Hall of Fame in Fort Lauderdale, Florida. For many years, members of the swimming fraternity longed to establish a shrine to honor the greatest male and female athletes of their sport, as well as commemorate their outstanding achievements throughout history. When the dream of the Hall of Fame at last became reality, the newly formed board of directors selected 21 individuals for the first induction ceremony to be held in December of 1965. As the "Greatest Swimmer of the Half-Century," Johnny was the first of the original inductees (which also included Buster Crabbe, Gertrude Ederle, and Duke Kahanamoku, all compatriots of Johnny's from the Olympic campaigns of 1924 and 1928). The international swim meet that was part of the gala grand opening celebration, was the first of four meets during 1965 and 1966 that were televised internationally by CBS Television. Johnny, along with Buster Crabbe and Eleanor Holm, were the guest commentators of CBS's Jack Whitaker, host of the Sports Spectacular.

The planned Hall of Fame complex would eventually include a museum, library, auditorium, and a million dollar swimming pool that was dedicated at the nationally televised Grand Opening International Meet in December of 1965. At the "halftime" induction ceremonies, Johnny Weissmuller and the rest of the inductees were introduced to the stars of the 1964 Olympics, which had been held in Tokyo. Among the five-thousand swimming fans, civic leaders and celebrities in attendance were numerous friends from Johnny's lifetime, including golfing comrade and boxing champion Rocky Marciano, pro golfers Sam Snead and Julius Boros, baseball great Ted Williams, and Olympic diver Wally Colbath (who was famed as the radio voice of "Jack Armstrong, All-American Boy").

Chosen as the director of the new Swimming Hall of Fame (SHOF) was Buck Dawson, who bestowed upon Johnny Weissmuller the honorary title of "Founding Chairman of the Board." The 50-plus Board of Directors was presided over by Dr. James Counsilman of Indiana University, who was the swim coach of the 1964 U.S. Olympic team. Buck Dawson, who was the executive director of the SHOF for more than 20 years until his retirement in 1986, recalled many Weissmuller stories and memories in a 1984 tribute published in *Swimming World*:

"Johnny was still a spectacular swimmer in his late sixties and took almost daily swims in the Hall of Fame pool during his eight years with us between 1966 and 1973. He was the first Hall of Fame honoree. Johnny stood with Buster Crabbe and the Duke high over the pool one day as hundreds of college swimmers were doing the Salmon Run 50/50s . . . It was Day One at the Hall of Fame!

"Johnny really helped us launch the Hall of Fame just by being around, even though we could not afford to pay him. He got other stars, Jackie Gleason, Rocky Marciano and Sam Snead, to appear at our water shows. He helped us run the first two afternoon-long CBS International Meets television. I'll never forget the night we went to the Mai-Kai where the Hawaiians performed for their living god, Duke Kahanamoku and Tarzan, too. Probably my biggest thrill was a trip to Jamaica with Johnny to promote the upcoming Commonwealth Games." (Queen Elizabeth of England was also in Jamaica and personally told Johnny how much she had enjoyed his movies as a child. When the Tarzan films were released they were brought to the royal palace so that Elizabeth and her sister Margaret, young children at the time, could watch them.)

Johnny was so enthralled by the new Swimming Hall of Fame that he accepted Buck Dawson's offer to be a more permanent part of the organization as an ambassador-at-large, beginning in 1966. Johnny and Maria pulled up stakes and moved to Fort Lauderdale, lock, stock and barrel — this would be their home for the next several years. Eventually Johnny and Maria found a comfortable condo near the Coral Ridge Country Club, where Johnny could get in plenty of his "other" favorite pastime — golfing. (Johnny, by the way, had five holes-in-one during his lifetime — and if you asked him, he would tell you about each and every one of them!)

Johnny poured his heart and soul into the Hall of Fame, which struggled for cash in the early years but would have floundered hopelessly without Johnny's presence and reputation luring donations from individuals and organizations. (During the eight years that Johnny was with the SHOF, he helped to raise approximately one million dollars for new construction and swimming programs. The money was raised by personal appearances by Johnny as well as attending fundraisers, and Maria later recalled, "I never went to so many barbecues in my life! That money we raised for the Swimming Hall of Fame was hard earned!)

Ground was broken for the Hall of Fame museum in 1966 and christened in 1967, and the dedication of the 300-seat auditorium was in 1968. In 1969 the first national swimming conventions were held at the SHOF, along with the men's and women's Olympic Committee meetings, and the grand opening of the Museum-Shrine building.

Johnny would spend many afternoons at the SHOF, taking a swim himself and watching the youngsters training at the Hall of Fame pool: "I swim an hour a day during the week and twice as much on weekends," said Johnny. "Some of these 16, 17-year-old kids swim 12,000 yards a day," he noted in a voice tinged with incredulity. "That's almost seven miles!"

He would often join them in the pool for a water polo match, a sport in which he earned a bronze medal in the 1924 Olympics in Paris. "Lots of times," he admitted, "I blow the whistle and stop the play, and the kids want to know why. I tell them, 'Why? For gosh sakes, you squirts, I'm 65-years-old, that's why!'"

Johnny recalled that the kids still knew him as Tarzan, a character way before their time: "I paddle around the pool with the kids. You'd think they wouldn't know Tarzan the way their parents and grandparents did. But, thanks to television showing my old movies, I'm still Tarzan to them. Like I said, it's been a wonderful life."

1966 inductees to the SHOF encompassed 25 of the greatest swimmers (and coaches) of all-time, including a sentimental choice for Johnny: his old coach, William Bachrach. "Big Bill" was Johnny's coach at the Illinois Athletic Club and perhaps his dearest friend, and was also the coach of the 1924 and 1928 Olympic Games. Other 1966 selections who were close friends of Weissmuller were Arne Borg, Pete Desjardins, Eleanor Holm, and Esther Williams. Eventually, the balance of Johnny's closest friends and competitors from the swimming wars and the Olympics, joined him in the SHOF, including: Sybil Bauer, Teddy Cann, and Norman Ross in 1967; Harry Hebner and George Kojac in 1968; USC swim coach Fred Cady and Ethyl Lacke in 1969; Helen Meany, a former flame of Johnny's, in 1971; Andrew Charlton, "Boy" Charlton in 1972; and Walter Laufer in 1973.

When Johnny introduced Australian Andrew Charlton at the induction ceremonies in 1972, he said with a broad grin to his old friendly rival, "Me Tarzan, you Boy!" (Charlton was known as "Boy" because he was a 16-year-old lad when he won a gold medal at the 1924 Olympics in the 1500-meter freestyle. Charlton finished third in the

400-meters that year to — of course — Johnny Weissmuller.)

Johnny was always willing to help Buck Dawson get publicity for the SHOF, and in 1967 he joined Buck along with Buster Crabbe and current swimming star Donna deVarona in an appearance on the Ed Sullivan show. Johnny went way back to the 1920s with Sullivan, who had been engaged to his friend and fellow Olympian, the late Sybil Bauer.

After making his home in Fort Lauderdale, Weissmuller noted his growing endearment with the town and the people: "I have grown to love this city," said Johnny. "Coming here was one of the best things that ever happened to me. Fort Lauderdale is one of the fastest growing, most exciting cities I have ever come in contact with, and I plan to be a part of the Gold Coast scene for a long time to come."

Johnny Weissmuller was invited to a Tarzan "reunion" in September of 1966, as part of a publicity drive for the new Tarzan TV series starring Ron Ely. Of the ten former Tarzan actors who were invited to the reunion held at the Churubusco studios in Mexico, only three were able to make the date: Weissmuller, Jock Mahoney (1962-63), and silent film Tarzan James Pierce (1927). The four actors posed for several photographs together, including the former Tarzans garbed in loincloths and poised for action on a mighty tree limb with vine in hand. These photos appeared in all the major newspapers across the country, giving Johnny a rare opportunity to briefly portray Tarzan once again.

Johnny later recalled that there was some talk that he might join the cast of this new Tarzan TV series as the father of Tarzan (Ron Ely). Unfortunately, the dialogue was abandoned and Johnny was never even offered a guest role on the show. This was a major blunder by NBC, which missed a golden opportunity for publicity by bringing back the greatest Tarzan in a guest role. The show lasted two years before being canceled, as Tarzan literally disappeared from sight for more than a decade.

Around this time, Johnny reflected on his Tarzan years and the impact of the dozen adventures in which he starred as the hero of Edgar Rice Burroughs' literary works: "The movies are still going well, 'Tarzan' never grows old. Like a Western, it will be the same in 1989 as it was in 1949. The jungle, the animals, and man's love for escape from the civilized and routine big-city life. They are decent films, designed for family viewing. It is basically an idealistic, down-to-earth story about a man's love for animals and the care of his family. You know 'Tarzan' sees the white hunters invading his territory and killing animals, and he swings down from the tops of the trees warning them, 'Tarzan mad — you leave.'"

Fan mail for Weissmuller and his alter-ego of Tarzan was once in the thousands of letters per week during his heyday of the 1930s. Now in the late 1960s, Johnny would "only" get perhaps 200 letters per week, many coming from the four corners of the earth including Romania (where he was born). His old movies were still popular in major markets around the world, including Japan, Germany, South and Central America, Italy, and even Russia. Mail for Johnny throughout the years would most often come addressed simply: "Tarzan . . . Hollywood, California." The folks at the post office knew where Johnny lived and all of the thousands of letters each year addressed to "Tarzan" in any form were sent to his current address. (Of course it was impossible for Johnny to personally answer all of this mail, but letters with questions about health and fitness often caught his eye and he would write a personal reply.)

After the Ron Ely Tarzan series ended in 1968, Johnny was thinking out loud that his 28-year-old son, John Scott, would be perfect as the next screen Tarzan. "Johnny looks just like I used to look," noted the father with pride. "Can you imagine what people would think if they saw Johnny Weissmuller on the screen again? They'd say, 'How'd that guy stay so young?' "

In 1969, Johnny and Maria became involved with a vitamin company called "Golden Fifty" which was headquartered in Chicago. Their main product was a high-potency vitamin supplement, which they offered on a free trial offer that was endorsed by Johnny. By mailing a magazine coupon to the company, a thirty-day supply was returned to the customer free of all charges. Endorsing a vitamin product was a natural for an athlete such as Johnny, who didn't endorse any product in which he didn't believe. Johnny and Maria did endorsements and magazine ads for this company for several years, and Johnny later became associated with his own national chain of health food stores.

Johnny eventually did get involved with another Tarzan project: a recreation park in Titusville, Florida called "Johnny Weissmuller's Tropical Wonderland." Located one and a half miles north of the Kennedy Space Center, Johnny had wanted to call this major undertaking "Johnny Weissmuller's Tarzanland." Some of the exhibits would have included Tarzan's Tree House, Jane's Lagoon, Cheeta's Island, and Boy's Tree Slide. However, he was stonewalled by Edgar Rice Burroughs, Inc., which politely declined to allow Johnny to use the name "Tarzan" in conjunction with his commercial enterprise. The Burroughs organization said: "We'd like to help Weissmuller, because he's our friend. In fact, Weissmuller is Tarzan. But we can't let him use the name because if we do, others also will use it — and we'll lose control."

The 60 acres of Johnny's Tropical Wonderland included enough exhibits to keep a family entertained an entire day, including a children's petting zoo, snake farm, bird aviary, alligator pit, and monkey island. There was also a jungle walk through the beautiful tropical settings, a scenic river boat ride, an authentic Seminole Indian village, an excursion train ride around the entire grounds, plus a midway and arcade. You could also enjoy lunch at the "Tree House" restaurant and lounge, and shop at several different gift boutiques including the "White Hunter" gift shop and the "Tiger" toy shop. "Tropical Wonderland is a fantastic magical place," said Johnny. "People come here and really get to enjoy the beauty and mystery of the jungle."

Future blueprints for Tropical Wonderland included a gigantic swimming pool, where Johnny hoped to host a high diving championship similar to the one held in Acapulco, and a Weissmuller museum where his immense stockpile of medals and trophies would be on display. Other proposals included a beautiful marina and luxury hotel, a boat and fishing pier, and a sight-seeing launch where visitors could view the lift-off of moon shots at the Kennedy Space Center. Johnny and Maria had purchased a home in Titusville on Knox McRae Drive, to be closer to what appeared to be a wonderful future for Tropical Wonderland. (Unfortunately, there would also be disappointment for Johnny and Maria — eventually they had the owners withdraw his name because they did not properly maintain the park and allowed it to become rundown.)

An ambitious Johnny also entered the world of franchising in 1969 with "Johnny Weissmuller's Jungle Hut, Inc.," which was headquartered in Fort Lauderdale. There were four major franchise ideas, all to be endorsed by Johnny Weissmuller, to include: Jungle Hut Restaurants; American Natural Food Stores; Safari Hut Gift Shops; and Umgawa Club Lounges.

As grandiose as these plans were, only the American Natural Food Stores actually came into being with several locations around the country. (Johnny's business agent advised him not to lend his name to the other ventures, which required a vast amount of start-up capital that was not available to the partners. The future appeared as if you would see Johnny's name on every corner of America, but the plans for these establishments were simply too monumental and too under-financed.)

Johnny appeared at the grand opening of the St. Louis health store, where eighteen-hundred fans of the former Tarzan mobbed Johnny for autographs and handshakes. He was greeted by similar turnouts of well-wishers at every one of his personal appearances to open a new location — the name of Johnny Weissmuller always had the magic that attracted people.

"My food stores serve all kinds of vitamin pills, organic foods, and protein candy bars," noted Johnny. "All good things which Mother Nature meant us to have but which modern living makes hard to get. In years to come, the environment is going to be so tough on our systems that only the very healthy will survive. Treat your body well and it'll see you through for many years."

Another colossal plan was for the establishment and construction of an ultramodern health and recreation complex, the Johnny Weissmuller Family Recreation Center, in the St. Petersburg, Florida area. An 86,000 square foot building would house Olympic-approved swimming and diving pools, bowling alleys, indoor golf putting and practice greens, all types of fitness and body conditioning equipment, sauna and steam rooms, a basketball court, and a "record and romp room" for teenaged dancing. This was just the tip of the iceberg, as the facility would also include a health food store, restaurant and lounge, children's nursery, billiard room, Judo and Karate classes, and a golf-pro shop.

More than anything, Johnny wanted these fitness centers to benefit the youth of America, and therefore a Johnny Weissmuller Scholarship Program would sponsor intramural competition in most sports. Local school coaches would be granted honorary memberships and would instruct and assist in the various sports classes and competitions. Family memberships would be reasonably priced and the gigantic complex would have a target goal of 5,000 memberships for families and individuals. Johnny was still advocating the tremendous value of swimming to the health of children, as he noted: "Swimming makes a child's muscles loose and supple. A child will be good at any sport if he (or she) is good at swimming."

With these monumental proposals in the planning stages, Johnny spoke of his philosophy of life in regard to health and fitness for the human race: "I have always been vitally interested and concerned with physical conditioning. And I have long believed that athletic competition among people and nations should replace violence and wars. I dedicate myself and my Family Recreation Centers to 'Unity Through Athletics,' and I pledge myself, and my associates, to do all we possibly can to create the peaceful atmosphere of athletic competition for all peoples. I look ahead to the speedy establishment of my Family Recreation Centers throughout this country and in many areas of the world."

These were incredibly ambitious and noble plans for the future involving Johnny, which required a tremendous amount of financial backing to come to fruition. During his eight years in the Fort Lauderdale area, working with the Swimming Hall of Fame, some of these plans became reality and others were unrealized dreams that simply didn't have the financial support to come true. But they were honorable plans and Johnny honestly believed that a better future was in store for mankind. As part of that dream, he had hopes of establishing a foundation to support young swimmers in the name of Johnny Weissmuller.

In remembering his own youth and the lucky break he had in hooking up with Bill Bachrach and the Illinois Athletic Club, Johnny hoped that through the foundation, top-flight swimmers would be ensured of a college education — something he never had the money or the opportunity to achieve.

In gratitude and recognition of the many contributions to the state including his work with the SHOF, Johnny was presented with a bronze Great Seal of Florida by Governor Claude Kirk. When asked about the possibility of retirement in the future, Johnny responded with a firm belief in keeping on with the current plan: "It's silly to retire. I don't know how to retire. I love life too much. I'll always be doing something. When people don't know me anymore or don't want my autograph, then I'll think about it. But not now when there is so much left to do."

"I've never had any real dark moments," noted Johnny. "I've been a pretty lucky fellow and I'm still enjoying life every day."

One moment that could have been dark for Johnny was when his Fort Lauderdale condominium was robbed by thieves, and two of his Olympic gold medals were part of the loot. Fortunately, the medals were replaced by the U.S. Olympic committee, so that Johnny once again had all five of his hard-earned gold medals.

In 1970, Johnny had a cameo role in his first film since his final Jungle Jim picture in 1955. *The Phynx* was intended to be a light-hearted comedy, but unfortunately brought only sparse laughter in a very limited release. The *Motion Picture Guide* said of the farcical comedy: "A disappointing all-star extravaganza with a silly plot that must have been sold to the assembled cast by one of the greatest con-men of all time."

The film reunited Johnny with his dear friend Maureen O'Sullivan, who also had a cameo role. It was their first motion picture together since 1942, in *Tarzan's New York Adventure*. Johnny and Maureen were among many great old celebrities in this one, including Ed Sullivan, Xavier Cugat, Joe Louis, former Bowery Boys Leo Gorcey and Huntz Hall, Guy Lombardo, Andy Devine, Dick Clark, Dorothy Lamour, Jay Silverheels, along with ventriloquist Edgar Bergen and his dummy, Charlie McCarthy.

Back in Fort Lauderdale, Johnny attempted to describe the plot — if you could call it that: "I read the script," said Johnny, "but it didn't help much. All I know is, 35 celebrities are abducted to Albania. Some beatniks are involved in the rescue. Ex-prize fighter Joe Louis had scenes before us and Dorothy Lamour after. It was frantic, and fun!" During his visit to Hollywood, Weissmuller looked up Johnny Sheffield, his young co-star in the Tarzan adventures. It was almost like the good old days, as Johnny was back together for a walk down Memory Lane with Jane and Boy.

Over the years, Johnny was on the cover of hundreds of magazines, mostly as his famous character, Tarzan. But the April 1970 issue of *Esquire* magazine devoted the cover to a current color photograph of Johnny and Maureen O'Sullivan (and one of Johnny's chimps, revealed when the front cover was fully opened). The title of the article: "Tarzan and other heroes come back once more." Johnny's photo in the article about the current lives of old-time muscle men, was in swimming trunks preparing for his daily swim at the SHOF. The cover photo of Johnny and Maureen, one of hundreds together but the first since their years as Tarzan and Jane, was probably the final portrait of the legendary couple.

Weissmuller was still in excellent trim at age 65, and explained his relatively strict diet: fruit juice, cereal, soup, no bread, lean meat (especially steaks), plenty of fruits and vegetables, and also a regular vitamin supplement to make up for the vitamins that were stripped by modern day food processing. He also noted the fun of making the Tarzan movies, and the danger of working with the elephants: "Once I was following my elephant by vine when he stopped suddenly and I ran into his tail-end and broke my nose." Johnny was smiling when he recalled this anecdote from yesteryear.

In the summer of 1972, a few weeks prior to the Olympics held in Munich, Johnny and four other past Olympic gold medal winners, Jesse Owens, Bob Mathias, Wilma Rudolph, and Peggy Fleming, were presented sets of sterling silver commemorative medals depicting great moments in Olympic history at a luncheon at the Four Seasons Restaurant in

New York on July 27th. The medals were designed by the noted sculptor, Seymour Chwaste, for the Franklin Mint, and the net proceeds from the 17-medal set were donated to the United States Olympic Committee.

The Associated Press published a new book in 1972 called *The Sports Immortals*, which highlighted the careers of 50 athletes they deemed to be the greatest of all time. On November 2, 1972, eight of the 50 immortals were honored at a luncheon at Jimmy's Restaurant on West 52nd Street in New York, and presented with the Dewar's Merit Award.

Howard Cosell acted as toastmaster at the affair, at which Johnny Weissmuller, Jack Dempsey, Willie Mays, Gordie Howe, A. J. Foyt, Willie Shoemaker, Kareem Abdul-Jabbar were recipients of awards, while Mrs. Babe Ruth accepted on behalf of her late husband.

This was pretty good company for Weissmuller, who had known Dempsey for years but got the opportunity to meet other great sport stars who were still making headlines in their chosen fields. Although the honored guests chatted informally of achievements in their respective sports (boxing, baseball, swimming, hockey, auto racing, thoroughbred racing and basketball), only Johnny stepped to the microphone for a brief self-revealing comment:

"How can a guy climb trees, say 'me Tarzan, you Jane' — and make a million?" Johnny's broad grin symbolized his marvelous sense of humor as well as his pride in being honored on this wonderful occasion.

When Johnny was interviewed by Dave Anderson of the *New York Times* in November of 1972, he noted that he was back in the swimming pool trade with his business partner, Jack Brown. According to Brown, General Pools Corporation had sold 500 pools in the first five months of operation.

Columnist Anderson, obviously a Weissmuller fan, spoke with Johnny concerning the recent Olympics in Munich, which Johnny had attended as a faithful fan of his chosen sport, swimming.

"Johnny Weissmuller remains a contemporary personality. Not so much for his Olympic swimming exploits nearly half a century ago, but for the 'Tarzan' motion pictures that are a television staple. 'All the kids know me,' said Johnny. 'They grow up watching me every Saturday morning.'

"He is 68-years-old, but he still looks like a movie Tarzan. His shoulders are enormous, dominating his trim 6-foot 3-inch frame. His brown hair curls over the collar of his jacket, as it did long before it was fashionable. He had a white bandana knotted inside the open neck of his red shirt, which had JOHNNY embroidered on each cuff. He made a lot of money and he spent a lot, too. But the Tarzan movies have obscured what a great swimmer this man was.

" 'I was better than Mark Spitz is,' said Johnny firmly in his squeaky voice. 'I never lost a [freestyle] race. Never. Not even in the Y.M.C.A. The closest I ever came to losing was on the last lap of the 400 in 1924 when I got a snootful. But I knew enough not to cough. If you don't cough, you can swallow it.'

"Weissmuller won five Olympic gold medals, three at Paris in 1924 and two at Amsterdam in 1928; he also earned a bronze medal in 1924 as a member of the United States water polo team. Spitz, of course, won seven gold medals at Munich this year, but four of his events did not exist in the Olympics when Weissmuller was competing. Spitz is a sprinter, but Weissmuller set 67 world records from 50 yards to 880 yards, the track equivalent of a 100-yard dash to a two-mile run.

" 'And it's easier to go faster now,' Weissmuller explained. 'On a turn, they don't have to touch with their hand, they just flip and push off, that's a split second. The platform is higher and the pool is deeper, so when you enter the water, that's a couple strokes. And the water's smoother. We didn't have the lane ropes, we had to get up higher in the water to avoid the little waves. It all adds up.'

"The showbiz concept of sports also is different now. Spitz is in Hollywood, surrounded by agents of the William Morris Agency, melting his medals into millions. Weissmuller popularized swimming as an Olympic sport in this country; but nobody considered him to be an instant commodity. Two years after the 1928 Olympics, his coach, Bill Bachrach, negotiated a swimsuit contract for him at $500 a week. Not long after that, he made the first of his 12 Tarzan movies.

" 'It was up my alley,' he said. 'There was swimming in it, and I didn't have to say much. You just had to have patience. Working with animals, especially a chimpanzee, they don't know what you're talking about, you have to do a scene five or six times.'

"His career as Tarzan ended in 1948, but soon he had another career as 'Jungle Jim' and a TV series. Now he's the chairman of the International Swimming Hall of Fame in Fort Lauderdale, Florida, where Spitz's medals are scheduled to be put on display next month. 'I was in Mexico City four years ago when he got beat a couple times and he didn't like it, he was a surly kid then,' Weissmuller said. 'But when he went to Indiana, his coach there, Doc Counsilman, got tough with him, and he's all right now. I was with his mother and father at Munich, but he avoided me. I think it was jealousy on his part. I'm a happy-go-lucky guy. I got nothing to lose. I don't know how he'll do as an actor. It depends what the William Morris Agency does for him. They handled me, too. In that business, you're only as good as your last picture. But if he hits it, he's got to go with it.'

" 'I'll see him at the Hall of Fame next month,' said Johnny as he took another sip of his bloody Mary and grinned. 'He avoided me, but I'll grow on him.' "

In the latter part of 1973, Johnny accepted an offer to join the public relations department at Caesar's Palace in Las Vegas. He and Maria had lived in south Florida for eight years, but Johnny was getting the itch to get back to the West Coast where his children, John Scott, Wendy, and Lisa, and his grand-children lived. He also missed the Hollywood scene, and his old friends from the movie business.

Johnny joined former heavyweight boxing champion Joe Louis, who had worked at the casino since 1967. (By this time, however, Joe Louis's health was in a severe decline and Weissmuller was expected to take over the role that the former champ had held the past several years. A third member of the public relations department was former tennis champion Pancho Gonzalez, who split the duties at the casino with Louis and Weissmuller.)

In his position with the public relations department, Johnny would roam the casino gaming hall until someone recognized him, and then he would reminisce about the past with the guests. There were still a great number of legendary celebrities that worked in Las Vegas in the 1970s, many of whom were old friends of Johnny's. The position at the casino had its drawbacks, as he would later note, but for the time Johnny was close to the spotlight and his comrades of yesteryear.

On December 20, 1973, Johnny suffered the first serious injury of his life at a sports banquet honoring Triple Crown winner Secretariat, which took place at the hotel. He slipped and fell from a wobbly chair while seating himself at the banquet table, and as a result broke his hip. Johnny underwent surgery to set the broken hip, and spent the Christmas holidays recovering in the South Nevada Memorial Hospital in Las Vegas.

Johnny was still in the hospital when the induction ceremonies were held for the current class of honorees at the Swimming Hall of Fame in Fort Lauderdale. He had been expected to be a guest for the ceremony, but instead placed a call to Buck Dawson extending his best wishes to the new inductees. In Johnny's words, "Give my best to the whole bunch." Johnny had been in superb health for most of his 69 years, and he recovered quite well from his busted hip. But it showed a crack in his armor, and proved that he was mortal and not as invincible as Tarzan.

May of 1975 found Johnny and Maria the guests of the Crystal Palace in the London borough of Twickenham, where he would be presenting prizes and medals at a swimming gala. Weissmuller fan Martin Smiddy recalled that Johnny was extremely gracious in signing a stack of old Tarzan photos — gazing at each one with fondness as he recalled the memories associated with that particular movie. Johnny had last been in London during a stopover en route to the Munich Olympics in 1972. Another longtime fan and the editor of *The Fantastic Worlds of Edgar Rice Burroughs*, Frank Westwood, recalled that he had met Johnny during this brief 1972 visit and that Mr. Weissmuller had cordially recalled a few stories from his Tarzan days — and signed his autograph for a millionth time (always accompanied by a warm smile and a firm handshake).

For the Labor Day weekend of 1975, Johnny was once again a special guest of the Burroughs Bibliophiles at their annual convention held in Los Angeles that year. Johnny was one of five Tarzans and six Janes who were among the honored guests, including Tarzan actors James Pierce, Denny Miller, Buster Crabbe, and Jock Mahoney. The "Janes" included Eve Brent, Joanna Barnes, Vanessa Brown, Joyce MacKenzie, Karla Schramm, and Louise Lorraine. Johnny looked dapper and fit in a blue suit, and attended all three days of the convention festivities.

In 1976, Johnny appeared in the final two films of his career — a cameo role in the comedy *Won Ton Ton, The Dog That Saved Hollywood*, and the MGM compilation extravaganza, *That's Entertainment: Part II*. Johnny looked to be healthy and dapper at age 71, and he sported a mop of dark brown hair (his own hair) that was reminiscent of his years as Tarzan. *Won Ton Ton* spoofed the silent picture era of the 1920s, and told a saga of three nobodies who become big Hollywood stars: a mutt German Shepherd; an actress who's desperate to catch any break (Madeline Kahn); and a wanna-be writer/ producer (Bruce Dern) who's currently driving a Hollywood tour bus.

Johnny's only scene was with Art Carney, who played a big-time director overrun with problems in his latest western epic (starring Won Ton Ton). Johnny's cameo bit was as a tall, rugged stagehand whose only line is to Carney: "You're wanted on the phone," barks Johnny. The frustrated producer has just threatened to fire everyone, and snaps back at the surprised stagehand, "You're fired, too!"

There were more than 50 cameo roles filled by stars of yesteryear, including Victor Mature as a mob "trigger" man; Walter Pidgeon as a butler; John Carradine as a drunk; Milton Berle as a blind man; Dorothy Lamour as an aging film actress; Ethel Merman as a gossip columnist; Rudy Vallee as an autograph hound; Peter Lawford as a slapstick star; Sterling Holloway as a bus rider; Rory Calhoun as a big western star; Dennis Day as a singing telegraph man; Yvonne De Carlo as a cleaning lady; Edgar Bergen as a vaudeville star; Keye Luke as a cook; Billy Barty as an assistant director; Huntz Hall as a moving man; Cyd Charisse and Zsa Zsa Gabor as film stars; and so on and so forth. The movie itself was only fair, but seeing all the old stars in cameo roles was worth the price of admission.

That's Entertainment: Part II was hosted by Fred Astaire and Gene Kelly, who presented film clips along with anecdotes from many of the greatest MGM classic films of all time. Although most of these films were musicals, there were also scenes from numerous dramatic films including *Tarzan, the Ape Man* (1932). Johnny did his splendiferous Tarzan yell, as well as the famous "me Tarzan — you

Jane" scene with Maureen O'Sullivan. The opening credits were done in a plethora of imaginative ways, with Johnny's name arriving like a message in a bottle.

This memorable film was a nostalgic look at the greatest stars of yesteryear, in some of their most famous roles and performances. Old hoofers Astaire and Kelly also did some new dance routines that proved they still had the dancing magic that made them legends. For Johnny Weissmuller, even though his segment was only a film clip, this would be the final screen credit of his long career that began in 1929.

Fittingly, and appropriately, he shared his moments in the spotlight with O'Sullivan, MaureenMaureen O'Sullivan, the marvelous lady who portrayed "Jane" in his greatest Tarzan adventures.

Johnny was also invited to a gala Hollywood party to simultaneously celebrate the premiere of *That's Entertainment* as well as the 50th anniversary of MGM. A group photograph of the fifty male and female stars gathered for the event included many of Hollywood's greatest heroes and heroines (including Lassie). Johnny Weissmuller was resplendent in a white tuxedo in his spot on the stage next to film legends James Stewart and Gloria Swanson.

CHAPTER THIRTY-THREE

Life Becomes
a Rocky Road

When Johnny reached his 72nd birthday on June 2, 1976, his life was in harmony and things were going well. He was maintaining his good health, and it seemed likely that he could continue making personal appearances as Tarzan for many years to come. His daily swimming regimen had helped him recover from the broken hip, along with the 40,000 letters that poured in from around the world, when his fans heard about the accident. "It's swimming that's kept me in excellent shape," noted Johnny, "even though a year ago I fell from a wobbly chair at a convention, and broke my hip.

"When I was ill and couldn't swim for a while, I got 'punchy' [like a boxer]. You know what I did? As soon as I could, I swam a lot. That's why I'm able to use my legs as well as before." (Around this time, realizing his own mortality, Johnny donated most of the medals he'd won as a swimmer to the Joseph

P. Kennedy Foundation, to help raise money for retarded children and adults. Today, all of Johnny's medals are held in trust for the Kennedy Foundation at the Swimming Hall of Fame in Fort Lauderdale, Florida.)

The Weissmullers owned a home on Laurie Drive in Las Vegas at this time, and Johnny had given up his job at Caesar's Palace in 1975, shortly before a trip he and Maria made to Europe. He was really quite fed up with the atmosphere at the casinos, as he recalled for *Modern Screen* in January of 1976: "Too much night life, too many banquets, and too many drunks," said Johnny. "I'm an outdoor man, and I don't like to do any work unless I want to." Now in his 70s, Weissmuller had earned the right to be picky when it came to working, and the casino job had become a burden rather than the enjoyable pastime it had started out to be.

There was always a busy schedule of personal appearances for Johnny, and he planned to be the guest of honor at the "Nostalgia Convention 1977" which was being held in New York City over Labor Day Weekend, September 2-5, at the Americana Hotel. Unfortunately, and tragically, Johnny suffered a stroke the last week of August, 1977 while in Los Angeles, and was hospitalized in the intensive care unit at the Valley Presbyterian Hospital in suburban Van Nuys, California. Under the dire circumstances he was unable to fulfil his commitment to the New York convention, and for all practical purposes this was the end of his public life.

As soon as his condition was stable, he was moved to the Motion Picture and Television Country Home and Hospital in Woodland Hills, California. Maria Weissmuller, meanwhile, sold their house in Las Vegas and moved in with her daughter Lisa in Los Angeles, so she could be close to her husband.

Johnny would live at the Country Hospital, a convalescent facility for veteran actors, for most of the next two years. (At one point an emergency tracheotomy had to be performed to improve his breathing, and Johnny nearly died.) Skyrocketing medical bills devoured the last of the Weissmuller's savings, but fortunately Maria was able to live on Social Security and Johnny's small pension from the Screen Actor's Guild.

In 1978, with Johnny's permission, the *National Enquirer* published an article about his protracted illness and his attempts to recuperate at the Country Hospital from the adversity of the strokes that robbed him of his good health. When Johnny's faithful fans saw the article, they sent him thousands of get-well cards, along with numerous gifts to include: a $10 check, one fan's own swimming medal, poems, pictures, and even a quarter from an eight-year-old who was touched by Johnny's plight. One favorite gift, said Maria, was a plastic giraffe sent by a boy in Ohio. When Johnny saw all the cards, letters, and small gifts he said through teary eyes, "Oh my God . . . they haven't forgotten me!"

In the spring of 1979, Johnny and Maria had to face another challenge when Jack Staggs, the executive director of the Country Home and Hospital, filed an affidavit in district court seeking conservatorship over Johnny. His intentions were to have Mr. Weissmuller committed to a mental institution, claiming that he was upsetting the other residents by shouting his famous Tarzan yell (which supposedly was frightening the other patients), and had repeatedly wandered away from the hospital grounds. The Weissmullers, including Johnny's stepdaughter Lisa, weren't the only ones upset about this action — old friend John Wayne also saw this maneuver as inappropriate. "I am deeply upset and shocked that Johnny should be in this situation," said the Duke. "I'm going to make sure that what they're doing is the right thing for him," vowed Wayne to Maria Weissmuller.

The Duke, himself fighting terminal cancer at this time, called the hospital several times to palaver with Staggs, and insisted that the action against Johnny be dropped. John

Wayne, always a strong persuader, made his point loud and clear to Staggs. "We all love Johnny," said Staggs to the press in explaining his request that he be institutionalized. "But we've had some problems with him, especially when he has attempted to leave the grounds of the hospital."

Just before Johnny's 75th birthday in June, a Superior Court judge denied the motion and awarded the conservatorship to Maria. "I'm glad they're not putting him in a mental institution," said Maria. "They did that to him once before. They kept him there for a month and it almost killed him. To do it again would be the end of John. He's not a mental patient, although we know he's suffering from some brain damage [from the strokes]. He was terrified about this court hearing. Johnny's a proud and gentle man. All he's ever wanted is to grow old peacefully with his family."

On Sunday, June 3rd, Maria, Lisa, and her daughter, 16-year-old Lisa Maria Salb, came to visit Johnny with a cake for his birthday. Johnny still enjoyed playing cards for money, and during the visit he recalled to his granddaughter the gin rummy games (a favorite pastime) they used to play. "Everything's completely under control," said Lisa Weissmuller. "My dad just has these memory lapses . . . just because he gives the Tarzan yell once in a while — that's a sign of good health to me," she added.

The whole situation was resolved when Johnny and Maria jointly decided to move down to Acapulco in October of 1979, and to stay temporarily at the Los Flamingos Hotel. Johnny's last Tarzan picture, *Tarzan and the Mermaids*, was filmed in an area called Pie de la Cuesta and he still had many fond memories of the kindly people of Mexico. Johnny felt deep inside that if he ever retired, he would like to do so in Mexico — he loved the sheer beauty of the nature and the landscape that surrounded Acapulco. Eventually they rented a house near the beach in Playa Mimosa (near Pie de la Cuesta) with a cliffside view of the Pacific Ocean, which would be their home for the next several years.

According to the *Hollywood Studio* magazine of March, 1980: "Five days after arriving in Acapulco, Johnny jumped in the pool and started swimming. This was the first time he had been near the water in over two and a half years. Doctors had predicted that it would be several months before he would be able to start swimming again." In the words of Maria, Johnny was happy again and he said, "Well, let's have some coffee and then take a swim."

Despite this optimistic report, Johnny's health was up and down for the next few years. At his 76th birthday on June 2, 1980, friends brought out a cake topped with a miniature Tarzan holding a knife with a tiny alligator at his feet. Johnny was so choked up with emotion, that he broke down and cried. Maria told *The Star* in June of 1980 that life wasn't the best for her husband anymore, but he still had his memories of the past: "Once in a while he mentions the old Hollywood Athletic Club and his pal Spencer Tracy. He used to adore dancing and was very good. Suddenly he will say, 'Let's go dancing.'

"On some days he will watch television, especially westerns. When the action begins, he will pound the chair and say, 'Get him. Get him.'"

Maria also told the *New York Times* in November of 1980 that her husband was "improving all the time," and that Johnny was taking strolls around their pool several times a day. According to his private nurse, Alice Miller, Johnny was doing well for all that he had been through with his health problems. "Sure, he's not as strong as he used to be," said Miller, "but he's eating regularly and getting stronger all the time. I'd say he's in good condition."

When Johnny celebrated his 78th birthday on June 2, 1982, he slowly raised his hand to signal Maria to cut the cake. Johnny was seated in a wheelchair, and he smiled that wonderful smile at the few close friends bearing gifts that had been invited by Maria to celebrate the occasion. He was also presented with the Key to the City of Acapulco by Mayor Febronio Figueroa, with all the local reporters present for the ceremony. The certificate that was presented to him was given a place of honor over his bedroom door, on the outside where it could be seen by visitors. Also on hand was his favorite musical trio, "Los Presidentes," who performed for Johnny the traditional Mexican birthday song "Las Mananitas" and other tunes.

Johnny had reached a certain peace with himself at this stage of his life, and he was no longer angry about the bad hand (the debilitating stroke) that life had dealt him. (Around this time a second tracheotomy had to be performed to improve his breathing, and a stomach tube for feeding was also necessary. Johnny's throat had been severely blocked by scar tissue, but his condition improved after the operation.)

One publication wrote about Johnny in his forced retirement: "He has accepted the fact he will not swim again and enjoys sitting by the pool looking out over the ocean. He also takes two walks daily with the help of his nurses.

"The once robust six-foot-three Olympic champion may be thin and weak, but his wife Maria is encouraged by his progress the past year. She prepares the strained vegetables, meat and fruit juices that are fed through the stomach tube. 'They must be fresh every day,' she said, 'and strained carefully and thoroughly.'

"It's evident that constant love and care have brought Weissmuller through another year." The article of course bespoke of the love and care of Maria, who stuck with Johnny in these toughest of times. For better or worse, richer or poorer . . . they had all of these situations in the final years of their two decades as husband and wife.

According to longtime friend Mike Oliver, the last time he and his wife Rita saw Johnny was a 1983 Thanksgiving party. Oliver also recalled that he would visit Johnny quite often during his final years in Acapulco, and "have a few drinks" with the former Tarzan, his boyhood idol. In a 1998 letter, Oliver fondly recalled, "I never once saw him lose his temper. He was always nice and had a smile for everything."

Mike Oliver also attended Johnny's final birthday party, when he reached his 79th birthday in 1983. "He still had that marvelous winning smile and would put his hand right out to shake yours," remembered Oliver.

Johnny received a great tribute in 1983 when he was one of the premiere inductees into the Olympic Hall of Fame which was established by the United States Olympic

Committee. Among the initial group of 1983 honorees were some illustrious Olympic heroes, including boxer Muhammad Ali; figure skaters Dick Button and Peggy Fleming; speed skater Eric Heiden; track and field stars Babe Didrikson Zaharias, Bob Beamon, Rafer Johnson, Bob Mathias, Jesse Owens, Wilma Rudolph, and Jim Thorpe; along with swimmers Mark Spitz, Don Schollander, and Johnny Weissmuller.

The induction ceremony was held in Chicago, the site of many of his greatest triumphs as a swimmer. His stepdaughter, Lisa Weissmuller, was there to accept the award on behalf of her father.

For more than forty years Johnny had been remembered as a champion swimmer and as Tarzan, arguably the most perfect physical specimen ever created and personified by Weissmuller on the silver screen. However, the final years of Johnny's life were a constant struggle to regain the good health that had made him a symbol of vitality and strength. With the help of his two male attendants, Johnny would go for a walk every day for fresh air and exercise.

But for each small step forward, each time there was a positive sign that he was regaining his strength, another small stroke would set Johnny back to the starting blocks. But he never quit. When 1984 arrived, Johnny was paddling slowly towards his 80th birthday which would be celebrated on June 2nd. Sadly, it was not to be.

Despite his valiant battle that lasted more than six years to recover from the big stroke of 1977, the war was finally lost on Friday evening, January 20, 1984, when Johnny Weissmuller passed away at his home in Acapulco. A spokesperson from the Acapulco Sinai Hospital, where Johnny had been treated as an outpatient from time to time, listed the official cause of death as pulmonary edema, or a blockage of the lungs. Meanwhile, Dr. Eustasio Ordaz Parades, the Weissmuller family physician, offered the opinion that he died of cerebral thrombosis — blood clotting of vessels in the brain. (Dr. Parades had also been the personal physician of the eccentric billionaire Howard Hughes.)

According to family friend Leonard Cashaback, when Johnny's moment came he "wrapped his arms around his wife, Maria, in a very forceful hug and kissed her — and then he took his last breath and passed away." Two weeks after Johnny's death, Cashaback told *The Star* that "Johnny lived happily in the last part of his life, and died happily in the Acapulco paradise where he'd made his last Tarzan film. Despite reports that he was senile and suffering his final days, the former Olympic champion was aware of things around him, exercised daily and was not in pain," added Cashaback.

Johnny's last wishes were that he be buried in Acapulco, which raised somewhat of a furor in the United States. "People were angry that he was buried in Mexico," said Cashaback. "But this is where he wanted to live and to die." Johnny had spent nine months in Acapulco filming *Tarzan and the Mermaids* in 1947, and had enjoyed many long weekends over the years in the picturesque seaside resort city where he was a part owner of the Los Flamingos Hotel. There were a lot of good memories in this city for Johnny, where many of the great stars of Hollywood also enjoyed their leisure time and were comrades of Johnny's. (As noted earlier, several of these same great stars were also partners with Weissmuller in the Los Flamingos — a luxurious resort hotel that never made any money, but was a veritable oasis for Hollywood luminaries to enjoy the high life when vacationing in Mexico.)

Johnny's funeral on Sunday, January 22, was attended by hundreds of his friends and Mexican neighbors, including his double in *Tarzan and the Mermaids*, Jose Estrada, and his longtime friend, Mike Oliver, the editor of the *Acapulco News*.

The funeral procession from the downtown Acapulco funeral home was escorted by six police motorcycles the twelve mile distance to the Valle de la Luz (Valley of the

Light) cemetery, and the burial took place at high noon. Representing the United States was L. J. Urbaneck, the United States Ambassador to Mexico, along with numerous Americans who had flown in to pay tribute to the man they had loved as Tarzan.

Maria, Johnny's beloved wife, said a few words softly in Spanish as the casket was lowered into the grave. Meanwhile, a tape of his famous Tarzan yell was played to the thrill of the many Tarzan fans that had come to pay their last respects to one of the great motion picture heroes. The flat marble marker at his grave is adorned with a cross and an open book (carved from stone), which simply says:

JOHNNY WEISSMULLER
1904-1984

Johnny Weissmuller was survived by his wife, Maria, daughters Lisa and Wendy, son John Scott, and six grandchildren. Although he was buried in Acapulco, Johnny was also honored in the United States on Wednesday, January 25th, with a memorial ceremony at the Good Shepherd Church in Beverly Hills. This service was attended by his children and grandchildren, and a small Hollywood contingent that came to remember their old comrade. Johnny was honored with a 21-gun salute by U.S. marines from the El Torro marine base, and Maria was presented with a flag of the United States. This was the first time that a celebrity was honored with a

21-gun salute, and the marines came to honor Johnny Weissmuller for his service during World War II instructing marines how to swim out from burning gasoline on water. (The 21-gun salute was an honor that Johnny deserved, but it was set in motion by Senator Ted Kennedy, an old friend of the family. Johnny Weissmuller, virtually loved by everyone, had friends on both sides of the political fence. He met every president from Coolidge to Nixon, and many of these American presidents called Johnny a close friend.)

Sadly missing from the circle of friends that had gathered to say good-bye to "Tarzan," was Johnny's longtime friendly rival Clarence "Buster" Crabbe, who had preceded his Olympic teammate in death by a few months. (Crabbe was in apparent good health when he suffered a fatal heart attack at age seventy-five on April 23, 1983.)

A separate memorial ceremony for Johnny was also held in Chicago at St. Michael's Catholic Church (located at Cleveland and Eugenie, a few blocks from where Johnny lived as a youth). The Rev. James Springer, pastor at St. Michael's, recalled at the memorial mass that Johnny had attended the parish school and had also served as an altar boy at St. Michael's before discovering his true passion in life — swimming.

Former Illinois Secretary of State Michael Howlett would often watch Johnny swim at the Illinois Athletic Club pool in Chicago, and recalled upon his death: "He was a remarkable athlete," said Howlett. "He was made for swimming . . . he was tall, slim and strong. His body rode high in the water.

"Today, with all the training and equipment, high school kids could tie records that he set. But back then . . . he was really something."

Lisa Weissmuller recalled one of her fondest memories of her father in a 1999 letter to the author: "In 1975 we were in Madrid, Spain, and some mothers brought their young children just to touch him. He got so nervous from the experience that he requested a beer to calm him down!" (Lisa Weissmuller is the mother of two of Johnny's six grandchildren: Lisa Maria Salb and Richard Anton Salb. Johnny's other grandchildren include Wendy's two sons, Nate and Adam; and John Scott's daughter, Heidi Grey, and stepson, David.)

Lisa also relayed a memory of Maria Weissmuller, who was married to Johnny for more than 20 years and now splits her time between Acapulco and Los Angeles: "When they were at San Clemente, President Nixon asked Johnny how he should handle the China 'situation.' My father (with his sense of humor) answered, 'Oh that's easy. Just swing over the China Wall like I swing from tree to tree . . . and you will reach your goal even if there isn't an elephant around to help!' "

(Today, in 2000, Lisa Weissmuller is associated with the "Johnny 'Tarzan' Weissmuller Foundation for the Homeless and Children of the Street," which raises money for the homeless in southern California. Her father always loved children around the world and devoted much of his life to presenting an image as a swimmer and as Tarzan that children especially could look up to and admire. Lisa Weissmuller firmly believes in the causes of the foundation, which has monumental goals to arrange shelter and employment for the large population of homeless people in Los Angeles.)

Buck Dawson, Johnny's close friend from the Swimming Hall of Fame, lamented the loss in 1984 of the greatest swimmer of all-time, as well as a fine gentleman:

"Weissmuller was one movie star who was for real," noted Dawson. "It is difficult to see how 'Tarzan' by any other name could perform greater athletic feats than Weissmuller in real life.

"The distance swum most often in the world was the 100-yard freestyle. Johnny set the world record in 1921, and it was 22 years before someone other than Johnny himself held the 100-yard record. It was another nine years *after* Allan Ford finally broke Johnny's record on Feb. 13, 1943, before anyone but Weissmuller or Ford went under 50 seconds. Eighteen years after Allan Ford broke Johnny's record, Steve Clark broke 48 seconds on April 1, 1961. Yet, the late Hall of Famer, Clarence Pinkston, swore until his death that Johnny had broken 48 [seconds] in a practice session in the Detroit Athletic's Club 20-yard pool nearly 35 years before."

"Johnny's close friend and rival, Duke Kahanamoku, had been Olympic champion and record holder for 12 years when Johnny beat him at the 1924 Olympics. Duke is responsible for the only record which Johnny still held late in his life. Many of Duke's fans insisted that Johnny only beat the Duke because he 'was better than the Duke on turns.' So they swam a match race in Hawaii on a 110-yard straightaway. Johnny won in 52.8, and the race has not been swum since.

"Weissmuller's world freestyle records were from 50-yards to the half-mile. All his performances were accomplished without a flip turn and without modern lane lines and starting blocks. Naturally, a comparison is made between Weissmuller and Mark Spitz. Each was the fastest in his time. Weissmuller's records lasted longer, and certainly he was more cavalier.

"Johnny Weissmuller was one of a kind and perhaps the best known swimmer not only of the first half-century of the 1900s, but of all time. You are one swimmer that will go on forever."

Of the many tributes that were written about Johnny after his death, the following from the *New York Tribune*, published on January 26, 1984, was perhaps the ultimate epitaph in honoring one of sport's greatest heroes and the immortal screen hero, Tarzan.

"Weissmuller Was Best, Noblest of Tarzans"

"In the 1930s, tens of thousands of young boys across our great nation spent their summers pounding their chests and trying their best to imitate the wild jungle cry of Tarzan.

"Some really believed they were the ape-man. They let their hair grow long. They fixed ropes to tree branches and swung their summers away. They were miniatures of the screen Tarzan, Johnny Weissmuller. He was their hero. These followers put up with Jane, but it was Tarzan they really loved. They would have gone with him to Africa and beyond.

"Oh, there were several movie Tarzans, but Johnny Weissmuller came first — at the right time and to the right place. He was the best. He could command elephants, outswim alligators and outrun gazelles. He was a friend to the tribes, from the tiny pygmy to the lofty Watusi.

"As a youth, Weissmuller swam to

685

strengthen his body. He swam so well he won five gold medals in the 1924 and the 1928 Olympic Games. Then he took up his film career. Tarzan was the creation of author Edgar Rice Burroughs. In Burroughs' books, Tarzan, the son of English nobleman Lord Greystoke, was abandoned as a baby in Africa and raised by a colony of apes. He was at once the noblest and most savage of noble savages. The 26 books of the Tarzan series have been translated into 30 languages and sold around the world.

"Now, the screen Tarzan, Johnny Weissmuller, is gone, dead at 79. After suffering several strokes, he decided to spend his declining years in Acapulco, the sun warm on his back. He was buried there last Sunday under a marble stone that says simply:

" 'Johnny Weissmuller 1904-1984'

"But he was more than Tarzan. He was a wonderful, healthy influence on American youth."

Perhaps that final statement from the unknown *New York Tribune* writer should be added to the marble stone that marks the grave of the man who was the world's greatest swimmer and Tarzan, too.

"Johnny Weissmuller: He was more than Tarzan. He was a wonderful, healthy influence on American youth."

AFTERWORD

The Wonderful World of Johnny Weissmuller

America truly loved their Johnny Weissmuller, who was an American hero perhaps more than any other sports legend or movie icon. Johnny was both of these, and thus was "twice the hero." If you also consider his real-life heroism in saving eleven lives in 1927 after the tragic disaster of the *Favorite*, Weissmuller would have to be crowned the ultimate hero.

Johnny also had a great sense of humor, and loved a gag or a well-timed joke that brought raucous laughter to himself and anyone who surrounded him. He also enjoyed telling humorous stories, often about his years on the Tarzan set. "I've led a charmed, lucky life," reminisced Johnny. "If it hadn't have been for Tarzan, I would have been nothing." In reality, nothing could have been further from the truth. But Johnny really was eternally grateful for his Tarzan role, and the international fame and adulation that it brought to him.

A favorite story of Johnny's was his routine for getting familiar with the tame lion — Jackie — that they used on the Tarzan films. "I used to go down to the compound on Ventura Boulevard about a month before filming started, and have lunch with the lions. I'd go into Jackie's cage and sit there — he's eating half a horse and I'm having a club sandwich. I'd say to the lion, 'How you doing, Jackie?' as he continued to feast upon his dinner. And he comes over and smells me, and I smelled him — he smelled awful! And so we'd get acquainted in this manner before we'd do the picture, so when he'd come on the set we'd be friends and I wouldn't get eaten alive!"

Johnny also recalled that he would ride home on the MGM bus from time to time with Jackie sitting beside him on the front seat. "The lion would ride with his head out of the window, and I'd be right next to him. A motorist would pull up beside us and Jackie would roar at him — the guy behind the wheel would practically jump out of his car he was so surprised to see a lion riding next to him on a bus! (And, with Tarzan sitting next to him!)

Jackie used to lick Johnny constantly whenever the beast was on the set because he liked the taste of the body makeup they used on the actors. "He had a tongue like sandpaper," recalled Johnny, "and rubbed me sore licking me all the damn time!"

The elephant that Johnny used to ride was 14 feet tall, and from time to time he would get thrown off the back of the beast when it was in a mood to be ornery. One time this happened and Johnny broke a toe after being thrown to the ground by the powerful beast. Johnny complained to the trainer, who told him to stick his finger in the elephant's eye the next time he was about to unseat Tarzan from his back. "Why didn't you tell me that in the first place," cried an anguished Johnny as he clutched his throbbing toe.

"All the jungle scenes were filmed at Sherwood Forest," noted Johnny, "and they used to clean off the bristly hairs on the elephants' heads with a blow torch. One day an elephant picked me up and threw me up on the back of his head. I felt like I landed on a pin cushion — I was a bloody mess. They'd forgotten to 'torch' the elephant's head."

Other injuries he received over the years included numerous scratches from lions, painful monkey bites, stone bruises on his feet from running barefoot, and a smashed nose from walking into the rear end of an elephant that was leading his safari through the jungle. Johnny did most of his own stunts in the Tarzan movies, and in 1980 he was inducted into the Hollywood Stuntman Hall of Fame for his fearless heroics in front of the camera.

When it came to fighting the wild animals, Johnny had a method that kept him relatively safe from harm. "As long as I hung on their backs I couldn't get hurt," he disclosed. "I jumped on May, a 3,000-pound rhino, and her trainer, George Emerson, said it was the first time anyone had ever ridden a rhino. Croc's were the hardest to ride. They thrashed around in the water something awful and had bumpy, scaly hides which ripped my legs up. Remember, I was practically naked. The water in the tank was heated to 85 degrees. You should have seen the steam coming off it on chilly mornings. We never hurt the animals, of course. I had a fake knife. Every time I'd plunge it in, the blade would slide into the hilt and red liquid, like blood, would come out. I never shed a drop of blood myself." (A close call came one day when a crocodile broke the tape around his jaws and chased Tarzan to the edge of the tank — if not for the champ's speed swimming it would have been Johnny for lunch!)

There was one scene where Tarzan jumps into the river to escape his captors, and overturns a canoe full of hostile natives. Johnny later recalled the irony in the following situation: "One fellow had lied to get the job as a native and said he could swim. He couldn't swim after all. I had to save him and it ruined the shot — Tarzan having to save one of the hostile natives was a no-no."

Concerning the chimpanzees in his Tarzan and Jungle Jim movies, Johnny didn't fool around when it came to training them so they'd obey his commands. "I got along with all of them just fine. I'd give them a crack on the head with the handle of my jungle knife, but they kept biting those Englishmen we had in the Tarzan pictures. The monkey trainer was a 'dese and doser' from Texas and the chimps were used to a Texas drawl. An English accent drove them bananas, so they bit the Limeys every time," said Johnny with a laugh.

There were three chimps that were used in the early Tarzan films, two brothers and a sister. "One of them ran away one time and we never did find him," lamented Johnny. After the Tarzan pictures ended, the original male Cheeta (real name Skippy) was put out to pasture at the Griffith Park Zoo in Los Angeles. Johnny used to go visit his old friend from time to time, until the ancient chimp finally died at the ripe old age of 34 in 1955.

Maureen O'Sullivan remembered that Johnny had a way with the chimps, and also a way with the jokes he often played on her on the Tarzan set:

"I couldn't feel much sympathy for Cheeta the chimp, who adored Johnny Weissmuller but was terribly jealous of me. All the apes were always trying to wrap their paws around Johnny's thighs.

"I was sad and miserable a lot of the times while making those films because I had one cold after another and never seemed to be without an ache or a pain. I was never completely comfortably warm and was constantly bitten by the monkeys. But it would be wrong to give the impression that it was all misery.

"There were good times too and I was extremely fond of Johnny. He was what you'd expect of a big athlete and didn't pretend to be a great intellectual giant. But he would drive me crazy with his practical jokes.

"I remember once on my birthday he bought me a huge birthday cake and as I put the knife in it to cut it, the whole thing exploded in my face!"

"We were dear friends," recalled Maureen fondly in 1992. "He was simple, unpretentious, without conceit — a wonderful big kid."

Buck Dawson, the director of the Swimming Hall of Fame, recalled that he and Johnny would often have lunch at the Student Prince, which was Johnny's favorite restaurant on the Fort Lauderdale strip. "One day we were having the special — a knackwurst with sauerkraut and German potato salad, all for 60 cents," said Dawson. "How can they afford to do this for 60 cents?" I asked Weissmuller. "Easy," remarked Johnny, "they have a string on the wienie so when you turn your head they give the wienie a yank and zip — it's back in the kitchen!"

Another funny story from Dawson involved a case of mistaken identity, as Buck recalled: "Everybody recognized Big John's ability to get along with animals. During the '64 Olympics, I was visiting the Bepo Zoo in Japan with Adolph Kiefer when Kiefer [the great American backstroke champion] received a nasty bite from a monkey. 'Pardon me,' said a polite Japanese to Kiefer, 'but, aren't you Johnny Weissmuller?' Kiefer, still in considerable pain, said, 'Certainly not, madam, no monkey would bite Weissmuller!' "

In the late 1960s Johnny and Arne Borg, a close friend and also an Olympic champion, were being honored at the Swimming Hall of Fame with cement casts of their feet. Borg, helping Johnny keep his balance as he placed his feet in the cement, joked, "Yonnie, no wonder you always beat me. Your foots are bigger!" Not to be outdone, Johnny wisecracked to Arne, "When I was growing up in Chicago, nobody voluntarily put his feet in cement!" (Weissmuller was referring to growing up in Chicago during the 1920s, where a wrong turn in Capone's town could get your feet dipped in cement and a quick trip to the bottom of the Chicago River.)

Another Weissmuller story that is certainly more myth than truth, had Johnny swimming offshore in Lake Michigan one warm sunny day. Suddenly he yelled out to the sunbathers on an unfamiliar beach, "Is this Milwaukee?" A reply was shouted back in unison, "No, it's Chicago!" A surprised but undeterred Johnny waved his thanks and headed back out to sea to continue his journey.

Back in the 1930s, Johnny forged a friendship with John Wayne that began at the Hollywood Athletic Club and lasted a lifetime. Wayne was among the many admirers who used to watch Johnny perform his daily swimming workouts at the H.A.C., when he first came to Tinseltown in 1931. Johnny and the Duke were both "real men" who enjoyed many of the same pastimes, including sailing and drinking with the boys. (Although Johnny didn't drink alcohol at all when he first arrived in Hollywood, he picked up the habit after he married Lupe Velez in 1933.)

Sometime around 1934, Wayne, JohnJohn Wayne and his clan of drinking buddies formed a men's club satirically dubbed "The Young Men's Purity Total Abstinence and Snooker Pool Association." None of the members of this club had any desires to join the snobbish social clubs that currently existed, and in fact none of them would probably ever have been invited to join. These self-named social outcasts did their drinking and smoked cigars in one of the upstairs rooms of

694

the Hollywood Athletic Club, where the manager set up a bar to accommodate some of his very best customers. Members of the original club included Duke Wayne and his closest friends John Ford and Ward Bond; actors Frank Morgan, Preston Foster, and Weissmuller; writers Liam O'Flaherty and Dudley Nichols; along with producers and directors Harry Wurtzel, Gene Markey, Wingate Smith, Merian Cooper, and Tay Garnett.

By the late 1930s they changed the name of the club to "The Emerald Bay Yachting Club" and applied for admission in the prestigious Southern California Yachting Association. Johnny and Lupe were ardent yachting enthusiasts and owned their own schooner, *Allure*, which would be anchored year-round at Catalina Island. Johnny remained friends with John Wayne his entire life, and it all got started in the steam rooms of the Hollywood Athletic Club.

Johnny's sense of humor was at its best when he was invited to be the guest of honor at the Burroughs Bibliophiles luncheon, held in Boston in conjunction with the 29th World Science Fiction Convention on September 4, 1971. Johnny received the "Golden Lion Trophy," a prestigious award that was presented to him for his long tenure as the screen hero Tarzan, the character created by Edgar

Rice Burroughs. Leading up to the introduction of the guest of honor, club vice-president Stan Vincent gushed on and on about Johnny's heroics in the swimming pool and his years in the jungle fighting all manner of villains as Tarzan.

Admittedly, Stan went a little overboard in his lengthy praise of Johnny, who at one point interjected from his seat, "My coach had a big whip!" — which brought a flood of laughter from the crowd. As Stan introduced Johnny, and presented him with his awards, he said, "If my voice is shaking, its because I'm standing next to Tarzan." At which point the six-foot-three Johnny — who towered over Vincent — broke through with the best line of the day, in a voice tinged with mock incredulity: "Are you standing up?" The entire audience roared with genuine laughter, and Stan himself laughed so hard there were tears in his eyes.

The 67-year-old Weissmuller, looking healthy and fit in a blue and white striped shirt and tailored white pants, began by thanking the fans that had supported him for so many years. "I've been a member of the Burroughs' 'family' for so many years, I feel like I'm related — and perhaps they don't really know how much I love them [the fans].

"Years ago on the set of the first Tarzan movie, I met 'Daddy' Burroughs and he was a wonderful man. He wanted to know how I could look so natural as Tarzan. I guess it was because I had been running around in a pair of swim trunks practically all my life."

Johnny recounted memories about making the Tarzan films and also recalled his audition in 1931 for the role of the ape-man: "They asked me if I could run, so I did some running. They asked me if I could climb a tree, so I climbed the tree. They asked me if I could pick up the girl, and I could sure do that," laughed Johnny. "They said I could go and they'd call me. I was selling swim suits for B.V.D. at the time, so I headed up to Oregon — that's when they called and said I got the job as Tarzan. So that's how it all started."

Later, one fellow asked Mr. Weissmuller if it wasn't extremely difficult to be climbing in trees and swinging on vines. The reply from Tarzan brought another wave of laughter from his appreciative audience. "Oh, that wasn't so hard," admitted Johnny with tongue-in-cheek. "You're not going to let go of a vine when you're 25-feet up in the air — are you?"

It was a great time for every Tarzan fan in attendance, each of whom got a chance to shake hands with Weissmuller and get his autograph at the conclusion of the festivities. Johnny, always a congenial guest, seemed to genuinely enjoy mixing with the fans who came to honor the man who unabashedly was their hero. "You have a lot of these memories as you get older, you know," he said after his stroll down memory lane. "You get as old as I am, you remember a lot of things." Johnny concluded his speech by saying, "I think Tarzan should live forever. There should always be a Tarzan."

The president of the Burroughs Bibliophiles, Vern Coriel, spoke the final word on Weissmuller's participation as an honored guest: "This luncheon is just our way of saying thanks to Johnny for being such a true Tarzan and helping to make Burroughs and science fiction famous."

During his lifetime, the favorite Tarzan of Edgar Rice Burroughs was Weissmuller. The author of the Tarzan stories offered the definitive praise of the man who was the screen Tarzan for seventeen years, when he said, "To me ... Johnny Weissmuller IS Tarzan."

Mr. Burroughs was so enamored with Johnny as Tarzan that he included him in his 1948 novel, *Tarzan and the Foreign Legion.* As the story progresses, one of the characters — Jerry Lucas — recognizes Tarzan in Sumatra, and is asked by "Shrimp" Rosetti:

"Is dat Johnny Weissmuller?"

Denny Miller, who starred in the 1959 version of *Tarzan, the Ape Man,* recalled in 1999 his own memories of the man who was the original Tarzan.

"Johnny Weissmuller was 'Tarzan' when I was a kid, so he still is Tarzan to me. One time at a golf benefit tournament he pulled the LONGEST driver out of his golf bag I ever saw (or have seen since). He proceeded to hit the ball a MILE with it.

"He gave off the Tarzan yell everywhere [upon request]. Hotel lobbies, out his hotel window, on the street. He was good at it, too — I wasn't. He was giving the yell one time at a gathering and someone said to us, 'What a loud guy!' Buster Crabbe was also there and said to the guy, 'He may be loud, but I was an Olympic champion and I never beat that man in a race!' The guy, whoever he was, shut up. Johnny was always friendly and giving to his fans. Never saw him mad. Easy to like and I really liked him."

Johnny was known as a down-to-earth guy who considered himself just an "ordinary Joe." And he wasn't above doing a favor for a stranger (without expecting any thanks), as Carol Joy Ross of the *Christian Science Monitor* recalled after interviewing him in 1969: "On leaving the restaurant interview, some of what the local chamber of commerce likes to call 'liquid sunshine' began to fall. Passing an empty, rather battered car open to the elements, Mr. Weissmuller muttered, 'Think I'll do this fellow a favor,' and rolled up the windows.

"It was a friendly sort of thing to do. Which

is the sort of chap Johnny Weissmuller is."

Perhaps the most famous golfer of them all, Arnold Palmer, recalled in a 1999 letter that he "played golf several times out West [California and Nevada] with Johnny Weissmuller." Arnie described the former Tarzan as a "fairly-good" player, which is a decent evaluation considering Johnny was well into his 50s when he played with Arnie, who was in his prime 30s during his matches with Weissmuller. Johnny played with practically every major celebrity who was also a golfer, including Babe Didrikson Zaharias, Babe Ruth, Rocky Marciano, Joe Louis, Bing Crosby, Bob Hope, Mickey Rooney, Joe. E. Brown, Forrest Tucker, and many others that crossed his path during three decades of celebrity pro-am tournaments.

Swimming and golf were only two of the many sports in which Johnny excelled — others included water polo, diving, tennis, squash, ocean surfing, sailing, skin diving, boxing (as a teenager), and running. (Remember, he was always running like crazy to save somebody in all those Tarzan and Jungle Jim films!)

As a diver he was capable of executing classic high dives like the swan dive, jackknife, one-and-a-half somersault, and the full gainer. Later in life when he gave up the dangerous sport of high diving, he recalled that the highest dive he ever did was 76 feet off a cliff into a river — for the opening shot of a Jungle Jim film.

Johnny had great endurance as an athlete, which is probably the main reason he never lost a freestyle swimming race; there always seemed to be a reserve of energy for him to draw upon when he needed a final burst to win yet another championship or gold medal. Hall of Fame swimming coach Robert Kiphuth, winner of the Presidential Medal of Freedom in 1963 (the highest civilian honor), saw Johnny in competition many times during his prime in the 1920s. Kiphuth offered the following testimonial to Weissmuller: "I've seen the most durable of athletes: Nurmi in track; Cobb in baseball; Dempsey in boxing. But I'd have to say Weissmuller has the most fantastic endurance of any champion."

It was also the methods of relaxation that he learned from coach Bachrach that helped to make Johnny a cut above his competitors, as he recalled later in life: "Even as a kid," said Johnny, "I didn't tense up. Not even the Olympics bothered me."

Johnny first met diminutive Pete Desjardins, the "Little Bronze Statue from Florida," when Desjardins competed in Chicago for the national diving championships in 1924, and they were team-mates on the 1924 and 1928 Olympic squads. Desjardins matched Weissmuller's total of two gold medals at the 1928 Amsterdam Games, and he and Johnny started a friendship that would last their entire lives. From the 1987 book, *Tales of Gold*, Pete Desjardins remembered the good times with his pal, Johnny Weissmuller:

"I was 17-years-old when I won my silver medal at Paris in 1924. That was a really great Olympics! I enjoyed watching the track meets, but one of the greatest races at Paris was between Johnny Weissmuller and Boy Charlton of Australia in the 400-meter swimming competition. It was very, very thrilling because they were neck and neck, turn to turn, and finally, in the last 25 meters, Johnny just burst out and won by a couple of lengths.

"Later on I got to know Johnny Weissmuller very well. I stayed with him in Los Angeles for about six months in 1937. He was married to Lupe Velez at the time, and she had just left to do a musical show in New York, so he invited me to come and stay with him. He was a very likable guy. He didn't seem to have a care in the world, and he was always happy-go-lucky and never got in an argument that I can remember. When I went out with him in L.A., he was too much for me; he'd be out all night. He had a little gym in his house, and he'd get up at seven in the morning and do some exercises and go out and play 27 holes of golf, and at night he wanted to go out again to a nightclub. I did that with him for about three weeks, and it nearly killed me.

"If Johnny Weissmuller had trained like today's swimmers train, no one would have come close to him in a race. Today these swimmers are in the pool at six in the morning, do God knows how many laps, go to school, get out of school, and then do it all over again. But Johnny was carefree: I don't think he really trained seriously until about two weeks before a meet. He had big hands and feet and was well-coordinated. He had so much natural ability that it was a pleasure to watch him swim. He was also very colorful, and by that I mean he had a lot of personality in the water.

"He was also playful. He liked to get in the pool and kid around. We were a funny pair; he was about six-foot-four, a little more than a foot taller than I. We gave exhibitions together, and we used to do the comedy act that he and Stubby Kruger first did together. I was so small that Johnny could pick me up off the board, and I didn't know if he was ever going to put me down again. But he was a lot of fun.

"When Mark Spitz won his races, he had some real competitors who were pushing him, but Weissmuller won his races without too much competition. He could break any record. I remember a story going around about his coach, Bill Bachrach. When they were going around the country giving exhibitions, it seems that Bachrach didn't want Johnny to break any record by too much so that at the next pool where he gave an exhibition he would break the record again and get worldwide publicity all over again. By doing it that way he'd set a new world record just by shaving a fraction of a second off the world record that he had just set the day before. Johnny was such a fine swimmer that he was capable of doing that."

Another good friend of Johnny's from the Olympic years was Clarence "Bud" Houser, who won three gold medals in the shot put and discus between the 1924 and 1928 Olympics. Houser had been chosen to carry the American flag during the opening ceremonies in Amsterdam, with Johnny carrying the sign with the name of the country on it. This was explained to Bud and Johnny by General MacArthur, who would be walking right behind these two athletes representing the United States.

Later, they were supposed to meet with MacArthur and some other officials to work out the details at the general's hotel. The meeting room was packed with people, and when MacArthur came in Johnny and Bud were squeezed towards the back of the room as everyone was trying to get the general's attention. Always a jokester, Johnny concocted a plan that he shared with his good friend, Houser:

"Bud, I'll tell you what," said Johnny. "Why don't we start talking loud and calling each other 'general,' and maybe somebody'll notice we're here, too." So they started their routine, hoping to draw some attention. "General Johnny, how're things going with you?" "Fine, General Bud, and you're looking well." The two of them kept yapping away in this manner, and they finally caught the attention of General MacArthur, who turned around and said to the upstarts: "Listen, you generals, I'm going to take you out for dinner after this meeting. You might get back to the boat a little bit late, but I think I can fix it up for you."

And so Johnny and Bud not only got to represent the United States in the opening and closing ceremonies, but they had dinner with one of the greatest generals in American history. Undoubtedly, there were some interesting stories shared at that table along with a meal that was probably unforgettable.

Concerning Johnny's swimming records, it is a legitimate truth that he never lost an individual freestyle race over a seven year period from his official debut in August of 1921 until his retirement in January of 1929. Johnny competed long before the innovations of the flip turn, lane lines, and starting blocks, which helped modern swimmers to erase his swimming records. Goggles and swim caps were at best primitive in his era, and lightweight swimsuits were light years away — Johnny competed in a wool suit with shoulder straps.

His unique style of swimming was called "hydroplaning," as he swam with his head and shoulders out of the water, his back arched, his feet low in the water to produce a deep flutter kick that minimized resistance. Some purists called Johnny's style of swimming unorthodox, others dubbed the talented Chicago lad to be revolutionary. As Weissmuller churned through the water like a human hydroplane, it was this unique style that made him the greatest swimming champion of all time.

The closest he ever came to a loss was an exhibition match with his friend, Arne Borg, the Swedish champion who had come to the United States specifically to train with Weissmuller at the Illinois Athletic Club in 1926. Johnny and Borg were close friends, teammates, and road roommates, as part of coach Bachrach's barnstorming road tour of the country. Bachrach had halted his star's training in the longer races, as he was preparing Borg to compete in the 400-meter freestyle in the coming 1928 Olympics. (There was no room for *prima donnas* on a swimming squad coached by William Bachrach — but with both Weissmuller and Borg on the I.A.C. team, it was necessary to bend the rules a little bit to keep both of his champions happy.)

During one out-of-town meet, the crowd began chanting for Johnny and Borg to go head-to-head in a 500-yard race, a distance that was Borg's specialty. Johnny wanted to swim the race but coach Bachrach said no, realizing that his star swimmer had not been training for the longer races. As the crowd clamored for the two stars to race, Bachrach relented but took Borg aside and warned him that this was just an exhibition and not to mess with Johnny's incredible winning streak that had begun in 1921. When the starter's gun cracked, it was even until the last leg when Borg broke his word to Bachrach and forged ahead of Johnny. Five yards from the finish Borg came to a complete halt in the pool, and yelled to his teammate, "Come on, 'Yonnie,' I let you win."

It counted as a win for Johnny, even though Borg could have had a tarnished victory. Wisely, Borg chose not to ruin Johnny's priceless winning streak in a meaningless exhibition match — or Bachrach might have put him on the next boat back to Sweden! Johnny had beaten Arne in the 400-meters in the truest test of a champion, the 1924 Olympics in Paris, and thus he had nothing to

707

prove to Borg or any other swimmer. (The only other freestyle race that Johnny ever lost was a 400-yard relay event in 1926 in which Walter Laufer and his Cincinnati YMCA team outraced Johnny and his I.A.C. teammates at the national championships in Chicago. Relay races are considered team events, and thus cannot be counted against Johnny as an individual loss.)

In comparing Weissmuller's swimming career with champions of other eras, Johnny's seven-year unbeaten streak in freestyle races in distances from 50-yards to the half-mile, along with the intangibles that truly defined him as a great champion, make him the all-time "King of the Swimmers."

In sports historian Bert Sugar's 1995 book, *The 100 Greatest Athletes of All Time*, Johnny Weissmuller is the only swimmer in this definitive history of immortal athletes. In Sugar's introduction, he defines the qualities that were used to select the so-called "greatest" athletes of all time: "It was a combination of things, an equation that included dominance, perceived greatness, consistent performance, accomplishments transcending time, and overall excellence that illumined an athlete's greatness."

Sugar concludes his essay on Weissmuller with the following statement: "Today, Johnny Weissmuller is best remembered not as a swimming great who set sixty-seven world records, who held every record from 50-yards to the half-mile, and who was never beaten, but as Tarzan. It is a fame that drowns out an appreciation of his skills — skills that made him one of the all-time great athletes."

Assuredly, it is unfair when Johnny is overlooked as one of the greatest athletes of all time, simply because he is better remembered for his wonderful career as Tarzan. Of all the athletes who are considered "greatest of all time," only Weissmuller went on to be more famous in another field of endeavor — in Johnny's case that was the motion pictures, and his remarkable screen character of Tarzan. Let's put it to rest once and for all — Weissmuller was the greatest swimmer of all time and deserves to be mentioned in the same breath as the other great athletes of the "Golden Age of Sports."

After the war ended in the late 1940s, the younger generation was already beginning to forget that Johnny was a great athlete before be became famous as Tarzan. Sports editor George T. Davis of the *Los Angeles Herald-Express* helped to revive the Weissmuller legend by noting: "Swimming records are being broken almost daily, but the greatest merman of them all — without even a rival, in the opinion of experts — is still Johnny Weissmuller."

A legendary swimming coach of that era,

Fred Cady, recalled that Johnny was a one-of-a-kind athlete unlikely to be seen again in the swimming arena: "They broke the mold with Weissmuller. He was Mr. Swimming himself and there's never been anyone like him. I don't care whether his records are broken or not, Johnny was by far the greatest of 'em all. He had power, form and competitive ability to a greater degree than any swimmer of all time and ranks in his sport along with such other champions as Bobby Jones, Bill Tilden, Babe Ruth, and Jack Dempsey."

Perhaps the most legendary sports writer of them all was Grantland Rice, who lived and breathed sports his entire life and saw all of the greats of the "Golden Age of Sports" during his long career. From his 1954 book, *The Tumult and the Shouting*, Rice summed up that wonderful age and the most memorable of the remarkable athletes of the era: "Looking back and reflecting on that golden, crazy age — from 1919 to 1930 — I'm convinced, more than ever, that no decade in history produced the likes of Ruth, Dempsey, Jones, Hitchcock [polo star], Man O'War, Weissmuller — my all-time swimmer — and Bill Tilden. They had the indefinable but 18-carat touch called 'color,' that put them above the greats of any age. Call it crowd appeal, class, warmth, personality — whatever it was they had it!"

*Crowd appeal, class, warmth, personality —
when describing Johnny Weissmuller, that really
says it all!*

According to the 1972 book, *The Sports Im-
mortals*, which was published by the Associ-
ated Press and honored the 50 greatest
athletes of all time, Johnny is grouped with
the following ten super athletes of The
Golden Era: Babe Ruth, *Savior of Baseball*;
Helen Wills Moody, *Queen of Tennis*; Jack
Dempsey, *Fists of Cement*; Bobby Jones, *The
Grand Slam*; Sonja Henie, *Symphony on Sil-
ver Skates*; Bill Tilden, *Court Jouster*; Bronco
Nagurski, *The Big Ukrainian*; Babe Didrikson
Zaharias, *Wonder Woman*; Jesse Owens, *The
Master of Race*; and Johnny Weissmuller,
Olympic Tarzan.

The Weissmuller chapter in *The Sports Immortals* was penned by Hubert Mizell, who lamented that Johnny no longer receives his
just respect as an athlete, since he became
immortalized as Tarzan after his swimming
career ended: "History may unduly chronicle
Johnny Weissmuller as Tarzan, mighty hero
in movie versions of Edgar Rice Burroughs'
jungle classics, who lived in a tree house with
a cute swinger named Jane and a chimp
called Cheeta. The real story of Johnny
Weissmuller is much deeper."

The pages of this biography have told the

"real story" of Johnny Weissmuller, a man whom fortune smiled upon. I will leave you with some of his words of wisdom — as usual, he will be brief, humorous, and directly to the point. Johnny used to say, "Old Tarzans never die." He was also known for giving advice to new Tarzan actors that accepted the role. "The best advice I can give is . . . don't let go of the vine, when you're swinging through the jungle!"

Johnny Weissmuller was a lovable hero, who appreciated his adoring public as much as they loved him. He was humble, honest, and human — he realized that fame and money were tangibles that could be fleeting. And although his money was gone long before his death, his fame would never be fleeting. Not for Johnny — who became a better known Tarzan than the pulp fiction character created by author Edgar Rice Burroughs.

Johnny also had a knack for putting things in perspective in simple terms, as he recalled what made Tarzan such an ideal hero: "They ask me why Tarzan was so big," reflected Johnny. "I have an idea it was the freedom thing. People say, 'Boy, I wish I could live in a treehouse without any problems and have all the animals in the world as pets. And no worries. Gee, that'd be great!' "

When someone once asked Johnny if he could change anything about his life, he responded with pure honesty when he said,

"How could I change anything? I have been the luckiest man alive and I love the people who made me what I am. I could do it all again, easy. All twelve Tarzan films and fifty Jungle Jim shows. It's been a wonderful life!"

Weissmuller the champion swimmer became larger than life after he assumed the mantle of Tarzan, and he remains a legendary icon many years after his death. Johnny was more than just one of the actors that portrayed the ape-man on screen — he has been immortalized as the greatest Tarzan.

The kid raised in Chicago would have been the first one to admit, with all the good fortune he had in his life, that "somebody up there truly liked Johnny Weissmuller."

That goes for me, too.

Motion Picture Filmography

1. GLORIFYING THE AMERICAN GIRL • 1929 Paramount

Cast: Mary Eaton (*Gloria Hughes*), Edward Crandall (*Buddy*), Olive Shea (*Barbara*), Dan Healey (*Miller*), Kaye Renard (*Mooney*), Sarah Edwards (*Mrs. Hughes*), Eddie Cantor, Rudy Vallee, Florenz Ziegfeld, Billie Burke, Ring Lardner, Noah Beery, Texas Guinan, Otto Kahn, Irving Berlin, Adolph Zukor, Charles Dillingham, Helen Morgan, Norman Brokenshire (*Narrator*), Evelyn Groves (*Aphrodite*), *Johnny Weissmuller* **(Adonis)**. **Credits:** *Directed by* Millard Webb; *Produced by* Florenz Ziegfeld; *Story by* J. P. McEvoy, Millard Webb; *Artistic Director*, John W. Harkrider; *Running time:* 96 minutes (restored version). *Release date:* December 1929

2. TARZAN, THE APE MAN • 1932 M-G-M

Cast: Johnny Weissmuller (*Tarzan*),

Maureen O'Sullivan (*Jane Parker*) Neil Hamilton (*Harry Holt*), C. Aubrey Smith (*James Parker*), Doris Lloyd (*Mrs. Cutten*), Forrester Harvey (*Beamish*), Ivory Williams (*Riano*) **Credits:** *Directed by* W. S. Van Dyke; *Produced by* Bernard H. Hyman; *Based upon the characters created by* Edgar Rice Burroughs; *Adaptation by* Cyril Hume; *Dialogue by* Ivor Novello; *Photography by* Harold Rosson and Clyde de Vinna; *Film Editors,* Ben Lewis and Tom Held; *Recording Director,* Douglas Shearer; *Art Director,* Cedric Gibbons; *Production Manager,* Joseph J. Cohn; *Animal Supervision,* George Emerson, Bert Nelson, Louis Roth, Louis Goebel; *Photographic Effects,* Warren Newcombe; *Additional Cinematography,* William Snyder; *Opening Theme,* "*Voodoo Dance*" *by* George Richelavie, *Arranged by* Fritz Stahlberg, P. A. Marquardt. *Running time:* 99 minutes. *Release date:* March 1932

3. *TARZAN AND HIS MATE* • 1934 *M-G-M*

Cast: Johnny Weissmuller (*Tarzan*), Maureen O'Sullivan (*Jane*), Neil Hamilton (*Harry Holt*), Paul Cavanagh (Martin Arlington), Forrester Harvey (*Beamish*), Nathan Curry (Saidi), William Stack (Tom *Pierce*), Desmond Roberts (*Henry Van Ness*), Paul Porcasi (*Monsieur Perron*), Everett Brown (*native bearer*) **Credits:** *Directed by*

715

Cedric Gibbons (*uncredited direction by* Jack Conway); *Produced by* Bernard H. Hyman; *Based upon the characters created by* Edgar Rice Burroughs; *Screenplay by* James Kevin McGuinness; *Adaptation by* Howard Emmett Rogers and Leon Gordon; *Photographed by* Charles G. Clarke and Clyde de Vinna; *Film Editor,* Tom Held; *Recording Director,* Douglas Shearer; *Art Director,* Arnold Gillespie; *Production Manager,* Joseph J. Cohn; *Second Unit Directors,* James McKay, Erroll Taggart, Nick Grinde; *Animal Supervision,* George Emerson, Bert Nelson, Louis Roth, Louis Goebel; *Special Effects,* James Basevi; *Art Effects,* Warren Newcombe; *Photographic Effects,* Irving Ries; *Sound Effects,* T. B. Hoffman, James Graham, Mike Steinore; *Opening Theme, "Voodoo Dance" by* George Richelavie, *Arranged by* Fritz Stahlberg, P.A. Marquardt; *Closing Theme, "My Tender One" by* Dr. William Axt. *Running time:* 116 minutes at preview, 95 minutes in general release. *Release date:* April 1934

4. *TARZAN ESCAPES* • *1936 M-G-M*

Cast: Johnny Weissmuller (*Tarzan*), Maureen O'Sullivan (*Jane*), John Buckler (*Captain Fry*), Benita Hume (*Rita Parker*), William Henry (*Eric Parker*), Herbert Mundin (*Herbert Henry Rawlins*), E. E. Clive (*Masters*), Darby Jones (*Bomba*), Monte

Montague (*Riverboat Captain*) **Credits:** *Directed by* Richard Thorpe; *Associate Producer,* Sam Zimbalist; *Screenplay by* Cyril Hume; *Based upon the characters created by* Edgar Rice Burroughs; *Recording Director,* Douglas Shearer; *Art Director,* Elmer Sheeley; *Photographed by* Leonard Smith; *Film Editor,* W. Donn Hayes; *Set Decorations,* Edwin B. Willis; *Special Effects Director,* A. Arnold Gillespie; *Photographic Effects,* Thomas Tutwiler; *Art Effects,* Warren Newcombe; *Opening Theme, "Cannibal Carnival" by* Sol Levy; *Closing Theme, "My Tender One" by* Dr. William Axt. *Running time:* 95 minutes. *Release date:* November 1936

5. *TARZAN FINDS A SON* • *1939* M-G-M

Cast: Johnny Weissmuller (*Tarzan*), Maureen O'Sullivan (*Jane*), Johnny Sheffield (*Boy*), Ian Hunter (*Austin Lancing*), Henry Stephenson (*Sir Thomas Lancing*), Frieda Inescort (*Mrs. Austin Lancing*), Henry Wilcoxon (*Mr. Sande*), Laraine Day (*Mrs. Richard Lancing*), Morton Lowry (*Richard Lancing*), Gavin Muir (*Pilot*), Uriah Banks (*Mooloo*) **Credits:** *Directed by* Richard Thorpe; *Produced by* Sam Zimbalist; *Screenplay by* Cyril Hume; *Based on the characters created by* Edgar Rice Burroughs; *Recording Director,* Douglas Shearer; *Art Director,* Cedric Gibbons; *Associate,* Urie McCleary;

Photographed by Leonard Smith; *Film Editors,* Frank Sullivan and Gene Ruggiero; *Special Effects,* A. Arnold Gillespie, Warren Newcombe, Max Fabian; *Animal Trainer,* George Emerson; *Assistant Director,* Dolph Zimmer; *Musical Director,* David Snell; *Music by* Sol Levy and Dr. William Axt. *Running time:* 95 minutes. *Release date:* June 1939

6. *TARZAN'S SECRET TREASURE* • *1941 M-G-M*

Cast: Johnny Weissmuller (*Tarzan*), Maureen O'Sullivan (*Jane*), Johnny Sheffield (*Boy*), Reginald Owen (*Professor Elliot*), Barry Fitzgerald (*O'Doul*), Tom Conway (*Medford*), Philip Dorn (*Vandermeer*), Cordell Hickman (*Tumbo*), Everett Brown (*Joconi chief*), Martin Wilkins (*headman*) **Credits:** *Directed by* Richard Thorpe; *Produced by* B. P. Fineman; *Screenplay by* Myles Connolly and Paul Gangelin; *Based upon the characters created by* Edgar Rice Burroughs; *Photography,* Clyde de Vinna; *Recording Director,* Douglas Shearer; *Art Director,* Cedric Gibbons; *Set Decorations,* Edwin B. Willis; *Film Editor,* Gene Ruggiero; *Special Effects,* Warren Newcombe; *Assistant Director,* Gilbert Kurland; *Musical Score,* David Snell; *Music by* Sol Levy and Dr. William Axt. *Running time:* 81 minutes. *Release* date: December 1941.

7. TARZAN'S NEW YORK ADVENTURE • 1942 M-G-M

Cast: Johnny Weissmuller (*Tarzan*), Maureen O'Sullivan (*Jane*), Johnny Sheffield (*Boy*), Virginia Grey (*Connie Beach*), Charles Bickford (*Buck Rand*), Paul Kelly (*Jimmy Shields*), Chill Wills (*Mountford*), Cy Kendall (*Sargent*); Russell Hicks (*Judge Abbotson*), Howard Hickman (*Blake Norton*), Charles Lane (*Beaton*), Elmo Lincoln (*roustabout*)

Credits: *Directed by* Richard Thorpe; *Produced by* Frederick Stephani; *Screenplay by* William R. Lipman and Myles Connolly; *Story*, Myles Connolly; *Based upon the characters created by* Edgar Rice Burroughs; *Photography*, Sidney Wagner; *Recording Director*, Douglas Shearer; *Art Director*, Cedric Gibbons; *Set Decorations*, Edwin B. Willis; *Film Editor*, Gene Ruggiero; *Special Effects*, Arnold Gillespie, Warren Newcombe; *Opening Theme*, "*Cannibal Carnival*" *by* Sol Levy; *Musical Score*, David Snell. *Running time:* 71 minutes. *Release date:* August 1942

8. TARZAN TRIUMPHS • 1943 Sol Lesser/RKO

Cast: Johnny Weissmuller (*Tarzan*), Johnny Sheffield (*Boy*), Frances Gifford (*Zandra*), Stanley Ridges (*von Reichart*), Sig Ruman (*Sergeant*), Pedro de Cordoba (*Patriarch*), Philip Van Zandt (*Bausch*), Stanley Brown (*Achmet*), Rex Williams (*Schmidt*), Otto

Reichow (*German soldier*), Sven Hugo Borg (*German soldier*) **Credits:** *Directed by* William Thiele; *Produced by* Sol Lesser; *Screenplay by* Roy Chanslor and Carroll Young; *Story,* Carroll Young; *Based upon the characters created by* Edgar Rice Burroughs; *Director of Photography,* Harry Wild; *Art Director,* Hans Peters; *Film Editor,* Hal Kern; *Production Design,* Harry Horner; *Asst. Director,* Clem Beauchamp; *Wardrobe,* Elmer Ellsworth; *Sound Technician,* John C. Grubb; *Music Director,* Constantine Bakaleinikoff; *Music by* Paul Sawtell. *Running time:* 78 minutes. *Release date:* February 1943.

9. *STAGE DOOR CANTEEN* • *1943*
United Artists/Sol Lesser

Cast: Cheryl Walker (*Eileen*), William Terry (*Ed "Dakota" Smith*), Marjorie Riordan (*Jean Rule*), Lon McCallister (*"California"*), Margaret Early (*Ella Sue*), Michael Harrison (*"Texas"*), Dorothea Kent (*Mamie*), Fred Brady (*"Jersey" Wallace*), Marion Shockley (*Lillian*), Patrick O'Moore (*Australian*), Ruth Roman (*Girl*), Judith Anderson, Henry Armetta, Kenny Baker, Tallulah Bankhead, Ralph Bellamy, Edgar Bergen and Charlie McCarthy, Ray Bolger, Helen Broderick, Ina Claire, Katharine Cornell, Lloyd Corrigan, Jane Cowl, Jane Darwell, William Demarest, Virginia Field, Dorothy Fields, Gracie Fields, Lynn Fontanne, Arlene Francis,

Vinton Freedley, Billy Gilbert, Lucile Gleason, Vera Gordon, Virginia Grey, Helen Hayes, Katharine Hepburn, Hugh Herbert, Jean Hersholt, Sam Jaffe, Allen Jenkins, George Jessel, Roscoe Karns, Virginia Kaye, Tom Kennedy, Otto Kruger, June Lang, Betty Lawford, Gertrude Lawrence, Gypsy Rose Lee, Alfred Lunt, Bert Lytell, Harpo Marx, Aline MacMahon, Elsa Maxwell, Helen Menken, Yehudi Menuhin, Ethel Merman, Ralph Morgan, Alan Mowbray, Paul Muni, Elliott Nugent, Merle Oberon, Franklin Pangborn, Helen Parrish, Brock Pemberton, George Raft, Lanny Ross, Selena Royle, Martha Scott, Cornelia Otis Skinner, Ned Sparks, Bill Stern, Ethel Waters, Arleen Whelan, Dame May Whitty, Ed Wynn (*Stage Door Canteen Stars*), **Johnny Weissmuller. Credits:** *Directed by* Frank Borzage; *Produced by* Sol Lesser; *Screenplay by* Delmer Daves; *Photography*, Harry Wild; *Production directors*, Harry Horner, Clem Beauchamps; *Editor*, Hal Kern; *Music*, Freddie Rich; *Musical Director*, Constantin Bakaleinikoff; *Art Director*, Hans Peters, *Set Director*, Victor Gangelin; *Costumes*, Albert Dano. *Running time*: 132 minutes

10. TARZAN'S DESERT MYSTERY • 1943 Sol Lesser/RKO

Cast: Johnny Weissmuller (*Tarzan*), Johnny Sheffield (*Boy*), Nancy Kelly (*Connie Bryce*),

Otto Kruger (*Paul Hendrix*), Joe Sawyer (*Karl*), Robert Lowery (*Prince Selim*), Lloyd Corrigan (*Sheik*), *also featuring*: Frank Puglia, Phil Van Zandt, Nestor Paiva, Frank Faylen. **Credits:** *Directed by* William Thiele; *Produced by* Sol Lesser; *Screenplay by* Edward T. Lowe; *Story*, Carroll Young; *Based upon the characters created by* Edgar Rice Burroughs; *Associate Producer*, Kurt Neumann; *Photography*, Harry Wild and Russ Harlan; *Art Directors*, Hans Peters and Ralph Berger; *Interiors*, Victor Gangelin and Stanley Murphy; *Film Editor*, Ray Lockert; *Assistant Director*, Derwin Abrahams; *Wardrobe*, Elmer Ellsworth; *Sound Technicians*, Jean L. Speak and Bailey Fesler; *Musical Director*, Constantine Bakaleinikoff; *Music Score by* Paul Sawtell. *Running time:* 70 minutes. *Release date*: December 1943

11. *TARZAN AND THE AMAZONS* • *1945 Sol Lesser/RKO*

Cast: Johnny Weissmuller (*Tarzan*), Brenda Joyce (*Jane*), Johnny Sheffield (*Boy*), Henry Stephenson (*Sir Guy Henderson*), Maria Ouspenskaya (*Amazon Queen*), Barton MacLane (*Ballister*), Shirley O'Hara (*Athena*), Don Douglas (*Andres*), J. M. Kerrigan (*Splivers*), Steven Geray (*Brenner*). **Credits:** *Director and Associate Producer*, Kurt Neumann; *Produced by* Sol Lessor; *Screenplay by* John Jacoby and Marjorie L. Pfaelzer;

Based upon the characters created by Edgar Rice Burroughs; *Photography*, Archie Stout; *Production Design*, Phil Paradise; *Art Director*, Walter Koessler; *Interiors*, James E. Altweis; *Film Editor*, Robert O. Crandall; *Assistant Director*, Scott R. Beal; *Wardrobe*, Earl Moser; *Makeup Artist*, Norbert Miles; *Sound Technician*, Jean L. Speak; *Music Score by* Paul Sawtell. *Running time:* 76 minutes. *Release date:* April 1945

12. TARZAN AND THE LEOPARD WOMAN • 1946 Lesser/RKO

Cast: Johnny Weissmuller (*Tarzan*), Brenda Joyce (*Jane*), Johnny Sheffield (*Boy*), Acquanetta (*High Priestess Lea*), Edgar Barrier (*Dr. Lazar*), Tommy Cook (*Kimba*), Dennis Hoey (*Commissioner*), Anthony Caruso (*Mongo*), George J. Lewis (*Corporal*), Doris Lloyd (*Superintendent*). *Also featuring*: King Kong Kashey, Robert Barron, Marek Windheim, Louis Mercier, Georges Renavent; *and as the Zambesi maidens:* Iris Flores, Lillian Molieri, Helen Gerald, and Kay Salinas. **Credits:** *Director and Associate Producer*, Kurt Neumann; *Produced by* Sol Lesser; *Story and Screenplay by* Carroll Young; *Based upon the characters created by* Edgar Rice Burroughs; *Photography*, Karl Struss; *Production Design*, Phil Paradise; *Art Director*, Lewis Creber; *Dance Director*, Lester Horton; *Film Editor*, Robert O. Crandall; *As-*

sistant Director, Scott R. Beal; *Wardrobe*, Robert Martien; *Makeup*, Irving Berns; *Sound Technician*, John R. Carter; *Unit Manager*, Clem Beauchamp; *Music Score by* Paul Sawtell. *Running time:* 72 minutes. *Release date:* February 1946.

13. SWAMP FIRE • 1946 Paramount

Cast: Johnny Weissmuller (*Johnny Duval*); Virginia Grey (*Janet Hilton*); Buster Crabbe (*Mike Kalavich*);Carol Thurston (*Toni Rousseau*); Edwin Maxwell (*Capt. Moise*); Pedro De Cordoba (*Tim Rousseau*); Pierre Watkin (*Mr. Hilton*); Marcelle Corday (*Grandmere Rousseau*); *also starring* David Janssen, William Edmunds, Charles Gordon, Frank Fenton. **Credits:** *Directed by* William Pine; *Produced by* William Thomas, William Pine; *Screenplay by* Geoffrey Homes; *Photography*, Fred Jackman, Jr.; *Musical Director*, Rudy Schrager; *Editor*, Howard Smith; *Art director*, Paul Sylos. *Running time:* 69 minutes. *Release date:* April 1946

14. TARZAN AND THE HUNTRESS • 1947 Sol Lesser/RKO

Cast: Johnny Weissmuller (*Tarzan*), Brenda Joyce (*Jane*), Johnny Sheffield (*Boy*), Patricia Morison (*Tanya Rawlins*), Barton MacLane (*Paul Weir*), John Warburton (*Karl Marley*), Wallace Scott (*Smitty*), Charles Trowbridge (*King Farrod*), Maurice Tauzen (*Prince Suli*),

Ted Hecht (*Prince Ozira*), Mickey Simpson (*Monak*). **Credits:** *Director and Associate Producer,* Kurt Neumann; *Produced by* Sol Lesser; *Story and Screenplay by* Jerry Gruskin and Rowland Leigh; *Based upon the characters created by* Edgar Rice Burroughs; *Photography,* Archie Stout; *Production Design,* Phil Paradise; *Art Director,* McClure Capps; *Film Editor,* Merrill White; *Associate Editor,* John Sheets; *Asst. Director,* Bert Briskin; *Sound Technician,* Frank McWhorter; *Production Manager,* Clem Beauchamp; *Music by* Paul Sawtell. *Running time:* 72 minutes. *Release date:* April 1947

15. *TARZAN AND THE MERMAIDS* • *1948 Sol Lesser/RKO*

Cast: Johnny Weissmuller (*Tarzan*), Brenda Joyce (*Jane*), Linda Christian (*Mara*), George Zucco (*Palanth*), John Laurenz (*Benji*), Fernando Wagner (*Varga*), Edward Ashley (*Commissioner*), Gustavo Rojo (Tiko), Andrea Palma (*Luana*), Matthew Boulton (*Inspector General*). **Credits:** *Directed by* Robert Florey; *Produced by* Sol Lesser; *Story and Screenplay by* Carroll Young; *Based upon the characters created by* Edgar Rice Burroughs; *Photography,* Jack Draper; *Art Director,* McClure Capps; *Film Editor,* Merrill White; *Associate Editor,* John Sheets; *Assistant Director,* Bert Briskin; *Costumes by* Norma; *Sound Supervisor,* James Fields; *Production Manager,*

725

Ray Heinz; Music *Composed and Directed by* Dimitri Tiomkin. *Running time:* 68 minutes. *Release date:* March 1948

16. *JUNGLE JIM* • *1948 Columbia Pictures*

Cast: Johnny Weissmuller (*Jungle Jim*), Virginia Grey (*Hilary Parker*), George Reeves (*Bruce Edwards*), Lita Baron (*Zia*), Rick Vallin (*Kolu*), Holmes Herbert (*Commissioner Marsden*), Tex Mooney (*Chief Devil Doctor*). **Credits:** *Directed by* William Berke; *Produced by* Sam Katzman; *Story and Screenplay by* Carroll Young (*based on the comic strip "Jungle Jim" created by Alex Raymond*); *Photography,* Lester White; *Editor,* Aaron Stell; *Musical Director,* Mischa Bakaleinikoff; *Art Director,* Paul Palmentola; *Set Director,* Sidney Clifford. *Running time:* 71 minutes

17. *THE LOST TRIBE* • *1949 Columbia Pictures*

Cast: Johnny Weissmuller (*Jungle Jim*), Myrna Dell (*Norina*), Elena Verdugo (*Li Wanna*), Joseph Vitale (*Calhoun*), Ralph Dunn (*Capt. Rawling*), Paul Marion (*Chot*), Nelson Leigh (*Zoron*), George J. Lewis (*Whip Wilson*), Gil Perkins (*Dojek*), George DeNomand (*Cullen*), Wally West (*Eckle*), Rube Schaffer (*Lerch*). **Credits:** *Directed by* William Berke; *Produced by* Sam Katzman; *Screenplay by* Arthur Hoerl, Don Martin

726

(*based on the comic strip* "*Jungle Jim*" *created by Alex Raymond*); *Photography*, Ira H. Morgan; *Editor*, Aaron Stell; *Musical Director*, Mischa Bakaleinikoff; *Art Director*, Paul Palmentola. *Running* time: 72 minutes

18. *CAPTIVE GIRL* • 1950 *Columbia Pictures*

Cast: Johnny Weissmuller (*Jungle Jim*), Buster Crabbe (*Baron*), Anita Lhoest (*Joan*), Rick Vallin (*Mahala*), John Dehner (*Hakim*), Rusty Wescoatt (*Silva*), Nelson Leigh (*missionary*). **Credits:** *Directed by* William Berke; *Produced by* Sam Katzman; *Story and Screenplay by* Carroll Young (*based on the comic strip* "*Jungle Jim*" *created by Alex Raymond*); *Photography*, Ira H. Morgan; *Editor*, Henry Batista; *Musical Director*, Mischa Bakaleinikoff; *Art Director*, Paul Palmentola. *Running time*: 73 minutes

19. *MARK OF THE GORILLA* • 1950 *Columbia Pictures*

Cast: Johnny Weissmuller (*Jungle Jim*), Trudy Marshall (*Barbara Bentley*), Suzanne Dalbert (*Nyobi*), Onslow Stevens (*Brandt*), Robert Purcell (*Kramer*), Pierce Lyden (*Gibbs*), Neyle Morrow (*head Ranger*), Selmer Jackson (*Warden Bentley*). **Credits:** *Directed by* William Berke; *Produced by* Sam Katzman; *Story and Screenplay by* Carroll Young (*based on the comic*

727

strip *"Jungle Jim"* created by *Alex Raymond*);
Photography, Ira H. Morgan; *Editor*, Henry
Batista; *Musical Director*, Mischa
Bakaleinikoff; *Art Director*, Paul Palmentola.
Running time: 68 minutes

20. *PYGMY ISLAND* • *1950 Columbia Pictures*

Cast: Johnny Weissmuller (*Jungle Jim*), Ann
Savage (*Capt. Ann Kingsley*), David Bruce
(*Major Bolton*), Steven Geray (*Leon Marko*),
William Tannen (*Kruger*), Tristram Coffin
(*Novak*), Billy Curtis (*Makuba*), Tommy
Farrell (*Captain*), Pierce Lyden (*Lucas*),
Rusty Wescoatt (*Anders*), Billy Barty
(*Tembo*). **Credits:** *Directed by* William Berke;
Produced by Sam Katzman; *Story and Screenplay by* Carroll Young (*based on the comic strip
"Jungle Jim" created by Alex Raymond*); *Photography*, Ira H. Morgan; *Editor*, Jerome
Thomas; *Musical Director*, Mischa
Bakaleinikoff; *Art Director*, Paul Palmentola.
Running time: 69 minutes

21. *FURY OF THE CONGO* • *1951 Columbia Pictures*

Cast: Johnny Weissmuller (*Jungle Jim*),
Sherry Moreland (*Leta*), William Henry
(*Ronald Cameron*), Lyle Talbot (*Grant*), Joel
Friedkin (*Dunham*), George Eldredge
(*Barnes*), Rusty Wescoatt (*Magruder*), Blanca
Vischer (*Mahara*), Pierce Lyden (*Allen*),

Juhn Hart (*guard*). **Credits:** *Directed by* William Berke; *Produced by* Sam Katzman; *Story and Screenplay by* Carroll Young (*based on the comic strip "Jungle Jim" by Alex Raymond*); *Photography*, Ira H. Morgan; *Editor*, Richard Fantl; *Musical Director*, Mischa Bakaleinikoff; *Art Director*, Paul Palmentola. *Running time:* 69 minutes

22. JUNGLE MANHUNT • 1951 Columbia Pictures

Cast: Johnny Weissmuller (*Jungle Jim*), Bob Waterfield (*Bob Miller*), Sheila Ryan (*Ann Lawrence*), Rick Vallin (*Bono*), Lyle Talbot (*Dr. Mitchell Heller*), William P. Wilkerson (*Maklee Chief*). **Credits**: *Directed by* Lew Landers; *Produced by* Sam Katzman; *Story and Screenplay by* Samuel Newman (*based on the comic strip "Jungle Jim" created by Alex Raymond*); *Photography*, William Whitley; *Editor*, Henry Batista; *Musical Director*, Mischa Bakaleinikoff; *Art Director*, Paul Palmentola. *Running time:* 66 minutes

23. JUNGLE JIM IN THE FORBIDDEN LAND • 1952 Columbia

Cast: Johnny Weissmuller (*Jungle Jim*), Angela Greene (*Linda Roberts*), Jean Willes (*Denise*), Lester Matthews (*Commissioner Kingston*), William Tannen (*Doc Edwards*), George Eldredge (*Fred Lewis*), Fredric Berest (*Zulu*), Clem Erickson (*Giant Man*), Irmgard

H.H. Raschke (*Giant Woman*), William Fawcett (*Old One*), Frank Jacquet (Quigley). *Credits:* Directed by Lew Landers; *Produced by* Sam Katzman; *Story and Screenplay by* Samuel Newman (*based on the comic strip "Jungle Jim" by Alex Raymond*); *Photography*, Fayte M. Brown; *Editor*, Henry Batista; *Musical Director*, Mischa Bakaleinikoff; *Art Director*, Paul Palmentola. *Running time:* 64 minutes

24. *VOODOO TIGER* • 1952 Columbia Pictures
Cast: Johnny Weissmuller (*Jungle Jim*), Jean Byron (*Phyllis Bruce*), James Seay (*Abel Peterson*), Jeanne Dean (*Shalimar*), Rick Vallin (*Sgt. Bono*), Charles Horvath (*Wombulu*), Robert Bray (*Major Bill Green*), Michael Fox (*Carl Werner*), John Cason (*Jerry Masters*), Paul Hoffman (*Michael Kovacs*), Richard Kipling (*Commissioner Kingston*), Fredric Berest (*Native Chief*), William R. Klein (*Co-Pilot*), Alex Montoya (*Native Leader*). *Credits:* Directed by Spencer Gordon Bennet; *Produced by* Sam Katzman; *Story and Screenplay by* Samuel Newman (*based on the comic strip "Jungle Jim" created by Alex Raymond*); *Photography*, William Whitley; *Editor*, Gene Havlick; Musical Director, Mischa Bakaleini- koff; *Art Director, Paul Palmentola; Set Director*, Sidney Clifford. *Running time:* 67 minutes

25. *SAVAGE MUTINY* • *1953 Columbia Pictures*

Cast: Johnny Weissmuller (*Jungle Jim*), Angela Stevens (*Joan Harris*), Lester Matthews (*Major Walsh*), Nelson Leigh (*Dr. Parker*), Charles Stevens (*Chief Wamai*), Paul Marion (*Lutembi*), Gregory Gay (*Carl Kroman*), Leonard Penn (*Emil Bruno*), Ted Thorpe (*Paul Benek*), George Robotham (*Johnson*). **Credits:** *Directed by* Spencer Gordon Bennet; *Produced by* Sam Katzman; *Story and Screenplay by* Sol Shor (*based on the comic strip "Jungle Jim" created by Alex Raymond*); *Photography,* William Whitley; *Editor,* Henry Batista; *Musical Director,* Mischa Bakaleinikoff; *Art Director,* Paul Palmentola. *Running time:* 73 minutes

26. *VALLEY OF THE HEADHUNTERS* • *1953 Columbia Pictures*

Cast: Johnny Weissmuller (*Jungle Jim*), Christine Larson (*Ellen Shaw*), Robert C. Foulk (*Arco*), Steven Ritch (*Lt. Barry*), Nelson Leigh (*Mr. Bradley*), Joseph Allen, Jr. (*Pico Church*), George Eldredge (*Kingston*), Neyle Morrow (*Cpl. Bono*), Vince M. Townsend, Jr. (*M'Gono*), Don Blackman (*Bagava*), Paul Thompson (*Gitzhak*). **Credits:** *Directed by* William Berke; *Produced by* Sam Katzman; *Story and Screenplay by* Samuel Newman (*based on the comic strip "Jungle Jim" created by Alex Raymond*); *Pho-*

tography, William Whitley; *Editor*, Gene Havlick; *Musical Director*, Mischa Bakaleinikoff; *Art Director*, Paul Palmentola. *Running time:* 67 minutes

27. KILLER APE • 1953 Columbia Pictures

Cast: Johnny Weissmuller (*Jungle Jim*), Carol Thurston (*Shari*), Max Palmer (*Man-Ape*), Burt Wenland (*Ramada*), Nestor Paiva (*Andrews*), Paul Marion (*Mahara*), Eddie Foster (*Achmed*), Rory Mallinson (*Perry*), Ray Corrigan (*Norley*), Nick Stuart (Maron). **Credits:** *Directed by* Spencer Gordon Bennet; *Produced by* Sam Katzman; *Screenplay by* Carrol Young, Arthur Hoerl (*based on the comic strip "Jungle Jim" created by Alex Raymond*); *Photography*, William Whitley; *Editor*, Gene Havlick; *Musical Director*, Mischa Bakaleinikoff; *Art Director*, Paul Palmentola. *Running time: 73 minutes*

28. JUNGLE MAN-EATERS • 1954 Columbia Pictures

Cast: Johnny Weissmuller (*Jungle Jim*), Karin Booth (*Bonnie*), Richard Stapley (*Bernard*), Bernie Hamilton (*Zuwaba*), Lester Matthews (*Commissoner Kingston*), Paul Thompson (*Zulu*), Vince M. Townsend, Jr. (*Chief Bogando*), Louise Franklin (*N'Gala*), Gregory Gay (*Latour*). **Credits:** *Directed by* Lee Sholem; *Produced by* Sam Katzman;

Story and Screenplay by Samuel Newman (*based on the comic strip "Jungle Jim" created by Alex Raymond*); *Photography*, Harry Freulich; *Editor*, Gene Havlick; *Musical Director*, Mischa Bakaleinikoff; *Art Director*, Paul Palmentola. *Running time: 67 minutes*

29. CANNIBAL ATTACK • 1954 Columbia Pictures

Cast: Johnny Weissmuller (*Johnny*), Judy Walsh (*Luora*), David Bruce (*Arnold King*), Bruce Cowling (*Rovak*), Charles Evans (*Commissioner*), Steve Darrell (*John King*), Joseph A. Allen, Jr. (*Jason*). **Credits:** *Directed by* Lee Sholem; *Produced by* Sam Katzman; *Story and Screenplay by* Carroll Young; *Photography*, Harry Freulich; *Editor*, Edwin Bryant; *Musical Director*, Mischa Bakaleinikoff; *Art Director*, Paul Palmentola. *Running time: 69 minutes*

30. JUNGLE MOON MEN • 1955 Columbia Pictures

Cast: Johnny Weissmuller (*Johnny*), Jean Byron (*Ellen Marston*), Helen Stanton (*Oma*), Bill Henry (*Bob Prentice*), Myron Healy (*Mark Santo*), Billy Curtis (*Damu*), Michael Granger (*Nolimo*), Frank Sully (*Max*), Benjamin F. Chapman, Jr. (*Marro*), Kenneth L. Smith (*Link*), Ed Hinton (*Regan*). **Credits:** *Directed by* Charles S. Gould; *Produced by* Sam Katzman; *Screenplay* *by* Dwight V. Babcock, Jo Pagano (*based on a story by Jo Pagano*); *Photography*, Henry Freulich; *Editor*, Henry Batista; *Musical Director*, Mischa Bakaleinikoff; *Art Director*, Paul Palmentola. *Running time:* 69 minutes

31. *DEVIL GODDESS* • *1955 Columbia Pictures*

Cast: Johnny Weissmuller (*Johnny*), Angela Stevens (*Nora Blakely*), Selmer Jackson (*Prof. Carl Blakely*), William Tannen (*Nels Comstock*), Ed Hinton (*Joseph Leopold*), William M. Griffith (*Ralph Dixon*), Frank Lacteen (*Nkruma*), Abel M. Fernandez (*Teinusi*), Vera M. Francis (*Sarab'na*), George Berkely (*Bert*). **Credits:** *Directed by* Spencer Gordon Bennet; *Produced by* Sam Katzman; *Screenplay by* George Plympton (*story by Dwight Babcock*); *Photography*, Ira H. Morgan; *Editor*, Aaron Stell; *Musical Director*, Mischa Bakaleinikoff; *Art Director*, Paul Palmentola. *Running time:* 70 minutes

32. *PHYNX, THE* • *1970 Cinema Organization/Warner Brothers*

Cast: A. Michael Miller, Ray Chippeway, Dennis Larden, Lonny Stevens (*The Phynx*), Lou Antonio (*Corrigan*), Mike Kellen (*Bogey*), Michael Ansara (*Col. Rostinov*), George Tobias (*Markevitch*), Joan Blondell (*Ruby*), Martha Raye (*Foxy*), Larry Hankin (*Philbaby*), Teddy Eccles (*Wee Johnny*), Ultra Violet (*herself*), Pat McCormack (*Father O'Hoolihan*), Joseph Gazal (*Yakov*), Bob Williams (*No. 1*), Barbara Noonan (*Bogey's Secretary*), Sally Ann Struthers (*World's No. 1 Fan*), Rich Little (*Voice in Box*), Sue Bernard, Ann Morrell, Sherry Miles (*Belly* Girls), Patty Andrews, Busby Berkeley, Xavier Cugat, Fritz Feld, John Hart, Ruby Keeler, Joe Louis, Marilyn Maxwell, Harold "Oddjob" Sakata, Ed Sullivan, Rona Barrett, James Brown, Cass Daley, Leo Gorcey, Louis Hayward, Patsy Kelly, Guy Lombardo, Butterfly McQueen, Richard Pryor, Col. Harland Sanders, Rudy Vallee, Edgar Bergen and Charlie McCarthy, Dick Clark, Andy Devine, Huntz Hall, George Jessel, Dorothy Lamour, Trini Lopez, Pat O'Brien, Jay Silverheels, Clint Walker, Maureen O'Sullivan, ***Johnny Weissmuller*** (*cameos*). ***Credits:*** *Directed by* Lee H. Katzin; *Produced by* Bob Booker, George Foster; *Written by* Stan Cornyn (based on a story by Booker, Foster); *Photographed by* Michel Hugo (Technicolor); *Editor*, Dann Cahn; *Production designer*, Stan Jolley; *Set decorator*, Ralph S. Hunt; *Costumes*, Donfeld; *Music and lyrics* by Mike Stoller, Jerry Leiber. *Running time:* 91 minutes

33. WON TON TON, THE DOG WHO SAVED HOLLYWOOD • 1976 Paramount

Cast: Bruce Dern (*Grayson Potchuck*), Madeline Kahn (*Estie Del Ruth*), Art Carney (*J. J. Fromberg*), Phil Silvers (*Murray Fromberg*), Teri Garr (*Fluffy Peters*), Ron Leibman (*Rudy Montague*), Dennis Morgan (*Tour Guide*), Shecky Greene (*Tourist*), Phil Leeds, Cliff Norton (*Dog Catchers*), Romo Vincent (*Short Order Cook*), Sterling Holloway (*Old Man on Bus*), William Demarest (*Studio Gatekeeper*), Virginia Mayo (*Miss Battley*), Henny Youngman (*Manny Farber*), Rory Calhoun (*Philip Hart*), Billy Barty (*Assistant Director*), Henry Wilcoxon (*Silent Film Director*), Ricardo Montalban (*Silent Film Star*), Jackie Coogan (*Stagehand 1*), Aldo Ray (*Stubby Stebbins*), Ethel Merman (*Hedda Parsons*), Yvonne De Carlo (*Cleaning Woman*), Joan Blondell (*Landlady*), Andy Devine (*Priest in Dog Pound*), Broderick Crawford (*Special Effects* Man), Richard Arlen (*Silent Film Star 2*), Jack LaRue (*Silent Film Villain*), Dorothy Lamour (*Visiting Film Star*), Nancy Walker (*Mrs. Fromberg*), Gloria DeHaven (*President's Girl 1*), Louis Nye (*Radio Interviewer*), Stepin Fetchit (*Dancing Butler*), Ken Murray (*Souvenir Salesman*), Rudy Vallee (*Autograph Hound*), George Jessel (*Awards Announcer*), Rhonda Fleming (*Rhoda Flaming*), Ann Miller (*President's Girl 2*), Dean Stockwell (*Paul Lavell*), Dick Haymes

(*James Crawford*), Tab Hunter (*David Hamilton*), Robert Alda (*Richard Entwhistle*), Fritz Feld (*Rudy's Butler*), Janet Blair (*President's Girl 3*), Dennis Day (*Singing Telegraph Man*), Mike Mazurki (*Studio Guard*), The Ritz Brothers (*Cleaning Women*), Jesse White (*Rudy's Agent*), Jack Carter (*Male Journalist*), Victor Mature (*Nick*), Barbara Nichols (*Nick's Girl*), Fernando Lamas (*Premiere Male Star*), Zsa Zsa Gabor (*Premiere Female Star*), Cyd Charisse (*President's Girl 4*), Huntz Hall (*Moving Man*), Doodles Weaver (*Man in Mexican Film*), Edgar Bergen (*Prof. Quicksand*), Morey Amsterdam, Eddie Foy, Jr. (*Custard Pie Stars*), Peter Lawford (*Slapstick Star*), Patricia Morison, Guy Madison (*Stars at Screening*), Regis Toomey (*Burlesque Stagehand*), Alice Faye (*Secretary at Gate*), Ann Rutherford (*Grayson's Studio Secretary*), Milton Berle (*Blind Man*), John Carradine (*Drunk*), Keye Luke (*Cook in Kitchen*), Walter Pidgeon (*Grayson's Butler*), Augustus Von Schumacher (*Won Ton Ton*), **Johnny Weissmuller (Stagehand 2).** **Credits:** *Directed by Michael Winner; Produced by* David V. Picker, Arnold Schulman, Michael Winner; *Written by* Arnold Schulman, Cy Howard; *Photographed by* Richard H. Kline; *Music by* Neal Hefti; *Editor,* Bernard Gribble; *Art Director,* Ward Preston; *Set Decorator,* Ned Parsons. *Running time:* 92 minutes

34. THAT'S ENTERTAINMENT, PART II • 1976 MGM/UA

Cast: Fred Astaire, Gene Kelly, Judy Garland, Mickey Rooney, Bing Crosby, Robert Taylor, Greer Garson, Clark Gable, Kathryn Grayson, Leslie Caron, Jeanette MacDonald, Nelson Eddy, Doris Day, Ann Miller, Ann Sothern, Frank Sinatra, Jimmy Durante, Eleanor Powell, John Barrymore, Louis Armstrong, Joan Crawford, Ronald Colman, Elizabeth Taylor, William Powell, Jean Harlow, Melvyn Douglas, Greta Garbo, Esther Williams, Ethyl Waters, W. C. Fields, Bud Abbott, Lou Costello, Jack Benny, Robert Benchley, Stan Laurel, Oliver Hardy, The Marx Brothers, Nanette Fabray, Lena Horne, Debbie Reynolds, Ginger Rogers, Bobby Van, Dinah Shore, Cyd Charisse, Donald O'Connor, Grace Kelly, Marge and Gower Champion, Betty Hutton, Howard Keel, Lassie, Spencer Tracy, Katharine Hepburn, Maureen O'Sullivan, *Johnny Weissmuller. Credits: New sequences Directed by* Gene Kelly; *Produced by* Saul Chaplin and David Melnick; *Narration by* Leooard Gershe; *Music arranged and conducted by* Nelson Riddle; *Photography,* George Folsey; editors, Rod Friedgan and David Blewitt. *Running time:* 133 minutes.

JUNGLE JIM TELEVISION SERIES • 1955-56 Screen Gems

Cast: Johnny Weissmuller (*Jungle Jim*), Martin Huston (*Skipper*), Norman Fredric (*Kaseem*), Tamba (*Jim's chimpanzee*), Trader (*Skipper's dog*). **Credits:** *Executive Producer*, Harold Greene; *Director*, Don McDougall; *Music*, Alec Compinsky

"The Golden Parasol" (airdate: Sept. 17, 1955)

"Code of the Jungle" (airdate: Sept. 24, 1955)

"Wild Man of the Jungle" (airdate: Oct. 1, 1955)

"Safari into Danger" (airdate: Oct. 8, 1955)

"Blood Money" (airdate: Oct. 15, 1955)

"Striped Fury" (airdate: Oct. 22, 1955)

"The Scared Scarab" (airdate: Oct. 29, 1955)

"The Lagoon of Death" (airdate: Nov. 5, 1955)

"Voodoo Drums" (airdate: Nov. 12, 1955)

"Treasure of the Amazon" (airdate: Nov. 19, 1955)

"The Avenger" (airdate: Nov. 26, 1955)

"Return of the Tauregs" (airdate: Dec. 3, 1955)

"The Silver Locket" (airdate: Dec. 10, 1955)

"Gift of Evil" (airdate: Dec. 17, 1955)

"White Magic" (airdate: Dec. 24, 1955)

"Man Killer" (airdate: Dec. 31, 1955)
"The Power of Darkness" (airdate: Jan. 7, 1956)
"Land of Terror" (airdate: Jan. 14, 1956)
"The King's Ghost" (airdate: Jan. 21, 1956).
"A Fortune in Ivory" (airdate: Jan. 28, 1956)
"The Eyes of Manoba" (airdate: Feb. 4, 1956)
"The Leopard's Paw" (airdate: Feb. 11, 1956)
"Precious Cargo" (airdate: Feb. 18, 1956)

SWIMMING RECORDS
and MEDALS

Olympic Gold Medals

1924 (Paris, France)
100-meter freestyle (Olympic record time 59.0)
400-meter freestyle (Olympic record time 5:04.2)
4 x 200-meter relay (World record time 9:53.4)

1928 (Amsterdam, Holland)
100-meter freestyle (Olympic record time 58.6)
4 x 200-meter relay (World record time 9:36.2)

Special Awards
and Honors

1922 American Swimmer of the Year
(Helms Athletic Foundation Lifetime Award presented in 1949)
1923 Athlete of the Year, North America
(Helms World Trophy Award Winner Life-

time Award, 1949)

1949 Helms Swimming Hall of Fame
(Elected by Helms Hall Board)

1950 "Greatest Swimmer of the Half-Century 1900-1950"
(Chosen by the Associated Press and the Sportswriters of America)

1965 First Inductee Swimming Hall of Fame, Ft. Lauderdale, FL
(Johnny also served as Founding Chairman of the Board 1966-1973)

1968 Awarded "Sportsman's World Award/Swimming"

1971 Awarded "American Patriot Award"

1972 Awarded Honorary Sixth Gold Medal at Munich Olympics

1972 Declared "Sportsworld King"

1972 Awarded Dewars Merit Awards "Sports Immortal"

1974 Declared "King of Swimming" Undefeated
(Honored by the International Palace of Sports)

1980 Inducted into the Hollywood Stuntman Hall of Fame

1983 Inducted into the United States Olympic Hall of Fame

National Championships and World Records

Johnny Weissmuller won *52 National Championships* and set *67 World Records* and over *100 American Records* during his career. His record-smashing time of *57.4 seconds in the 100-meter freestyle* in 1924 was a record that would last for an incredible ten years! His world record time of *51 seconds flat in the 100-yard freestyle* set in 1927 lasted for nine years before being broken! (Johnny also set the American record in this event with a faster time of 49.8 seconds.)

Outdoor Nationals	*Year*
50-yard freestyle	1921
220-yard freestyle	1921
50-yard freestyle	1922
100-yard freestyle	1922
220-yard freestyle	1922
440-yard freestyle	1922
100-yard freestyle	1923
440-yard freestyle	1923
100-yard freestyle	1925
440-yard freestyle	1925

100-meter freestyle	1926
440-yard freestyle	1926
100-meter freestyle	1927
440-yard freestyle	1927
880-yard freestyle	1927
100-meter freestyle	1928
440-yard freestyle	1928

Relays

4x220-yard relay	1923
4x220-yard relay	1924
4x220-yard relay	1925
4x220-yard relay	1926
4x220-yard relay	1927
4x220-yard relay	1928

Indoor Nationals	Year
100-yard freestyle	1922
220-yard freestyle	1922
500-yard freestyle	1922
50-yard freestyle	1923
100-yard freestyle	1923
150-yd backstroke	1923
220-yard freestyle	1923
500-yard freestyle	1923
50-yard freestyle	1924
100-yard freestyle	1924
220-yard freestyle	1924
500-yard freestyle	1924
50-yard freestyle	1925
100-yard freestyle	1925

100-yard freestyle	1927
220-yard freestyle	1927
500-yard freestyle	1927
100-yard freestyle	1928
220-yard freestyle	1928
500-yard freestyle	1928

Relays

4x50-yard relay	1922
4x100-yard relay	1922
4x100-yard relay	1923
4x50-yard relay	1924
4x100-yard relay	1924
4x100-yard relay	1925
4x75-yard medley	1927
4x75-yard medley	1928
4x100-yard relay	1928

Johnny also won *National Championships* in the *Pentathlon* (five swimming and diving events) in 1922 and 1923, and was a member of the *National Championship water polo teams* in 1924 and 1927.

Acknowledgments

I would certainly like to thank Johnny Weissmuller for having such a wonderful career as to inspire the writing of this book. I'd love to shake his hand, if only I could. Probably my best opportunity to meet Johnny would have been at the Edgar Rice Burroughs' convention in September of 1971 when he was the Special Guest of Honor. Checking my memory banks, at that precise moment I was pounding a typewriter at the military base in Cholon, Vietnam, during my tour of duty in the Army.

In researching this book, I fell heir to a great deal of information — and misinformation. By digging as deeply as I could into the facts, this biography hopefully represents a truthful, accurate, and interesting view of the life of Johnny Weissmuller.

I'm grateful to Johnny for the information contained in his own 1930 autobiography, *Swimming the American Crawl*, that he wrote in collaboration with Clarence A. Bush. This book was especially helpful in researching Johnny's career as a champion swimmer, and his early life up to the age of his 25th year. I'd also like to acknowledge Narda Onyx and her 1964 biography, *Water, World, and Weissmuller*, and a host of other writers who have written stories and interviewed Johnny over the years.

There are many people whom I would like to thank for contributing to this book, especially Maureen O'Sullivan, "Jane" in Johnny's early Tarzan pictures, and Johnny Sheffield, who was kind enough to author the Foreword for "Twice the Hero." Both of these close friends of Johnny's were very generous in sharing their memories of working with him in the Tarzan pictures, as well as recalling the lighter side of his personality. A gracious tip of the hat to artist Thomas Yeates for his original drawing of Johnny as Tarzan.

My extreme gratitude goes to Lisa Weissmuller, Johnny's daughter, and Maria Weissmuller, Johnny's wife. Thank you so much for your support, information, and photographs.

Hank Brown and Rudy Sigmund contributed information, photographs, and their editing skills. George McWhorter was wonderful (as usual) in loaning many Tarzan photographs from the Burroughs Bibliophiles collection, and a wealth of Weissmuller clippings from his files. I'd also like to thank the many other friends who contributed their time, memories, clippings, and photographs, including: Jerry Spannraft, Frank Westwood, Martin Smiddy, Denny Miller, Bob Hyde, Matt Winans, Rudy

Behlmer, Geoff St. Andrews, Bob Barrett, Harry Habblitz, Mike Oliver, Altha Edgren, Carolin Kopplin, and my proofreader supreme, Carol Furry. (I'm truly sorry if I forgot anyone . . . it was not an intentional oversight.)

Organizations and individuals that were very helpful include Dr. Robert Morris at the National Archives and Records Administration; Maria M. Antenorcruz at Ellis Island; Preston Levi at the International Swimming Hall of Fame; Martha L. Selner, Map Librarian at the University Library, University of Illinois at Chicago; Julie Thomas, Research Specialist at the Chicago Historical Society; the Hennepin County Libraries and Librarians in the wonderful state of Minnesota; the United States Olympic Committee in Colorado Springs, Colorado; Julie A. Satzik, Assistant Research Archivist at the Archdiocese of Chicago; and the kind folks at St. Michael's Catholic Church in Chicago.

Photographic credits

My sincere gratitude goes to the contributors of photographs in this volume, including:

George McWhorter and the Burroughs
    Bibliophiles
Frank Westwood and the Edgar Rice
    Burroughs Society

Henning Library at the Swimming Hall
  of Fame
Martin Smiddy
Jerry Spannraft
Rudy Sigmund
Lisa and Maria Weissmuller
(all other photos are from the author's
  collection)

Front dust jacket photo from the collection of
Rudy Sigmund

Many thanks to the motion picture studios
and the photographers who captured Johnny
Weissmuller in all his glory from 1931 to
1956, including:

Metro-Goldwyn-Mayer
RKO Radio Pictures
Columbia Pictures
Screen Gems

Bibliography

Books

Addams, Jane *Twenty Years at Hull House* (Macmillan, 1910)

Associated Press *The Sports Immortals* (Rutledge Books, 1972)

Bowles, Jerry *The Story of the Ed Sullivan Show* (G. P. Putnam Sons, 1980)

Carlson, Lewis H. *Tales of Gold* (Contemporary Books, 1987)

Crabbe, Clarence "Buster" *A Self-Portrait* (Karl Whitezel, 1997)

Conner, Floyd *Lupe Velez and Her Lovers* (Barricade Books, 1993)

Cromie, Robert *A Short History of Chicago* (Lexikos, 1984)

Crosby, Bing *Call Me Lucky* (Simon and Schuster, 1953)

Dawson, Buck *Weissmuller to Spitz* (Swimming Hall of Fame, 1986)

Essoe, Gabe *Tarzan of the Movies* (Citadel Press, 1968)

Fenton, Robert *The Big Swingers* (Prentice Publishers, 1967)

Fury, David A. *Kings of the Jungle: Tarzan History and Filmography* (McFarland and Co., 1994)

Gelman, Steve *Young Olympic Champions* (Norton Press, 1974)

Holtzmark, Erling B. *Edgar Rice Burroughs* (Twayne Publishers, 1986)

Kieran, John/Daley, Arthur *Story of the Olympic Games* (J. B. Lipincott, 1965)

Lake, John *Greatest Athletes of the Century* (Random House, 1966)

Lowe, David *Lost Chicago* (Houghton Mifflin, 1975)

Myers, Jeffrey *Gary Cooper: American Hero* (William Morrow, 1998)

Onyx, Narda *Water, World & Weissmuller* (Vion Publishing, 1964)

Pacyga, Dominic A. and Skerrett, Ellen *Chicago: City of Neighborhoods* (Loyola University Press/Chicago)

Parish, James Robert *The RKO Gals* (Rainbow Books, 1974)

Pierce, James H. *The Battle of Hollywood* (House of Greystoke, 1978)

Porges, Irwin *Edgar Rice Burroughs . . . The Man Who Created Tarzan* (Brigham Young University Press, 1975)

Rice, Grantland *The Tumult and the Shouting* (A. S. Barnes, 1954)

Roberts, Randy and Olson, James S. *John Wayne: Ameican* (The Free Press, 1995)

Sugar, Bert *100 Greatest Athletes of All Time* (Citadel Press, 1995)

Wagenknecht, Edward *Chicago* (University of Oklahoma Press, 1964)

Wallechinsky, David *Complete Book of the Olympics* (Little, Brown, 1991)

Wayne, Pilar *John Wayne: My Life with The Duke* (McGraw Hill, 1987)

Weissmuller, Johnny and Bush, Clarence A. *Swimming the American Crawl* (Houghton Mifflin Company, 1930)

Zaharias, Babe Didrikson *This Life I've Led* (A. S. Barnes, 1955)

Ziegfeld, Richard *Life and Times of Florenz Ziegfeld, Jr.* (Harry Abrams, 1993)

Magazines and Newspapers

Albert, K. *"Hey! Hey! Here comes Johnny"* (Photoplay June 1932)

Anderson, Dave "Tarzan Was Better Than Mark Spitz Is"
(*New York Times*, November 4, 1972)

Behlmer, Rudy "Tarzan, Hollywood's Greatest Jungle Hero" (*American Cinematographer* Jan. & Feb. 1987)

Behlmer, Rudy "Johnny Weissmuller: Olympics to Tarzan"
(*Films in Review* July/August 1996)

Evans, Harry "Tarzan and His Mate" (*The Family Circle* May 25, 1934)

Esquire "Tarzan and other heroes come back once more" (April, 1970)

Garnett, Richard E. "Interview with Johnny Weissmuller" (1972)

Hampton, J. "Lupe and Johnny were lovers" (*Photoplay* June 1934)

Hyde, Clarence "Bob" "Interview with

Johnny Weissmuller" (1967)

Lahue, Kalton C. "E.R.B and the Silent Screen" (*ERB-dom* 20 and 21, 1967)

Literary Digest "Boy who has broken all swimming records" (May 27, 1922)

Literary Digest "Swim said the doctors, and Johnny swam" (July 4, 1931)

Literary Digest "Weissmuller swims to films" (April 16, 1932)

Mueller, Arlene "Hot Stove" (*Sports Illustrated*, August 6, 1984)

Reader's Digest "Best advice I ever had" (July, 1958)

Reinman, T. R. "Shining star from the Golden Era"

San Diego Tribune, 8-11-1984)

Schneider, Jerry L. *"On Location at the Arboretum"*
(Burroughs Bulletin #11 July, 1992)

Sherwood, Robert E. "The Movie Album" (*Richmond Times*, 4-7-1932)

Weissmuller, Johnny "My Greatest Sport Thrill" (*Male Magazine*, Jan. 1951)

The employees of Thorndike Press hope you have enjoyed this Large Print book. All our Large Print titles are designed for easy reading, and all our books are made to last. Other Thorndike Press Large Print books are available at your library, through selected bookstores, or directly from the publisher.

For more information about titles, please call:

(800) 223-1244
(800) 223-6121

To share your comments, please write:

Publisher
Thorndike Press
295 Kennedy Memorial Drive
Waterville, ME 04901